Kathleen Ja Sook Bergquist, PhD
M. Elizabeth Vonk, PhD
Dong Soo Kim, PhD
Marvin D. Feit, PhD
Editors

International
Korean Adoption
A Fifty-Year History
of Policy and Practice

*Pre-publication
REVIEWS,
COMMENTARIES,
EVALUATIONS . . .*

"*International Korean Adoption* is a noteworthy collection of research and writings on the topic of international adoptions from Korea. This book probes beneath the surface of the lives of Korean adoptees to discern the historical, political, and social forces that have caused the dispersal of tens of thousands of Korean children across the globe and the impact this 'social experiment' has had on the lives of adoptees and their families. Some of the historical material will be familiar to adoption researchers and professionals. However, there are unexpected findings and hypotheses that bring fresh and nuanced meanings to this complex global phenomenon. Notable are Catherine Ceniza Choy's in-depth exploration of the diverse institutional networks that helped launch international adoptions after the Korean War; Eleana Kim's insightful observations of awkward encounters between visiting adoptees and the state of South Korea; Hosu Kim's analysis which brings the otherwise absent voices of Korean birth mothers to the forefront of adoption analysis; and articles that shed light on the experiences of adoptees from The Netherlands, Australia, and other non-U.S. countries that highlights the truly global nature of this form of child migration.

As an adoptee and an independent filmmaker, I found this book to be both informative and provocative. For adoptees, adoption professionals, and researchers, this book will be a rare and useful resource for years to come."

Deann Borshay Liem
Independent Filmmaker;
Director/Producer,
First Person Plural

More pre-publication
REVIEWS, COMMENTARIES, EVALUATIONS . . .

"**F**or over fifty years, the world has been engaged in an unplanned social experiment of children born in one country being raised by parents in another country. While adoption has been a part of many cultures and countries almost from the beginning of recorded history, international or transnational adoption is a relatively recent phenomenon.

International Korean Adoption coalesces the voices of the adoption triad—birth parents, adoptive parents, and adoptees—into original writings from multiple disciplines and perspectives in the social and behavioral sciences. It will become the seminal work on Korean adoption. Ideas and writing about Korean adoption are verified and challenged. It is interesting and provocative, social science and personal essay, recrimination and celebration. The lessons learned have not only implications for policy and practice, but serve to outline an agenda for further scholarship into the multiple perspectives and issues in transnational adoption in general and Korean transnational adoption in particular."

Victor Groza, PhD
Professor, Mandel School
of Applied Social Sciences,
Case Western Reserve
University

The Haworth Press
New York

NOTES FOR PROFESSIONAL LIBRARIANS
AND LIBRARY USERS

This is an original book title published by The Haworth Press, Inc. Unless otherwise noted in specific chapters with attribution, materials in this book have not been previously published elsewhere in any format or language.

CONSERVATION AND PRESERVATION NOTES

All books published by The Haworth Press, Inc., and its imprints are printed on certified pH neutral, acid-free book grade paper. This paper meets the minimum requirements of American National Standard for Information Sciences-Permanence of Paper for Printed Material, ANSI Z39.48-1984.

DIGITAL OBJECT IDENTIFIER (DOI) LINKING

The Haworth Press is participating in reference linking for elements of our original books. (For more information on reference linking initiatives, please consult the CrossRef Web site at www.crossref.org.) When citing an element of this book such as a chapter, include the element's Digital Object Identifier (DOI) as the last item of the reference. A Digital Object Identifier is a persistent, authoritative, and unique identifier that a publisher assigns to each element of a book. Because of its persistence, DOIs will enable The Haworth Press and other publishers to link to the element referenced, and the link will not break over time. This will be a great resource in scholarly research.

International Korean Adoption

A Fifty-Year History of Policy and Practice

HAWORTH Health and Social Policy
Marvin D. Feit, PhD

Maltreatment and the School-Age Child: Developmental Outcomes and Systems Issues by Phyllis T. Howing, John S. Wodarski, P. David Kurtz, and James Martin Gaudin Jr.

Health and Social Policy by Marvin D. Feit and Stanley F. Battle

Adolescent Substance Abuse: An Empirical-Based Group Preventive Health Paradigm by John S. Wodarski and Marvin D. Feit

Long-Term Care: Federal, State, and Private Options for the Future by Raymond O'Brien and Michael Flannery

Health and Poverty by Michael J. Holosko and Marvin D. Feit

Financial Management in Human Services by Marvin Feit and Peter Li

Policy, Program Evaluation, and Research in Disability: Community Support for All by Julie Ann Racino

The Politics of Youth, Sex, and Health Care in American Schools by James W. Button and Barbara A. Rienzo

Race, Politics, and Community Development Funding: The Discolor of Money by Michael Bonds

Changing Welfare Services: Case Studies of Local Welfare Reform Programs edited by Michael J. Austin

Accountability in Social Services: The Culture of the Paper Program by Jill Florence Lackey

Voices of African-American Teen Fathers: "I'm Doing What I Got to Do" by Angelia Paschal

Making Business Districts Work: Leadership and Management of Downtown, Main Street, Business District, and Community Development Organizations edited by David Feehan and Marvin D. Feit

International Korean Adoption: A Fifty-Year History of Policy and Practice edited by Kathleen Ja Sook Bergquist, M. Elizabeth Vonk, Dong Soo Kim, and Marvin D. Feit

International Korean Adoption
A Fifty-Year History of Policy and Practice

Kathleen Ja Sook Bergquist, PhD
M. Elizabeth Vonk, PhD
Dong Soo Kim, PhD
Marvin D. Feit, PhD
Editors

The Haworth Press
New York

For more information on this book or to order, visit
http://www.haworthpress.com/store/product.asp?sku=5734

or call 1-800-HAWORTH (800-429-6784) in the United States and Canada
or (607) 722-5857 outside the United States and Canada

or contact orders@HaworthPress.com

The Haworth Press, Inc., 10 Alice Street, Binghamton, NY 13904-1580.

PUBLISHER'S NOTE
The development, preparation, and publication of this work has been undertaken with great care. However, the Publisher, employees, editors, and agents of The Haworth Press are not responsible for any errors contained herein or for consequences that may ensue from use of materials or information contained in this work. The Haworth Press is committed to the dissemination of ideas and information according to the highest standards of intellectual freedom and the free exchange of ideas. Statements made and opinions expressed in this publication do not necessarily reflect the views of the Publisher, Directors, management, or staff of The Haworth Press, Inc., or an endorsement by them.

Identities and circumstances of individuals discussed in this book have been changed to protect confidentiality.

Cover design by Marylouise E. Doyle.

Library of Congress Cataloging-in-Publication Data

International Korean adoption : a fifty-year history of policy and practice / Kathleen Ja Sook Bergquist . . . [et al.], editors.
    p. cm.
Includes bibliographical references and index.
ISBN: 978-0-7890-3064-1 (hard : alk. paper)
ISBN: 978-0-7890-3065-8 (soft : alk. paper)
    1. Intercountry adoption—Korea (South)—History. 2. Intercountry adoption—History. 3. Interracial adoption—History. I. Bergquist, Kathleen Ja Sook.

HV875.58.K6I58 2007
362.734095195—dc22
                                    2006038230

We would like to dedicate this book
to all Korean adoptees, both adults and children.
This body of work is a testimony
to their continued journey . . .

CONTENTS

About the Editors   xiii

Contributors   xv

Foreword   xix
    Paull H. Shin

Preface   xxi

PART I: SOCIOHISTORICAL BACKGROUND   1

Chapter 1. A Country Divided: Contextualizing Adoption
  from a Korean Perspective   3
    Dong Soo Kim

  Historical and Cultural Background   4
  Korean Conflict and Its Impact on Families   4
  The Origin of Korean International Adoption   5
  International Adoption As a Permanent Institution   7
  Motivation for International Adoption   9
  Globalization of Korean International Adoption   11
  Questions and Issues   14
  Recent Developments   17

Chapter 2. Institutionalizing International Adoption:
  The Historical Origins of Korean Adoption
  in the United States   25
    Catherine Ceniza Choy

  A World Vision   28
  From Rescue to Rivalry   31
  Independent Adoption Schemes: An Uneven Legacy   38

PART II: FORMING NEW FAMILIES   **43**

**Chapter 3. A Long-Term Follow-Up of Transracially
Adopted Children in Their Young Adult Years**   **45**
   William Feigelman

Methods   48
Results   50
Discussion   56

**Chapter 4. Choosing Korea: Marketing
"Multiculturalism" to Choosy Adopters**   **61**
   Kristi Brian

The Trouble with "Culture"   63
Themes of the Dominant Institutional Discourse   64
Conclusion: Shifting the Practice Paradigm Toward
   a Problem-Oriented View of Adoption Culture   74

**Chapter 5. Korean Adopted Children's Ethnic Identity
Formation**   **79**
   Nam Soon Huh

Ethnic Identity   80
Ethnic Identity Development and Adoption   80
Method   83
Results   84
Discussion   92
Implications for Practice   94

**Chapter 6. Transracial Adoptive Parents' Thoughts
About the Importance of Race and Culture in Parenting**   **99**
   M. Elizabeth Vonk
   Sung Hyun Yun
   Wansoo Park
   Richard R. Massatti

Methodology   101
Results   102
Discussion   108
Implications   110

PART III: REFLECTIONS ON KOREAN ADOPTION   113

**Chapter 7. Remembering Loss: The Koreanness
of Overseas Adopted Koreans**   115
Eleana Kim

Introduction   115
Points of Reentry   116
The Global Family of Korea   119
Wedding Citizenship and Culture   124
Conclusion   127

**Chapter 8. Mothers Without Mothering: Birth Mothers
from South Korea Since the Korean War**   131
Hosu Kim

Trauma and the Figure of the Birth Mother   134
Intercountry Adoption and Korea   135
Three Cohorts of Birth Mothers' Characteristics in Korea   139
Affect Economy and the Figure of the Birth Mother   142
The Child As Gift or Adoption As Gift?   145
Activating the Memory of Birth Mothers   147

**Chapter 9. A Sociological Approach to Race, Identity,
and Asian Adoption**   155
*Jiannbin L. Shiao
Mia H. Tuan*

Introduction   155
The Asian Adoption Phenomenon   155
The Desirability of Asian Adoptees   157
Controversy Over Black-White Adoption Placements   157
Asian Adoption As an Area of Sociological Investigation   159
Research   160
Clues from the "Asian Immigrants in White Families:
   Korean Adoptees in America" Study   163
Conclusion: From Family Adjustment to Diverse Meaning
   and Contexts   167

Chapter 10. Lifting the Shroud of Silence: A Korean Adoptee's Search for Truth, Legitimacy, and Justice   **171**
Rebecca Hurdis

Prologue   171
Christianity and the Korean War   172
Illegitimate Motherhood   176
Daughters of the Ghost   178

PART IV: BIRTH-COUNTRY PERSPECTIVES   **187**

Chapter 11. Recent Trends in Child Welfare and Adoption in Korea: Challenges and Future Directions   **189**
Bong Joo Lee

Introduction   189
A Brief History of Adoption in Korea   191
Trends in Adoption   195
Challenges and Future Directions of Adoption in Korea   199
Conclusion   204

Chapter 12. Korea's Overseas Adoption and Its Positive Impact on Domestic Adoption and Child Welfare in Korea   **207**
Tai Soon Bai

Introduction   207
Domestic Adoption Practice in Korea   209
Impact of International Adoption on the Development of Domestic Adoption and Child Welfare Practices   213
Conclusion   216

Chapter 13. The Korean Adoption Issue and Representations of Adopted Koreans in Korean Popular Culture   **221**
Tobias Hübinette

The Importance of Popular Culture   222
The Development of the Korean Adoption Issue   223
Susanne Brink's Arirang   224
From the Spectacular to the Natural   226
Sad Songs About Adoption   228
The Construction of a Discourse on Adopted Koreans   229

PART V: GLOBAL PERSPECTIVES   **235**

**Chapter 14. Identity and International Adoptees:
A Comparison of the Vietnamese and Korean
Adoptee Experience in Australia**   **237**
    Kim Gray

Brief Background on International Adoption in Australia   237
Aim   238
Methodology   239
Recruitment of Participants and Data Collection   240
Data Analysis   241
Sociopolitical Context   241
International Adoptees and Cultural Identity   243
"Difference" and Diversity in Adoptee Experiences   245
Results   246
The Impact of Multiculturalism and the Construction
    of "Difference"   249
Korean-Australian Identities   250
Dealing with Racism   254
Discussion and Conclusions   257

**Chapter 15. A Longitudinal Study of Korean Adoptees
in the Netherlands: Infancy to Middle Childhood**   **263**
    Femmie Juffer
    Marinus H. van IJzendoorn

Introduction   263
Adoption in the Netherlands   263
The Longitudinal Adoption Study   265
Early Childhood   266
Middle Childhood   270
Discussion and Conclusions   272

PART VI: IMPLICATIONS FOR PRACTICE   **277**

**Chapter 16. Utilization of Structural Equation Modeling
to Predict Psychological Well-Being Among Adopted
Korean Children**   **279**
    Dong Pil Yoon

Literature Review   280

Method 283
Data Analysis 285
Results 286
Discussion 289

**Chapter 17. Once Upon a Time: A Critical Look
at How Children's Literature Contextualizes
Adoption for Asian Adoptees** **295**
Kathleen Ja Sook Bergquist

Survey of the Literature About Asian Adoption 298
Themes in Literature About Asian Adoption 301
Bibliotherapy and Asian-American Adoptees 308

**Chapter 18. Reconstruction of the Psychosocial World
of Korean Adoptees in the United States: A Search
for New Meanings** **315**
Daniel B. Lee

The Meaning of Homecoming for Adopted Korean
Youths and Young Adults: Case Examples 318
Search for Cultural Roots and Biological Kin:
Homecoming Experiences 320
Research Project 320
Findings and Discussions 324
Conclusion 336

PART VII: RESOURCES **339**

**Chapter 19. International Korean Adoption:
A Selective Bibliography** **341**
Janet H. Clarke

Korean Adoption 342
Asian Adoption—General 369

Conclusion **385**
M. Elizabeth Vonk
Kathleen Ja Sook Bergquist

Index **389**

ABOUT THE EDITORS

Kathleen Ja Sook Bergquist, PhD, is an Assistant Professor in the School of Social Work at the University of Nevada, Las Vegas. She completed her PhD in counselor education at the College of William and Mary, and her MSW at Norfolk State University. Her areas of interest and research are international adoption, diaspora studies, and culturally relevant practice. Dr. Bergquist is an adoption researcher, Korean adoptee, and Korean adoptive parent.

M. Elizabeth Vonk, PhD, is an Associate Professor and Director of the Doctoral Program at the School of Social Work at the University of Georgia. She is the author of numerous articles on transracial adoption and provides workshops for transracial adoptive parents and children. Her other research interests include practice evaluation and post-traumatic stress disorder treatment. Dr. Vonk is an international transracial adoptive parent of two.

Dong Soo Kim, PhD, is a Professor of Social Work at Norfolk State University. He completed his doctorate at the University of Chicago and MSW at the University of Pittsburgh. He also holds an MDiv from the Pittsburgh Theological Seminary. Dr. Kim was one of the earliest researchers of Korean adoption, completing the first longitudinal study examining self-concept and adjustment.

Marvin D. Feit, PhD, is Dean and Professor in the Norfolk State University Ethelyn R. Strong School of Social Work in Norfolk, Virginia. He is the author or co-author of several books and has written many articles and chapters in the areas of group work, substance abuse, health, and practice. Dr. Feit has made numerous presentations at national, state, and local conferences and has served as a consultant to for-profit and nonprofit organizations, federal and state agencies, and numerous community-based agencies. He is the founding editor of the *Journal of Health and Social Policy* (Haworth) and of the *Journal of Evidence-Based Social Work* (Haworth). In addition, he is a co-founding editor of the *Journal of Human Behavior in the Social Environment* (Haworth).

International Korean Adoption
© 2007 by The Haworth Press, Inc. All rights reserved.
doi:10.1300/5734_a

CONTRIBUTORS

Tai Soon Bai is a Professor in the Department of Social Welfare at Kyungnam University. She completed her MSW at the University of Michigan and her PhD from the University of Chicago. From June 1978 to September 1981, she worked for the State of Michigan as an adoption worker in the Intercountry Adoption Program, and was the President of the Korean Society of Child Welfare from 1998 through 2000.

Kristi Brian is a doctoral candidate in Temple University's Department of Anthropology. Her dissertation research questions center around constructions of culture and race and the degree to which adoption professionals incorporate the perspectives of Korean adopted adults.

Catherine Ceniza Choy is an Assistant Professor of American Studies at the University of Minnesota, Twin Cities, and the author of *Empire of Care: Nursing and Migration in Filipino American History* (Duke University Press, 2003). Her current research project focuses on the history of the international adoption of Asian children in the United States.

Janet Hyunju Clarke is Associate Librarian at Stony Brook University. She has a PhD in English with a special interest in Asian-American Literature.

William Feigelman completed his doctorate in sociology at the State University of New York at Stony Brook in 1987. Presently he is Professor of Sociology at Nassau Community College, Garden City, New York. Over the course of his career, besides studying adoptions, he has pursued a wide range of research interests, such as youth political protest, voyeurism, religious commitments, intergroup relations, youth drug abuse, tobacco use and cessation, and gambling. He has received research grant support from a variety of funding agents including the National Institute of Mental Health, National Science Foundation, the Research Foundation of the State University of New York, and the California Department of Health Services. The author of seven books and more than thirty-five journal articles, his most recent work on adoptions compares the differences in psychosocial adjustments between teenage adoptees living with one parent and non-adoptees living with one parent (*American Journal of Orthopsychiatry,* forthcoming).

Kim Gray is a sociology doctoral candidate at the University of Newcastle, New South Wales, Australia, and adoptive parent to two Korean children. Her chapter in this book forms part of her doctoral research, which considers the experiences of adolescent and adult international adoptees growing up in Australia and issues of race, culture, and identity. The doctoral research follows on from her earlier study on adoptive families' experiences of the intercountry adoption process in Australia and the politics of race, culture, and identity.

Tobias Hübinette (Korean name: Lee Sam-dol) is an adopted Korean and has a PhD in Korean studies from Stockholm University, and he is conducting research on the Korean adoption issue. He received a bachelor's degree in Irish studies from Uppsala University in 1991, and a master's degree in Korean studies from Stockholm University in 2000. In addition, he writes and lectures on issues of postcoloniality, Orientalism, international adoption, and racism, and has published internationally as well as in Sweden.

Nam Soon Huh is the Dean of the College of Social Science and a Professor in the Department of Social Welfare, Hallym University, Hallymdaehak-gil, Chuncheon City, Korea. She graduated from the Department of Social Work at Ewha Women's University in Korea with an MA. She then completed her MSW at the University of Minnesota and her PhD from the School of Social Welfare, University of New York at Albany. She worked at adoption agencies both in Korea and in the United States before she joined Hallym University as a faculty member.

Rebecca Hurdis is a doctoral candidate in the Comparative Ethnic Studies Program at the University of California, Berkeley. Her work interrogates the intersection of race and gender in relation to the social, political, and personal complexities of transnational and transracial adoption from Asia. Born in Korea and adopted at the age of six months, her formative years were spent in New England. She has resided in California for the past seven years.

Femmie Juffer received her MA and PhD in Child and Family Studies in from Utrecht University. In 1993, she joined the faculty of Leiden University, Center for Child and Family Studies, as a postdoctoral researcher and later became Assistant Professor and then Associate Professor. In 2000 she was appointed as a Professor of Adoption Studies. In 2001 she became Head of the Department for Child and Family Studies.

Eleana Kim is a second-generation Korean-American currently completing her PhD in Cultural Anthropology at New York University. Her dissertation research focuses on the Korean adult adoptee community and their relationships to Korea. Her articles on Korean adoption have been recently published in *Visual Anthropology Review* and *Social Text*.

Hosu Kim is a doctoral candidate in the PhD program in Sociology and the Women's Studies Certificate Program at the Graduate Center of the City University of New York. She is teaching as an instructor in the department of Sociology, Hunter College. Her research interests are intercountry adoption and language.

Bong Joo Lee is an Associate Professor at the Department of Social Welfare, Seoul National University, Korea, and a faculty associate at Chapin Hall Center for Children at the University of Chicago. He holds a PhD in Social Service Administration from the University of Chicago, and has held an Assistant Professorship at Boston University School of Social Work. His research focuses on child poverty, child welfare, and social service reform issues.

Daniel B. Lee is a faculty member and Associate Dean in the School of Social Work at Loyola University, Chicago. He completed his DSW at the University of Utah and his MSW at Florida State University. He is founder of the Transcultural Family Institute and also a cofounder and former president of the Global Awareness Society International. His research interests include issues of intercultural communication, transgenerational family relations, immigrant and relocation stressors, interdisciplinary care and intervention, and marital and family treatment.

Rick Massatti is a Social Science Research Specialist for the Ohio Department of Mental Health. He received his master's degree in Social Work from Ohio State University and has bachelor's degrees in Psychology and German Studies from Ohio University. His research interests include cross-cultural issues, spirituality in treatment, and transfer of mental health technology in the international arena.

Wansoo Park is Assistant Professor in the School of Social Work at University of Windsor in Ontario, Canada. She completed her graduate studies in social work at Ohio State University and her PhD from the University of South Carolina. Her primary research interests include acculturation, cultural competence, women's health, health communication, and parenting.

Jiannbin Lee Shiao is an Associate Professor of Sociology at the University of Oregon. He is the co-principal investigator (with Mia Tuan) for the project "Asian Immigrants in White Families: Korean Adoptees in America," supported by the Russell Sage Foundation. He is also finalizing a book on organizational diversity policy for Duke University Press and teaches courses on racial and ethnic diversity, race relations, education, the Asian American experience, and racial theory/intersectionality for both the Sociology Department and the Ethnic Studies program.

Mia Tuan is an Associate Professor of Sociology at the University of Oregon, where she specializes in racial/ethnic identity, immigrant adaptation, and intergroup relations. She received her BA from University of California, Berkeley, and MA/PhD from University of California, Los Angeles. She is the mother of two fabulous daughters, Macy and Cleo.

Marinus H. van IJzendoorn is Professor at the Centre for Child & Family Studies at Leiden University, the Netherlands. He is director of the Leiden Attachment Research Program. The focus of the research in this program is on the development and sequelae of attachment relationships and representations across the life span. These attachment relationships and representations are studied in a wide variety of settings, such as in different cultures, various family settings including adoptive families, day care settings, and in different nonclinical populations. He is involved in research based on two complementary approaches: (1) empirical studies of antecedents and sequelae of attachment in "normal" children and their families as well as in children and families at risk, and (2) theoretical and historical research of the foundations and methods of child and family research, including the meta-analytic synthesis of empirical findings in child and family studies.

Dong Pil Yoon is an Assistant Professor at the School of Social Work, University of Missouri–Columbia. He has conducted a number of studies on intercountry adoption, religiousness/spirituality, and rural social work. The article "Causal Modeling Predicting Psychological Adjustment of Korean-Born Adolescent Adoptees" was published as part of the special "Psychosocial Aspects of the Asian-American Experience" issues of the *Journal of Human Behavior in the Social Environment*.

Sung Hyun Yun is a doctoral candidate at the School of Social Work, University of Georgia, Athens, Georgia. In addition, he is Assistant Professor at the School of Social Work, University of Windsor, Ontario, Canada. Prior to beginning his doctoral studies, he was Program Director of The Center for Pan Asian Community Services, Inc., in Georgia, where he developed a culture-specific intervention program for Korean-American domestic violence perpetrators.

Foreword

As a scholar, elected official, adoptee, and as one who has adopted Korean children, I applaud this effort to examine the phenomenon of Korean adoption in a comprehensive and systematic way. This body of research will serve as a kind of "encyclopedia" that will enable the reader to better understand the depth and breadth of issues related to international transracial adoption.

I, for one, consider it a great blessing to be adopted. Most Korean adoptees, like myself, have found successful, meaningful lives in the United States, and many have contributed positively to the betterment of their communities. While I cannot speak for other parts of the world, studies suggest that Korean adoptees have made positive adjustments throughout the world. Despite my own personal success as an adoptee, adoption has always raised difficult questions and challenges related to self-identity, perception, and discrimination. It is my feeling that all Korean adoptees approach the question of identity, at least to some degree. Some Koreans, whether for better or for worse, have chosen to return to Korea. Some have returned to find their biological parents, others to pursue job opportunities, and others to explore the land of their heritage. Although I was adopted by a family that provided me with a loving home and an education, I too had a keen interest in exploring my heritage. It is for this reason that I support adoptees who return to Korea, for whatever reason, if it aids their quest for success and fulfillment in life. I will remain eternally grateful to those who have found it in their heart to adopt Korean children. We thank you for giving us a new beginning, but we also invite you to become part of our heritage. The key to success is finding the balance between preserving one's distinct cultural background on the one hand, and assimilation to mainstream society on the other.

I am confident this collection of work will provide scholars, adoptees, and adoptive parents with answers to many unresolved questions and will

International Korean Adoption
© 2007 by The Haworth Press, Inc. All rights reserved.
doi:10.1300/5734_c

serve as the basis for further exploration into the origins, development, and institutionalization of Korean adoption. I express my sincere gratitude to the authors who have contributed their time and expertise to this worthwhile endeavor.

Paull H. Shin, PhD
Washington State Senator

Preface

This collection of scholarly work commemorates fifty years of Korean international adoption, the most significant and longstanding form of international child welfare practice. The transplanting of these children into families in the United States, Australia, and several Western European countries has both provided homes for orphans who might have otherwise lingered in institutional care and made available children for parents amid rising infertility rates and decreasing availability of healthy infants. This practice has also profoundly challenged previously held assumptions about family formation, situated discourses on race and commodification in the living rooms and neighborhoods of middle-class Caucasian families, reinforced South Korea's dependency on the West, and, most significantly, positioned children and families to navigate racialized notions of community, family, and self.

PURPOSE/FOCUS OF THIS BOOK

This book is aimed at furthering the interdisciplinary discourse on the construction, context, and impact of international transracial adoption by assembling works from scholars who have engaged in research on Korean adoption. Originating out of the academic disciplines of psychology, ethnic studies, sociology, social work, and anthropology, the authors seek to share with fellow scholars, practitioners, parents, adoptees, and the adoptive community at-large critical reflections and up-to-date research. The group of contributors includes established adoption researchers (i.e., Dong Soo Kim, William Feigelman, and Nam Soon Huh) as well as newer researchers who are keeping the study of international adoption in the forefront. The breadth of contributions not only across disciplines but also across national borders reflects the complexity and global impact of this practice.

While developing the collection, we chose to solicit contributions addressing international Korean adoption in a general sense, and then orga-

International Korean Adoption
© 2007 by The Haworth Press, Inc. All rights reserved.
doi:10.1300/5734_d

nized the essays around emerging themes. This was purposeful in two ways: it allowed us to cast a broader interdisciplinary net while not restricting us—or the authors—in considering this multifaceted phenomenon. The essays therefore run the gamut from Tobias Hübinette's reflections on international adoption located in Korean popular culture to Hosu Kim's metaphorical conceptualization of Korean adoptees as embodying the American dream.

The collection comprises the following seven sections:

1. Sociohistorical background: Much of the existing literature characterizes the onset of Korean adoption as an outcome of the Korean War, without serious discussion or analysis of the deeply rooted sociopolitical contexts that precipitated and sustained it. This section offers interconnected yet distanced historical perspectives on the inception and institutionalization of the unilateral practice of placing Korean children into Western homes.

2. Forming new families: Notions of family in relation to international adoption are stretched beyond heredity, traversing national borders, and situated within the geopolitical discourse of race and neocolonialism. This section explores how Korean children and their adoptive families navigate these third spaces, which are their homes, and the negotiation of their roles and identities as parent, child, and self.

3. Reflections on Korean adoption: The integration of the personal and political is explored in essays that seek to capture the voices and experiences of adoptees. Findings and discussion from multimodal research are interspersed with exercises in academic inquiry.

4. Birth-country perspectives: Literature representing the accommodation of international adoption both in practice and the psyche of the Korean people is virtually absent, at least for Western consumption. This section most uniquely provides thoughtful consideration of adoption in Korea as a child welfare practice and the integration of it into the public conscience.

5. Global perspectives: Korean children were placed in the diaspora through intercountry adoption, finding homes in the United States, Australia, Canada, Sweden, and other European countries. This section provides insight into the varied contexts and experiences of adoptees and their families transnationally.

6. Implications for practice: Although Korean adoption represents the longest-standing form of international child welfare practice, there is a marked absence in the literature of writing and research that reflect a fifty-year history of practice. The need for evaluation, evidence-based

practice, and the development of best practices is significant. This section represents a token collection of works offering critical consideration of Korean adoption practice.

7. Resources: This section serves as a repository for indexing archival, historical, and current resources on Korean adoption. It also necessarily includes related resources that deal with international adoption, in general, and also the connected arenas of transracial and other Asian adoptions.

CONTRIBUTION TO EXISTING LITERATURE

In seeking to commemorate and provide a meaningful contribution to the existing literature, we became aware of both the wealth of current scholarly inquiry as well as a dearth in birth-country/birth-parent representation accessible to Western audiences. We have included, in this collection, essays that will challenge readers to entertain, if not accommodate or refute, varied perspectives and critical analyses of this borderless child welfare practice. Each piece has been selected for its important and unique contribution to critical inquiry and discourse. As a collection, we intend this book to be a depository for representative current work and a marker for future research.

Its value lies not only in its focus on Korean international adoption but in its relevance to the broader context of global child welfare and allied fields such as international family law, diaspora and migration studies, sociology, psychology, and anthropology; and other scholarships that consider children and families within a geopolitical context. The interdisciplinary background of the contributors makes this collection accessible and germane to the individual authors' fields and also to those who are positioned to impact adoption policy and practice.

PART I:
SOCIOHISTORICAL BACKGROUND

International adoption has become a highly visible and institutionalized practice wherein it is not uncommon for most North Americans to have at least second- or thirdhand knowledge of a family who has adopted from Asia, Latin America, or one of the former Eastern Bloc countries. However, public awareness about the precipitating conditions that place children in the diaspora as orphans is generally limited to textbook or evening news summaries of poverty, war, or gender preferences in sending countries.

The following essays examine the institutionalization of Korean international adoption from equally important and differing lenses and from both sides of the Pacific. Dong Soo Kim examines the complex social, economic, and political history that divided Korea and devastated families. He provides a birth-country perspective and context that is virtually absent in the literature. Catherine Ceniza Choy's exploration of independent adoption schemes through archival research leads her to "documents that speak to the multiple controversies surrounding international and transracial adoption." Both authors illuminate the pivotal and dichotomous role that the United States has played in relationship to Korean adoption. Kim describes the United States' interest in the political tug-of-war over North and South Korea, which positioned children as victims, measured against the humanitarian responses of adoptive American families. Ceniza Choy further juxtaposes adoption agencies' responsibility in guarding "the best interests of the child" against the commodification of Korean children. The contributors' candid analyses of the context of Korean adoption provide a firm grounding and direction for the collection.

Chapter 1

A Country Divided: Contextualizing Adoption from a Korean Perspective

Dong Soo Kim

Korea is a small peninsula in Far East Asia with a little over seventy-one million people living in 85,228 square miles (CIA, 2005). Forcefully divided for sixty years, Korea is the only remaining vestige of the old East-West ideological conflicts in the world today. Once known as "a Hermit Kingdom" to the Western world, the nation's history goes back to 2,333 BC with her distinctive cultural heritage throughout various political triumphs and turmoil for many centuries. For the past half-century, Korea has experienced a tragic civil war, dire poverty, rapid social change, vigorous industrialization, and political unrest, all in the context of national division and conflict between the North and South. Historical development of this divided small peninsula has been the stage on which the drama of massive and permanent child transfer and placement was performed beyond national, racial, and cultural boundaries to create an international adoption practice in the global community.

The purpose of this chapter is to review the overall context of international adoption from the Korean perspective. Korea's historical background, sociocultural environment, perspectives on adoption, global trends, associated issues and problems, and recent new developments will be discussed. Statistical data and scholarly literature also will be referenced.

An edited version of this chapter originally appeared in *Korean Quarterly,* 9(2) (winter 2005/2006), 14-17. Reprinted by permission of the author.

International Korean Adoption
Published by The Haworth Press, Inc., 2007. All rights reserved.
doi:10.1300/5734_01

HISTORICAL AND CULTURAL BACKGROUND

Korea has been a traditional agro-feudal society with its own language, culture, history, and beliefs for many centuries. Traditionally, Korean cultural patterns have been strongly influenced by Confucianism, even though Shamanism and Buddhism were also prevalent as religions. The old society has been singularly characterized by patriarchy with a heavy emphasis on family tradition and filial piety. In a patriarchal society, the family system has a male-dominated and extended family structure, with built-in provisions for total allegiance and care for all members. In such a cultural context, blood ties have been highly valued to preserve the family system. Adoption, when it occurred, was simply to continue the family bloodline, usually among relatives or within the same surnames. Accordingly, adopting a child of nonrelated or unknown origin was a very foreign concept. Furthermore, the adoption of a child born from "wrong blood" or mixed blood was especially not culturally acceptable (Kim, 1978b).

The traditional culture was drastically shattered, however, as Korean society experienced massive destruction and rapid changes in the last century. In fact, Korea has been invaded and intruded upon by powerful neighboring countries, like China, Japan, and Russia. Korea served often as a battleground among competing and invading foreign powers, and yet it managed to maintain its political independence and cultural identity for so long.

In 1910, the Japanese Empire forcefully annexed and colonized Korea for thirty-six years, destroying much of Korean traditional culture and national spirit. With the end of World War II, Korea was liberated from Japanese rule, but the North was occupied by USSR forces and the South by the United States, thus creating the frontline of an East-West ideological cold war. The South embraced a fragile form of democracy with an American capitalistic system and the North the Stalinist state of Communism, with central planning and controlled economy system. The division of the country along the thirty-eighth parallel begot the separation or loss of many family members.

KOREAN CONFLICT
AND ITS IMPACT ON FAMILIES

In June 1950, the Korean War broke out between the North (Democratic Peoples' Republic of Korea, or North Korea, for short) and the South (Republic of Korea or South Korea). The United States and sixteen other nations soon joined the war on behalf of South Korea under the United

Nations' sanction through the Security Council Resolution 83 (June 27, 1950), and in return Communist China (Peoples' Republic of China) soon supported North Korea with their "Volunteer Army." This war lasted for three years with crisscrossing frontlines before the conflict came to an end with a military armistice agreement between the two camps. This brought massive destruction to the entire peninsula with about five million casualties. According to various statistical reports, it is estimated that the total deaths reached 2,800,000 among Koreans and non-Koreans, both combatants and civilians. Also, approximately 200,000 widows and 100,000 orphans were created by the war. About 80 percent of industries, public facilities, and transportation system were destroyed (Korean Institute of Military History, 2001; Wikipedia, 2005). The total number of U.S. military casualties alone reached 54,746 deaths and 103,284 wounds (Department of Defense, 2005). The ensuing chaos and hardships of the war brought much disintegration to the traditional family system. The greatest victims of this war, as in any military conflict, were children. There were hundreds of thousands of lost, abandoned, neglected, and orphaned children both in the North and South whose needs for care and support were unmet.

With the devastating obliteration and very limited social infrastructure, parentless children were crowded into some 500 shelters and orphanages that were developed through foreign aid organizations in the South. Many overflowed onto streets to scavenge and beg for their survival. The situation in North Korea, one can assume, must have been even worse because of the greater number of casualties, devastating destruction, and limited foreign aid. While being a welfare state in theory, the poverty-stricken North was not in a position to provide much for the survival needs of the numerous orphaned children.

For the most part, Korea's traditional family system was no longer functional. Its structure was so weakened that families were isolated and fractured, many headed by women. Unemployment and poverty were rampant. The Korean War resulted in many families with children becoming helpless victims of dependency and disintegration.

THE ORIGIN OF KOREAN
INTERNATIONAL ADOPTION

The misery of the aftermath of Korean War brought great sympathy and support to the South from the international community, especially from many U.S. charity organizations such as Save the Children's Fund, World Vision, Compassion, Church World Services, and Catholic Charities. In

1955 Harry Holt traveled to South Korea from Oregon to adopt orphaned children. *The Seed from the East* chronicles the Holts' personal account of adopting eight Korean GI orphans, their adjustment to their new home, and other inspiring stories about the origins of the project that developed into the world's largest international adoption program (Holt, 1956; Holt International Children's Services, 1976). These pioneering adoptions were widely publicized and inspired many U.S. families to adopt Korean children in ever-increasing numbers. In 1961, the Korean government promulgated a special law, Extraordinary Law of Adoption for the Orphan Child, in order to encourage foreigners to adopt Korean children. According to a government report, the number of international adoptions had been growing each year, with the placement of increasingly more full-Korean children (74.2 percent). From 1955 to 1973, Korea sent 21,890 children overseas for adoption (Ministry of Health and Social Affairs, 1974).

Of course, the initial and primary receiving country of Korean children has been the United States for the past fifty years. However, international adoption was virtually unknown to the United States before World War II. In 1948 the U.S. Government enacted the Displaced Persons Act to help war orphans (up to 3,000) get settled in, with or without adoption. Immediately following the war, 500 Korean orphans were allowed to enter the United States every year for adoption. However, due to the great need for homes for Korean War orphans, the Refugee Relief Act allowed 4,000 orphans to the United States for adoption until 1956. The following year the cap on orphan visas was removed by Congress, and immigration for the purpose of adoption was "normalized" with the Immigration and Nationality Act in 1961, which became a *de facto* legal tool of international adoption (Babb, 1999).

The continued pressure for the international adoption of Korean children was also matched by powerful advocacy activities of adoptive and prospective adoptive parents in the United States. In 1967 an adoptive mother, Betty Kramer, founded Parents of Korean and Korean-American Children. The following year the name was changed to the Organization for a United Response (OURS), becoming the largest international adoption support group in the country (Kramer, 1975). With continued evolution and restructuring, OURS later became Adoptive Families of America (AFA). The organization's award-winning national adoption magazine, *Adoptive Families,* has been the leading adoption information source in print and online for families before, during, and after adoption (AFA, 2005). Through their support and advocacy, Korean, Vietnamese, and other foreign children continued to be adopted in the United States throughout the post-Vietnam era. However, Korea remained the leading source for international adoption until 1995. During the first forty years following the Korean War, more children were brought into the United States from Korea than from all other countries combined. Not until the opening of Eastern Europe and China for adoption in the 1990s did the picture of international adoption change. In 1997 *Adoptive Families* reported that Russian and Chinese children were adopted more than children from all other countries combined. Thus, what was originally started as a critical rescue mission in Korea has now become a permanent institution of child welfare services on an international level.

INTERNATIONAL ADOPTION AS A PERMANENT INSTITUTION

As indicated in the preceding text, the "temporary" practice of Korean international adoption continued and grew as time went by. In spite of some enhanced measures of security and stability in South Korea in the 1960s, and improving economic conditions in the 1970s, Korea's international adoptions continued and flourished. Most biracial children born to Korean women and American servicemen were ostracized in the "pure blood" monoethnic society. Consequently, out of necessity and moral mandate, they were prime candidates for foreign adoption. In the 1980s and 1990s, South Korea experienced dramatic economic growth and development, along with intermittent political turmoil and social unrest. Hundreds of thousands of poor women were oppressed and exploited with little provision for building a future. The rapid social change in turn increasingly disintegrated family and community functions, resulting in many illegitimate and abandoned children.

These children were mostly left in institutional care and not considered adoptable domestically. This was largely due to the cultural bias against nonrelative open adoptions and also public reluctance, or inability, to develop and invest in its own social service resources. Thus, ever more nonwar orphans were sent away for international adoption. Those considered hard to place, such as older, handicapped, or "problem" children, were placed overseas with families who were eager and ready to provide adoptive homes.

Table 1.1 shows comprehensive statistics of Korean overseas adoption since the war until 2004. There have been some noticeable fluctuations in the number of adoptions in the past fifty years, significantly reflecting the Korean government policy on international adoption (GAIPS, 2005).

According to Table 1.1, the number of adoptions has steadily grown, with some interludes or downward trends. In 1976, in the face of increasing criticism and uneasiness about the "child export business," a new law was

TABLE 1.1. Korean Overseas Adoption by Year

Year	Number	Year	Number	Year	Number
–	–	1971	2,725	1991	2,197
–	–	1972	3,490	1992	2,045
1953	4	1973	4,688	1993	2,290
1954	8	1974	5,302	1994	2,262
1955	59	1975	5,077	1995	2,180
1956	671	1976	6,597	1996	2,080
1957	486	1977	6,159	1997	2,057
1958	930	1978	5,917	1998	2,443
1959	741	1979	4,148	1999	2,409
1960	638	1980	4,144	2000	2,409
1961	660	1981	4,628	2001	2,436
1962	254	1982	6,434	2002	2,365
1963	442	1983	7,263	2003	2,287
1964	462	1984	7,924	2004	2,258
1965	451	1985	8,837	–	–
1966	494	1986	8,680	–	–
1967	626	1987	7,947	–	–
1968	949	1988	6,463	–	–
1969	1,190	1989	4,191	–	–
1970	1,932	1990	2,962	–	–
Subtotal	10,997	Subtotal	113,576	Subtotal	31,669
Grand Total	156,242				

Source: Ministry of Health and Welfare, Overseas Koreans Foundation (2005).

created by the military government of Korea which was intended to promote in-country adoption by restricting overseas adoption by 20 percent each year (Extraordinary Law, 1976). There was some decline the four or five years that followed, but due to mounting pressure from all quarters—including adoption agencies in the United States—the law was eventually rescinded and the growth trend resumed until it reached a peak in 1985. Starting in 1990, however, the number was significantly reduced and stabilized with approximately 2,000 children being adopted overseas per year. In Korea, this decrease seemed to reflect a combined effect of public sentiment, comparatively increased in-country adoption, greater social and familial stability, and an increased supply of children from other countries in the international adoption market.

The foreign adoption of Korean children survived for one-half century, starting with biracial children, war orphans, abandoned and poor children, older and handicapped children, to now any adoptable child. Even though the number has significantly decreased and stabilized, international adoption is here to stay and has become a permanent institution of Korean child welfare.

MOTIVATION FOR INTERNATIONAL ADOPTION

It has often been alleged that the movement of children across national borders is motivated by profit. Contrary to the initial humanitarian action to save poor children in Korea, the continuing flow of children has raised suspicion that somehow children were exploited to benefit adoption organizations, adoption brokers, adoptive parents, or even biological parents, if known. Largely because of tight governmental controls in Korea, and the physical distance between Korea and receiving countries, the illegal trafficking of children was never a serious issue, unlike in some Latin American countries. All Korean adoptive children had to be "legally adoptable," either having been abandoned or voluntarily relinquished by biological parents, usually mothers.

For many years, even after the War ended, there were many abandoned children as well as orphans. From 1955 to 1970, a total of 80,250 children have been abandoned by an unknown number of parents in Korea; the number may be significantly underestimated because of incomplete reporting procedures (Miller, 1971). Traditionally, leaving babies in front of wealthy or prospective caretakers' homes was a common practice in Korea. But institutional requirements that a child be parentless became a contributing factor to the large-scale phenomenon of child abandonment. Most children were abandoned because of an inability to care for them financially rather than the social stigma usually attached to single mothers. The implications of requiring children to be parentless was not fully understood until 1956, when an infant was found abandoned with a simple note, addressed to the superintendent of Baby's Home, that stated the child was "now a real orphan." The body of the writer was found nearby a few days later. This highly publicized dramatic event helped modify many orphanage policies to accommodate some children with known parents.

With the relaxation of the policy and public education, the number of children abandoned gradually decreased and the number of voluntary relinquishments steadily increased, reaching 1,232 within the first six months of 1975 (Central Child Welfare Committee, 1975). Voluntarily relinquishing one's child has complex psychosocial factors, dictated by situational reality. If a woman in Korea had a mixed-race child, her best choice for the child was considered to be obvious, that is, adoption abroad, since the child would be otherwise subject to lifelong discrimination in racist Korea. These children were not accepted in the racially homogeneous Korean society not only because of their different skin color but also because of the condemned status of their mothers, ironically called "U.N. madams," "comforters," or "Western queens." These children experienced open and inhumane rejection, accompanied by others' cultural bias, shame, fear, and hostility, from infancy.

Along with these children, increasingly more full-Korean children were being adopted abroad. If a mother was unmarried, deserted, divorced, or simply had too many children without adequate familial or financial resources, her challenge was sheer survival for herself and her children. She seemingly had little choice but to abandon or relinquish him to unknown (foreign) parents. One empirical study on maternal motivation for relinquishment indicated that most reasons given were socially, legally, or psychologically forced situations in which parents, especially birth mothers, had few acceptable alternatives but to give up their children. Also, they clung to "the vague expectation that relinquishment will guarantee the child and the parents a better life" (Whang, 1976, p. 98).

These mothers' acts of relinquishment seem to be based in sad but noble motivations. A small book, *I Wish for You a Beautiful Life,* is a rare collection of letters from Korean birth mothers who voluntarily gave up their children. A few lines from one of those letters seems to sum up the mothers' sad yet loving motivation very well: "You needed to be loved by family members, and you could have that love only if you were in a family. I couldn't give that love by myself. Therefore, adoption was my gift to you" (Dorow, 1999, back cover).

The rapid proliferation of international adoption was also due in part to the changing adoption field in the United States. During the 1970s, birth and fertility rates steadily began to decline, while the number of healthy white infants available for adoption also decreased (Barabba, 1975). Legalized abortion, following the landmark Roe v. Wade case (1973), wider availability of reliable contraception (birth control pills), and an increased prevalence of single mothers choosing to raise their own children were contributing factors (Nutt, 1974).

Despite such a short supply of available white children for adoption, childless couples were compelled, by their own desire to parent and/or societal expectations, to pursue the "second best" option of international adoption, often bypassing available children-of-color in the United States. In fact, at some level Americans' sense of entitlement tends to defy more conventional boundaries of human relationships than in other societies, with regard to marriage, family, business, class, or race. By adopting a child from another racial or cultural group, white American couples sought to satisfy their parental desires (Kim, 1978a).

Infertility, which is typically the primary reason couples seek to adopt, was not the main motivating factor in the case of international adoption. According to one nationwide study of international adoption, adoptive parents ranked infertility as the fourth most cited reason for adopting, while "love of children and parenting" and "humanitarian/religious concerns" were ranked most highly. In fact, many parents who adopted overseas also had birth children. Many were motivated by a desire to rescue poor children, an altruism reportedly based in religious or spiritual beliefs (Kim, 1976).

The humanitarianism, parental caring, and spiritual motivations of Korean adoptive parents are impressively deep and real. However, there seems to be also some discrepancies in their altruism, if not hypocrisies, in that their concern and love for poor homeless children were color-biased and somewhat romanticized with "those problems far away." In the same study cited here, when adoptive parents were asked to rank their willingness to adopt within ten categories of "hard-to-place children," black children were ranked in eighth place. Most prospective parents who were eager to adopt Korean children were somehow reluctant to consider black children. The need for adoptive homes for children-of-color in the United States was even greater, yet the children were relegated to an overburdened foster care system or institutional care for a long period of time (Herzog et al., 1972).

GLOBALIZATION OF KOREAN INTERNATIONAL ADOPTION

The continued short supply of adoptable (white) children in the United States and the ever-recurring needs for caring homes for many orphans and refugee children throughout the world have led to multilateral international adoptions. According to the Child Welfare League of America (2003), well over 100 million children are estimated to live without adequate caregivers in Asia (sixty-five million), Africa (thirty-four million), and Latin America

and the Caribbean (eight million), and an unknown number of institutionalized children in the former Eastern Europe. According to a recent report of
Children on the Brink 2004, there were 143 million orphans ages zero
through seventeen years around the world in 2003 (UNICEF, 2004).

Thus, the pressure for further expansion of international adoption is ever
mounting each year. Figure 1.1 shows the continuing increase of international adoption.

A recent U.S. Department of State report (Table 1.2) shows detailed immigrant visas issued to orphans coming to the United States for adoption,
broken down by year and country. According to this report, the numbers for
2003 and 2004 were further increased to 21,616 and 22,884, respectively.
The number of countries involved in sending children is even more striking.
The following alphabetized list represents nations from which a significant
number of children were sent for adoption, primarily to the United States
and about a dozen European countries.

> Brazil, Bulgaria, Cambodia, China, Columbia, Ecuador, El Salvador,
> Ethiopia, Georgia, Guatemala, Haiti, Honduras, Hungary, India, Kaz-
> akhstan, Mexico, Mongolia, Paraguay, Peru, Philippines, Poland, Ro-
> mania, Russia, Taiwan, Uganda, Ukraine, Thailand, and Vietnam.
> (U.S. Department of State, 2005b, p. 28)

There are also a couple of dozen sending countries that participate in international adoption on a much smaller scale: Albania, Armenia, Azer-
baijan, Belarus, Bolivia, Chile, Costa Rica, Dominican Republic, Estonia,
Hong Kong, Jamaica, Japan, Latvia, Liberia, Luthuania, Moldova, Nepal,
Panama, Sierra Leone, South Africa, Sri Lanka, etc. (JCICS, 2005; U.S. Department of State, 2005b). According to the Canadian Immigration Bureau,

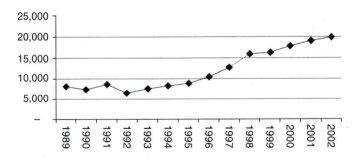

FIGURE 1.1. Number of International Adoptions (*Source:* U.S. Department of
State, 2005b.)

TABLE 1.2. Number of Children and Top Twenty Source Countries for International Adoptions by Year

Country	2004	2003	2002	2001	2000	1999	1998
China	7,044	6,859	5,053	4,681	5,053	4,101	4,206
Russia	5,865	5,209	4,939	4,279	4,269	4,348	4,491
Guatemala	3,264	2,328	2,219	1,609	1,518	1,002	911
S. Korea	1,716	1,790	1,779	1,770	1,794	2,008	1,829
Kazakhstan	826	825	819	672	399	113	–
Ukraine	723	702	1,106	1,246	659	321	180
India	406	472	466	543	503	499	478
Vietnam	–	382	766	737	724	709	603
Colombia	287	272	334	266	246	231	351
Bulgaria	110	198	260	297	214	221	151
Cambodia	–	124	254	407	402	249	249
Haiti	356	250	187	192	131	96	121
Philippines	196	214	221	219	173	195	200
Romania	57	200	168	782	1,122	895	406
Belarus	202	191	169	129	–	–	–
Ethiopia	289	135	105	158	95	103	96
Poland	102	97	101	86	83	97	77
Thailand	69	72	67	74	88	77	84
Azerbaijan	–	62	–	–	–	–	–
Mexico	89	61	61	73	106	137	168
Top Twenty	21,831	20,443	19,139	18,193	17,579	15,365	14,817
World Totals	22,884	21,616	20,099	19,137	18,537	16,396	15,774

Source: U.S. Department of State, Office of Visa Processing, September 2004 (2005b).

even the United States sent 786 children to Canada from 1993 to 2002 (Adoption Council of Canada, 2003). The major players in international adoption in recent years are China, Russia, and Guatemala, with Korea steadily taking the third position since 1995 and the fourth position since 2002. Table 1.2 shows the top twenty sending nations in the past seven years based on visas issued by the US State Department (2005b).

In view of the international transfer of children throughout the world, there have been considerable concerns about the protection of children's rights and interests. Most nations developed the necessary legislation and policies, but finally the Hague Convention culminated into a multinational agreement on international child adoption. The Hague Convention on Intercountry Adoption is a multilateral treaty designed to apply to all international adoptions between countries that ratify it. This treaty provides guidelines for streamlining and standardizing international adoption in order to prevent illegal child trafficking and abuse. Developed in 1994 under the Conference on Private International Law, the Convention is the result of a five-year process involving participants from sixty-six prospective member countries, which the U.S. Congress ratified in 2000 (U.S. Department of State, 2005a).

Thus, adoptions of Korean children, originally started by concerned American individuals as an emergency measure, have become a permanent institution of child welfare services on a global level.

QUESTIONS AND ISSUES

In the past fifty years since the first wave of Korean adoptions, about 160,000 Korean children, plus an unknown number of children privately arranged, have been placed for adoption in the United States. The initial preoccupation in this child transplant was with an efficient "rescue mission" without the luxury of thinking about their future. For those biracial children, it was assumed that there was no choice but international adoption. As the number increased drastically, more somber questions were raised from both sending and receiving sides—if and how the children would adjust in the new socially and culturally different home environments. A few initial adjustment observations and studies indicated that they did fare rather well considering their earlier deprivation or desertion (for example, CWLA, 1960; DiVirgilio, 1956; O'Conner, 1964; Valk, 1957; Young, 1963).

As those adoptive children aged, along with the massive flow of older and full-blood Korean children, more serious questions were asked about their long-term adjustment in terms of school performance, relationship with parents, socialization, cultural adaptation, self-esteem, mating, ethnic identity, etc. Several studies were conducted in this regard and important factors were identified for the healthy long-term adaptation and ethnic identity development (for example, Bergquist, 1997; Huh & Reid, 2000; Kim, 1977, 1978b; Simon & Altstein, 1987; Yoon, 2001). Korean adoptive children's overall outcome has been affirmative and positive. One more recent *JAMA* publication based on a large-scale meta-analysis of ninety-eight articles from 1950 to 2005 reported that international adoptees presented fewer behavior problems and were less often referred to mental health services than domestic adoptees (Juffer & van IJzendoorn, 2005). Some heartwarming "success stories" of individual adult Korean adoptees abound.

Yet, it cannot be denied that there have been some negative outcomes of international adoption, including maladaptation, placement failures, and mental health problems. The possibility of emotional and psychological scars for adoptees and their Korean parents is undeniable. Many biological parents, in spite of their sacrificial love and prudent decisions, might have suffered lifelong shame and pain because of their decision to relinquish their children. Likewise, although the Korean adoptees may have grown up relatively happily in American families, they might still have suffered a sense of being abandoned or cut off from their original family, culture, and roots. Many adoptees search for their roots and some have managed to visit the land of their birth. Many feel *fortunate* to be able to reunite with their biological parents, although those reunions sometimes end with eventual disappointment. Many adoptees have carried certain burdens, and sometimes the burdens, though full of great treasures, were heavy. Thus, Koreans perceive international adoptions with enduring guilt and hidden joy at the same time. When Koreans see a perfectly groomed Korean-American adoptee on an upper stage in their various professions, they feel sadly happy about them.

Still, the large-scale ongoing export of Korean children could not free the modern Korean society from the fundamental mandates and obligations for "the best interest of the children." The Joint Council on International Children's Services (JCICS) is the oldest and largest affiliation of licensed, nonprofit international adoption organizations in the world, with a membership of over 200 including adoption agencies, child welfare organizations, parent support groups, and medical specialists with an interest in intercountry adoption. The JCICS (2005) advocates on behalf of children in need of permanent families, preferably in birth countries and, only when not feasible, promotes ethical practices in intercountry adoption.

By all economic measures, Korea has been capable of caring for its own homeless children for some time. Thanks to aggressive economic development, South Korea was no longer regarded as a poor nation by the mid-1970s. South Korea joined the Organisation for Economic Co-operation and Development (OECD, 2005) in December 1996, which is an exclusive international club of relatively affluent thirty member countries sharing a commitment to democratic government and the market economy. Korea's Gross Domestic Product (GDP) per capita was $10,391 in 1994. As of 2004, South Korea commands the eleventh largest economy in the world. Now, with adequate economic resources on hand, increasingly more groups have banded together to challenge international adoption policy and the continuing neglect of children, Korea's most precious resource, and betraying its obligations for the welfare of all children.

In a sense, international adoptions served as an easy and inexpensive means for Korea to resolve the chronic social problems, namely, unwanted children of the nation (Byma, 1974). Particularly, children with handicaps and disabilities were conveniently placed into adoptions abroad. Ironically, the maintenance of international adoption has been necessary to take care of large numbers of children waiting in institutional care, and yet it might have contributed to help deter or delay the serious need for aggressive development of in-country adoptions. Such a deterrence and consequent lack of domestic adoption resources in turn justified the continued reliance on international adoption. It appeared to be a classic case of a vicious cycle of social policy failure, with the catch-22 dilemma. By default and by design, the Korean society seemed to have accepted the mass export of children as an inevitable path in the development of a welfare state.

It is not surprising, then, that Korea has retained notorious fame as the nation with the largest "child export." This becomes a political embarrassment in the international community, especially vis-à-vis the archenemy of North Korea. North Korea often criticizes the South Korean policy of "selling children." In North Korea, as they faced gravely desperate orphan problems during and after the Korean War, unknown numbers of war orphans were shipped to the Soviet Union and other Eastern European countries for foster or institutional care. They were accompanied by teachers and years later were brought back home.

The United States and other Western nations, the recipients of these transplanted children, are also not free from the blame associated with this trade. In the early years in the United States, large-scale international adoptions caused some uneasiness and objections, especially from the African-American community. International adoption in a significant way influenced the domestic minority adoption movement in the mid-1960s and 1970s, involving black foster care children and American-Indian reservation children (Fanshel, 1972; Jones, 1972). Main objections came from the then rising black militant movement as well as from the classic white racism or its realistic recognition of racism (Anderson, 1971). Many black professionals felt that placing and raising a black child in a white home and community might deprive the child of the essential developmental opportunity for his racial consciousness, pride, identity, and capability to deal with the reality of racism in the United States (Billingsley, 1968; Chestung, 1972; NABSW, 1972).

Korean international adoption as transracial and transcultural child place-ment was perceived with the same or more doubts and reservations. Child welfare professionals were concerned, at least initially, with the immediate adjustment of the Korean foreign children in U.S. society. This concern was justified in view of the daring amateur-like disregard in the international adoption process of the then conventional practice by child adoption pro-fessionals of "home study," "matching," "sealing records," etc. (CWLA, 1959). The uncertainty of long-term outcomes of the experiment of interna-tional adoption was viewed as truly worrisome in view of the uprooting and transplanting of foreign children.

But the continuing practice of international adoption shows an increas-ingly alarming trend. According to the Department of State statistics (U.S. Department of State, 2005b), immigrant visas issued to orphans coming from mostly poor nations to the United States are ever growing, as shown in Table 1.2. The importation of foreign children is almost always from third world countries and from former Communist bloc countries. This trend seems to suggest a deepening division between the "have and have-not countries" and another form of exploitation by powerful rich nations. Hollingsworth (2003) criticized international adoption practice, using Rawls' egalitarian concept of a distributive method of social justice. Inter-national adoption practice is now a long-term, worldwide phenomenon of exploitation whereby nonwhite children from poor nations are transferred to families in rich, white nations. That transfer might be viewed as taking advantage of the dreadful and helpless situations of economic, social, polit-ical underdevelopment in those countries. Hoksbergen, one of the research-ers in the Holland adoption field, advocated "long-distance sponsorship" as an alternative to international adoption, with "institutional supports to pro-vide them with educational opportunities, economic security, and healthy emotional ties" within their homeland (Altstein & Simon, 1991, p. 190). The division and conflict of the nation from which the whole drama of interna-tional adoption was originated has brought now quite dissimilar perspec-tives and different perceptions. Korean society may share mixed feelings about this new development.

RECENT DEVELOPMENTS

Pressured largely by a rising national pride and embarrassment in the international community that an increasingly prosperous country kept sending so many children away, a deliberate change in adoption policy was attempted in Korea more than once in order to decrease international adoptions. Since the Seoul Olympics in 1988, the Korean government authority set an ambitious goal of reducing the number of international adoptions. The country set an unofficial quota of about 2,000 children a year and aimed to halt them altogether by 1996. But the goal was not met at all due to chronic cultural bias and public unwillingness to adopt homeless children (Reitman, 1999). Also, such external factors as the International Monetary Fund (IMF) crisis in late 1997 and an ensuing severe recession were a major blow to the in-country adoption campaign.

Recently, with enactment of special laws and procedures to promote in-country adoption, Korea has made concerted efforts to increase domestic adoption and decrease international adoption (Extraordinary Law for Promotion of Adoption and Its Procedure, 2000). Specifically the Ministry of Health and Welfare launched a new policy for increased domestic adoption with various new programs, including subsidy and other support services (MOHW, 2005). At the present time, there are eighteen professional in-country adoption agencies and four in-country/international adoption agencies operating in Korea. Also, there are numerous support/self-help/information groups on domestic adoption, online and offline (GAIPS, 2005). Table 1.3 shows the comparative numbers of international and in-country adoption in recent years (GAIPS, 2005).

It is somewhat encouraging that, while the rate of international adoption has remained steady with over 2,000 children level each year, in-country adoption has also been slowly increasing. Nonetheless, international adoption accounts for about 150 percent of in-country adoption. In collaborative

TABLE 1.3. Overseas and Domestic Adoption of Korean Children

Year	Overseas	Domestic
2003	2,287	1,564
2002	2,365	1,694
2001	2,436	1,770
2000	2,360	1,686
1999	2,409	1,726
1998	2,443	1,426
1997	2,057	1,412
1996	2,080	1,229
1995	2,180	1,025

Source: Ministry of Health and Welfare and the Overseas Koreans Foundation (2005).

efforts to encourage in-country adoption, several civic organizations and social agencies have promoted special programs. For example, MPAK is an organization that is dedicated exclusively to the mission to promote adoption in Korea by advocating the needs of homeless children, by removing the negative social stigma attached to homeless children and adoptees, and by enabling Koreans to overcome fear in adoption (MPAK, 2005).

Being uprooted from the country of their birth, Korean adopted children and adults have been in great need of being reconnected to the country, culture, and heritage of their birth. In the past fifteen years or so, there have been some heartening developments, both in Korea and abroad, for international adoption in the form of adoptees' groups, information dissemination, support services, and cultural/heritage enrichment programs, etc.

The Global Adoption Information & Post Service (GAIPS) Center provides the most comprehensive adoption information and post-services, both domestic and overseas. With the common interest in establishing a coordinated and specialized post-service system, the Center started under the auspices of Korea's four representative adoption agencies—Social Welfare Services, Eastern Social Welfare Society, Korea Social Services, and Holt Children's Services. Now, the GAIPS Center has become an independent organization focused on providing an improved quality of adoption information and post-services to both domestic and overseas adoption triads—adoptees, adoptive families, and birth parents.

There are about fifty active and not-so-active adoptee/adoptive family Web sites in English. They share and coordinate various membership activities, research, fellowship, and publications. For example, Korean American Adoptee Adoptive Family Network (KAAN, 2005), which was developed to provide cultural programs, support groups, and adoption information, lists twenty-eight culture camps, twenty-two Korean schools, thirteen trips to Korea programs, and six performance groups throughout the United States. Holt was the first agency to establish tours back to birth countries, beginning with Korea Motherland Tours in 1974. Motherland and Family Tours are now offered to other countries in Holt's overseas programs, which have been replicated by many organizations. The AFA Web site (2005) lists seventy-two Korean and international support groups throughout the United States. Korean Focus (2005) operates an extensive discussion list, which is a forum for multicultural adoptive families with children from Korea, for adult Korean adoptees, and for anyone with an interest in Korean adoption. These services may help enrich cultural heritage among Korean adoptees and their adoptive families as well.

All these developments may enhance the quality of international adoption services, benefiting Korean adoptees, adoptive parents, and adoption workers both in Korea and the United States. More important, they have set a new direction, and moderate progress has been made to increase and improve in-country adoption in Korea. In the foreseeable future, hopefully most children can be helped to grow happily in their homeland, and their bodies and souls can be nurtured in the more familiar cultural environment of their kinship.

The history of Korean international adoption was witnessed by the global community as an innovative prototype of the compassion and care for poor children beyond national, racial, and cultural boundaries. It is also hoped then that the same spirit of love and care from American families, and other receiving parties, may help develop a bold and effective support system model for all needy children anywhere in the world without having to uproot them from their homeland and transplant them into foreign territory. After all, true love can embrace all possibilities and create provisions for all needs.

REFERENCES

Adoption Council of Canada (2003). Canadians adopt almost 20,000 children from abroad. Retrieved August 4, 2005, from http://www.adoption.ca/news/031212 cicstats.htm.

Adoptive Families of America (AFA) (2005, July/August). *Adoptive Families.* Retrieved August 4, 2005, from http://www.adoptivefamilies.com.

Altstein, H., & Simon, R. (Ed.). (1991). *Intercountry adoption: A multinational perspective.* New York: Praeger.

Anderson, D. (1971). *Children of special value: Interracial adoption in America.* New York: St. Martin's Press.

Babb, A. (1999). *Ethics in American adoption.* Westport, CT: Bergin & Garvey.

Barabba, V. (1975). United States population. *The world almanac and book of facts 1975.* New York: Newspaper Enterprise Association, Inc.

Bergquist, K. (1997). *Identity formation in adult Korean Americans who were transracially adopted.* Unpublished master's thesis, Norfolk State University School of Social Work.

Billingsley, A. (1968, October). Black children in White families. *Social Work, 41*(5).

Byma, S. (1974, May/June). Overseas adoptions threaten development of local services. *Canadian Welfare, 50,* 7-11.

Central Child Welfare Committee (1975). *The sixth report on child welfare seminar.* Seoul, Korea.

Central Intelligence Agency (CIA) (2005, July). *The world factbook—Korea North/ South.* Retrieved August 4, 2005, from http://www.cia.gov/cia/publications/ factbook/geos/kn.html.

Chestung, L. (1972, May). The dilemma of bi-racial adoption. *Social Work, 17*(3), 100-105.

Child Welfare League of America (CWLA) (1959). *Standards for adoption service.* New York: CWLA.

Child Welfare League of America (1960). *Adoption of Oriental children by American white families: An interdisciplinary symposium.* New York: CWLA.

Child Welfare League of America (2003, November). Intercountry adoption: Trends and issues. *National Data Analysis System.* Retrieved August 4, 2005, from http://ndas.cwla.org/include/pdf/InterntlAdoption_FINAL_IB.pdf.

Department of Defense (2005). Korean War casualty summary. *Directorate for Information Operations and Reports.* Retrieved August 4, 2005, from http://web1.whs.osd.mil/mmid/CASUALTY/KOREA.pdf.

DiVirgilio, L. (1956, November). Adjustment of foreign children in their adoptive homes. *Child Welfare, 35,* 15-21.

Dorow, S. (Ed.) (1999). *I wish for you a beautiful life: Letters from the Korean birth mothers of Ae Ran Won to their children.* St. Paul, MN: Yeong & Yeong Book Company.

Extraordinary Law for Adoption (Law No. 2977; 1976.12.31). Republic of Korea.

Extraordinary Law for Promotion of Adoption and Its Procedure (Law No. 6151, Amended, 2000.1.12); Enforcement Ordinance of the above Law (Presidential Order No. 16252; Amended, 1999.4.19); Enforcement Regulations of the above Law (Ministry (MOHW) Order No. 109; Amended, 1999.5.19) (http://gaips.or.kr/adoption/adoption2.php).

Fanshel, D. (1972). *Far from the reservation: The transracial adoption of American Indian children.* Metuchen, NJ: The Scarecrow Press.

Global Adoption Information & Post Service (GAIPS). (2005, July). *Overseas adoption statistics.* Retrieved August 4, 2005, from http://gaips.or.kr/adoption/adoption.php.

Herzog, E. et al. (1972). *Families for black children: The search for adoptive parents.* Washington, DC: Office of Child Development, HEW.

Hollingsworth, L. D. (2003, April). International adoption among families in the United States: Considerations of social justice. *Social Work, 48*(2), 209-217.

Holt, B. (1956). *The seed from the east.* Los Angeles: Oxford Press.

Holt International Children's Services (1976). *1975 Annual report.* Eugene, OR.

Huh, N. S., & Reid, W. (2000). Intercountry, transracial adoption, and ethnic identity: A Korean example. *International Social Work, 43*(1), 75-87.

Joint Council on International Children's Services (JCICS) (2005). Retrieved August 4, 2005, from http://www.jcics.org.

Jones, E. (1972). On transracial adoption of black children. *Child Welfare, L*(3), 156-164.

Juffer, F., & van IJzendoorn, M. I. (2005, May). Behavior problems and mental health referrals of international adoptees: A meta-analysis. *Journal of American Medical Association (JAMA), 293*(20), 2501-2515.

Kim, D. S. (1976). *Intercountry adoptions: A study of self-concept of adolescent Korean children who were adopted by American families.* Unpublished doctoral dissertation, University of Chicago, Illinois.

Kim, D. S. (1977, March-April). How they fared in American homes: A follow-up study of adopted Korean children in the United States. *Children Today, 6*(1), 2- 6.

Kim, D. S. (1978a, Spring). From women to women with painful love: A study of maternal motivation in intercountry adoption process. *Korean Women in a Struggle for Humanization: Association of Korean Christian Scholars in North America, 3,* 117-169.

Kim, D. S. (1978b, October). Issues in transracial and transcultural adoption. *Social Casework, 59*(8), 477-486.

Korean American Adoptee Adoptive Family Network (KAAN) (2005). *Korean cultural programs.* Retrieved August 4, 2005, from http://www.kaanet.com/korean_programs.

Korean Focus (2005). Korean focus discussion list. Retrieved August 4, 2005, from http://groups.yahoo.com/group/KoreanFocus.

Korean Institute of Military History (2001). *The Korean war.* Lincoln, NE: University of Nebraska Press.

Kramer, B. (Ed.). (1975). *The unbroken circle: A collection of writings on interracial and international adoption.* Minneapolis, MN: Organization for a United Response.

Miller, H. (1971, Summer). *Korea's international children.* New York: Lutheran Social Welfare Conference of America.

Ministry of Health and Social Affairs (1974). *Yearbook of public health and social statistics* (pp. 390-391). Seoul: Republic of Korea.

Ministry of Health and Welfare (MOHW) (2005, May 1). *Child welfare service programs guides 2005.* Children Welfare Policy Bureau, Republic of Korea. Retrieved August 4, 2005, from http://www.mohw.go.kr/index.jsp.

Mission to Promote Adoption in Korea (MPAK) (2005). Retrieved August 4, 2005, from http://www.mpak.com/HomeEnglish.htm.

National Association of Black Social Workers (NABSW) (1972). *Position paper.* The Third North American Conference on Adoptable Children, Washington, DC.

Nutt, T. (1974). Issues in supply and demand in adoption. *Proceedings of the Fourth North American Conference on Adoptable Children.* Washington, DC: Council on Advocacy for Children.

O'Conner, Jr., L. (1964). *The adjustment of a group of Korean and Korean-American children adopted by couples in the United States.* Unpublished master's thesis, School of Social Work, University of Tennessee, Knoxville.

Organisation for Economic Co-Operation and Development (OECD) (2005). *OECD factbook 2005: Macroeconomic trends.* Retrieved August 4, 2005, from http://ocde.p4.siteinternet.com/publications/doifiles/302005041P1T008.xls.

Reitman, V. (1999). S. Korea tries to take care of its own with domestic adoptions. *Los Angeles Times* (March 6), Part-A; 2.

Simon, R., & Altstein, H. (1987). *Transracial adoptees and their families.* New York: Wiley.

UNICEF (2004). *Children on the brink 2004: A joint report of new orphan estimates and a framework for action.* Retrieved August 4, 2005, from www.unicef.org/publications/cob_layout6-013.pdf.

U.S. Department of State (2005a). *Hague Convention on intercountry adoption.* Retrieved on August 4, 2005, from http://travel.state.gov/hagueinfo2002.html.

U.S. Department of State (2005b). *Immigrant visas issued to orphans coming to the United States.* Retrieved August 4, 2005, from http://travel.state.gov/family/adoption/stats/stats_451.html.

Valk, M. (1957). *Korean-American children in American adoptive homes.* New York: CWLA.

Whang, M. S. (1976). *An exploratory descriptive study of inter-country adoption of Korean children with known parents.* Unpublished master's thesis, University of Hawaii.

Wikipedia (2005). *Korean War.* Retrieved August 4, 2005, from http://ko.wikipedia.org.

Yoon, D. P. (2001). Causal modeling predicting psychological adjustment of Korean-born adolescent adoptees. *Journal of Human Behavior in the Social Environment, 3*(3-4), 65-82.

Young, M. J. (1963). *Inter-racial adoption: An exploratory study of non-Oriental parents who adopted Oriental children.* Unpublished master's thesis, Graduate Department of Social Work and Social Science, Bryn Mawr College, Pennsylvania.

Chapter 2

Institutionalizing International Adoption: The Historical Origins of Korean Adoption in the United States

Catherine Ceniza Choy

A number of scholarly studies and mainstream news reports have acknowledged the historical significance of U.S. and Korean relations in the phenomenon of international adoption. According to *Los Angeles Times* staff writer Bettijane Levine, the orphans of the Korean War who were primarily adopted by white American families became "the first mass wave of international, interracial adoptions ever on the planet, the forerunner of all those that have since become commonplace" (Levine, 2000, p. E1). Between 1958 and 1990, families in Western nations adopted approximately 130,000 Korean children. While France and Sweden were among the major receiving countries of Korean adoptees, the United States has been the top receiving country of Korean children, adopting over 50 percent (approximately 80,000) of the world total (A/K/A World, 1999). The numerical dominance of Korean adoptees in the United States and other Western nations explains why Korean case studies of international adoption are important for illuminating our understanding of the past and present state of international adoption.

While scholarly studies about international adoption often include Korean adoptees, the historical origins and development of Korean adoption in the United States over time have yet to be documented. Although recently published book-length studies on the history of U.S. domestic adoption—most notably E. Wayne Carp's (1998) *Family Matters: Secrecy and Disclosure in the History of Adoption* and Barbara Melosh's (2002) *Strangers and Kin:*

International Korean Adoption
© 2007 by The Haworth Press, Inc. All rights reserved.
doi:10.1300/5734_02

The American Way of Adoption—have noted the rise of international adoption in the United States after the end of the Korean War in 1953, this phenomenon has received scant attention in these studies. Scholarly studies often acknowledge the various U.S. and Korean political and cultural contexts that indicate the rise of international adoption in the second half of the twentieth century (Kim, 1995). In the United States, these contexts include the decline of the availability of U.S.-born white infants after the introduction of birth-control pills in 1960, the legalization of abortion in 1973, the increasing social legitimacy of single parenthood, and the racial tensions over the adoption of black and American Indian children by white American families (Patton, 2000). In Korea, the rise of the availability of Korean orphans after the Korean War, especially mixed-race Korean children (born to Korean women and U.S. white and black servicemen) who were socially ostracized in Korean society, provided a source of adoptive children. However, these important historical and sociological contexts do not explain why Korea became the leading sending country of adoptive children to the United States.

This chapter is part of my current book-length project that seeks to address and help close this gap in the scholarly literature through its focus on the historical origins of the adoption of Asian children in the United States and the development of this phenomenon over time. I pose the following major questions that have yet to be addressed in the scholarship on international adoption: Why has Korea emerged in the late twentieth century as the world's leading supplier of adoptive children? Why have tens of thousands of predominantly white American families adopted Korean children?

In order to explore these lines of inquiry, I am conducting archival research in the voluminous, yet hitherto underutilized, records of the International Social Service, United States of America Branch, Inc., held in the Social Welfare History Archives at the University of Minnesota, Twin Cities.* In 1924, social workers founded the International Migration Services, which was renamed the International Social Service (ISS) in 1946. The formation of the ISS emerged after delegates from seventeen nations met to discuss the need for an international social service agency that could pro-

---

*The historical records of the International Social Service, United States of America Branch, Inc. (ISS-USA, located in Baltimore, MD) on which this study is based are held by the Social Welfare History Archives at the University of Minnesota (SWHA, in Minneapolis, MN). Permission for their use in this research project was granted by ISS-USA. For more information, see http://www.iss-usa.org and http://special.lib.umn.edu/swha.

Points of view in this presentation and/or document are those of the author and do not necessarily represent the official position or policies of International Social Service, United States of America Branch, Inc. (ISS-USA).

vide casework services to individuals and families whose problems necessitated coordinated efforts in two or more countries. In the first half of the twentieth century, much of the ISS work focused on U.S. and European cases and specifically the provision of services to migrants, refugees, and displaced persons. By the second half of the twentieth century, however, the bulk of their casework involved international adoptions by U.S. families, and the adoption of Korean children was central to this work (ISS, n.d.).

The ISS-United States of America Branch, Inc. (ISS-USA) records contain numerous administrative files, program and service records, and correspondence between ISS-USA and other organizations, U.S. states, and countries. My research to date has focused on the ISS-USA folders on *independent adoption schemes* between 1953 and 1972. Although the word *scheme* connotes a crafty or secret program, in these records *independent adoption schemes* refer to nonsocial service organizations that participated in facilitating international adoption in the United States. My preliminary research findings based on these records illuminate an important, yet neglected, theme in the scholarly literature on migration: the institutionalization of migration (Goss & Lindquist, 1995). The institutionalization of migration signifies the ways that institutions (in this particular case, social service agencies and independent organizations) create, facilitate, and sustain specific migrant flows. In this essay, I explore the ways the adoption of Korean children by primarily white American families in the 1950s and 1960s was institutionalized through a complex network of social service agencies and independent organizations in the United States and Korea. While most news stories of international adoption focus on individuals' motives and experiences, I argue that this network of institutions in addition to individual efforts encouraged as well as enabled international adoption between Korea and the United States in the 1950s and subsequent decades.

My preliminary research findings have already revealed that this network of social service agencies and independent adoption organizations was much more complex than the depictions given by existing historical studies on U.S. adoption. The summaries of the history of Korean adoption in the United States typically acknowledge the efforts of a few charismatic individuals: most notably, writer Pearl S. Buck, who publicized the plight of mixed-race Amerasian children born to U.S. servicemen and Asian women; and, Oregon farmer Harry Holt and his wife Bertha Holt, who organized mass adoptions of Korean War orphans by American families soon after the end of the Korean War. Although the ISS-USA records, like all archival collections, are limited and subjective because they feature documents related to the concerns of their organization, these records reveal the sheer number of social service agencies and independent adoption organizations involved in Korean adoption overseas in the 1950s. These social service agencies included the Child Placement Service in Korea and various U.S. state departments of public welfare in addition to the ISS-USA. In the United States, each of the states regulates adoption law, and so ISS-USA officials had to coordinate not only the social service efforts between the two countries, Korea and the United States, but also the legalities of U.S. state adoption practices. In addition to Harry Holt's adoption program and Pearl S. Buck's Welcome House, other independent adoption organizations involved in facilitating Korean adoption in the United States included World Vision, Christ Is the Answer Foundation, and Everett Swanson Evangelistic Association.

A focus on the institutions illuminates the multiple tensions surrounding international adoptions such as the massive multilevel government bureaucracy associated with the process, and the conflicting agendas among social service agencies, independent adoption schemes, and adoptive parents about how the process should function. Although much has changed in international adoption since the 1950s—with some of the major changes being the decline of adoption from Korea beginning in the late 1980s and the rise of China as the top sending Asian nation of adoptive children overseas—these tensions undoubtedly persist in more recent times. My hope is that this chapter helps inform practitioners, policymakers, and individual members of the adoptive community at-large of the ways that contemporary international adoption processes might be better understood in relation to a more complete and complex understanding of the past.

A WORLD VISION

Many scholars have contextualized the rise of international adoption against the backdrop of postwar political and humanitarian efforts. Relatively few studies have emphasized the role that international adoptive children play as immigrants (Lovelock, 2000; Weil, 1984). Placing Korean adoption in the historical contexts of U.S. immigration as well as the Cold War is useful for understanding the radical nature of this phenomenon. For much of the first half of the twentieth century, exclusion was a dominant theme in the history of Asian immigration to the United States. U.S. legislation historically marked various Asian peoples—Chinese, Japanese, Koreans, South Asians, and Filipinos—as strange, dangerous, and inassimilable. These differences were codified in the U.S. immigration laws, for example, which by 1924 had virtually banned Asian immigration to the United

States. By contrast, the practice of international adoption from Asia created a vision of the world in which national, cultural, and political borders could be crossed. Section 5 of the Refugee Relief Act of 1953 enabled the immigration of Korean adoptees by allocating 4,000 special nonquota immigrant visas to eligible orphans under the age of ten years. The Act defined an eligible orphan as a child who has "lost both parents through death, disappearance, abandonment, desertion, or separation, or who has only one parent who is incapable of providing care for such orphan and has in writing irrevocably released the child for emigration and adoption" and "who has been lawfully adopted abroad by a United States citizen and spouse or received commitment by a United States citizen and spouse to adopt the child and care for the child properly if the child is admitted."

However, immigration laws alone could not sustain the vision of the world that legitimized a global sense of family. New attitudes and beliefs about U.S. involvement in Asia had to be cultivated to put new legal provisions in use. In 1950, Christian Minister Dr. Bob Pierce founded an organization in Portland, Oregon, appropriately named World Vision, which facilitated international adoption from Asia. He described World Vision broadly as an "interdenominational missionary service organization seeking to help meet emergency needs in crisis areas through existing evangelical agencies."[1] By the late 1950s, World Vision provided aid to children in nineteen countries. However, Korea (and specifically the emergency needs of Korean War orphans) was the key crisis area in the founding of this organization. Among World Vision's five major areas of activity was Christian social welfare service, which involved the administration of a sponsorship program that organized monetary assistance to Asian orphans and destitute children. According to a 1950s World Vision newsletter, "North American friends who provide $10 each month ($11 in Canada) as 'parents' for 'their' child—a precious little one in some distant part of the world" participated in the sponsorship program, which built "Christian hospitals, clinics, milk bars and schools throughout the Orient."[2]

World Vision's sponsorship program in Asia was not new, but rather a part of a broader cultural movement in the United States that forged bonds between Asia and America in familial, and more specifically in parental, terms in which American *parents* sponsored their poor and helpless Asian *children*. In 1938, Presbyterian Minister Dr. J. Calvitt Clarke founded the Children's Christian Fund (originally the China's Children Fund) to raise money for homeless and orphaned Chinese children of the Sino–Japanese War. Scholar Christina Klein documents that the appeal to prospective American donors by representing their relationship with the children they sponsored as one of *adoption* was a fund-raising innovation of Dr. Clarke (Klein, 2000). Thus, by

1954, when World Vision's Overseas Director Erwin Raetz collected pictures and case histories of 1,200 Korean orphans for sponsorship, at least some of their potential American donors were already aware of their parental obligations to Asian children.[3] Klein argues that these sponsorship programs complemented U.S. political and military agendas in Asia during the Cold War by cultivating a sense of obligation to Asia among Americans who might not initially support U.S. political and military intervention in Asia. These organizations and their sponsorship programs also set in motion another phenomenon: the legal adoption of Asian children by families in the United States.

The following example illustrates that, although sponsorship and legal adoption were distinct, the two could go hand in hand with the initial sponsorship of a child resulting in desires for legal adoption.[4] In 1955, an excerpt from a letter from the Multnomah County Public Welfare Commission in Portland, Oregon, reported that a Mr. and Mrs. C were interested in adopting a particular mixed-race Korean female infant. Mrs. C was the head of the *adoption unit* of World Vision, a unit that filed pictures of orphans and distributed literature that solicited donations from the United States. While looking through these pictures, Mrs. C found a picture of the infant, and she and Mr. C *sponsored* her by sending her money and clothing. After several months of sponsorship, they contacted the county's public welfare commission to discuss the possibility of bringing her to the United States for legal adoption.

Perhaps the most famous example of international legal adoption during this time period was the adoption of eight Korean children by Harry and Bertha Holt of Oregon. World Vision again played an instrumental role in helping to secure the twelve Korean adoptive children that Harry Holt brought to the United States in October 1955. Three other American families (including Mr. and Mrs. C) adopted four of these children. Because Section 5 of the Refugee Relief Act of 1953 limited each U.S. citizen and spouse to two nonquota immigrant visas for eligible orphans, special legislation was needed to enable Harry and Bertha Holt to adopt eight children. In June 1955, Erwin Raetz wrote a letter to Oregon Senator Richard Neuberger to urge Congress to pass the special legislation. According to Raetz, Harry Holt was at that time residing in a World Vision missionary's home in Seoul, Korea, while waiting for the processing of the children. On behalf of World Vision, Raetz communicated to Senator Neuberger that "we all appreciate your interest in this splendid effort of his, and wish you every success in having the enabling act passed before Congress adjourns for the summer." Raetz' tone was filled with urgency as he characterized the conditions under which the children were being processed as "deplorable." He described Holt's visit to Korea as a "most worthy and humanitarian" mission.[5] In his address to the U.S. president, Senator Neuberger echoed that sentiment with great rhetorical drama:

> What nobler and more unselfish deed could there be than to bring to the security and comfort of America, eight small children from the ravages and tormented country of Korea? If the brotherhood of man still has meaning in this troubled world, then that sentiment is exemplified by Harry Holt and his family.[6]

The mainstream news media publicized Harry Holt's delivery of twelve Korean children in October 1955 with much celebration and fanfare. A *Washington Post* article described Harry Holt as a "pied piper" who "shepherded twelve Korean-American babies through [the] crowded Tokyo International Airport . . . to a plane taking them to new homes in the United States" (Kramer, 1955). Such publicity mistakenly created the impression that this historical moment was the product of a sole individual's efforts. However, in addition to World Vision's participation, the ISS-USA also played a fundamental role by endorsing the immigration papers of nine of the twelve children. Nevertheless, while a news story in the *Oregonian* (1956) acknowledged World Vision's help in the matter, it concluded, "But the spark of initiative and the flame of determination were Mr. Holt's . . . He has virtually given life to hundreds of children. Given his example, can anyone doubt the power of the individual?" With politicians and the press on his side, Holt's efforts did not end there. With the provisions of the 1953 Refugee Act about to expire in December 1956, he started to organize mass international adoptions of several hundred children from Korea by appealing to thousands of American families through written correspondence. His fervor contributed to major controversies about who should oversee the process of international adoption and how it should be done.

FROM RESCUE TO RIVALRY

The favorable publicity given to Holt's story generated outright confusion and critical concerns about the role of nonsocial service agencies in international adoption practice. ISS-USA archival records reveal that the 1955 adoption activities of World Vision and Holt sparked numerous inquiries between World Vision and individual U.S. state welfare departments, and between these departments and the ISS-USA. For example, in August 1955, World Vision's Erwin Raetz—clearly aware of individual U.S. states' regulation of adoption practice—sent correspondence to governors' offices in Wisconsin and Nevada requesting a transcript of state laws governing adoption, a copy of state welfare department requirements and procedures, and the contact information of the state agency authorized to make home investigations of prospective adoptive parents.[7] Unfamiliar with the World Vision organization and its interest in international adoption, individual state departments contacted the ISS-USA about the ways to proceed.

In the mid-1950s, the ISS-USA was unprepared for the volume of these inquiries. ISS-USA Assistant Director Susan Pettiss wrote to the state public welfare commission of Oregon, where World Vision was incorporated, claiming that their office was "being swamped with requests for advice from many of the departments and [was] at somewhat of a loss as this organization has only recently come to our attention."[8] By the end of the year, Pettiss communicated with Bob Pierce, the founding president of World Vision, and inquired if there was a way to work together to finding a solution to their mutual interest in alleviating "the plight of orphaned Korean-American children."[9] Pettiss explained that, although the ISS had developed an "effective machinery" to deal with social service problems that cut across national boundaries—including the international adoption of children by American families since the end of World War II—the ISS did not have a branch in Korea. She related, however, that the ISS-USA was working closely with the American-Korean Foundation, the Church World Service, the Child Placement Service in Seoul, and Korean governmental bodies.

Gestures to work together and the mutual interest in the plight of Korean War orphans could not overcome the political and personal differences over minimum standards in adoption practice. Social service agencies, such as the ISS-USA and individual U.S. state welfare departments, firmly maintained that the welfare of adoptive children necessitated minimum standards of investigation, placement, and supervision conducted only by social work professionals. Independent adoption organizations, such as Holt's adoption operations, flouted these minimum standards, for example, by practicing and promoting proxy adoptions. In proxy adoptions, U.S. citizens designated a proxy agent to act in their place and to adopt a child in a foreign court. According to the Adoption History Project,

> during the 1950s, proxy adoptions were the most publicized means of international adoption. . . . Proxy adoptions revealed how inadequate federal policy was in dealing with family-making across national borders. Until the passage of the Immigration and Nationality Act of 1961, which incorporated international adoption, the migration of foreign-born children to the United States had no place in permanent

law. (Adoption History Project, n.d., para. 1-2. Quoted with permission.)

Rather, a series of provisional refugee and displaced persons acts, such as Section 5 of the 1953 Refugee Relief Act, enabled the immigration of *eligible orphans* from war-torn countries.

Children adopted by proxy immigrated to the United States as the legal children of adoptive parents, without any endorsement from a social service agency. However, social service agencies, such as the ISS-USA, believed these endorsements to be integral to the welfare of the adopted child. As Susan Pettiss emphasized,

> We take very seriously our commitment to the United States Government in endorsing the DSR-5 assurance forms for the immigration for adoption of foreign children coming to the United States . . . We are deeply concerned about the future of each one of these Korean-American orphans and want to be sure that they are placed in suitable homes as quickly as possible with the slightest possible margin of error.[10]

Harry Holt's operations further challenged the expertise and autonomy of social work professionals by employing a private company to conduct the investigations that determined whether or not prospective adoptive families' homes were suitable. Holt's primary concern was that the adoptive families be *saved* and *born-again* Christians. As he explained to prospective adoptive families in a 1955 letter, "If we help to place a child in a home, we are responsible before the Lord. . . ." Holt concluded the letter with a *personal word:* "It is our desire that these children go into the homes of born again believers."[11]

These differences developed into a rivalry among the various organizations involved in Korean adoption in the United States. In one of his letters to prospective American adoptive families, Harry Holt claimed that "we are not in competition with the [social] welfare [agencies]." He insisted that his sole motivation was the knowledge that "little boys and girls are dying in Korea for want of homes, and we know that many people have their hearts and homes open to these little ones." Yet, in his letters to prospective adoptive families, his comparison of the methods of adoption "through welfare and international social service" and those of adoption "by proxy" characterized adoption by proxy as more efficient and advantageous, in effect functioning as an advertisement for proxy adoptions. Under the heading of *Adoption by Proxy,* Holt touted:

People who are financially able and can spend two or three months in a foreign country can adopt war orphans; however, most people who have big hearts are not able to do this. The only answer that we know is for them to have someone be their proxy and adopt the child or children in the foreign country under the laws of that country . . . Then the child or children enter the country as the sons and daughters of the adoptive parents. They do not have to be adopted in the states.[12]

In contrast to the seemingly easy method of adoption by proxy, Holt represented the method of adoption though welfare and international social service agencies as time-consuming and unrealistic. Holt sarcastically critiqued social service workers' methods with the following description:

First, one has to contact the local welfare and ask them to make an inspection of the home. This may involve months of questioning. In time the home may be approved. If so, then the local welfare sends its report to the International Social Service at New York, and after due process the International Social Service contacts its agencies in the foreign country to find a child to fit the home. It is very hard to pass on the physiological background of some little child that was found abandoned in a ditch, but they always try. This takes time. If they find a child which they think is suitable, the couple in the States is allowed to sponsor the child's entry into the country, and it may be placed in their home, where it is kept under the watchful eyes of the local welfare for six months or a year. If after this trial period the child is all right and the welfare are satisfied, the child may be placed in an American orphanage for readoption.[13]

Social service workers in various states criticized Holt's methods, such as his bulk mailing of letters like the preceding one. Sibyl Thompson, supervisor of the adoption unit of Minnesota's Department of Public Welfare, had brought this Holt letter to the attention of the director of the ISS-USA in April 1956. She characterized Holt's procedures as "unsound" and the Holt operation as a "problem," and wanted to know what the ISS-USA thought about the matter before her unit gave any response. Thompson concluded her letter by writing that "it will be most helpful if we knew what steps are being taken to prevent further importation of children for purposes of adoption in this manner carried out by this fervent but misguided group."[14] Lucile Kennedy, chief of California's Division of Child Welfare, also wrote to the ISS-USA during the same time period about the "activities of Mr. Holt and World Vision," which she similarly characterized as a "very serious problem" that would attract and enable unfit families to adopt. Kennedy gave the example of a Mr. and Mrs. L, who wrote repeatedly to their agency expressing interest in international adoption. The agency expressed doubts about Mr. and Mrs. L's suitability as adoptive parents of mixed-race foreign children after they made comments while residing in Texas, such as "[We] love the southern people and we know their [sic] wouldn't be any mixed blood as here in California." Later, the Ls wrote to say that they had heard from "some cotton pickers that it would be possible to go to Morro Bay, California, and adopt a child immediately as two boats full of children came in."[15]

Despite social welfare workers' disapproval of his methods, Holt continued to send similar bulk letters to prospective American adoptive families the following year. Aware of social service workers' opposition to his methods, Holt strongly criticized them for what he believed to be their own self-interest:

> Welfare groups [are] building up strong opposition against adoption by proxy, as social workers have no authority over and do not get any income from children adopted by proxy. This irritates them and they are going all out to influence congress to turn it down early this session.

Holt urged readers to engage in the political battle over international adoptions: "Explain that if adoption by proxy is stopped you will not be able to get a child . . . It is very important that you write these letters today to all your congressmen. If they receive a flood of letters they will do something about it."[16]

As before, these letters were brought to the attention of individual state departments of public welfare, often by local citizens who were interested in international adoption from Korea. Heber Robertson, a child welfare worker in Utah's Department of Public Welfare, forwarded the Holt letter to the ISS-USA. Robertson relayed, "We were quite alarmed to see that he is encouraging people to continue with the proxy adoption program and also interested in a statement he makes regarding social workers."[17] The ISS-USA did not take Holt's criticisms lightly. Assistant Director Susan Pettiss characterized his zeal as a troubling "Messiah complex," and with great prescience, she sadly remarked ". . . we are all aware of the serious damage being done to the future of these kids being brought in by proxy adoption or the potential danger to them."[18]

Such harsh criticisms and name-calling might best be understood in the context of the chaotic situation in postwar Korea, situations that created trauma for war orphans and frustrating desperation among those who sincerely wanted to help. Pettiss acknowledged the sincerity of Holt's desire to give opportunities to Korean mixed-race children, and she praised his "generosity in making available his financial resources to help bringing these children to the United States."[19] Yet, because of their disagreements over international adoption methods, both Holt and the ISS-USA staff members accused one another of being uncooperative and detrimental to the welfare of Korean orphans. In an April 1956 letter, Susan Pettiss aired the ISS-USA's frustrations:

> Things are happening so fast here in regard to Korea that we find it hard to keep up with them . . . Sometimes I feel as if I am punching a pillow in attacking each of the major problems in handling these Korean cases. You have no idea of the repercussions which are resounding all over the United States about Mr. Holt's activities. I was in Washington two days last week and met in several places his accusations against the ISS as obstructing his plans.[20]

Despite the unpleasant aspects of the rivalry, both sides of the international adoption methods controversy raised significant awareness about salient issues in international adoption practice. Holt's methods brought to light the frustrating ways in which the multilevel bureaucracy associated with domestic adoption practice was in many instances unrealistic and overly time-consuming in the context of international adoption practice, especially in the immediate postwar period. Even the American-Korean Foundation, which sympathized with Susan Pettiss about the "serious questions about Mr. Holt's plan to complete adoptions by proxy" and the "dubious aspects of employing a business firm to make home studies," urged the ISS-USA to find another plan through which home studies or investigations of prospective American adoptive families could be conducted more expeditiously. In a 1956 letter to Pettiss, Lucile Chamberlin, chief of the welfare division of the American-Korean Foundation, emphasized that Korean President Rhee and the Korean Ministry of Health and Social Affairs' "number one welfare project" was the sending of as many Korean War orphans to adoptive homes in the United States. Chamberlin noted that many of the Korean War orphans were "really badly abused" and that "this fact together with the great pressure of the government to get them out of Korea makes this program very important from the standpoint of the welfare of the children and also from a public relations aspect."[21]

In the early 1960s, American adoptive parents who had encountered frustrating bureaucratic situations with various U.S. state welfare departments formed the group Parents for Overseas Adoption. Parents for Overseas Adoption advocated for proxy adoptions. In a 1963 letter, Mr. B documented his and his wife's ordeal as they tried to adopt a second Korean child while they were living in Minnesota. Their story illuminates the inadequacy of state adoption legislation and resources to deal with international adoption during that time period and the ways that U.S. state and national bureaucracy combined to make the process more confusing and frustrating. Mr. B related:

> Federal law required that we meet the adoption requirements of the State. To our amazement, the State of Minnesota had a requirement that the adoptive child must be a resident of the state for a six-month period. It was immediately obvious that a child in Korea could not meet such a requirement. They gave me encouragement and indicated that they would assist us in getting the child to this country if I met all other state requirements. I proceeded to do this, to include a home study by the County Welfare office even though we had already been carefully examined and studied by the Naturalization and Immigration Service. The Welfare office would not consider their report at all. I had continued to maintain contact with the State Welfare during November, December, and January. I discovered that little or nothing was being done for my case in late December . . .

Such experiences led Mr. B to conclude that "delaying tactics were being employed by the State Welfare" and that their ordeal was "uncalled for and unnecessary simply because we wished to become parents of these children who might have otherwise died in their poverty and unwanted condition."[22]

Yet, social service workers' bureaucratic methods pointed to an important issue regarding the welfare of Korean adoptive children: accountability upon their arrival in the United States. In the summer of 1957, a Douglas County grand jury in Roseberg, Oregon, indicted Edith Ott with second-degree murder in the death of her adopted Korean daughter. According to the indictment, twenty-two-month-old Korean adoptee Wendy Kay Ott died after being struck on the head. Edith Ott had adopted the girl through Holt's program in October 1956. Rather than accept any responsibility for or raise critical questions about what had transpired, Bertha Holt lashed out at social service workers who, in her mind, had promoted negative publicity about the Otts, whom she referred to as "this wonderful Christian family."[23] In the 1950s and early 1960s, the Holts' and some adoptive parents' assumptions about the inherent goodness of Christian adoptive families blinded them to the very real possibilities of brutality in the United States.

INDEPENDENT ADOPTION SCHEMES:
AN UNEVEN LEGACY

Despite the rivalry between social welfare agencies and the Holt adoption program, new independent adoption programs continued to form in the early 1960s. Individuals such as V.A. Kelley, Lillie Reed Smith, and Everett Swanson engaged in work very similar to that of Bob Pierce and Harry Holt. Like their predecessors, Kelley, Smith, and Swanson were Christian evangelists whose adoption methods directly or inadvertently flouted social service workers' minimum standards.

V.A. Kelley operated a private adoption agency called Christ Is the Answer Foundation in Vandalia, Illinois. With the help of Oak Soon Hong of Korea's Child Placement Service, he himself adopted two Korean children in 1956. Social welfare workers criticized the "unorthodox" adoption methods of Kelley, which included home studies of prospective adoptive parents that he conducted himself using forms that emphasized the importance of "no smoking or drinking, church attendance, and family prayer" in addition to work record, income, and insurance.[24] ISS representatives in Korea also suspected that Kelley benefited from child placement referrals from the Korean Child Placement Service after he gave the service enough money monthly to employ a driver, typist, and social worker.[25]

In Denton, Texas, retired Methodist missionary Lillie Reed Smith embarked on finding adoptive homes for Korean children after a 1958 visit to Seoul, where she visited several orphanages. Smith claimed that the directors of the orphanages urged her to find adoptive homes for those children less than fourteen years of age. According to Smith, these directors told her that the ISS would "handle the investigation and take full responsibility of securing the adoption papers and expense incurred therein and also arrange transportation." In a 1960 letter addressed to the ISS in Korea, she claimed:

> I spent all of 1959 contacting couples who wanted to adopt a Korean orphan. Through our church papers, I received more than 150 letters of inquiry as to how and where they could apply for a child in one of these three orphanages. I sent them 2 application blanks and full information together with a personal letter. When they stated the age and sex of child desired, I referred them to the orphanage having those ages and sex.

Smith expressed frustration toward the ISS, who she assumed had been processing these adoption applications all along. She continued:

Now, I have no way of knowing where and what were the results of their applications to these 3 Directors. Seldom do they write me the second time unless they have grown tired in not being able to hear whether your agency is processing their application or not . . . I have had letters from many fine Christian couples, most of them childless and young and in good circumstances who crave to have a child to love and rear, and many of them will be disappointed and censure me unless the directors and you live up to your obligations and the children are missing a most wonderful opportunity to be loved and reared in some of the best Christian homes in Texas.[26]

However, in later correspondence, Susan Pettiss wrote to Smith claiming that only one orphanage in Korea, the Holy King Orphanage, had been in touch with the ISS representative in Korea and had corresponded with them about four prospective adoptive families. The ISS contacted the four families, suggesting that they get in touch with their state department of public welfare to locate an authorized child welfare agency near them to help them meet the multiple requirements for international adoption. Furthermore, the ISS representative had not heard anything from the other two orphanages in question, Green Meadows and Mapo.[27] In a separate letter to Commissioner John Winters of the Texas State Department of Public Welfare, Pettiss urged him to contact Smith "in order to explain the complexities of any intercountry child placement program and why it is not such a simple matter to undertake the transplanting of children from one country to another."[28]

In Chicago, Illinois, the Everett Swanson Evangelistic Association headed by former Presbyterian Minister Everett Swanson operated a *sponsorship plan* to help Korean orphans. American individuals who participated in the Swanson plan paid $8 monthly to assist a child they had selected. Similar to the sponsorship plan of World Vision, the relationship between the American sponsor and Korean child was represented in parental and other familial terms. As one advertisement for the Everett Swanson Evangelistic Association beckoned: "Be a 'Daddy and Mommie' or 'Big Brother or Sister' to a Korean orphan who will know you as sponsor."[29] Although Swanson's association did not operate a legal adoption program, its sponsorship plan led some "parents" and "big siblings" to want to legally adopt their sponsored child. Similar to Holt, Swanson advocated adoption only by born-again Christians and, unsurprisingly, referred prospective adoptive families to the Holt adoption program.[30]

In the 1950s and 1960s, multiple individuals and institutions in the United States and Korea participated in promoting and facilitating international adoption. The sheer volume of this activity challenges the notion that this phenomenon was the result of the efforts of a few individuals. This preliminary research on the institutionalization of international adoption points to the need for more research, documentation, and analysis of the history of international adoption. Although this research thus far has illuminated the controversies and complexities of the phenomenon, its emphasis on past troubles can pave the way for future, and hopefully more productive, conversations about how international adoption should work.

NOTES

1. Bob Pierce, "Dear Friend," World Vision, Inc. brochure, International Social Service-United States of America Branch, Inc. (hereafter ISS-USA) papers, Box 10, File # 29, Social Welfare History Archives, Minneapolis, MN.

2. Christian Social Welfare Service, World Vision, Inc. brochure, International Social Service-American Branch (hereafter ISS-USA) papers, Box 10, File # 29, Social Welfare History Archives (hereafter SWHA), Minneapolis, MN.

3. Margaret Leal to Mrs. Pettiss, August 17, 1955, ISS-USA papers, Box 10, File #29, SWHA, Minneapolis, MN.

4. Excerpt from Multnomah County Public Welfare Commission letter, May 31, 1955, ISS-USA papers, Box 10, File #29, SWHA, Minneapolis, MN.

5. Erwin W. Raetz to Richard Neuberger, June 30, 1955, ISS-USA papers, Box 10, File "Children-Independent Adoption Schemes, Harry Holt, 1955-1957, Vol. 1," SWHA, Minneapolis, MN.

6. "Excerpt from *Congressional Record* of July 30, 1955," ISS-USA papers, Box 10, File "Children-Independent Adoption Schemes, Harry Holt, 1955-1957, Vol. 1," SWHA, Minneapolis, MN.

7. Erwin W. Raetz to Office of the Governor in the state of Wisconsin, 1 August 1955 and Erwin W. Raetz to Office of the Governor in the state of Nevada, 1 August 1955, ISS-USA papers, Box 10, File #29, SWHA, Minneapolis, MN.

8. Susan T. Pettiss to Andrew F. Juras, 19 August 1955, ISS-USA papers, Box 10, File #29, SWHA, Minneapolis, MN.

9. Susan T. Pettiss to Bob Pierce, 22 November 1955, ISS-USA papers, Box 10, File #29, SWHA, Minneapolis, MN.

10. Susan T. Pettiss to Bob Pierce, 22 November 1955, ISS-USA papers, Box 10, File #29, SWHA, Minneapolis, MN.

11. Harry Holt, "Dear Friends," 14 December 1955, ISS-USA papers, Box 10, File "Children-Independent Adoption Schemes, Harry Holt, 1955-1957, Vol. 1," SWHA, Minneapolis, MN.

12. Harry Holt, "Dear Friends," no date given, ISS-USA papers, Box 10, File "Children-Independent Adoption Schemes, Harry Holt, 1955-1957, Vol. 1," SWHA, Minneapolis, MN.

13. Harry Holt, "Dear Friends," no date given, ISS-USA papers, Box 10, File "Children-Independent Adoption Schemes, Harry Holt, 1955-1957, Vol. 1," SWHA, Minneapolis, MN.

14. Sibyl Thompson to William T. Kirk, 11 April 1956, Harry Holt, "Dear Friends," no date given, ISS-USA papers, Box 10, File "Children-Independent Adoption Schemes, Harry Holt, 1955-1957, Vol. 1," SWHA, Minneapolis, MN.

15. Lucile Kennedy to Susan T. Pettiss, 26 April 1956, ISS-USA papers, Box 10, File "Children-Independent Adoption Schemes, Harry Holt, 1955-1957, Vol. 1," SWHA, Minneapolis, MN.

16. Harry Holt, "Dear Friends," 27 December 1956, ISS-USA papers, Box 10, File "Children-Independent Adoption Schemes, Harry Holt, 1955-1957, Vol. 1," SWHA, Minneapolis, MN.

17. Heber W. Robertson to American Branch, International Social Service, 1 February 1957, ISS-USA papers, Box 10, File "Children-Independent Adoption Schemes, Harry Holt, 1955-1957, Vol. 1," SWHA, Minneapolis, MN.

18. Susan T. Pettiss to Ralph W. Collins, 23 April 1956, ISS-USA papers, Box 10, File #29, SWHA, Minneapolis, MN.

19. Susan T. Pettiss, "Report: Trip to the West Coast and Ohio," March 11, 1956, ISS-USA papers, Box 10, File #29, SWHA, Minneapolis, MN.

20. Susan T. Pettiss to Lucile L. Chamberlin, 30 April 1956, ISS-USA papers, Box 10, File #29, SWHA, Minneapolis, MN.

21. Lucile L. Chamberlin to Susan Pettiss, 23 March 1956, ISS-USA papers, Box 10, File #29, SWHA, Minneapolis, MN.

22. Mr. B to Rev. Norman Minard, 20 August 1963, ISS-USA papers, Box 10, File #26, SWHA, Minneapolis, MN.

23. "Woman Accused by Jury of Killing Korea Orphan," newspaper clipping, ISS-USA papers, Box 10, File "Children-Independent Adoption Schemes, Harry Holt, 1955-1957, Vol. 1," SWHA, Minneapolis, MN.

24. D. Adjemovitch to Ruth Elsenraat, 23 December 1959, ISS-USA papers, Box 10, File #15, SWHA, Minneapolis, MN.

25. Virginia Baumgartner to Susan T. Pettiss, 11 July 1958, ISS-USA papers, Box 10, File #15, SWHA, Minneapolis, MN.

26. Lillie Reed Smith to International Social Service Agency, 22 March 1960, ISS-USA papers, Box 10, File "Children-Adoption Independent Schemes, Miscellaneous, 1955–," SWHA, Minneapolis, MN.

27. Susan T. Pettiss to Lillie Reed Smith, 16 May 1960, ISS-USA papers, Box 10, File "Children-Adoption Independent Schemes, Miscellaneous, 1955–," SWHA, Minneapolis, MN.

28. Susan T. Pettiss to John H. Winters, 16 May 1960, ISS-USA papers, Box 10, File "Children-Adoption Independent Schemes, Miscellaneous, 1955–," SWHA, Minneapolis, MN.

29. "Help Heal a Child's Broken Heart," Everett Swanson Evangelistic Association, Inc. advertisement, ISS-USA papers, Box 10, File #28, SWHA, Minneapolis, MN.

30. Susan T. Pettiss to Garner J. Cline, 29 April 1963, ISS-USA papers, Box 10, File #28, SWHA, Minneapolis, MN.

REFERENCES

Adoption History Project (n.d.). *Proxy adoptions*. Retrieved on May 1, 2003, from http://darkwing.uoregon.edu/~adoption/topics/proxy.htm.

A/K/A World (1999). *Korean adoptees: Statistics*. Retrieved February 2, 1999, from http://akaworld.org/Koreanstat.html.

Carp, E. W. (1998). *Family matters: Secrecy and disclosure in the history of adoption.* Cambridge, MA: Harvard University Press.

Goss, J., & Lindquist, B. (1995). Conceptualizing international labor migration: A structuration perspective. *International Migration Review, 29*(2), 317-351.

International Social Service (ISS). (n.d.). *About ISS*. Retrieved February 18, 2003, from http://www.iss-ssi.org/About_ISS/body_about_iss.html.

International Social Service, American Branch (ISS-USA). (n.d.) *Dear friend* [Brochure]. Minneapolis, MN: World Vision, Inc, Box 10, File # 29, Social Welfare History Archives, Minneapolis, MN.

Kim, W. J. (1995). International adoption: A case review of Korean children. *Child Psychiatry & Human Development, 25*(3), 141-154.

Klein, C. (2000). Family ties and political obligation: The discourse of adoption and Cold War commitment to Asia. In C. G. Appy (Ed.), *Cold War constructions: The political culture of United States imperialism, 1945-1966* (pp. 35-66). Amherst, MA: University of Massachusetts Press.

Kramer, G. (1955, October 14). "Pied Piper" corrals 12 Korean babies, flies them to America for adoption. *Washington Post.*

Levine, B. (2000, June 21). For orphans of the forgotten war, the past is shrouded in questions. *Los Angeles Times,* E1-E3.

Lovelock, K. (2000). Intercountry adoption as a migratory practice: A comparative analysis of intercountry adoption and immigration policy and practice in the United States, Canada, and New Zealand in the post WW II period. *International Migration Review, 34*(3), 907-949.

Melosh, B. (2002). *Strangers and kin: The American way of adoption*. Cambridge, MA: Harvard University Press.

"Mr. Holt Moves the World." (1956, April 9). *Oregonian*. ISS-USA papers, Box 10, File "Children-Independent Adoption Schemes, Harry Holt, 1955-1957, Vol. 1," SWHA, Minneapolis, MN.

Patton, S. (2000). *Birthmarks: Transracial adoption in contemporary America.* New York: New York University Press.

Refugee Relief Act, 1953, Section 5 (a). Pub. L. No 83-203, §14(a), 67 Stat. 400, 406.

Weil, R.H. (1984). International adoptions: The quiet migration. *International Migration Review, 18*(2), 276-293.

PART II:
FORMING NEW FAMILIES

Early adoptees integrated families, neighborhoods, and communities in ways that profoundly challenged the notions of family and race. Parents were advised to minimize their children's differences and to raise them as *Americans*. Parental motivations—which include altruism, charitable inclinations, response to infertility, and desire to parent—intersected with the children's psychosocial and affiliation needs to be nurtured, to be loved, to feel *normal,* and to develop a congruent and integrated sense of self in the home. Researchers have sought to understand how adoptive families navigate private and public spaces.

Researchers William Feigelman and Nam Soo Huh offer retrospective studies that provide insight into developmental processes for adoptees. Feigelman contrasts the adjustment of Asian, African-American, and Latino adoptees raised in white homes with white adoptees raised within race, while Huh updates her original seminal work with William Reid in exploring ethnic identity development, in which they interviewed adoptees ages eleven to fourteen and their parents. The last two chapters in this section mark a shift in research, which more directly addresses how race, ethnicity, and culture are constructed in the adoption process, and the implications of parental cultural competence for their Korean children. This shift parallels an increasing awareness that adopting from Asia does not circumvent the challenges of raising children-of-color in a racially stratified society and a growing public espousal of a multicultural ideology. More specifically, Kristi Brian looks at how adoption facilitators "market" international adoption to prospective parents. Both Brian (Chapter 4) and Vonk et al. (Chapter 6) examine the ways in which international adoption is constructed and the relationship of that construction to parental motivations and cultural competence.

Chapter 3

A Long-Term Follow-Up
of Transracially Adopted Children
in Their Young Adult Years

William Feigelman

In the United States, nearly forty years ago, the subject of transracial adoption, especially of Korean children adopted into white American homes, evoked considerable controversy, even generating front-page news stories when, with the fall of the Saigon government, large numbers of Vietnamese war orphans were brought to the United States for adoption. This was at a time when transracial adoptions were greatly increasing, and then, as now, many debated whether these adopted children would remain outsiders, unable to adjust well to their new families and to the American social landscape. Many also wondered whether these children would remain confused about their racial identities and whether they would lose altogether any sense of having a national or ethnic heritage beyond their American one.

This selection is revised and updated from an earlier work titled "Adjustments of Transracially and Inracially Adopted Young Adults" that appeared in *Child and Adolescent Social Work Journal,* Vol. 17, No. 3, June 2000, pp. 165-184.

I am deeply grateful to Richard Barth, Devon Brooks, and Jill Duerr Berrick. Thanks to their resourceful and painstaking enterprise, respondents to a survey taken thirteen years earlier were successfully tracked for the present work. I am also grateful for their generosity to share this data. This work was also supported by grants from the U.S. Children's Bureau, the Office of Planning and Evaluation, and the Department of Health and Human Services.

International Korean Adoption
doi:10.1300/5734_03

This debate still persists. Yet, despite the differences of opinions, the flow of children to the United States from other countries continues to grow; along with Korean and Vietnamese adoptions, there are now increased adoptions from China, Russia, Romania, and Central and South America (Pertman, 2000). For the first time ever, the 2000 census enumerated the adoption statuses of U.S. households. It was found that, of the 2,000,000 homes with adopted children (nearly 3 percent of all homes with children), 250,000 consisted of homes with foreign-born adopted children. It was further noted that over 50,000 of the foreign-born adoptees were Korean, comprising the largest single group of internationally adopted children in the United States (Kreider, 2003).

Transracial adoption still remains controversial among the public at-large and among social service practitioners. As social workers and policymakers continue to challenge each other on its benefits and deficiencies, a community-based survey of Latinos in California showed evenly divided public opinion on its value (Bausch & Serpe, 1997). Previous community studies undertaken with African-American respondents have shown generally favorable opinions for it when the alternative is institutionalization (Howard, Royse, & Skerl, 1977; Simon, 1978).

Yet, the experts remain divided on transracial adoption, debating whether transracially adopted children ultimately lose their cultural identity in the process. One controversial question is whether the transracial adoptee becomes marginalized in the majority society (where they may be regarded as an outsider because of their physical distinctiveness) and within the minority community, too (where they may also become estranged because of their Anglo/Caucasian adoptive parentage). Transracial adoption critics argue that the cultural confusion, and conflict connected to this unique adoption situation, ultimately will undermine the adjustment of the transracial adoptee. So far, although occasional cases of culturally confused individuals have been found in some transracial adoption studies, no systematic evidence has emerged documenting this result as a pervasive adaptation.

On the other side of the ledger, advocates favoring transracial adoption have amassed an impressive body of information documenting its success. An outpouring of research, beginning in the early 1970s and extending to the present, has consistently established that transracially adopted children are well adapted. Placements have been found to be as successful as those placed inracially, and transracial adoptions are no more likely to disrupt than other types of adoptions (Barth & Berry, 1988; Fanshel, 1972; Feigelman & Silverman, 1983; Grow & Shapiro, 1974; Ladner, 1977; Simon & Altstein, 1977; Simon & Altstein, 1992; Zastrow, 1977). Studies of young, transracially adopted adolescents also show favorable adaptations, compared with those adopted inracially (Kim, 1976; McRoy & Zurcher, 1983; Shireman & Johnson, 1988; Simon & Altstein, 1992). Most of this documentation has been with regard to younger adoptees, where, at that age, racial identification issues are less salient in the life of the person. However, during one's late adolescence and early adult years, the recognition of one's racial or ethnic identity becomes more important. At this time, more than at any other during the life course, having a confused or uncertain racial identity could give rise to problems. Thus far, the evidence established on older adolescents and young adults has documented positive adaptations on the part of transracial adoptees. No studies have uncovered any serious adjustment difficulties.

Simon, Altstein, and Melli (1994), in a twenty-year follow-up of their original respondents, found no evidence of dysfunction among the transracially adopted blacks and Koreans in comparison with inracially adopted whites. They reported that most adapted harmoniously within their transracial families (with siblings and parents) and possessed positive viewpoints about their racial identities. Most regarded themselves as racially mixed and were positively adapted within their communities with work, school, friendships, and marriage. Yet, the study may leave transracial adoption critics with some lingering uncertainty. From the original study of 157 transracially adopted children in 1971, only fifty-five were followed up in 1991, and no analysis was given to the nonresponse issue.

Vroegh (1992) had greater success with a seventeen-year follow-up of a sample of transracially and inracially adopted African-American adoptees from Chicago. From the original eighty-seven adoptive parent couples studied from 1970 to 1972 by Shireman and Johnson (1988), fifty-five were followed up seventeen years later. Vroegh found most of the adopted children to be doing well. Identified problems were found to be similar to those noted in the general population. Adoptive parents and adoptees were highly satisfied with the adoptions. Transracial adoptees had generally harmonious relations with their siblings, had good self-esteem, had pride in being black, and had comfortable interaction with both blacks and whites. Yet, given that this sample was drawn exclusively from only two Chicago adoption agencies, doubt remains whether the sample represents transracial adoptees in general.

Thus, the jury is still out on settling transracial adoption's central controversies. The present study is by no means the definitive one for settling the transracial adoption debate. In the present analysis, I submit the responses of a large and diverse group of transracial and inracial white adoptive parents who provided information about their young adult children.

One of the neglected issues of past adoption research has been the failure to study adoptees as adults. This is beginning to be addressed more often in current research, including in the work of Barth and Brooks (1997), who compare family structural, gender, and racial correlates linked with differences in adult adoptive adjustments. In another study, using data from the National Longitudinal Survey of Youth, I compare and contrast adoptees in early adult years who grew up in intact adoption homes with their counterparts who were raised in comparable biological two-parent homes (Feigelman, 1997). The present study attempts to shed more light on the behavior of young adult adoptees as well.

METHODS

The original baseline survey, from which present respondents were drawn, began in 1975. The original sample of transracial and inracial adoptive parents were taken from membership lists of adoptive parent organizations and from lists of names furnished by several large adoption agencies known to be specialists in international and transracial placements. Also included were names of other adopting families who were not members of these organizations, but were known to the officers of the adoptive parent groups.

The original survey aimed to maximize the numbers of transracial adoption families with the most frequently occurring international adoptions of that time (i.e., of children born in Korea, Vietnam, and Colombia). In addition, efforts were made to represent white U.S.-born adopted children and African-American children adopted by white parents, for comparison.

Over 3,000 names of possible respondents were originally collected, and depending upon a group's potential for fulfilling desired sample characteristics, names were chosen either randomly or by its membership's entire listing. Of the 1,121 questionnaires sent to families in 1975, 737 were returned (66 percent). From that total, twenty nonwhite adoptive parent respondents were excluded because they did not meet the comparative transracial study criteria.

The original sample yielded sufficient numbers of transracially and inracially adopted children. It included 58 African-Americans, 442 Korean-and Vietnamese-born children (some of whom counted as African-American/ Vietnamese/white adoptions), forty-six Colombian-born children, and ninety-six white children born in the United States. Children came from a variety of sources, including domestic and foreign private agencies, regional social service departments, and independent adoptions.

In 1980 and 1981, when most children were enrolled in the early grades of primary school, a second wave of surveys was collected. At that time, 26 percent of respondents proved to be unreachable. Families had moved and postal forwarding requests had expired. From 545 possible respondents, 68 percent cooperated, yielding a total of 372 families.

In the most recent survey of 1993, conducted under the auspices of the School of Social Welfare at the University of California at Berkeley, some 532 questionnaires were mailed out to respondents of the first two surveys. Approximately 14 percent were returned as undeliverable. Twenty-six respondents wrote back, declining to participate in the latest survey. Two additional respondents returned questionnaires that later proved to be unusable, yielding a total of 240 usable responses.

The third survey was undertaken eighteen years after the first study had begun, at a time when most original adopted children were in their young adult years. The average age of these adoptees in 1993 was twenty-three. Considering the long lapse between follow-ups, the 1993 response rate (64 percent) seemed to be more than satisfactory.

Of course, a crucial question to ascertain in any longitudinal study is whether patterns of nonresponse contribute to making current respondents different from those who had participated in earlier surveys. Although the detailed tabulations have not been presented here, analysis of the demographic characteristics of the 1993 respondents showed extremely high convergence with those who participated in the two earlier surveys. Furthermore, there was no serious attrition of respondents who had reported child problems in earlier surveys. Consistent levels of participation were noted among those parents who reported child problems in the prior survey.

As in all prior survey analyses, I used parental judgments and reports to assess problem behavior. Two scales were used to assess problematical adjustments. The first was the Global Assessment Scale (GAS). This rating scale is based on a 100-point range, asking respondents to use a list of described adaptations and to offer numerical ratings on an adoptee's level of functioning, with 100 as the highest possible score and 0 reflecting total dysfunction. The description "no symptoms, superior functioning in a wide range of activities . . ." would rate as 100, while the description "needs constant supervision for several days to prevent hurting self or others . . ." would rank between 1 and 10. The scale offered a page-long list of adaptations, and their corresponding numerical values for raters to choose from, between these two extreme descriptions. This instrument has been widely used in community mental health research (Endicott, Spitzer, Fleiss, & Cohen, 1976). The second scale was an index of dysfunction created for the present research from responses to five behavioral questions. Parent respondents gave information on various behaviors of their children including whether their child ever had (a) run away from home, (b) been expelled from school, (c) experienced problems with the law, (d) drug or alcohol problems, and/or (e) received counseling for emotional problems. The top of Table 3.1 displays the frequencies for this index of dysfunction. Forty percent of parents reported none of these problems for their children ($N = 94$); 23 percent reported only one problem ($N = 54$); 15 percent reported two problems ($N = 36$); and 21 percent reported three or more problems ($N = 21$). From these items a five-point scale was created.

The five-item dysfunction scale correlated -0.55 with the GAS scale, and each of the scale items were highly intercorrelated with one another, with correlation coefficients ranging from a low of 0.18 to a high of 0.51. Because ten fewer missing cases were reported with the index of dysfunction, I relied more on this measure than on the GAS responses.

RESULTS

Table 3.1 displays the cross-tabular analysis of each of the components of the index of dysfunction against transracial adoption status. None of the components were significantly associated with being transracially adopted. Thus, transracial adoptees were no more likely to run away from home than inracial white adoptees. They were not more likely to have experienced problems with drugs or alcohol. They were not more likely to have gotten arrested or been in trouble with the police.

Two relationships approached significance. Latino and other adoptees were somewhat more likely to have seen doctors or counselors for emotional problems than all other subgroups; Asians were the least likely of all subgroups to have seen counselors (approaching significance at the 0.07 probability level). It should be noted that high levels of care-getting were experienced among these respondents. Fifty-five percent of all parents reported seeing counselors for their children's emotional or behavioral problems at some time or other, testifying the heavy reliance on mental health professionals among adoptive parents.

Another near significant association was noted in the case of those expelled from school (approaching significance at the 0.06 level), showing inracially adopted whites more likely to have experienced this event than any of the transracially adopted subgroups. On this dimension, Latino transracial adoptees showed the least likelihood of being expelled or suspended from schools.

TABLE 3.1. Adoptees' Ethnicity and Kinds of Youth Difficulties

	White (N = 37)	Asian (N = 151)	Black (N = 33)	Latino/Other (N = 19)	Total 100%	Base 240
			Percentages			
Has your child ever run away from home?						
No	75.7	82.6	66.7	73.7	78.5	187
Yes	24.3	17.4	33.3	26.3	21.4	51
Base	37	149	33	19	238	
Has your child ever seen a doctor/counselor for emotional or behavioral problems?						
No	45.9	50.7	31.3	26.3	45.4	108
Yes	54.1	49.3	68.8	73.7	54.6	130
Base	37	150	32	19	238	
Has your child ever had a problem with alcohol or drugs?						
No	75.7	81.9	71.9	78.9	79.3	188
Yes	24.3	18.1	28.1	21.1	20.7	49
Base	37	149	32	19	237	
Has your child ever been arrested or in trouble with the police?						
No	81.1	80.1	69.7	78.9	78.8	189
Yes	18.9	19.9	30.3	21.1	21.2	51
Base	37	151	33	19	240	
Has your child ever been expelled or suspended from school?						
No	67.6	84.8	75.8	89.5	81.3	195
Yes	32.4	15.2	24.2	10.5	18.8	45
Base	37	151	33	19	240	
Mean Global Assessment Scale Score/N	81.3/35	81.3/140	80.0/32	75.8/17	80.7	224

Source: International Adoption Survey, 1993, Univ. of California, Berkeley, Sch. of Social Welfare.

A one-way analysis of variance (ANOVA) test showed no significant differences between any of the transracial adoptive subgroups (with each other) and the inracially adopted whites on the GAS. The null hypothesis assumed GAS scores would be normally distributed about the mean and the same for each category of respondents. Test results did not come close to rejecting the null hypothesis.

Table 3.2 displays the cross-tabular analysis of the five-item index of dysfunction tabulated against a variety of possible factors associated with

TABLE 3.2. Index of Dysfunctionality by Various Characteristics

	No Problems (N = 94)	One Problem (N = 54)	Two Problems (N = 36)	Three or More Problems (N =49)	Base
			Percentage		
Age					
18-23	42.3	21.9	17.5	18.3	137
24+	37	26.1	10.9	26.1	92
					229
Adoption type					
White/White	35.1	18.9	21.6	24.3	37
Black/White	25.8	19.4	22.6	32.3	31
Asian/White	46.6	24.7	10.3	18.5	146
Latino/White	26.3	26.3	31.6	15.8	19
					233
Adoption type					
White/White	35.1	18.9	21.6	24.3	37
All TRAs	41.3	24.0	14.3	20.4	196
					233
*Gender**					
Male	40.4	21.2	10.1	28.3	99
Female	40.3	24.6	19.4	15.7	134
					233
Parents' marital status					
Intact	43.1	22.7	15.5	18.8	181
Split	30.4	23.9	17.4	28.3	46
					227
Age at adoption					
<l year	41.5	21.8	15.0	21.8	147
2-5 years	39.3	25.0	8.9	26.8	56
>6 years	25.0	30.0	35.0	10.0	20
					233

Source: International Adoption Survey, 1993, Univ. of California, Berkeley, Sch. of Social Welfare.

*Four-way chi-square probability <.05.

youth problems. Consistent with the results shown in Table 3.1—whether I compared all transracial adoptees with the inracially adopted whites, or whether each racial subset was separately compared with one another and to the whites—there was no significant association between any of the adoption types and poor adjustments. Thus, transracial adoptees as a group showed no greater adjustment deficits compared with inracially adopted whites.

Table 3.2, however, shows some important differences between the transracially adopted subsets. The overall probability value for this table—displaying each of the four ethnic subsets—was 0.08, below the customary 0.05 significance level. Yet, the table showed that about twice as many black transracial adoptees reported for three or more adjustment problems compared with Latino transracial adoptees (32 percent as compared with 16 percent). In a separate comparison (not shown) of all transracial adoptees, and excluding the inracially adopted whites, this difference between the blacks and the Latinos proved to be a statistically significant one (at the 0.03 level). Asian transracial adoptees also exhibited fewer problems than African-American transracial adoptees. Thus, there is evidence showing significant variation in the adjustments of transracial adoptees among racial subsets when whites are excluded from the analysis.

Table 3.2 also shows statistically significant differences in gender and adjustment. Male adoptees were more likely to have problems than females, with almost twice as many having three or more adjustment problems than the females. The data also showed that variations in young adult adjustments did not seem linked to whether adoptive parents remained married or not.

Following up on earlier findings that showed adjustment deficits for those adopted later in life, I found no adjustment differences among young adult adoptees adopted during their first year of life, those adopted between ages two and five years, and those adopted at age six years or later. Those adopted later showed somewhat fewer problems than the infant adoptees, but these differences did not come close to approaching statistical significance.

Table 3.3 displays the responses of all transracial adoption families and excludes inracially adopted whites. This effort was aimed at assessing whether experiencing racial antagonism was associated with more adjustment problems. All three of the hypotheses I tested confirmed this supposition with statistically significant results. Results showed higher levels of adjustment difficulties reported when children encountered more discrimination, more negative comments about their background, and when they experienced more appearance discomfort.

Investigating the frequency of discrimination among each of the three transracial adoptee subgroups, I found slightly more than half of the parents of black children (53 percent) said their child was discriminated against sometimes or often, compared with 32 percent of parents of Asian transracial adoptees and 11 percent of Latino transracial adoptees making similar reports. This chi-square measure was significant at the 0.01 level. This evidence suggests that African-American transracial adoptees were

TABLE 3.3. Index of Dysfunctionality by Racially Exclusionary Experiences[a]

Index of Dysfunctionality*	Hardly Never/Never	Sometimes/Often	Base
	Percentage		
Has your child ever been discriminated against because of his/her race/ethnic background?			
No problems	47.7	28.6	79
One problem	25.0	22.2	46
Two problems	10.9	20.6	27
Three or more problems	16.4	28.6	39
			191
Have you or members of your household received negative comments because of your child's race/ethnic background?			
No problems	45.6	22.6	80
One problem	23.1	32.3	47
Two problems	10.6	32.3	27
Three or more problems	20.6	12.9	37
			191
Has your child ever displayed any discomfort over his/her racial/ethnic appearance?			
No problems	46.6	35.6	80
One problem	30.1	17.8	47
Two problems	8.7	20.0	27
Three or more problems	14.6	26.7	39
			193

Source: International Adoption Survey, 1993, Univ. of California, Berkeley, Sch. of Social Welfare.

[a]Based on the responses of transracial adoption families only (*N* = 203).

*Chi-square probability <.05.

subjected to the most intense antiminority mistreatment. Regarding negative comments and discomfort about the child's appearance, evidence showed similar (and statistically undifferentiated) responses among the four different ethnic subgroups under investigation. About 17 percent of families encountered negative comments about their child's ethnicity, and about half of all transracial adoptees' parents felt their child had experienced discomfort about their appearance.

An assumption of enlightened transracial adoptive parenthood is the idea that parents, recognizing and accepting their adoption family as a biracial one, can help their children to cope more effectively with American racism. I suspected this would be reflected in the children's perceptions of themselves, especially in feelings of discomfort about their appearance. In brief, I sought to investigate whether parental behavior toward fostering an adopted child's ethnic or racial identity would help their child to reduce his or her discomfort about his or her appearance.

Table 3.4 shows several hypotheses aimed at accounting for variations in children's perceived discomfort about their appearance; this analysis was confined exclusively to the 203 transracial adoptees in the sample. Whether their child was judged to be identified as "American only" or whether the parent felt their child was "Korean/American" or "Colombian/American" or identified only with his or her country of birth did not seem to matter in the child's experience of any discomfort. However, whether parents lived in a predominately white neighborhood was associated with significantly greater feelings of discomfort among their transracially adopted children. Separate calculations of the tables were also completed among African-American transracial adoptees only and among the Asian transracial adop-

TABLE 3.4. Discomfort About One's Appearance Based on Parental Behavior Patterns[a]

How does your child identify him/herself?			
Appearance Discomfort	American Only/Other Only	American-Hyphen-Other	Base
No	51.1	53.8	88
Yes	48.9	46.3	80
			168
How many whites live in the community where you now live?			
Appearance discomfort*	Whites and some nonwhites	Whites only	Base
No	75.0	48.8	104
Yes	25.0	51.2	94
			198
How many nonwhites live in the community where you now live?			
Appearance discomfort*	Few nonwhites	Many nonwhites	Base
No	41.6	60.2	92
Yes	58.4	39.8	92
			184

Source: International Adoption Survey, 1993, Univ. of California, Berkeley, Sch. of Social Welfare.

[a]Based on the responses of transracial adoption families only (*N* = 203).

*Chi-square probability <.05.

tees. These results showed the same pattern displayed in Table 3.4; i.e., that those living in racially mixed areas had children who felt less discomfort about their appearances than those who lived in predominately white areas. It was not possible to do this calculation meaningfully for the Latino transracial adoptees with only nineteen cases available for analysis. The data also showed that parents of Latino transracial adoptees were the most likely of all to live in predominately white neighborhoods. Ninety-four percent lived in all-white neighborhoods, compared with 89 percent of the parents of Asian transracial adoptees and 66 percent of the parents of black transracial adoptees.

DISCUSSION

Making assessments about adoptees' adjustments from information supplied by their parents can be a hazardous enterprise. Parents may be poorly informed on many points and may not be able to provide accurate data on their children's activities and feelings. For example, how a transracially adopted child identifies oneself in racial or cultural terms is probably beyond the apprehension of many transracial adoptive parents. Yet, parents should be able to provide accurate information about much of their children's conduct. They should know whether their child had ever run away from home, had been expelled from school, had trouble with the law or with drugs, or had ever sought counseling for behavioral problems. There is certainly no basis for assuming that transracially adoptive parents would be any less informed about these matters than the parents of white inracially adopted children. Therefore, findings showing no significant differences between transracial adoptive parents and inracial adoptive parents on adult children's adjustments seem adequately demonstrated.

Transracial adoptive and inracial adoptive parents also provided information on feelings of satisfaction with their adoption, i.e., whether they had close and warm relationships with their adopted children and whether adopted children had positive and close (or conflicted) relations with their siblings. Almost three-fourths of all the sampled adoptive parents reported being highly satisfied with their adoptions. Only 14 percent reported some serious dissatisfaction. Nearly four-fifths of parents reported having warm and positive relations with the adopted child at the time of the survey, and only 18 percent reported frequent sibling conflict between these adoptees and their siblings. When I contrasted each of the three subgroups against one another and against inracially adopted whites, again results showed comparable responses between subgroups. Thus, all the parent-based data showed no elevated levels of adjustment problems associated with being transracially adopted.

One of this study's most striking findings showed that the transracial adoptive parents' decisions on where to live had a substantial impact on their children's adjustments. Transracial adoptive parents residing in predominately white communities tended to have adoptees who experienced more discomfort about their appearance than those who lived in integrated settings. Adoptees feeling more discomfort, in turn, were more likely to have adjustment difficulties.

Thus, one important recommendation is to advise prospective transracial adoptive parents to relocate to more culturally heterogeneous neighborhoods if they wish to strengthen their children's adjustments. The evidence suggesting this was especially clear for the African-American and Asian transracial adoptive parents, but less convincing for the Latino transracial adoptive parents, given their smaller numbers in the sample. It would be especially hazardous to speculate on what the nineteen Latino cases represent, but I found only 11 percent of the parents of Latino children reported their child was discriminated against sometimes or often, as compared with 53 percent for the parents of blacks and 32 percent for the Asians (chi-square $p < .05$).

This analysis also confirmed findings uncovered in many studies of nonadopted youth, i.e., males are more problem-prone than females. Somewhat surprising, perhaps, was the failure to confirm greater levels of youth dysfunction among the adoptees whose parents had divorced. Although differences were noted in the predicted direction, results fell considerably short of the 0.05 significance level.

Early studies have found an association between the child's age at adoption and adjustment problems. Those adopted as infants were found to be far less problem-prone than those whose adoptions were initiated when they were older. Yet, analysis of this data, obtained when children had reached adulthood, showed no adjustment differences between those adopted as infants and those adopted at older ages. It seems that this sample of mostly transracially adopted children—comprised of only 9 percent who were adopted after age six years—represented a population of predominately infant adoptees. This fact alone could account for these unanticipated findings.

Yet, it is also possible that developmental problems troubling the later-age adopted children during their youth could vanish as these children eventually develop deeper bonds of trust with their adoptive parents over the longer term. If future studies confirm this, there may be encouraging news to the many prospective adoptive parents who remain wary about adopting older children, fearing they will inevitably encounter a lifelong struggle in managing their child's adjustment.

Young adults comprise a crucial testing ground for assessing whether transracial adoptees are confused about their personal and cultural identities. If transracial adoptees are more confused about their identities (compared with their inracially adopted peers), then we would expect them to show evidence of greater adjustment difficulties. Yet, the results obtained here suggested otherwise. Parents of transracial adoptees reported no more adjustment problems among their children than those reported by the parents of inracially adopted whites. Thus, the present study supports the viability of transracial adoption for many, mostly minority, children now denied opportunities of family living.

The evidence acquired here suggested that extra-family forces, such as societal racism, did impact negatively adjustment outcomes of adolescents and young adults, and in that, black and Asian children, who appear unmistakably different from whites, were most likely to encounter societal discrimination. Based on the present data, it seems safe to conclude that when transracially adoptive parents live in racially mixed neighborhoods, their children will be able to thrive better than when parents live in more segregated settings.

REFERENCES

Barth, R. P., & Brooks, D. (1997). A longitudinal study of family structure and size and adoption outcomes. *Adoption Quarterly, 1,* 29-55.

Barth, R. P., & Berry, M. (1988). *Adoption and disruption.* New York: Aldine de Gruyter.

Bausch, R. S., & Serpe, R. T., (1997). Negative outcomes of interethnic adoption of Mexican American children. *Social Work, 42,* 136-143.

Endicott, J., Spitzer, R. L., Fleiss, J. L., & Cohen, J. (1976). The global assessment scale. *Archives of General Psychiatry, 33,* 766-771.

Fanshel, D. (1972). *Far from the reservation: The transracial adoption of American Indian children.* Metuchen, NJ: The Scarecrow Press.

Feigelman, W. (1997). Adopted adults: Comparisons with persons raised in conventional families. *Marriage and Family Review, 25,* 199-223.

Feigelman, W., & Silverman, A. R. (1983). *Chosen children: New patterns of adoptive relationships.* New York: Praeger.

Grow, L., & Shapiro, D. (1974). *Black children–white parents: A study of transracial adoption.* New York: Child Welfare League of America.

Howard, A., Royse, D. D., & Skerl, J. A. (1977). Transracial adoption: The black community perspective. *Social Work, 22,* 184-189.

Kim, D. S. (1976). *Intercountry adoptions: A study of self concept of adolescent Korean children who were adopted by American families*. Unpublished doctoral dissertation, University of Chicago.

Kreider, R. (2003). *Adopted children and stepchildren: Census 2000 special reports*. Washington, DC: U.S. Department of Commerce.

Ladner, J. (1977). *Mixed families*. Garden City, NY: Doubleday Anchor.

McRoy, R., & Zurcher, L. A. (1983). *Transracial and inracial adoptees*. Springfield, IL: CC Thomas.

Pertman, A. (2000). *Adoption nation: How the adoption revolution is transforming America*. New York: Basic Books.

Shireman J., & Johnson, P. (1988). *Growing up adopted*. Chicago, IL: Chicago Child Care Society.

Simon, R. J. (1978). Black attitudes toward transracial adoption. *Phylon, 39*, 135-142.

Simon, R. J., & Altstein H. (1977). *Transracial adoptees and their families*. New York: Wiley.

Simon, R. J., & Altstein, H. (1992). *Adoption, race and identity: From infancy through adolescence*. New York: Praeger.

Simon, R. J., Altstein H., & Melli, M. S. (1994). *The case for transracial adoption*. Washington, DC: American University Press.

Vroegh, K. (1992, April). *Transracial adoption: How it is 17 years later*. Unpublished report. Chicago, IL: Chicago Child Care Society.

Zastrow, C. H. (1977). *Outcome of black children–white parent transracial adoptions*. San Francisco: R & E Research Associates.

Chapter 4

Choosing Korea:
Marketing "Multiculturalism"
to Choosy Adopters

Kristi Brian

We just thought it was more interesting if we were going to adopt, to kind of adopt another culture as well. And that was fine with us. We had no problems going outside our race, going outside our country.

Mrs. Morrison,[1]
Adoptive mother of three Korean children

One of the most striking changes in Korean-American adoption practice in recent years has been the emergent focus on *culture*. While the vast majority of families formed through international Korean adoption have never had the option of "hiding" their adoption the way "racially matched" adoptive families have, to varying degrees, many adoptive families have hidden their child's birth culture out of an impulse or desire to thoroughly Americanize the adoptee. However, now that the discourse within adoption practice has morphed from an edict of cultural assimilation into one of celebrated multiculturalism, new questions arise about how this turn toward culture is intersecting with matters of race and international hierarchies of privilege.

Furthermore, with the dramatic increase and rapid globalization of adoption services over the past decade, it appears that international adoption practices are becoming far more consumer-oriented than problem-oriented. As adoption agencies model a neoliberal approach to problem solving by

International Korean Adoption
doi:10.1300/5734_04

hastily adding more sending countries to their list of partners to provide more "multicultural" choices to American family-builders, they compromise their ability to attend to the specific crises in each particular sending nation. They also fail to give sufficient attention to the historical patterns of racism and class stratification that have conditioned our ideas about adoption in the United States.

In light of this deficiency, as nonprofit and for-profit agencies multiply and expand across the globe, it does not seem unreasonable to begin to demand that facilitators and agency CEOs alike clearly convey how the *business* of adoption is actually working toward the elimination of the need for international adoption in the various sending countries with whom they partner. To expect this of facilitators is to expect that such agencies exist for the purpose of effecting real social change, rather than for the purpose of fulfilling American dreams of nuclear-family-building by way of the misfortunes of others.

In an effort to ultimately raise questions about whose interests are being served through a reliance on particular culture-based discourses, this chapter looks specifically at the ways in which adoption facilitators "produce knowledge" on the subject of Korean-American adoption (KAA). With training usually in the fields of social work, psychology, or law, adoption facilitators currently working in the United States have become the key "knowledge producers" propagating ideas on the need for, and "shared benefits" of, adoption. They assign meaning to adoption that is mediated, interpreted, or reproduced by adoptive parents and other adoptive family members including the adoptees themselves.

Through ethnographic research within adoptive families and adoption agencies, I have identified some common discursive elements used across agencies in the promotion of KAA. I suggest that these common elements or themes help to fortify the notion that KAA is a mutually beneficial arrangement for both participating nation-states, as well as for all individual participants involved. One narrative theme takes the form of an "adopter-centered" marketing model that caters to adopters' desire for controlled, timely, cost-effective family-building. Another theme imagines Korea as a nonpolitical, cultural "other." And a third theme revolves around a paradigm that detrimentally equates the consumption of "multiculturalism" to race consciousness in adopters. Before turning to the specific examples that expose these discursive themes, I want to first address the centrality of common "culturalist" paradigms in nation-building narratives that have undoubtedly influenced international adoption discourse.

THE TROUBLE WITH "CULTURE"

Any conversation about international adoption is embedded in partial and competing notions of culture. Indeed, culture, as literary critic Raymond Williams (1976) suggests, " . . . is one of the two or three most complicated words in the English language" (p. 87). More to the point, as Michaela di Leonardo (1992) once stated, in a discussion of the misguided uses of culture, *our guild* (meaning anthropologists) "invented the damn term, which has become a Frankenstein monster, rampaging across the landscape of national life" (p. 441).

A look at how culture has been deployed in dominant U.S. nation-building narratives over the past half-century in which KAA has taken place helps to explain the troubled nature of the concept within KAA discourse. At its inception in the late 1950s, KAA was ensconced within the pervasive, albeit highly debatable, image of the U.S. military as "liberators" in Korea (Yuh, 2002) and its convergence with nation-building narratives at home that articulated cultural assimilation as an American ideal. Embedded in these nation-building narratives is what Judith Goode (2001) calls a version of "culturalist essentialism" (p. 436). Goode argues that culturalist essentialism, which conceptualizes culture as a bounded set of fixed rules, is used in both earlier melting pot prescriptions for national unity as well as in the more recent master narratives based on ethnic pluralism. The former imagined that unity could only be forged through a "nation of immigrants" losing their ties to their ancestral homeland and becoming absorbed into an Anglo-American ideal. The later narratives, which emerged after the civil rights movements and the celebrated American bicentennial, deploy the new imagery of the *mosaic, tapestry,* or *salad.* These latter images attempt to give the impression that all cultures are valued equally for their unique contribution in crafting a unified and richly diverse nation. Both the *melting pot* and the *unity through diversity* narratives rely on the notion that ethnic cultures are separate and distinct from one another. Unfortunately, as these narratives entrench ideas of immutable racial/ethnic differences, they potentially discourage us from imagining how alliances can form based on class or other shared interests for social change.

Like Goode, Frank Wu (2002) observes that the melting pot approach, which he describes as an intense "dissolving operation," did not vanish, but is experiencing resurgence in the new language of multiculturalism (p. 229). Wu suggests that both assimilation and multiculturalism together place Asian Americans in a "no-win bind" as they both serve "as a description of how people behave and a prescription for how they ought to behave" (p. 237).

In agreement with Wu's argument that the problems with assimilation are not solved by the assumptions of multiculturalism, Korean-American adoptee Pauline Park (1999) states:

> [Multiculturalism] nonetheless does a disservice to Korean adoptees by constructing a binary opposition between "Korean" and "American"—a false dichotomy—that traps Korean adoptees in the crevice between the White dominant culture from which they are often alienated and a traditional Korean culture to which they may feel no integral connection. (p. 11)

Thus, in order to harness offhand uses of culture and multiculturalism, those that reduce culture to race, aesthetics, traditions, or essentialist expectations for behavior, it is useful to illustrate the complexity of cultures by considering aspects of political economy. This theoretical approach views culture as a manifestation of shifting power relationships and historical processes involving racism, sexism, class stratification, and other discriminatory structures—all of which can be linked to larger political and economic constraints on people's lives. Therefore, approaching the subject of KAA from this line of inquiry requires an attentiveness to matters pertaining to the extreme economic transitions of post-war Korea, the military and economic relationship between the United States and Korea, the gendered and class-based family ideologies in both nation-states, as well as the racial hierarchies that have conditioned adoption practices and adoptive family life. Though these cultural factors may not be as easy to consume as ethnic dishes or traditional costumes, they are just as fundamental to the fabric of cultural complexity.

THEMES OF THE DOMINANT
INSTITUTIONAL DISCOURSE

In order to understand the particular discourses of culture found in the context of Korean-American adoption, I interviewed adoption facilitators, adoptive parents of Korean children of different generations, and adult Korean adoptees. Also, I attended several adoption conferences, meetings, and functions in various agencies during the months of September 2001 to February 2003. This chapter is based primarily on the in-depth interviews I conducted with six adoption facilitators who conduct Korean-American adoption through one of four private, nonprofit agencies in the Mid-Atlantic region of the United States. It is also based on my observations of the nine general information meetings and three preadoption training sessions for adoptive parents hosted by different agencies.

All of the agency meetings and trainings I attended were facilitated by white/European American women. Five of the adoption facilitators interviewed for this study are also white women.[2] One is an adopted Korean woman. Four of the facilitators I interviewed are also adoptive parents. While this sample is not intended to be representative of the adoption profession, it does reflect the reality of the high number of white adoptive parents working in the field of international adoption. Though the adoption agencies observed differ in size, mission, and procedural technicalities, they are strikingly similar in the way they address matters of race and culture in KAA. My analysis focuses on these similarities among the consumer and culture-based narratives articulated by the three agencies and, at times, considers how these narratives are also articulated by adoptive family members.

Meeting the Consumer Needs of the Target Market

In the early stages of researching KAA, I expected to find international adoption, in general, promoted in a manner that appealed to prospective parents' sense of altruism or international relief efforts. Much to my surprise, I found, instead, adoption facilitators focused primarily on appeasing adoptive parents' expectations for consumer choice and efficient adoption services. While adoptive parents increasingly use the Internet to compare adoption agency programs and services, the official point of entry into the field of international adoption is typically a general information meeting hosted by an adoption agency. In these information meetings, referred to by one facilitator as *marketing meetings,* the "best interests of the children" are given the perfunctory nod, which seem to lurk in the shadows of the demands of well-meaning Americans who find themselves in the throes of nuclear-family-building, in many cases after years of physical and emotional struggles with infertility.

These introductory meetings are often facilitated by social workers or representatives who have previously adopted children internationally. These facilitators sometimes offer their impressions of other agencies they encountered through their own adoption process or eliminated from their list of possible agencies. In other words, facilitators can often give a survey of the market that comes from their own experience as adoptive parents, not just facilitators. In efforts to demonstrate the agency's ability to personalize the adoption process and provide prospective adopters with ample amounts of sensitivity, affirmation, and options, it is not uncommon for facilitators to say such things as "we really hold your hand through the process" and "we want you to be sure to find a child that is just right for your family."

In contrast to the unexpected disappointments and feelings of uncontrollable circumstances with infertility, many adopters are eager to engage in a more controlled process of family-building with somewhat predictable outcomes. Thus, in addition to empathizing with parents' vulnerability around issues of infertility, facilitators are well aware that prospective parents, especially those arriving at an adoption agency for the first time, are likely "shopping around" for a reputable and reliable adoption source.

At least to some degree, adoptive parents' "choosiness" is catered to by adoption agencies' zeal to add more sending countries or adoption options to their list of programs. While adding new programs can be superficially rationalized as providing homes for a greater number of children throughout the world, such expansion must also be seen as both congruent with and conditioned by other processes of globalization that favor "private sector solutions over the public sector" and downplay power asymmetries for the sake of competitive growth and dominance within a market (Goode & Maskovsky, 2001, p. 5). All the adoption agencies I observed for this study facilitate international adoptions with multiple countries (between three and twelve countries per agency) throughout Latin America, Asia, and Eastern Europe.

Though some private nonprofit agencies have contracts with the state to facilitate domestic adoption or run their own non-state-affiliated domestic infant programs, information meetings for domestic adoption and international adoption are usually held separately. Thus, neither the stressed, fractured, and racialized state of the American child welfare system (Roberts, 2002) nor the thousands of children awaiting adoption in the United States are generally mentioned at meetings geared to those interested in international adoption. Therefore, whether or not prospective parents have already consciously chosen not to adopt an American child, these meetings do not generally provide new information on U.S. adoption for parents to consider. Adoption facilitators are aware of the fact that many adoptive parents come to their first information meeting having already decided from which country they want to adopt and, therefore, tailor the meetings according to these desires.

While adoption facilitators may differentiate KAA from other adoption choices in informational meetings, the specificity granted to this form of adoption usually focuses on KAA's "well-tested" history and streamlined efficiency. Therefore, the longevity of KAA is applauded and carries a great deal of sway in adoptive parents' decision to choose Korea over other options. KAA has another appealing convenience feature for many adopters in that it is generally the only form of international adoption offered that does not require adopters to travel to the birth country to retrieve the child. Thus facilitators and parents speak positively of KAA, often characterizing it as one of the safest, easiest, and quickest routes to a young healthy baby.

However, it is important to note that the requirement of heterosexual marriage mandated by KAA policy eliminates this form of adoption as an option for single, gay, or lesbian parents. Furthermore, the application and processing fees involved in most forms of international adoption, including KAA, make this style of family-building cost-prohibitive for low-income families. Thus, the promotion of KAA is primarily "targeted" to white, middle-class, heterosexual couples, while ideas about class and race consciousness as well as discussion about rigid sexuality norms remain underdeveloped dimensions of adoption "marketing" discourse.

Korea As a Nonpolitical, Cultural "Other"

While the complicated military and economic relationship between the United States and Korea and the relevance of this to Harry Holt's endeavors are generally absent from agency discussion, the continued *need* for international adoption from Korea is always expressed, usually in culturalist or moralistic terms. The culture-based narratives that facilitators offer to account for the continued need for Korean international adoption tend to focus on three main Korean factors. The one-sentence explanation offered by a facilitator during an information meeting for prospective parents addressed two of the three factors. As she succinctly stated without any follow-up comments, "Korea is still a culture that does not accept [domestic] adoption or out-of-wedlock births." Promoters of KAA across agencies asserted with consistency that Korean women bearing children out of wedlock are ostracized and hence turn to adoption, usually international, to avoid shaming their families.

A third and related cultural explanation for KAA that facilitators routinely mention is the importance of having a child's name entered on a family registry, or *hojuje,* an act which only the father can perform, and is unlikely to if he is not married to the mother of his child. As facilitators explain, without a documented family lineage, Korean children born out of wedlock are likely to be broadly discriminated against within their own birth culture.[3] These needs for KAA are usually stated as "social facts," and mentioned merely as a preface to the bulk of most agency discussions centered on the requirements, costs, and timelines for adopting a Korean baby.

While these cultural factors are indeed relevant to the historical trajectory of KAA, to focus too heavily on these aspects of the practice is to oversimplify the adoption context and the motives of those participating in it. Blanket statements about single mothers being ostracized and adoption being culturally unacceptable tend to present birth parents as an undifferentiated mass constrained by a "traditional" society. Such explanations downplay the various ways in which such "traditions" or cultural constraints are also resisted or overcome. When facilitators omit this latter point, they risk perpetuating a manufactured polarity between the supposed limitations of non-Western, "traditional" society and the freedoms of modern Western liberal democracy. After hearing a simple culturalist explanation about the need for KAA in a training session for prospective adoptive parents, one adoptive-father-to-be shook his head and said, "Can you believe how backward they are over there?"

As Seungsook Moon (2002) urges, with regard to gender hierarchies that are often associated with "traditions," such as Confucianism in Korean society, it is necessary to give careful consideration to *how* "tradition" is differently constructed at particular historical moments. Otherwise, it is as though "tradition persists automatically or that it tenaciously refuses to go away" (p. 82). Instead of portraying KAA as intimately tied to the rapid industrialization, urbanization, and political volatility of Korean society, it often gets portrayed as the best solution for a society crippled by its own traditions. Rather than encouraging adopters to consider the ways in which South Korea has been engulfed in processes, forcefully supported by American capital, which have dramatically conditioned everything from social welfare priorities to gender relations, sexuality, class consciousness, and consumer culture (Cho, 2002; Kendall, 2002; Lee, 2002), facilitators tend to focus on the nobleness of allowing children to be adopted internationally.

When asking adoption facilitators to reflect on Korea's economic motivation for sustaining the practice, I often framed my question with reference to the infamous episode during the 1988 Olympics in Seoul, when American newscaster Bryant Gumbel questioned the ethics of Korea's "profitable" international adoption program on national television (Kim, 2000, p. 63). To this query regarding Korea's profit-motive in adoption, facilitators responded in distinctively noneconomic, moralist terms.

For example, when I asked one facilitator, Paula, who is the mother of two adopted Korean children, how she interpreted the negative media coverage, she said:

> They don't profit . . . The Korean people are a very proud and loving people and want the best for their children, and I commend them for being one of the first countries to step out of the box and say we have got to do something that is best for these children. I think they truly

want to have these children remain in their country, but at this point, they don't have a way.

Similarly, another facilitator summarized her favorable impression of KAA in the following way:

> Korea is brave for participating in international adoption. Over all these years she has been saving her children. These are children born out of wedlock, so they would have that stigma to live with, so it's better that they are adopted. The mothers are brave because they have not chosen abortion but adoption. How wonderful for these kids.

None of the facilitators I observed granted any attention to organizations such as the Mission to Promote Adoption in Korea (MPAK), an organization formed by families in Korea who actively promote domestic Korean adoption and who have established economic incentives for families willing to adopt. Nor were facilitators forthcoming about adult adoptee organizations in either Korea or the United States who support international adoptees returning to Korea and who attempt to broaden dialogue around the practice of adoption within Korea (Elliot, 2002; Seo, 2001).[4] Although such organizations may be relatively new to the KAA landscape, their inclusion in the discourse would be beneficial if for no other reason than to dispute the misconception that Koreans are unanimously, "culturally" intolerant of adoption and to reveal the fact that international adoption is indeed contested terrain.

Moreover, rather than relying on the lazy language of "tradition," facilitators would offer a greater understanding of the context if they were to offer concrete examples of the actual structural (economic and political) barriers to parenting that Korean birth parents face. Whether the birth parents are teenage students, farmers facing massive urbanization, wage earners in factories, or middle-class social climbers, their diverse reasons for either considering or deciding against adoption ought to be contextualized in adoption discourse, just as Americans' reasons for choosing to adopt from Korea ought to be included.

Assumptions of Race Consciousness in "Culture"-Consuming Parents

Adoption social workers often advocate international adoption over public domestic adoption by claiming that first-time parents may not be equipped to parent the older children-of-color that are most commonly available through the U.S. foster care system. Because facilitators view their role as helping families exercise as much personal choice as possible in building their families according to cultural preferences as opposed to domestic social welfare needs, they rarely seem to challenge or discourage parents' decision to adopt repeatedly from the same country abroad. This allows adopters to further defend their adoption choices in cultural terms, while submerging their motives that may be based on race or other discriminating factors.[5] For example, the Morrisons, who have adopted from Korea three times since 1992, after years of infertility treatment and miscarriages, described to me the process they went through in selecting a birth country from the thirteen different countries on the agency's list. The adoptive mother stated:

> We took all of the countries [offered by the agency] and he sat down [referring to her husband] and listed the ones he would or would not consider and I sat down and did the same thing. Then we compared our lists. And we agreed up front that if one of us would not consider a particular country we would not have to justify why. We immediately wrote off South America . . . but if there were any that we didn't agree on we just moved on because there were certainly enough to choose from . . . We thought at least for the first one we wanted a baby, we didn't care about the sex, but we wanted a baby.

This adoptive mother then explained that they ultimately decided to "go with an Asian country" because, in addition to her husband's being Dutch, they had an Asian connection too. Her husband went on to explain their connection to Asia more specifically. He explained that, though he had some Indonesian heritage down the line somewhere on his mother's side, he was the son of a Dutch naval officer. He captured his experiences in Indonesia by saying, "Since we were the Dutch colonists, we had a very good life there, servants, country club, things like that." This couple's approach of "not justifying" to one another why certain countries were or were not considered for their adoption was not challenged by any agency procedure and allowed them to evade the issues pertaining to racism or national superiority that were likely influencing their decision-making process.

The white adoption facilitators whom I interviewed and observed seemed very comfortable with their assumptions that international adopters from the United States were above average in terms of their race consciousness and "open-mindedness" about cultural difference. However, facilitators were not inclined to probe white adopters' level of comfort around American minority communities and, perhaps, even the degree to which this may have influenced the adopters' decision to choose Korea. Therefore, the adopters' eagerness to embrace a "new culture" through international adoption is viewed as virtuous, despite the fact that this embrace of "difference" happens precisely on adopters' own terms, in limited doses, and from a comfortable distance away from the adoptees' birth communities.

After a cultural awareness training session, I spoke with a white couple (in their early thirties) about their choice to adopt from Korea, and asked if they had considered adopting domestically. The husband said they had not. This soon-to-be adoptive father then told me a story about some friends who had their adopted child "taken away from them" when the child's "Puerto Rican father showed up on their doorstep." He went on to say that it is a problem adopting and "raising minorities in this country because you are never really able to replace that culture." He said, "There is always the chance that they are going to seek out that group of people and identify with them and see you, the parent, as the outsider; particularly with African-Americans, they are always going to have that group around." When I asked him why he was so sure he would not experience the same dilemmas with his Korean son, he said, "The Korean community is only in certain cities and in more isolated pockets, as opposed to spread out all over the country." He said, "Just four miles from my house there is a community that is predominantly African American," emphasizing the threateningly close proximity this group would pose if he were to adopt an African-American child.

As Goode (2001) argues, entrenched "culturalist essentialism" in popular American thought invokes the notion of cultures as bounded entities, which can be placed on hierarchies according to moral worth. The adoptive father mentioned here articulated such ideas when he implied that some American minorities are born into cultures that cannot be "replaced" and that some cultures are more easily contained than others. When adoption facilitators overemphasize adopters' right to choose a birth culture—one that appeals to the adopters' interests and lifestyle—they model a type of race-evasive and power-evasive thinking that allows culture to stand in as the "polite proxy for race" in the selection process while it does nothing to challenge the race consciousness of adoptive parents (p. 437).

If the choice to pursue KAA is related to the appeal it holds for white Americans who are fearful of having their adopted child taken away from them by the child's birth parents or symbolically taken away through their child's close association with groups who share the child's racial or ethnic identity, agencies do very little to point out the problems related to this appeal. Furthermore, the dynamics of whites selecting particular nonwhites to satisfy their own desires or to assuage certain fears, however well-intentioned, ought to appear jarringly comparable to other forms of exploitation of peoples of the world through slavery, colonialism, concubinage, and the like. If the association with other forms of appropriation does not seem fitting, then the evidence to support this venture as something entirely different from other forms of paternalism and domination in the hands of a white majority needs to be made abundantly clear. Though adoption facilitators may assume they are making this distinction clear, the fact that there is such a limited amount of attention granted to the social welfare crises at hand, coupled with unbridled opportunities for adopters to select and choose children according to their own preferences, leaves in place a familiar racialized power imbalance.

Having recognized white adopters' greater degree of comfort with Asian adoption over that of American transracial adoption, I asked facilitators to comment on how they address this hierarchy of "acceptableness," or the differential worth of adoptable children when they sense it from parents. For instance, I asked facilitators how they would proceed in an adoption if they recognized that parents had chosen to adopt from Korea specifically as a means of avoiding the idea of adopting an African-American or Latino child. One facilitator, Kelly, responded:

KELLY: Well, some parents just feel that a child won't have as negative of an experience because they are Asian.

K.B: Do you think that is true?

KELLY: It's just different. It's not that different though. But I see this assumption in parents. Even in the [domestic] program, they will adopt a Latino child or a biracial child before they will adopt an African-American child. Even with African-American couples, they will state they will take a light-skinned child but not a dark-skinned child. So we place children according to this preference. And I think that is okay. Because, like for me, I like [the country of her internationally adopted child] culture. Korean culture just doesn't hold the same appeal for me. So I think there is some legitimacy from adoptive parents' perspectives because we expect some interaction with that culture, the culture from which you are adopting; so if a particular culture doesn't call to you, then it will be harder for you to integrate it.

The language this facilitator used to describe her own and other parents' decision-making processes legitimizes American adoption as an act of choosy cultural consumption that is often based on racialized selection criteria. The point is that parents and facilitators who legitimize this aspect of the practice, in the name of "cultural sensitivity," virtually condone the logics of American entitlement, without attending to the ways in which the practice essentializes children as cultural commodities.

When I asked another facilitator, Paula, if she ever tried to gauge white adoptive parents' level of comfort or interaction with African-American communities or other American minorities, she dismissed the question as irrelevant. She told me that comparing white parents' level of comfort with African Americans and their willingness to incorporate their Korean child's birth culture was like "comparing apples and oranges." She stated that, since her agency does not place any children of African heritage, it is not important to assess this. She reiterated the assumption she mentioned earlier in the interview about adoptive parents' "unconditional acceptance of all races." She continued:

> You got to look at a couple that is going to cross-race into their home. [That couple] is going to be a pretty open couple in general. So I wouldn't say that those couples would be prejudiced. Whether they would have a preference, and they *should,* for a particular race to be in their home over another race, yes.

Considering the fact that several of the Korean adoptees in my study described the ways in which their adoptive parents modeled, rather than opposed, racist language and racialized thinking about American minority groups, Paula's assumption about adoptive parents' universal tolerance seems dubious.

However, my point is not to argue that adoptive parents as a group are any more racist in their thinking than the vast majority of Americans who have not successfully "undone" the media images and popular discourses that associate such things as crime, intelligence, work ethics, and poverty with particular racialized groups (Baker, 2001; Frankenberg, 1999; Wu, 2002); nor is it to suggest that white parents' comfort with, or willingness to, adopt an African-American child ought to be a litmus test for appropriate race consciousness. I call attention to facilitators' combined practice of assuming racial tolerance while encouraging racial/cultural selection because of its contradictory nature. It is a contradiction that risks leaving in place white parents' subconscious or conscious expectations about the ease of "whitening" Asian children. It also preserves the racialized status quo by avoiding issues of racial hierarchies in adoption in the interest of accommodating the desires of those who already hold the most power in the arrangement.

As is apparent from adopters' and adoptees' reflections on their adoption experiences, facilitators historically and to the present have done little to urge white adopters to develop well-thought-out plans for addressing matters of race within their families. Though facilitators claim that they discuss with prospective adopters their reasons for wanting to adopt internationally, most facilitators I interviewed seemed uncomfortable and reluctant to probe for adoptive parents' actual preparedness in the realms of race and culture, preferring to assume that adoptive parents had made an informed and appropriately race-conscious choice in selecting a particular birth country.

Paula, the facilitator who emphasized that adoptive parents "should" have a preference "for a particular race to be in their home," defended her position by stating: "choice makes commitment." Paula explained that, because international adoption involves making lifestyle choices to incorporate a new culture, parents have every right to choose that culture. Paula went on to equate choice in adoption to the kind of choice one expects when buying a home or selecting a school.

To further emphasize her point that "choice makes commitment," she spoke of her own decision to adopt two children from Korea, based in part on her interest and ability to incorporate Korean culture into her lifestyle. She said, "For example, I cook Korean food twice a month. I happen to like Indian food too, but I wouldn't particularly be open to cooking Indian food twice a month." Paula and other facilitators frequently made statements that equated adoptive parents' ability and willingness to display cultural inclusiveness through food choices, art, spirituality, and the like as a sufficient indication of parents' acceptance of diversity in their lifestyle. The problem is that, when facilitators merely encourage adoptive parents to bring an easy color-blindness or cultural openness to the adoption process, they fail to alert adoptive parents to the real traumas of racial isolation and misunderstanding that virtually all transracial/transnational adoptees confront at some point in their lives.

CONCLUSION:
SHIFTING THE PRACTICE PARADIGM TOWARD
A PROBLEM-ORIENTED VIEW OF ADOPTION CULTURE

In their review of empirical studies on transracial and international adoption, Simon and Altstein (2000) report that, while most studies suggest that adoptees' best interests were generally served by their adoptions, they also indicate that "not all of the parents recognized how much they needed to alter their lifestyles until several years after the adoption and sometimes not until the adoptees were adolescents" (p. 142). In the case of KAA, addressing this delayed response in parents would certainly involve confronting misguided assumptions about the ease of achieving actual multicultural lifestyles. Furthermore, many of the deficits in international adoption discourse could be effectively addressed by consistently incorporating the wide-ranging perspective of adult Korea adoptees in the adoption process—an initiative that agencies seem to be only slowly prioritizing.[6]

Especially for those adoptive parents who have endured long battles with infertility or other social dilemmas around childlessness, the finalized adoption of a child clearly represents a "happy ending." However, for the "transplanted child," an adoption placement often means the beginning of a lifelong journey of unsettling quandaries about identity and family. It is this stormy chaos, often endured by adoptees, that many American adoption facilitators have trouble adequately conveying to prospective parents.[7]

As I have tried to make clear, the turn toward culture in the current boom of international adoption in various ways deflects attention away from not only the real work involved in adoptive parenting but also from the globalized social crises in need of localized solutions. Public interest stories that feature American families exploring the "cultural roots" of their "kimchi kids" often portray the growing trend in international adoption as an emblem of America's unfaltering acceptance of multiculturalism and racial tolerance. When international adoption is represented in this way, adult adopted Koreans' struggles with identity construction and feelings of racialized isolation are depicted as vestiges of the unenlightened cultureless past, while the new adoptive parents' "cultured" enthusiasm is presented as a marker for how far adoption practice has come in its attention to racial/ethnic inclusion (Lin, 1999; Zhao, 2002).

Clearly, the history of international Korean adoption provides fertile ground for broadening our understanding of how the individual choices of birth and adoptive parents are embedded in, and help to maintain, the privileges, gendered relationships, and racial hierarchies of states and institutions (Riley, 1997). Thus international adoption discourse should be used as a way to shatter one-dimensional views of culture rather than perpetuate them.

Yet only when American adoption facilitators genuinely prioritize eliminating the need for international adoption entirely will they actually reposition the more marginalized, as opposed to the most powerful, at the center of their model of family-building. Therefore, before we can celebrate white Americans' selective ease with adopting thousands of children from various points on the globe as simply another sign of our benevolent interconnectedness, it behooves all members of the adoption triad, facilitators, and others of us concerned about this social practice to hold one another accountable not only to adoption policies and procedures but also to our representations of culture. In so doing, we will move closer to a more politicized and less "exoticized" version of cultural awareness—one that focuses on the fluidity of cultures and leads us to carefully question which elements of adoption culture in both the sending and receiving nations need to be preserved, eliminated, or radically transformed.

NOTES

1. Any names used in this chapter are pseudonyms.

2. The term "Caucasian" is widely used in the field of adoption to describe people of European heritage, but harkens back to the late eighteenth-century racial classifications and hierarchies of Johann Friedrich Blumenbach and his teacher Carolus Linnaeus. Blumenbach, who believed the light-skinned people of the Caucasus Mountains were "the most beautiful race of men," invented the term Caucasian to designate Europeans as the superior ideal against which all other human variation would be measured. Blumenbach's socially constructed, nonscientific racial rankings have persisted in various ways ever since the invention of this term (see Gould, 1994, for further discussion of Blumenbach's "unintended" racism). I choose to grant no further legitimacy to the term and use the other socially constructed terms "white" or European American to refer to people who are identified by their European heritage. I also use the term white, in an effort to contribute to social and historical studies, which have emerged over the past two decades to problematize both the racial domination and heterogeneity embodied in the concepts of "whiteness." See Frankenberg (1999) for a brief overview of this literature. Also see Ong (1996) and Goode (1998) for a specific look at how the process of "whitening" occurs in particular Asian immigrant communities.

3. In March 2004, male Korean biologist Choe Jae-Chun made headlines when he was awarded a prize from the Korean Women's Association United for his stance in favor of abolishing *hojuje*. The women's organization applauded Choe's forthright criticism of the patriarchal family registry tradition that maintains gender inequality (*Korea Herald,* 2004). For an in-depth look at the role of lineage, published genealogical tables, and inheritance laws see Mark Peterson (1996).

4. Also absent from the discussion are the SOS Villages that exist in South Korea as a way to keep children in their birth country while providing a home consisting of a house-mother and siblings similar to a foster care environment, but without the pursuit of adoption as the ultimate goal. For information on SOS Villages in the ROK, see www.koreasos.or.kr/sos_eng.htm, and http://www.geocities.com/sunny_jo888/sos.html

5. In her research with international adopters and their selection processes, Christine Gailey (2000, p. 44) found that "race was a submerged motive" which intersects with parents' wishes to have as much control as possible over the child's earliest environmental settings, the child's physical and mental health, and to have "unambiguous rights to [the custody of] the child" (Gailey 2000, p. 50).

6. Even agencies that have hired adult Korean adoptees for various full-time positions within their organizations do not necessarily ensure that prospective adoptive parents are exposed to both positive and critical adult adoptee perspectives. In

other words, *how and when* adult adoptees are inserted into the process is more important than how many adoptees adoption agencies hire.

7. The recently published memoirs of Katy Robinson (2002) and Jane Jeong Trenka (2003), and the documentary film *First Person Plural* by Deanne Liem Borshay (2000) are among the many works from Korean-American adoptees that offer deeply personalized perspectives on the various dilemmas that accompany the adoption experience. Also see http://www.transracialabductees.org for critical essays by adoptees on the subject of international adoption.

REFERENCES

Baker, L. (2001). The color-blind bind. In I. Susser & T. C. Patterson (Eds.), *Cultural diversity in the United States* (pp. 103-119). Malden, MA: Blackwell.

"Biologist challenges family registry system" (2004, March 8). *The Korea Herald.* Retrieved March 8, 2004, from http://www.koreaherald.com.

Borshay Liem, D. (Producer & Director). (2000). *First person plural.* [Video]. (Available from NAATA, 145 Ninth Street, Suite 350, San Francisco, CA 94103).

Cho, H. (2002). Living with conflicting subjectivities: Mother, motherly wife, and sexy woman in the transition from colonial modern to postmodern Korea. In L. Kendall (Ed.), *Under construction: The gendering of modernity, class and consumption in the Republic of Korea* (pp. 165-195). Honolulu: University of Hawai'i Press.

di Leonardo, M. (1992). Rape, race, and the myth of the underclass. *The Village Voice, 37*(33), 437-443.

Elliott, Louise. (2002). Battling pride and prejudice: Overseas adopted Koreans fight. *The Korea Herald,* August 30: Electronic Document.

Frankenberg, R. (1999). Introduction: Local whitenesses, localizing whiteness. In R. Frankenberg (Ed.), *Displacing whiteness: Essays in social and cultural criticism* (pp. 1-33). Durham, NC: Duke University Press.

Gailey, C. (2000). Ideologies of motherhood and kinship in U.S. adoption. In H. Ragone & F. Winddance Twine (Eds.), *Ideologies and technologies of motherhood: Race, class, sexuality, nationalism* (pp. 11-55). New York: Routledge.

Goode, J. (1998). The contingent construction of local identities: Koreans and Puerto Ricans in Philadelphia. *Identities 5*(1), 33-64.

Goode, J. (2001). Teaching against culturalist essentialism in anthropology. In I. Susser & T. C. Patterson (Eds.), *Cultural diversity in the United States: A critical reader* (pp. 434-456). Oxford, England: Blackwell Publishers.

Goode, J., & Maskovsky, J. (2001). Introduction. In J. Goode & J. Maskovsky (Eds.), *The new poverty studies: The ethnography of power, politics and impoverished people in the United States* (pp. 1-34). New York: New York University Press.

Gould, S. (1994, November). The geometer of race. *Discover Magazine,* 65-69.

Kendall, L. (2002). Introduction. In L. Kendall (Ed.), *Under construction: The gendering of modernity, class and consumption in the Republic of Korea* (pp. 1-24). Honolulu: University of Hawai'i Press.

Kim, E. (2000). Korean adoptee auto-ethnography: Refashioning self, family, and finding community. *Visual Anthropology Review, 16*(1), 43-70.

Lee, S. (2002). The concept of female sexuality in Korean popular culture. In L. Kendall (Ed.), *Under construction: The gendering of modernity, class and consumption in the Republic of Korea* (pp. 141-164). Honolulu: University of Hawai'i Press.

Lin, J. (1999, November 9). Keeping old homeland alive on a new shore. *Philadelphia Inquirer,* pp. A1, A10.

Moon, S. (2002). The production and subversion of hegemonic masculinity: Reconfiguring gender hierarchy in contemporary South Korea. In L. Kendall (Ed.), *Under construction: The gendering of modernity, class and consumption in the Republic of Korea* (pp. 79-113). Honolulu: University of Hawai'i Press.

Ong, A. (1996). Cultural citizenship as subject-making: Immigrants negotiate racial and cultural boundaries in the United States. *Current Anthropology, 37*(5), 737-762.

Park, P. (1999, Autumn). Deconstructing race: Intercountry adoptees and the discourse of authenticity. *Transcultured Magazine, 2*(1), 10-11.

Peterson, M. (1996). *Korean adoption and inheritance: Case studies in the creation of a classic Confucian society.* Ithaca, NY: Cornell University East Asia Program.

Riley, N. (1997). American adoptions of Chinese girls: The socio-political matrices of individual decisions. *Women's Studies International Forum, 20*(1), 87-102.

Roberts, Dorothy E. (2002). *Shattered bonds: The color of child welfare.* New York: Basic Civitas Books.

Robinson, K. (2002). *A single square picture: A Korean adoptee's search for roots.* New York: Penguin Group.

Seo, H. (2001, June 8). Adoptive parents strive to change adoption culture. *The Korea Herald.* Retrieved June 8, 2001, from http://www.koreaherald.com.

Simon, R., & Altstein, H. (2000). *Adoption across borders: Serving the children in transracial and intercountry adoption.* Lanham, MD: Rowman and Littlefield Publishers, Inc.

Trenka, J. J. (2003). *The language of blood: A memoir.* St. Paul, MN: Borealis Books.

Williams, R. (1976). *Keywords: A vocabulary of culture and society.* New York: Oxford University Press.

Wu, F. (2002). *Yellow: Race in America beyond black and white.* New York: Basic Books.

Yuh, J. (2002). *Beyond the shadow of Camptown: Korean military brides in America.* New York: New York University Press.

Zhao, Y. (2002, April 9). Living in two worlds, old and new: Foreign-born adoptees explore their cultural roots. *New York Times,* pp. B1-B2.

Chapter 5

Korean Adopted Children's Ethnic Identity Formation

Nam Soon Huh

Since 1953, over 100,000 Korean children have been adopted by American families (U.S. State Department, 2002). Korean children were the largest number of foreign-born children who were placed in American families until 1995. Even though the number of adoptions of Korean children has significantly decreased compared with the 1980s, 1,770 Korean children were still placed in American homes in 2001 (U.S. State Department, 2002). International adoptions, particularly from Asian countries such as Korea and China, have raised concerns in the field of child welfare. A strong argument against international adoptions concerns the development of a child's ethnic identity. If children are uprooted from their cultures, their sense of ethnic identity may become confused or conflicted (Friedlander, 1999). Ethnic identity develops as a result of cultural socialization within and across multiple contexts. Therefore, many adoption agencies often provide various cultural activity programs and encourage the adoptive families to participate in those programs. Some adoptive parents considerately accept the differences of their child's own ethnicity and tend to those activities actively, while others emphasize universal human identity and do not think it is necessary to teach Korean culture to their children.

Given the relative importance that agencies and adoption support groups place on this area, little is known about whether parents need to teach their children of their ethnic background and how the children would respond. Previous research and current agency practices relating to international adoptions raised several questions that prompted the present study: What sorts of ethnic identities are developed by children who have experienced

International Korean Adoption
© 2007 by The Haworth Press, Inc. All rights reserved.
doi:10.1300/5734_05

such adoptions? What factors appear to be associated with the development of those identities? More specifically, does family involvement in culturally related activities appear to be a factor? Is the development of ethnic identity related to other aspects of the child's adjustment? Do the children go through distinct stages in the development of ethnic identity? What factors are related to variations in this development?

This study will compare how adoptive parents' attitudes toward Korean culture (and other people's attitudes toward Korean children) influence the adopted child's development of ethnic identity. The main purpose of this study is to investigate the impact of cultural influences on the formation of ethnic identity for adopted Korean children.

ETHNIC IDENTITY

Ethnic identity is the integration of ethnicity and race into one's self-image. Definitions of ethnic identity vary according to the researchers' intent on resolving its conceptual meanings. Phinney (1990, 2000, 2003) defines ethnic identity as a sense of belonging to an ethnic group and the part of one's thinking, perceptions, feelings, and behavior that is due to ethnic group membership. Lee (2003) defines ethnic identity as an aggregate of ethnic pride, ethnic belonging, identity achievement, and culture-specific behaviors. Ethnic identity is influenced by racial, natal, symbolic, and cultural factors (Cheung, 1993). Racial factors involve the use of physiognomic and physical characteristics; natal factors refer to homeland or origins of individuals. The terms *race* and *ethnicity* have been used interchangeably in reference to both the physical and cultural characteristics of an individual as a member of his or her ethnic or racial group in much of the literature (Bernal, Knight, Garza, Ocampo, & Cota, 1990; Sollars, 1996).

ETHNIC IDENTITY DEVELOPMENT AND ADOPTION

Ethnic identity development is a very complex process that involves interaction of context (e.g., home, school, neighborhood, society, etc.) and development. Ethnic identity of internationally adopted children is a feeling of connection with both one's race or cultural past and one's present adoptive heritage. Issues relating to the ethnic identities of adopted children have been explored in a number of studies. For example, Baden and Steward (2000) developed the Cultural-Racial Identity Model. The Cultural-Racial Identity Model consists of four dimensions: adoptee culture dimension, parental culture dimension, adoptee race dimension, and parental race dimension. The adoptee culture dimension is the degree to which transracial adoptees identify with their own racial group's culture or birth culture, while on the other hand, the parental culture dimension signifies the degree to which transracial adoptees identify with their adoptive parents' racial group's culture. The adoptee race dimension is the transracial adoptee's level of comfort with his or her own racial group membership and with those belonging to his or her own group. Parental race dimension is the transracial adoptee's level of comfort with his or her racial group membership and those belonging to his or her adoptive parents' racial group. Baden and Steward (2000) stated parental attitudes and beliefs that either affirm or discount the transracial adoptees' culture and racial group membership would influence the development of various cultural-racial identities. Feigelman and Silverman (1983) also observed that, the stronger the parents' positive orientation toward the race of their adoptee, the greater the likelihood of a positive attitude on the part of the child toward his or her heritage. It has been argued that, if the parents recognize that the life of an international adoptive family involves the notion of defining themselves as an American-Korean (or American-Chinese) family, the children tend to acquire similar perceptions about themselves (Cole, 1992; Gross & Gross, 1988; Huh, 1985). Cole's study found that other important variables such as ethnic discussions within the home, parents having friends or work colleagues who are Asian, and the community in which the child lives could assist in fostering a positive ethnic identity in transracially adopted children. Feigelman and Silverman (1983) observed that adoptees who showed strong pride in their own background adjusted more easily than those who were less enthusiastic about their cultures of origin.

The findings thus far reported provide grounds for optimism about the development of ethnic identities of international adoptees. At the same time, however, not all findings are so sanguine. Some adoptive parents appear confused about how strong an emphasis should be placed on racial and ethnic heritage (Cole, 1992; Raynor, 1980). They seem concerned about becoming alienated from their adopted children. These parents were much more likely to reject the concept of "differentness" as it applied to their children and to minimize the differences between themselves and their adopted children. Many adoptive parents prefer a "color-blind" approach in which differences in their own and their children's race are deemphasized (Gill & Jackson, 1983; Howe, 1992; Kim, 1978; McRoy, Zurcher, Lauderdale, & Anderson, 1982).

Moreover, some studies have found that most adoptees have little ethnic identity and have little interest in exploring their own cultural heritage

(Bishoff & Rankin, 1997; Kim, 1976; Koh, 1993; Lydens, 1988). They have been found to identify themselves more with their adoptive parents' ethnic group than with their own (Gonzalez, 1990). In one study, the majority of children were described by their parents as being apathetic, embarrassed, or confused about their racial background and heritage (Chartrand, 1978). Actually, ethnic identity is achieved through an active process of decision making and self-evaluation (Baden, 2002; Phinney, 1990). Benson, Sharma, and Rohelkepartain (1994) reported that Asian adolescents sometimes felt ashamed or embarrassed about their racial background. Adoptees have also said that their identities are more challenged by their race than adoption.

These mixed findings highlight the tensions faced by internationally adopted children in reconciling their cultures of origin with their picked-up cultural realities. Benson et al. (1994) have stated the dilemma well:

> When the differences of the child and parents become a central issue in family life, it can thwart satisfactory adjustment because it is a constant reminder of adoption. Alternately, if the inevitable differences in appearance and temperament are not acknowledged and affirmed, a part of the individual feels rejected. The feelings of rejection interfere with the development of a positive identity. (p. 58)

While being judged by their ethnic label, internationally adopted children do not have many opportunities to develop positive identification with their culture of origin because they often have little or no exposure to their native country.

The developmental course of the ethnic identity of adopted children has been the subject of various studies, too. Some professionals have intuitively pointed out that internationally adopted children placed in racially different homes are deprived of developing a major aspect of identity—that of belonging to a specific racial or cultural group (Simon & Altstein, 1992; Wilkinson, 1985).

According to some investigations, ethnic identity begins to form at about the age of six years and simply increases with cognitive development (Bernal et al., 1990; Cole, 1992). Katz (1976) claims that a rudimentary concept of an ethnic group develops about the age of three years and includes the three components of attitude, perception, and cognition. Later steps involve the integration of these components and their elaboration.

Wilkinson (1985) described the forming of an ethnic identity as a life-long process moving from denial to an inner awakening (noticing others from the same culture of origin), verbal acknowledgment, identification, acceptance, and finally to the integration of ethnicity into identity. Unanswered by this body of research are questions about variations in such courses of development and factors that may be related to such variations. Some of the studies referred to earlier suggest that a sense of ethnic identity may not develop at all.

Having awareness of the various issues elaborated here, adoption agencies and professionals have taken steps to facilitate the development of ethnic identity in international adoptions. For instance, they usually advise the adoptive families of the need for sensitivity to the child's culture of origin. In addition, many adoption agencies provide cultural activity programs and encourage the adoptive families to participate in those activities. Some adoptive families eagerly attend these activities and hope to help their children to learn about their cultures of origin. Other adoptive families appear to be less interested in teaching their children about their cultural roots. Lee (2003) emphasized that the cultural socialization process is quite different in adoptive families because the adoptee's culture and ethnicity usually are introduced extrinsically.

METHOD

This study explored the formation of ethnic identity among forty Korean adopted children and their families. The researcher recruited participants through a child welfare agency in northeastern New York. The adoption program director of the agency wrote a letter explaining the purpose of research and the procedure, and introduced the researcher to the parents and children. The researcher also wrote a letter explaining the research and the brief questions that the researcher intended to ask children. The agency sent out a mailing to the 115 families whose children met the following criteria: (1) adopted as infants (under fifteen months); (2) at least nine years of age at the time of the study; (3) fully Korean. Further, the families resided within ninety minutes' driving distance from the adoption agency. Finally, if a family consisted of more than one adopted Korean child, then all Korean adoptees who were nine years or older were selected as subjects.

Thirty adoptive families and forty children responded and agreed to participate. Researchers conducted interviews with thirty adoptive families including their forty Korean children in their homes. Semistructured, in-depth interviewing with children and their parents separately was the primary method of data collection.

The children ranged in age from nine to fourteen years, with a median age of eleven years. The parents were all Caucasians. The majority were in their forties, well educated with college degrees or higher, and employed in professional or technical occupations.

To increase the reliability of the subject's memory and to reduce bias, adoptees and their parents were asked to describe specific events. The request for descriptions of specific events was followed with probes and cross-checked between children and parents. All interviews that were tape-recorded and later transcribed were done at the individual families' homes by the author, who is Korean. Interviews with each subject lasted from one to two hours.

The study made use of a combination of quantitative and qualitative methods. More specifically, the quantitative component consisted of constructing and applying scales to measure (1) the extent of family involvement in Korean cultural activities; (2) the extent of the child's identification with Korean culture; (3) ease of communication between parents and children concerning the adoption. The scales for content analysis were applied to all of the interviews by the author and by a second coder to nine of these interviews. Percentages of agreement between the author and coder exceeded 80 percent across all scales. On the other hand, qualitative aspects of the study were guided by grounded theory (Strauss, 1987; Strauss & Corbin, 1990), which was used primarily to understand the development of Korean identity formation as it relates to parents' attitudes toward Korean culture.

RESULTS

Factors Associated with the Extent of Ethnic Identity

Our statistical analysis (multiple regression) suggested that two factors were significantly associated ($R^2 = .52$, $p < .05$) with the extent of ethnic identity in the children: the children's participation in Korean cultural activities and ease of communication between the children and their parents concerning the adoption. The children's participation in cultural activities was by far the strongest factor. To express this finding another way, children who were judged to be high participators in Korean cultural activities ($n = 23$) had a mean identity score of $+9.2$ (on a scale ranging from -10 to $+10$); the mean for the relatively low participators ($n = 17$) was 2.6. There was statistically significant difference between the high and low participators in their identity score ($p < .001$). As findings in the next section will make clear, participation in Korean cultural activities, such as attending Korean "culture camps," was instigated by the parents whose Korean cultural participation score was highly related to that of their children's ($r = .92$, $p < .001$ correlation).

It is not surprising that parents and children who have been more intensely involved in Korean cultural activities would find it easier to communicate about the child's Korean origins—the adoption process—than those less intensely involved ($p < .012$). Somewhat unexpected, however, were findings concerning the relation between the extent of ethnic identity and the children's ethnic self-designations. Children were asked to describe how they thought of themselves in ethnic terms. Response options were American, Korean, Korean-American, "just a person," or "haven't thought about it." Of those with high Korean ethnic identity scores, 80 percent identified themselves as Korean-American, in contrast to only 20 percent with low identity scores. For the latter group, the most popular response was, interestingly enough, "Korean" (53 percent), and the next highest a response in the combined category of "American," "just a person," or "haven't thought about it" (27 percent). The results were similar when high participators in Korean cultural activities were compared with low participators. It is not immediately apparent why children scoring high on Korean identity and cultural participation should see themselves as Korean-American while their low-scoring counterparts tended to see themselves as just Korean. A possible answer is that the high scorers on these variables had been able to achieve a better integration between their Korean and American identities than the low scorers, yet the answer does not explain the process by which such integration might be achieved. However, a sense of identity that incorporates one's cultural origins as well as ease in communicating about these origins might be seen as valued attributes in themselves.

The Development of Ethnic Identity

Data from both parents and adoptees were used to trace the processes of the adoptees' identity formation. Respondents were asked to recall events concerning developmental processes that occurred prior to the child's current age. The picture that emerged should help clarify the quantitative findings presented in the preceding text.

Recognizing and Rejecting Differences
(Age: Four to Six Years)

Recognition of differences began when children entered a new situation such as kindergarten. They were still not able to grasp the idea of ethnicity. They knew that they came from Korea, but they did not understand what that meant. Lambert and Klineberg (1967) found that children in this age group did not understand the concentric relationships among town, region, country, and the world. National differentiations are often too abstract for young children to comprehend. One child said, "In nursery school, I knew I kind of looked different, but when I was in first grade, I knew I came from Korea."

In general, girls recognized the differences earlier than boys, though there were individual variations. One parent said, "My son did not have a clue he looked different for the first seven years of his life, while my daughter noticed the differences even before she went to kindergarten."

When adoptees recognized differences, they sometimes wished to change their appearance. One girl said, "When I was five or six, it really hit me that I was different, and I wanted to look like my mom." In the initial stage of recognizing differences, children's ethnic identification is still undeveloped. Some children were still confused about their ethnicity. One parent said, "One time my son asked whether he was considered black. It was summertime, and he tans very well." Similarly, Cole (1992) concluded from her study that Korean children of this age assumed that, if they were not white, they were black.

Parents played an important role in exposing their children to their ethnic culture at this stage of recognizing differences. During this age period, most parents tried to introduce their children to Korean culture or gave them a chance to meet Korean children. However, when the children started kindergarten, some parents continued to take active roles in exposing children to different cultural activities, while other families became more neutral. One child said, "That's when they started bringing me to Camp Mu Ji Gae and got me into some Korean stuff like that . . . It was all Korean kids, and I could learn more about my heritage."

However, one parent said, "We were a part of a Korean-American club. However, we stopped that because we felt that we were alienating them. She wanted to be just the same as every other kid in her school." Like this parent, some parents explained that their child's lack of exposure to Korean culture was not due to the parent's unwillingness but rather to the child's reluctance to participate.

The Beginning of Ethnic Identification
(Age: Seven to Eight Years)

Beginning about the age of seven, the children began to learn that their ethnicity and facial structure would remain constant across time even as they grew into adulthood. They began to understand that Korea is another country and that was the reason why they looked different from their parents. Children were able to identify themselves as Korean. Bernal et al. (1990) state that ethnic identification develops at a later developmental period than either gender or racial identification.

Even though children were aware of the ethnic differences and knew that they were from Korea, some of them still perceived themselves as American or become very self-conscious about being Korean. Ethnic identification involves one's relationship with others—parents, friends and neighbors, etc. Therefore, the children had a hard time identifying themselves as Korean since they did not know anything about Korea. However, questions about their ethnicity and teasing from other children frequently made the children aware they were different. Most children said that they experienced a great deal of teasing at this stage. While teasing was hard for all the children, the way they coped with it varied. Some children had negative feelings about themselves while other children felt angry toward the teaser. One child said, "When I was little, I really wished that I was American because I would get funny looks from other people. When I am with all my friends, I would like to fit right in." Another child said, "Sometimes people would call me Chinese. I didn't like that because I was Korean."

These kinds of external factors pushed the children to develop certain attitudes toward their Korean identity. At this point the role of the parents seemed to be especially important. Since Korean adoptees did not have an immediate reference group, adoptive parents took a primary role in helping their children develop a positive attitude toward their ethnicity. Moreover, the parents' actions often helped bring about reinforcing responses from peers and teachers. One parent said:

> My son was confused and asked me why they were calling him Chinese. So we took him to see a film on China. He was fascinated. He was pleased to see all the beautiful countryside and the Chinese people. Then he could understand why people might think he looked like a Chinese person. Then we took him to the Korean cultural camp and he really enjoyed it. Then after that he naturally had a lot of pride in it because we talked it up. It just gave him some connection. He impressed his schoolteachers with the fact that he knew something about this country on the other side of the world and could find it on the atlas and go over to it on the globe and pinpoint it when he was in second grade.

One child said, "My mom brought Korean food to school and explained about Korea in the class. My friends liked that because they learned new things. I was very proud of that." Such interactions, involving parents, peers, and teachers, helped the adoptees develop a positive sense about being Korean. In some cases, however, such interactions did not occur. For example, some teachers did not want to devote class time to having parents or children talk about Korea.

Also, some children tended to react against what they saw as a parental overemphasis on Korean things. They began to feel alienated from American culture. As one child said, "I just wanted to talk about it a little bit less. I know I am Korean. And my parents tried to remind me a little bit too much that I am Korean. I gave them clues to ease back."

Some parents did not feel strongly that they needed to teach Korean culture to their children. One parent said, "We will support her if she wants to learn about Korean culture, but we will not push her. I don't see her as Korean. I think other people in the community see her as American." Following their parents' lead, these children began to see themselves as American or just human beings. They did not see being Korean as significant to their sense of self.

According to the interview, children hold more pro-Korean attitudes if their parents are active and believe in promoting the Korean culture. This finding is congruent with many researches (Baden & Steward, 2000; Friedlander, 1999; de Haymes & Simon, 2002; Lee, 2003).

Acceptance of Difference versus Ethnic Dissonance
(Age: Nine to Eleven Years)

With the development of the knowledge of different ethnic groups in society, children developed certain attitudes toward their own Korean ethnicity. Some children accepted their differences and had good feelings about themselves. They liked the way they looked and it became a source of pride. They indicated their uniqueness as strength: "I am proud because I am special." They developed a positive attitude toward Korean culture and wanted to learn more about Korea. Parents sent their children to Korean cultural camp, read Korean storybooks at bedtime, or attended Korean events in the community as a family. These were the children who tended to identify their ethnicity as Korean-American. These children tended to immerse themselves in Korean culture—to learn Korean, to attend Korean cultural camp, and to go to Tae Kwon Do centers. The adopted children expressed how much they enjoy attending different Korean activities and being in the majority at Korean camps.

However, children who did not have much experience with Korean culture began to identify themselves as American or Korean, or did not know how to indicate their ethnicity. These children's ethnic identities tended to be dominated by an American concept of ethnicity. They believed that other people saw them as part of the human race or just a person. They downplayed their differences from other children. As one child commented, "I am really American. I just look like a Korean." When the researcher asked how she would answer the question "What is your nationality?" she said "I would say Korean. It is easy to answer. If I say American, they would ask more questions." They seem to stay at the stage of ethnic identification even though their biological age advances and cognitive ability develops.

In some cases, lack of interest in Korean culture seemed to be the outgrowth of an interaction between the parents and child. For example, some parents responded to their child's perceived disinterest in learning about Korean culture by becoming inactive themselves. As one parent put it,

> We've never had a strong Korean identity. There's really nothing here in our household that we do that's truly Korean. Last year Kim (eleven years old) went to Mu Ji Gae with Sandy. She didn't want to go back. It didn't really mean a whole lot to her. I don't even know if people see her as Korean anymore. Basically she's just like an American kid.

Apropos here are the observations of Johnson, Shireman, and Watson (1987) that "when a parent no longer thinks of the child as different, the child's sense of racial identity stops growing" (p. 54).

The self-esteem or self-confidence of the children in this latter group, however, seemed no different from those who identified with their ethnic culture. Cross (1971) explains this by stating that personal identity and group identity are different,

> the price of assimilation for a member of a given group is not necessarily "poor mental health" but rather the development of a world view that can frequently inhibit one's knowledge about, and one's capacity to advocate for, political and cultural interests that flow from the frame of reference of the nonassimilated members of that group. (p. 13)

In this stage, children still experience teasing, but it is less and they develop better coping skills. In general, at this stage boys experience teasing more than girls. However, it still makes the children conscious of their ethnicity. By this time, most of them have developed ways of handling the teasing and do not tell their parents of the incidents. One boy's comments were typical:

The teasing? Much better, actually. The kids try to get my attention and I just ignore them. I can tell they are getting frustrated. Now they are doing it less and less often. I just take a deep breath, don't show them . . . I try and force myself to smile and turn around and say, "Huh?" or "What did you say?"

They get really frustrated. You just have to look like you are enjoying it, then it will stop. It's hard to keep smiling. You don't go, "Shut up, jerk!", or something like that. Then aha! A reaction.

Integrating Korean Heritage and American Culture
(Age: Twelve to Fourteen Years)

At the age of twelve or thirteen, children's cognitive development entered a new phase. They were now capable of more abstract thinking. Most children who had been involved in Korean culture clearly identified themselves as Korean-American. They were able to explain how they integrated their Korean ethnic heritage and American culture. To the question of nationality, one said, "I would say probably Korean and American, because I was born in Korea, but I am also part American because I am living in America. I am used to the American ways and customs."

Children can also better articulate their reasons for ethnic pride or their need to learn more about Korean culture. Their desire to learn about Korea now stems more from inner needs and interests than from their parents' encouragement. As one child observed,

I think it is important to know what your background is and to know about where you came from. It makes you a little bit different from other people, instead of the only difference being that you have dark hair. I think it is important to learn about your country, its history, and what it is doing now. It is something you like to talk about with your friends.

School and friends take a bigger role in making children interested or proud of Korean ethnicity than parents do at this stage. Around the time that children enter the sixth grade, they learn about different countries at school. They have a chance to select countries they would like to present. Most children who were involved with Korean culture selected Korea for their presentation. It encouraged them to study more about Korea and helped them develop ethnic pride. In the words of one child, "I get to tell people about South Korea. I am just real proud because I know a lot of stuff, and I am teaching everybody else about it."

Children also learned what kinds of stereotypes are attached to Korean people. One girl remarked, "Koreans have a reputation for being hard workers. So if I don't turn in something in school, they say, 'You are Korean, so how come?'" Another child said, "my teacher expects me to do well in math and music because I am Korean but I am not good at math at all, although I am good at music. I do violin." Adoptees said that being Korean is good sometimes, but sometimes it is a burden because they do not fit the stereotypes. Other children's responses to Korean adoptees were also important with regard to their self-esteem. One girl said, "I get more compliments than I do put-downs. Everybody likes my hair, the color, everybody . . . they try to die it black and stuff . . . Children used to tease me. Now they don't." Their identification as Koreans and their pride in their own ethnicity are becoming based on more concrete knowledge about Korea rather than just about their differences or uniqueness. They wanted more specific knowledge, such as ancient Korean history, and the daily life of the children of their age. They also looked for Korean role models and Korean friends. According to one girl, "It is nice to have a Korean friend . . . It does not bother me, being different. I like being different, but I cannot really talk about Korea to anybody else because they don't really get it, but I think Brenda [who is a Korean adoptee too] does."

Children's interest in learning about Korean culture seemed to change from time to time. One parent said that her daughter was not interested in learning about Korea. "Last year I bought her that book on Korea. She looked through it once and she said, 'I am not really interested in this right now.' She is completely American. She thinks like an American and talks like an American." However, when the researcher interviewed the girl she said, "I am sort of interested right now in learning about Korea. We did some heritage projects in school and we had to do a family tree and I did one of my American families. It also made me wonder about learning about Korea."

At this stage, even some children who were not interested or not involved in Korean culture began to show a little interest because of school curriculum. One boy who identified himself as American said, "I feel more American, but sometimes I do get interested in finding out about Korea." When the researcher asked when this boy became interested in finding out about Korea, he said:

We had Korean Day at school. We got to learn some stuff, how to write in Korean and taste some Korean food, which was pretty good. I felt pretty special . . . At that time, I was interested in learning about Korea. The children in my school also said that they were interested and I was very proud of that. I wanted to tell them it is mine.

Another boy, who perceived himself as American, said, "For school once we had to find out where our relatives were from long ago. Instead of going to my American parents, I showed the class my Korean picture and my Korean flags and stuff. That kind of got me interested in learning more." With these children, however, their interest was inconsistent unless there was continuous stimulation about learning Korean culture. Such sporadic spurts of interest may offer parents opportunities to encourage further development of ethnic identity.

Most of the children said it should be up to the child about how much they want to learn about Korea. One child gave this piece of advice:

> Don't push them to learn, but ask the children if they want to learn about their Korean heritage. Don't make them learn about it if they don't want to. Try to help them understand that they are not really different than other people.

DISCUSSION

As anticipated, it was found that children who were high participators in Korean cultural activities scored higher on Korean identity than their low-participating counterparts. These findings can perhaps be best explained in interactional terms: Parents and their children who were favorably inclined to incorporate Korean culture into their lives actively participated in the cultural activities, which likely reinforced their Korean interests. High participators may also have achieved an identity more integrated with American culture than low participators, given their greater tendency to see themselves as Korean American. While high participators were not necessarily better adjusted, their better "integrated" identities and their greater ease in discussing their adoptions with their parents may be considered as desirable. This result is different from results of other researchers. Many researchers (Cole, 1992; Johnson et al., 1987; Kim, 1976, 1978; Lee, 2003; McRoy et al., 1982) found in their studies of transracial adoption that children whose parents emphasized children's ethnic culture or who had more contact with their ethnic culture saw themselves as with a single ethnic identity such as Korean or black. However, in this study, the opposite was found. More children who were exposed to Korean culture perceived themselves as Korean American. It seems that children who were involved in Korean culture were able to develop a biethnic identity earlier. Biethnic identity refers to an identification of oneself as from two ethnic groups: born in Korea and grew up in America. Cross (1987) said that minority children need to be raised to identify with both their own, and the majority, culture because such a bicultural view is functional. In the present study, it was found that many children who were not involved in Korean cultural activities were unable to integrate Korean-born ethnicity and American upbringing. Many children who stated that they were Korean were simply indicating their appearance and ethnicity. They were rather ambiguous concerning their ethnicity. Self-identification as Korean did not mean that they had strong identity as Korean or that they had a great interest in learning about Korea.

Qualitative analysis suggested two courses in the development of Korean identity: for children who were high participators in Korean cultural activities, the process of ethnic identification began to take hold in the seven to eight age range and became established by the beginning of adolescence; for low participators this process did not develop or became arrested prior to the attainment of an integrated sense of identity. Korean adoptees were forced to have identity conflict earlier than other children due to their adoption and minority status. Adopted children had questions about their identity, struggling with who and what they were earlier than other children. When parents discuss these questions frequently with the children and involve cultural activities actively, they resolve ethnic differences by age twelve or thirteen.

Parental encouragement and coparticipation in cultural activities seemed critical to the process. If such parental involvement were lacking, children seemed less likely to develop the Korean side of their identities. In some cases, lack of parental involvement seemed reactive to the child's lack of interest. However, it is possible that the children who showed a lack of interest were responding to subtle parental cues that might have discouraged such interests from developing in the first place.

Recognizing, understanding, and accepting children's ethnicity as well as learning to cope with racial differences are critical tasks for biracially adopted children (Vonk, 2001). Parents should acknowledge the differences of their family's ethnicity in positive ways and try to be involved in Korean cultural activities with their children. However, as Kim (1978) noted, when parents are insensitive about ethnic differences or want to *Americanize* their Korean adoptees, adoptees may choose American culture over the Korean culture. Adoptive families also need to redefine their family identity as an American-Korean family as a way of accepting the biracial and bicultural element of their family. In any case, the children's interest in their culture seemed to vary over time, particularly in early adolescence. Such variation would give parents additional opportunities to involve the child in activities that might foster ethnic identification.

These findings and conclusions must be regarded as quite tentative, given the limitations of the study. The sample was small and self-selected. The subjects' recall of earlier years may have been distorted by problems of memory and other biases. That the interviewer was herself Korean may have caused the children to be more self-revealing; on the other hand, it may have prompted the children and their parents to exaggerate their affiliation with Korean culture.

IMPLICATIONS FOR PRACTICE

As previously noted, the study has relevance for international, trans-racial adoptees, and the implications are offered with such children in mind. In developing implications from the study, we assume that there is value in helping adopted children develop ethnic identities that incorporate their culture of origin.

Social workers should help facilitate parental involvement with their children in activities that will foster their children's development of inte-grated ethnic identities. Such activities might include participation in cul-tural programs (that, hopefully, families, agencies, schools, community, and the Korean government would sponsor), helping children develop relation-ships with other children from their culture and providing cultural experi-ences in the home, such as serving ethnic food and accompanying their children on visits to their native country. In order to allow children to develop affection toward Korean culture, parents need to show an interest in Korean culture and participate in a variety of different Korean cultural programs themselves. Parents' encouragement that is absent of a true respect for or in-terest in their child's Korean background may be seen artificial and may discourage the child from learning about Korean culture. However, parents might be cautioned to be sensitive to their children's own interest in their birth culture. Parents might be advised to provide encouragement and stim-ulation, but not to push too hard if their children become resistant at a par-ticular point in time. However, parents should continue to be encouraging and wait for other opportunities, since children may show renewed interest at a later point as a result of school projects, friends, etc.

In addition, social workers might work with the schools to increase teacher sensitivity to the needs of adoptees. For example, teachers might be encouraged to give children opportunities to study and talk about their native cultures. It will enhance the Korean adoptee's identity. Diversity education might also be encouraged. Instruction in the children's native language might be also indicated if there are enough children from a given culture in a school or school district.

REFERENCES

Baden, A. (2002). The psychological adjustment of transracial adoptees: An application of the Cultural-Racial Identity Model. *Journal of Social Distress and the Homeless, 11*(2), 167-191.

Baden, A., & Steward, R. (2000). A framework for use with racially and culturally integrated families: The Cultural-Racial Identity Model as applied to transracial adoption. *Journal of Social Distress and the Homeless, 9*(4), 309-337.

Benson, P., Sharma, A., & Rohelkepartain, E. (1994). *Growing up adopted.* Minneapolis, MN: Search Institute.

Bernal, M., Knight, G., Garza, C., Ocampo, K., & Cota, K. (1990). The development of ethnic identity in Mexican-American children. *Hispanic Journal of Behavioral Sciences, 12*(1), 3-24.

Bishoff, T., & Rankin, J. (1997). *In the shadow of race: Growing up as a multiethnic, multicultural, and "multiracial" American.* Mahwah, NJ: Lawrence Erlbaum Associates.

Chartrand, W. E. (1978). *Application of selected components of a correspondence theory of cross-cultural adjustment to the adjustment of white families who have adopted older children from Korea.* Unpublished doctoral dissertation, University of Minnesota, Minneapolis.

Cheung, Y. W. (1993). Approaches to ethnicity: Clearing roadblocks in the study of ethnicity and substance abuse. *International Journal of Addictions, 28*(12), 1209-1226.

Cole, J. (1992). *Perceptions of ethnic identity among Korean-born adoptees and their Caucasian-American parents.* Unpublished doctoral dissertation, Columbia University, New York.

Cross, W. E. (1971). The negro to black conversion experience. *Black World, 20,* 13-27.

Cross, W. E. (1987). A two-factor theory of black identity: Implications for the study of identity development in minority children. In J. S. Phinney & M. J. Rotheram (Eds.), *Children's Ethnic Socialization* (pp. 117-133). Thousand Oaks, CA: Sage Publications.

Feigelman, W., & Silverman, A. (1983). *Chosen children: New patterns of adoptive relationships.* New York: Praeger.

Friedlander, M. L. (1999). Ethnic identity development of internationally adopted children and adolescents: Implications for family therapists. *Journal of Marital and Family Therapy, 25*(1), 43-60.

Gill, O., & Jackson, B. (1983). *Adoption and race.* New York: St. Martin's Press.

Gonzalez, E. (1990). *Effects of age at placement and length of placement on foreign and domestic adopted children.* Unpublished doctoral dissertation, the University of Akron, Ohio.

Gross, G., & Gross, J. (1988, October 15). *From trans-racial adoption to a bi-racial family identity.* Paper presented at Parsons and Sage Fall Institute, Albany, New York.

de Haymes, M. V., & Simon, S. (2002). Transracial adoption: Families identity issues and needed support services. *Child Welfare, 82*(2), 251-272.

Howe, D. (1992). Assessing adoptions in difficulty. *British Journal of Social Work, 22,* 1-15.

Huh, N. (1985). Adopted Korean children's adjustment in American families. *Korean Social Welfare, 83,* 82-101.

Johnson, P., Shireman, J., & Watson, K. (1987). Transracial adoption and the development of black identity at age eight. *Child Welfare, 66,* 45-55.

Katz, P. A. (1976). The acquisition of racial attitudes in children. In P. Katz (Ed.), *Toward the elimination of racism* (pp. 125-154). New York: Pergamon.

Kim, D. (1976). *Intercountry adoptions: A study of self-concept of adolescent Korean children who were adopted by American families.* Unpublished doctoral dissertation, University of Chicago.

Kim, D. (1978). Issues in transracial and transcultural adoption. *Social Casework, 59*(8), 477-486.

Koh, F. (1993). *Adopted from Asia: How it feels to grow up in America.* Minneapolis, MN: EastWest Press.

Lambert, W. E., & Klineberg, O. (1967). *Children's views of foreign peoples.* New York: Appleton Century Crofts.

Lee, R. M. (2003). The transracial adoption paradox: History, research, and counseling implications of cultural socialization. *The Counseling Psychologist, 31*(6), 711-744.

Lydens, L. A. (1988). *A longitudinal study of crosscultural adoption: Identity development among Asian adoptees at adolescence and early adulthood.* Unpublished doctoral dissertation, Northwestern University, Chicago.

McRoy, R., Zurcher, L., Lauderdale, M., & Anderson, R. (1982). Self-esteem and racial identity in transracial and inracial adoptees. *Social Work, 27,* 522-526.

Phinney, J. S. (1990). Ethnic identity in adolescents and adults: Review of research. *Psychological Bulletin, 108,* 499-514.

Phinney, J. S. (2000). Ethnic identity. In A. E. Kazdin (Ed.), *Encyclopedia of psychology, volume 3* (pp. 254-259). New York: Oxford University Press.

Phinney, J. S. (2003). Ethnic identity and acculturation. In K. Chun, P. B. Organista, & G. Marin (Eds.), *Acculturation: Advances in theory, measurement, and applied research* (pp. 63-81). Washington, DC: American Psychological Association.

Raynor, L. (1980). *The adopted child comes of age.* London: Allen and Unwin.

Simon, R., & Altstein, H. (1992). *Adoption, race, and identity.* New York: Praeger.

Sollars, W. (1996). *Theories of ethnicity: A classical reader.* New York: New York University Press.

Strauss, A. (1987). *Qualitative analysis for social scientists.* New York: Cambridge University Press.

Strauss, A., & Corbin, J. (1990). *Basics of qualitative research: Grounded theory procedures and techniques.* Thousand Oaks, CA: Sage.

U.S. State Department (2002). *Immediate relative visas issued, 1958-2001.* Reported by Adoption Institute: International Adoption Facts, Retrieved October 28, 2003, from http://www.adoptioninstitute.org/FactOverview/international.html.

Vonk, M. E. (2001). Cultural competence for transracial adoptive parents. *Social Work, 46*(3), 246-255.

Wilkinson, H. (1985). *Birth is more than once: The inner world of adopted Korean children.* Bloomfield Hills, MI: Sunrise Ventures.

Chapter 6

Transracial Adoptive Parents' Thoughts About the Importance of Race and Culture in Parenting

M. Elizabeth Vonk
Sung Hyun Yun
Wansoo Park
Richard R. Massatti

The need to strengthen or develop expertise related to race and culture among parents who adopt across race in order to assist their children with unique racial and cultural issues has been discussed among scholars of transracial adoption, adult Korean adoptees, and transracial adoption practitioners. Little is known, however, about transracial adoptive (TRA) parents' views of the importance of developing competence to assist their children with positive racial and ethnic identity development. The purpose of this study is to add to what is known about TRA parents' perceptions of the role of race, ethnicity, and culture in their parenting.

While numerous studies attest to satisfactory adjustment and functioning at home and school among domestic and international transracially adopted children (Rushton & Minnis, 1997; Tizard, 1991), many point out difficulties related to racial and ethnic identity development (Andujo, 1988; McRoy, 1994). In addition, adult Korean adoptees describe their identity struggles and lack of skills to cope with stereotypes and racism that they faced (Simon & Roorda, 2000). Adoption practitioners have added their concerns as well, describing difficulties of children- and adolescents-of-color who question where and with whom they belong (Crumbley, 1999; Steinberg & Hall, 1998).

International Korean Adoption
doi:10.1300/5734_06

Critics as well as supporters of the practice of transracial adoption insist that TRA parents need to possess certain attitudes, knowledge, and skills in order to help their children develop positive racial and ethnic identities, a sense of belonging within their birth cultures, and the ability to successfully cope with racism or discrimination (Andujo, 1988; McRoy, 1994; Rushton & Minnis, 1997). This constellation of knowledge, skills, and attitudes has been conceptualized as cultural competence for TRA parents (Vonk, 2001). Such competence includes racial awareness, including (1) awareness of how race, ethnicity, and related power status affects parents' and children's lives; (2) multicultural planning, the creation of avenues for the child to participate in his or her ethnic culture; and (3) development of survival skills and strategies to cope with prejudice and racism.

Recent research has provided empirical support for the importance of parental cultural competence to assist in the development of transracially adopted children's positive ethnic identity. Among Korean-born adoptees, consistent parental encouragement of ethnic socialization and co-involvement in cultural activities were found to be associated with the development of a positive sense of ethnic identity (Yoon, 2001) and with an ethnic identity that integrated both Korean and American cultures (Huh & Reid, 2000). In addition, children in families who participated regularly in Korean cultural activities, when compared with low participators, were found to experience a more positive relationship with parents, greater psychological adjustment (Yoon, 2001), and greater ease in discussing adoption-related concerns with parents (Huh & Reid, 2000).

Despite the growing awareness of and empirical support for development of cultural competence, little is known about what current TRA parents themselves think about the role of racial and cultural considerations in their parenting. Huh and Reid (2000) described some of the parents in their study as being "intensely involved in Korean cultural activities" (p. 79), while others allowed their children's interest level to determine participation. Although many families were involved in cultural activities during the child's preschool years, participation decreased or stopped when the child entered school, either because of the child's reluctance or the parent's belief that the child's identity was no longer Korean, but American.

The tendency for parents to place less emphasis over time on their children's racial identities was noted also by Bergquist, Campbell, and Unrau (2003). In a survey administered twice, with a seven-year interval in between, parents of Korean-born adopted children reported they thought of their children as more "American" and less "Korean" both in their appearance and in their racial identities at the second data point. In addition, the majority of families consistently saw themselves as "Caucasian with Korean children" rather than as a multiracial family unit. The parents also reported an increase in racially based teasing as the children grew older.

Transracial adoptive parents' beliefs and activities related to race and culture have been discussed also by Lee and Grotevant (2003), who reported that parents' cultural socialization beliefs were associated with engagement in cultural activities and racial socialization. In addition, parents were more likely to engage in culture-specific parenting if they were involved in postadoption groups, including Internet-based support groups.

While there is variation among families, the aforementioned studies suggest that parents seem to believe that ethnicity and race are important aspects of parenting, and yet they may tend to minimize the racial differences within their families and engage in decreasing levels of ethnic socialization activities over time. As it becomes clearer that the parents of TRA children are integrally involved in the development of the child's positive racial identity, it becomes more important to gain a deeper understanding of TRA parents' views about cultural competence in parenting. A deeper understanding of the concerns of TRA parents about cultural competence issues may help to improve the manner in which pre- and postadoption education and support is marketed and conducted by adoption professionals.

The purpose of this study is to add depth to the current understanding of TRA parents' concerns about cultural competence in parenting. While conducting a related study designed to test a standardized measure of cultural competence for TRA parents (Massatti, Vonk, & Gregoire, 2004), the authors received numerous unsolicited written comments, including letters and lengthy notes. A few of those who wrote letters declined to complete the standardized questionnaires included in the survey. Although the data were unexpected, we nonetheless thought it important to give voice to these parents' concerns, many of whom had spent a great deal of time and energy in their efforts to communicate with the researchers. We have therefore conducted a qualitative data analysis of the written material to capture and report on what the parents wanted us to know.

METHODOLOGY

The data consisted of comments and letters written to the investigators of a study of the Transracial Adoption Parenting Scale (TAPS). The original study used a cross-sectional survey design with a national nonprobability sample of 1,411 participants solicited through the Holt International Adoption Agency, located in Eugene, Oregon. All participants were parents who had adopted from China or Korea between the years 1991 and 2000. The purpose of the original study was to examine psychometric properties of the TAPS, which measures the cultural competence of transracial adoptive parents (Massatti, Vonk, & Gregoire, 2004). Each parent completed the TAPS and three other instruments, along with demographic questions.

All written comments, consisting of one or more complete sentences, whether written on the questionnaire or on separate pages, were included in the current study. Single words and short phrases were selected out of the sample. Comments from a total of 124 individuals, 8.8 percent of the original study sample, were selected for analysis. Of those included, 106 were sentences or paragraphs written on the questionnaire and 18 were letters.

Participants in the current study had similar demographic characteristics as the participants of the original study. The vast majority of the respondents were Caucasian, more than 60 percent of whom reported annual incomes over $75,000. Most respondents were female (72.6 percent) and married (89.4 percent). For the vast majority, the adoptive child's ethnic background was Asian (95.6 percent). Slightly over half of the children in the current sample were under the age of seven years at the time of the survey administration, and about 70 percent were female.

Data analysis was conducted using the Consensual Qualitative Research (CQR) method described by Hill, Thompson, & Williams (1997). Following transcription, the CQR method involved three steps: initial development of domains or themes, distillation of each respondent's comments into core ideas, and cross-analysis or categorization of core ideas. The two first authors, serving as the research team, conducted each step of the analysis independently, and then conferred with one another until reaching consensus about domains, core ideas, and categorization. In addition, the third author served as an auditor to independently examine the data and the team's results. The auditor then shared her questions and comments with the research team. At each step in the process, the research team further refined the results through a process of discussion and reflection on the original data. The auditor and research team repeated the process until a thorough understanding of the data emerged.

RESULTS

The qualitative analysis resulted in the identification of four major domains, each with several categories of core ideas. The domain names, category names, and percentage of respondents who made at least one comment in the given areas are shown in Table 6.1. Each domain and category will be presented and illustrated with the respondents' core ideas.

TABLE 6.1. Names of Domains and Categories with Respondent Rate (*N* = 124)

Domain	Category	*N*
Race and Culture Are Not of Primary Importance		93 (75.0%)
	Other qualities, values, or issues are more important	22
	We have challenges or benefits due to our location	21
	Only if the child is interested or has the need	21
	Our child is too young	18
	My own or spouse's ethnic or racial background changes things	14
	We have not experienced specific issues related to race and culture	14
	We need to balance American and birth cultures	10
Issues of Race and Culture Are Complex		66 (53.2%)
	Here's how we do it in our family . . .	35
	Situational and complex nature of responding to racism and dealing with differences	34
	We are immersed in American values and traditions	12
Race and Culture Do Not Matter		46 (37.1%)
	Loving family and/or good parenting is what matters	14
	My religious beliefs supercede	14
	People are the same	13
	I am angry that you asked	13
Training, Education, and Support		32 (25.8%)
	Preadoptive	23
	Postadoptive	18

Domain 1: Race and Culture Are Not of Primary Importance

"Race and Culture Are Not of Primary Importance" had the highest proportion of respondents and provides categories of ideas about why parents feel unable to or do not place primary importance on issues of race and culture in their parenting. It is comprised of seven categories of core ideas, which are as follows:

1. Other qualities, values, or issues are more important. In the largest category of this domain are core ideas related to the family's preferences or values that are considered more important than racial or cultural issues. For example, regarding choice of location, one parent stated, "I don't choose a neighborhood according to who lives there—regardless of race. I go by quality of neighborhood." Similarly, another parent stated, "Just because [school] is labeled multicultural, [it] doesn't mean there are good role models [of] discipline and good teaching." Yet another said, "I would [help my child establish relationships with adults from her birth culture] if they are good people."

Others in this category focused on children's needs. One parent stated, "My child is developmentally disabled, and I need to go with his developmental ability more than worry about his race or culture." The instillation of other values in their children was also expressed, such as in these statements: "I think talking to your child . . . about differences is important. Having love is also important and being open about adoption issues!!" "We [want to] give our children new experiences and hopefully to instill in them that the world is theirs if they work hard."

2. We have challenges or benefits due to our location. This category includes core ideas related to the perception of local opportunity for socialization in the child's birth culture. Some parents pointed out that diversity was not available in their locale, while others indicated extensive diversity. For example, one respondent stated that "[Multicultural schools are] not available," while another responded, "In the San Francisco area, there's a large Asian population . . . and we have experienced no racial prejudice . . . if we continue to live in S.F., it probably won't be necessary [to teach our child how to cope with racism]."

3. Only if my child is interested or has the need. In this category, parents expressed their intention to pursue socialization for their children in their birth cultures only if the interest or need is present within the child. One respondent expressed it this way: "We will leave the choice to study Korean culture up to the children, and provide support . . . But this desire has to come from them." Another parent stated, "[I would seek service providers, such as a doctor, of my child's race] if she had a special Asian disease, etc."

4. Our child is too young. In this category, respondents indicated that the ideas or behaviors related to race and culture are not perceived to be applicable because of the young age of their primarily preschool-aged children. For example, one person stated, ". . . depends on age, if appropriate to [talk to my child about racial differences]" and "several of these questions do not apply as my daughter came as an infant."

5. My own or my spouse's cultural, ethnic, or racial background changes things. In this category, respondents expressed core ideas related to the influence of their own or their partner's racial or cultural identities. Owing to their own experiences with diversity, they seemed to express confidence in their ability to handle issues of race and culture with their children. For example, "Each child has a parent of his or her culture, and we have an international marriage. So in teaching about these things, we teach our own lives." In addition, "I learned firsthand about the privilege of living outside of one's own birth culture and some of the not-so-great aspects of prejudice and racism. This has given me the gift of a great deal of insight when it comes to raising our Chinese-born daughter."

6. We have not experienced specific issues related to race or culture. The ideas in this category are related to parents' perceptions that their children have not experienced prejudice aimed toward the child or family. In addition, these parents express the idea that potential future issues related to the child's race will not be a problem for them. One parent stated, ". . . we haven't run into any prejudice yet with kids or adults. At least, nothing overt that needed to be . . . explained to our kids. I guess I don't think we need to bring it up until it's an issue for our family." Another addressed interracial dating or marriage, stating, "I have absolutely no 'negative' or 'positive' feelings about interracial dating or marriage. My concern is solely that my daughter learns how to develop emotionally healthy relationships with other emotionally healthy individuals."

7. Need to balance american culture and birth culture. Responses in this category were concerned with balancing attention to the two cultures. For example, "I have told her I am very proud for her to become a 100 percent U.S. citizen. I have also stressed that the Chinese are *very good people* and China is *also* a great nation."

Domain 2: Issues of Race and Culture Are Complex

This domain contains comments from just over half of the respondents. It consists of three separate categories of core ideas, all of which seem to be related to the parents' desire to provide nuances or details related to items on the instrument.

1. Here's how we do it in our family. This is one of the two largest categories in this domain. Although focused on varying concerns, all of the ideas within this category provide details about the ways that parents acknowledge race and culture in their families. Some of the parents' comments in this category were related to interaction with people of their children's birth culture. For example, "We have friends . . . from both the countries our sons were born in." Others were concerned with socialization in and understanding of child's birth culture. One parent stated, "Our home is full of Korean toys and artifacts. Our son's one year birthday party was done completely in Korean style (food, music, dress, gift). . . ." Still others were concerned with coping with prejudice or racism as in the following statement: "[I talked with] parents of other Korean adoptees [about coping with prejudice]."

2.Situational nature and complexity of responding to racism and racial differences. The core ideas in this category demonstrate the parents' desire to express their understanding of responding to racism and racial differences. Some of the ideas emphasized the need to tailor responses to insensitive remarks or racism that may be directed at a child according to the circumstances and child's needs. For example, one parent remarked, "It would depend on the situation if [it is best to ignore insensitive remarks]; and . . . pick your battles, but [insensitive remarks] shouldn't be totally ignored." Other parents expressed that issues of racial and cultural differences are complex. For example, "Adopting parents walk a fine line in developing useful and compassionate sensitivity to prejudice without engendering feelings of isolation and persecution." Another stated, "[Opportunities for my child to learn values and traditions of his birth culture] are important for understanding, not necessarily adherence."

3. We are immersed in American values and traditions. These comments were in response to several items that asked about the importance of aspects of American culture. These parents indicated understanding that their children will learn American cultural values and traditions through his or her daily surroundings. One parent summarized, "They live in the USA, they are exposed [to American culture] every day, whether I like it or not."

Domain 3: Race and Culture Do Not Matter to Me

"Race and Culture Do Not Matter to Me" is composed of core ideas that provide insight into the reasons that respondents think matters related to race and culture are of little significance or consequence to them and their families. Over one-third of the total number of respondents contributed ideas in this domain, with roughly the same number of respondents in each of four categories of responses.

1. Becoming a loving family and/or good parenting is what matters. This category contains core ideas related to parents' perception that the race or birth culture of their children is insignificant in the context of a loving family and good parenting. Some parents, as shown in the following succinct statement, expressed this idea in relation to their motivation to adopt from Asia. "They [children] were available and race is irrelevant." Another parent, reacting to the idea of providing cultural opportunities for the child stated, "I focus more on the family, not on my culture or my son's culture." Another stated, "[Extra responsibilities related to race] are not significant—there's so much to good parenting."

2. My religious beliefs supercede. The core ideas in this category are related to the parents' belief in God as the provider of parental guidance, from God's plan for the children to be a part of their families to every decision they make concerning child rearing. One parent stated, "The most important message regarding race that I have tried to instill in my daughter is the fact that God chose her for our family and our family for her. Only He knows why He desired her to be a Chinese adoptee or why He led us to adoption." Another emphasized, "Your questionnaire does not address the *crucial* need for instilling a spiritual relationship between the child and God. That is where I spend my time with my child—not teaching her Chinese or taking her to Chinese theater, etc."

In addition to guidance from God about parenting, parents indicated that teachings in the Bible or their relationship with God also direct their views of racial differences and their response to racial prejudice. For example, "God created people in His image, and we all have the same heart, so I feel that we should act as the Lord Jesus Christ would. We try to reflect to our son that color and race don't matter because God loves us all"; and "Our daughter knows God has a special plan for her life that racial prejudice will pale in comparison to. This will give her a solid foundation that will keep her appreciating the privilege God gave her rather than her focusing or whining over real or imagined racism."

3. People are the same. The next category in "Race and Culture Do Not Matter" contains core ideas related to the belief that the children's race is inconsequential because all children are the same in their humanity or by virtue of being Americans once adopted by American parents. One parent stated, ". . . so even though [our] children are of a different race from their European descendant parents, [our] main message to [our] children is they are the same race, *the human race*." The American theme was emphasized by this parent who stated, "My children are American and don't see themselves as Korean citizens."

4. I am angry that you asked. In this category are a variety of comments in which respondents expressed anger about the research questionnaire. While some of these ideas were also included in categories related to their content, the category was devised due to the high level of emotionality expressed, as in the following comments:

"News flash! Shocking as it may seem, there *are* people who believe that God of the Bible is in control!"

"Of course we [teach them about American values and traditions]; they live here and have since infancy!"

Domain 4: Training, Education, and Support

The fourth and final domain involves ideas about training, education, and support for transracial adoptive parents. There are two categories of responses: comments regarding preadoptive educational experiences and comments regarding postadoptive support.

1. Preadoptive. These comments indicated that parents received very minimal education from their agencies, and relied instead on educating themselves. For example, this parent said, "Yes, [we received training], but it was very minimal . . . only [through] books I purchased and read, and people I spoke to."

2. Postadoptive. In this category, parents described minimal or no participation at all in formal adoption support groups, but instead developed informal support mechanisms with friends, travel groups, or LISTSERVs on the Internet. Comments such as the following were typical: "We have an informal group which sees each other socially . . . We also have a group who lived in the same orphanage and meet once a year." "If e-mail counts, then [we have] more frequent [support] via participation on lists."

DISCUSSION

The results of this analysis of TRA parents' comments indicate that a majority of our respondents find aspects of race and culture important in their parenting, albeit complex and difficult to place in a position of primary importance in the lives of their families. These results are consistent with findings of previous studies that have also identified interest among TRA parents in supporting children's racial and ethnic identities (Bergquist, Campbell, & Unrau, 2003; Huh & Reid, 2000; Lee & Grotevant, 2003). The core ideas expressed in this study provide insight into TRA parents' perceived barriers to fully embracing cultural competence, as well as a sense of heightened sensitivity to the complexity of it. In addition, for a smaller group of TRA parents, the results suggest reasons that cultural competence is thought to be irrelevant to parenting.

Results in the "Race and Culture Are Not of Primary Importance" domain indicate that parents perceive many barriers to their ability to fully embrace or implement cultural competence in their parenting despite their awareness of its importance. A few of the barriers are not surprising. For example, the child's interest level as a factor in involvement in cultural activities was also identified by Huh & Reid (2000), and the family's location in nondiverse communities has long been identified as a problem for TRA families (Andujo, 1988).

Other perceived barriers may be related to the parents' level of racial awareness, which is thought to be the foundation for other parts of cultural competence such as development of coping strategies (Vonk, 2001). For example, parents who stated that their children were too young to notice racial differences may be unaware that children perceive such differences very early. In similar fashion, it is possible that a lack of racial awareness is at play among parents who stated their children and families had no experience of prejudice or were completely neutral about interracial dating and marriage.

Still other parents have placed racial and cultural concerns in a secondary position to more primary concerns, such as overall quality of neighborhoods, schools, service providers, and friends. While they do not negate the importance of race and culture in their decision making, the underlying thought seems to be that cultural diversity or access to the child's birth culture is considered separately from other quality indicators.

Interestingly, parents who lived in very diverse communities, had a history of life experience with diversity, or who were themselves people-of-color expressed they had the required insight and skills to meet the challenges related to race their children might face. These parents seemed to possess a confidence in their own cultural competence that was different from other respondents. It is impossible to assess from this study how their confidence was associated with their competence.

In the "Issues of Race and Culture Are Complex" domain, parents seemed to demonstrate heightened sensitivity to the complexities of issues related to cultural competence in parenting. Some parents seemed to be actively grappling with how to respond to racism and racial differences both in and beyond their families within the cultural context of their lives in the United States. Others seemed to want to disclose details about ways in which their families have engaged in cultural socialization efforts for the children.

The ideas in Domains 1 and 2 are interesting in relation to Bergquist, Campbell, and Unrau's (2003) finding that parents of Korean children became more sensitive about the role of race in their children's lives, and yet they deemphasized racial differences over time. In spite of heightened sensitivity, barriers identified here may be responsible for the parents' tendency to downplay the role of the child's ethnicity and birth culture over time.

A smaller, but still substantial, group of respondents contributed ideas in the "Race and Culture Do Not Matter" domain. These parents seem to believe that cultural competence is not a relevant parenting concern. Huh and Reid (2000) identified a similar group of parents who felt they did not need to teach children Korean culture. This study, however, suggests that these parents have strongly held beliefs or values related to religion, American nationalism, or parenting, which are perceived to be inconsistent with aspects of cultural competence, particularly those aspects associated with recognition of racial differences. This group of respondents seems to express beliefs compatible with a "color-blind" approach to raising their children. The parents in this domain were the most frequent participants to refuse to complete the instruments, write lengthy letters, and express anger related to cultural competence questions, potentially indicating they represent a more difficult-to-reach group of parents than those who readily volunteer to participate in TRA research.

Finally, about a quarter of respondents wrote about "Training, Education, and Support," almost all of whom indicated they did not receive much formal education or support on cultural competence issues. Many, however, indicated they had managed to put in place informal education and support systems by socializing with similar families, through reading, or via the Internet. These comments are particularly interesting in light of Lee and Grotevant's (2003) finding that those parents who participated more in support groups were more actively involved in cultural activities. Ongoing postadoption support group participation may be particularly important in light of Bergquist, Campbell, and Unrau's (2003) finding that TRA parents tend to deemphasize racial identity more over time.

IMPLICATIONS

While the results of this study must be viewed with caution because of limitations of the methodology related to data collection, there are tentative practice implications. First, attention to the perceived barriers to cultural competence might be helpful for providers of adoption education and support. For some TRA parents, greater racial awareness may lift barriers; for others, more creative methods of program delivery are needed. For example, parents living in locations lacking cultural diversity may be willing to make use of the Internet for Web-based classes or linkage with cultural mentors. In addition, some of the parents who feel more confident in their cultural competence may be willing to assist other families.

Creative programming may also be needed to reach the group of TRA parents who find cultural competence irrelevant to their parenting. While further research is needed to understand this group more fully, it may be that recognition and understanding of parents' values will be central to discovering a meaningful way to deliver information about the importance of cultural competence for their children. Ideally, this group of parents could come to see the possibility that cultural competence might coexist with their other beliefs and values.

Although this study adds to our knowledge of TRA parents' perceptions of the role of race and culture in parenting, questions have been raised for future research as well. The comments by parents-of-color, or parents with substantial diversity experience, raise questions about the relationship of cultural confidence and actual cultural competence. Are parents-of-color more helpful to their children, and if so, in what ways? In addition, as stated earlier, we need to learn more about parents who resist acknowledging racial differences. Are children of such parents at higher risk for racial identity and self-esteem issues? Is there a way to move such parents toward cultural competence? Another area deserving more attention is the parents' reliance on the child's interest level for cultural activity participation. Are there some parents who insist on participation in spite of interest level? More importantly, what results are seen in children of such parents? These and other questions deserve closer examination in order to inform best practices with and policies directed toward current and future families formed through transracial adoption.

REFERENCES

Andujo, E. (1988). Ethnic identity of transethnically adopted Hispanic adolescents. *Social Work, 33,* 531-535.

Bergquist, K. L., Campbell, M. E., & Unrau, Y. A. (2003). Caucasian parents and Korean adoptees: A survey of parents' perceptions. *Adoption Quarterly, 6*(4), 41-58.

Crumbley, J. (1999). *Transracial adoption and foster care.* Washington, DC: CWLA Press.

Hill, C. E., Thompson, B. J., & Williams, E. N. (1997). A guide to conducting consensual qualitative research. *The Counseling Psychologist, 25,* 517-572.

Huh, N. S., & Reid, W. J. (2000). Intercountry, transracial adoption and ethnic identity: A Korean example. *International Social Work, 43,* 75-87.

Lee, R. M., & Grotevant, H. (2003). *Cultural experiences of children adopted from South Korea.* Presented at Society for Research in Child Development, Tampa, FL.

Massatti, R. R., Vonk, M. E., & Gregoire, T. K. (2004). Reliability and validity of the Transracial Adoption Parenting Scale. *Research on Social Work Practice, 14,* 43-50.

McRoy, R. G. (1994). Attachment and racial identity issues: Implications for child placement decision making. *Journal of Multicultural Social Work, 3*(3), 59-74.

Rushton, A., & Minnis, H. (1997). Annotation: Transracial family placements. *Journal of Child Psychology and Psychiatry, 38,* 147-159.

Simon, R. J., & Roorda, R. M. (2000). *In their own voices: Transracial adoptees tell their stories.* New York: Columbia University Press.

Steinberg, G., & Hall, B. (1998). *An insider's guide to transracial adoption.* San Francisco: PACT, An Adoption Alliance.

Tizard, B. (1991). Intercountry adoption: A review of the evidence. *Journal of Child Psychology, Psychiatry, and Allied Disciplines, 32,* 743-756.

Vonk, M. E. (2001). Cultural competence for transracial adoptive parents. *Social Work, 46*(3), 246-255.

Yoon, D. P. (2001). Causal modeling predicting psychological adjustment of Korean-born adolescent adoptees. *Journal of Human Behavior in the Social Environment, 3*(3/4), 65-82.

PART III:
REFLECTIONS
ON KOREAN ADOPTION

More than fifty years ago the first Korean orphans ventured on a one-way trip to destinations throughout North America and Europe; today they are wives, husbands, parents, grandparents, aunts, uncles, sisters, and brothers. They have careers, their own homes, and have situated themselves within the social fabric of their respective adopted communities and countries. They have maturity and life experiences that enable them to reflect on the "social experiment" that was, and is, international adoption. The parallel maturation of adoptees and the practice of international Korean adoption moves researchers and scholars to capture a generational overview and engage in critical analysis of this institutionalized global child welfare practice.

Eleana Kim, in her chapter on "remembering loss," captures the voices of adult adoptees, locating them in an active search for meaning through participation in the Gathering, an international conference for adult adoptees, and the OKF Motherland Tour. In this section Hosu Kim and Rebecca Hurdis bring into focus the *figure* or *ghost* of the birth mother, who is too often absent in the discourse on international adoption. They place birth mothers whose children have been objects of both rescue and commodification within the context of illegitimacy and reproductive rights. Shiao and Tuan interviewed adult adoptees who were able to reflect upon their childhoods, ethnicity, identity, and society. All of these essays raise questions of legitimacy, identity, loss, and status, which facilitate a necessary discourse on the impact on adoptees in relation to birth country and birth mothers.

Chapter 7

Remembering Loss: The Koreanness of Overseas Adopted Koreans

Eleana Kim

INTRODUCTION

The relationship between overseas adopted Koreans and "Korea" complexly intertwines the deeply personal realms of identity, including notions of home, family, memory, and belonging, with the starkly impersonal realms of the social and political, spanning categories such as citizenship, nation, history, and culture. This relationship is peculiar and particular to each adoptee; it is simultaneously individual and collective, real and imagined, intimately embodied, distantly remembered, or entirely forgotten. It is also historically specific and sensitive to fluctuations in the economic and political relationships between nations, legislated through policies and structured and managed through programs intended to welcome overseas adoptees back to the "motherland."

Although some adoptees may have little or no interest in their biological families or country of birth, it is undeniable that, for many, Korea holds a central place in their imaginations about who they are, where they came from, and what they might have been otherwise. Many adoptee narratives express a yearning, sometimes laced with fear, to travel to South Korea, to explore cultural and biological "roots," and perhaps to locate missing pieces of the self.

This chapter offers an analysis of the dynamics between the South Korean state and adopted Koreans based on five years of dissertation research in the United States and South Korea. Two main sites that I examine here are the adoptee-organized "Gathering" conferences and a government-

International Korean Adoption
© 2007 by The Haworth Press, Inc. All rights reserved.
doi:10.1300/5734_07

sponsored "motherland tour" for adult adoptees hosted by the Overseas Koreans Foundation (OKF). OKF's Cultural Awareness Training Program for Overseas Adopted Koreans and the Gathering conferences provide lenses onto the complex ways in which Korean adoptees encounter Korea. Moreover, they show that the diversity of Korean adoptees' experiences frustrate any attempts at broad generalization. Not only do differences among them cut across personal histories and nationalities, but they also cross lines of class, race, gender, and sexuality, as well as religious, generational, and regional lines.

POINTS OF REENTRY

The 1988 Seoul Olympic Games marked a historic moment for South Korea, drawing honor and international recognition to the newly industrialized nation that had risen from the ashes of war to become a competitive player in the global economy within the span of just one generation. It also, however, marked another historic moment, drawing attention away from Korea's remarkable developmental achievements to its less praiseworthy practice of "exporting" its children for international adoption to the West. If 1988 was a symbolic coming of age for the Republic of Korea, it was also a coming of age for its adoptees. With its emergence on the world map, South Korea ceased to be a misty faraway land and became actualized for adoptees who began traveling there in increasing numbers during the late 1980s and early 1990s. Today, an estimated 3,000 to 5,000 adopted Koreans return annually, to discover their roots by enrolling in language or cultural classes, joining motherland tours organized by cultural institutions, adoption agencies, and the government, or by actively searching for birth family. Some returnees decide to remain as long-term sojourners, and a rough estimate would put their numbers at around 200.

The adoptees who started streaming back to South Korea after the 1988 Olympics largely took the South Korean government and adoption agencies by surprise. Adoption agency professionals in particular were unprepared to deal with the large number of requests by adoptees for information about their birth families. But the government began to nominally address the increasing adoptee presence with provisions in the 1995 Special Act Relating to the Promotion and Procedure of Adoption *(ibyang ch'okchin mit chôlch'ae kwanhan t'ûngnyepôp)* stipulating the establishment of programs and services to help those returning adoptees. Programs, including cultural education, language training, preferential job recruitment, and birth-family reunions, were further outlined in 1996.

To help address the needs of returnees, several European and American adoptees established Global Overseas Adoptees' Link (GOA'L) in 1998, a resource center that also advocates for adoptee rights in South Korea. GOA'L receives nominal financial and political backing from the Korean government, administrative support from native Korean staff and volunteers, and earned NGO status in 2004. Since the late 1990s, programs for adoptees in Korea have multiplied, with nonprofit religious and civic organizations offering cultural programs and assistance with birth-family search. In addition, university language programs regularly offer scholarships to adoptees. Adoptee artists like Mihee-Nathalie Lemoine are frequently exhibited, and adoptee activists have made important contributions and interventions into the public discourse of adoption in South Korea. Since 1991, Lemoine has been instrumental in helping over 500 adoptees search for their birth families and has been vocal about the need for adoption agency reform especially with respect to the search process and adoptees' rights to information. Recently, a group of progressive-minded adoptees have been organizing to make more direct interventions into adoption policies in Korea.

These organizations and activities are part of a broader network of adopted Koreans worldwide. The first Gathering was one of three major international conferences for adopted Koreans in 1999, representing a culmination of more than a decade of activity by regional organizations, smaller groups, and individuals, either isolated or connected only through the Internet. Its success spawned a number of minigatherings in U.S. cities, and more adoptee groups have formed to add to the dozen or so that have been established worldwide since 1986. A second Gathering took place in Oslo, Norway, in 2002, and the third in Seoul in 2004.

In tandem with this proliferation of adult adoptee activity, during his presidency, Kim Dae Jung and his wife, First Lady Lee Hee-ho, exhibited a remarkably open attitude toward adopted Koreans. Shortly after his inauguration in 1998, Kim invited twenty-nine overseas adopted Koreans to the presidential residence and offered them an unprecedented public apology. The next year, adoptees won legal recognition as "overseas Koreans" *(chaehoe tongp'o),* which legitimized their membership in the "global family of Korea," a diaspora of over seven million worldwide. This designation allows them visas to stay in Korea for up to two years that include rights to work, make financial investments, buy real estate, and to obtain medical insurance and pensions. Along with special visa rights, the 1999 opening of the "Adoption Center" by the Ministry of Health and Welfare and the inauguration in 1998 of the OKF Cultural Awareness Training Program for Overseas Adopted Koreans were further government gestures to acknowledge adult adoptees' needs. Over the past five years, representatives of the Korean state have regularly appeared at each of the major adoptee conferences, reiterating the state's interest in and inclusion of adoptees in the broader global Korean community.

Yet this recognition of adoptee political and economic citizenship disregards the difficulties of negotiating the "cultural citizenship" of adopted Koreans in South Korea and elsewhere. Lok Siu (2001) discusses anthropological theories of cultural citizenship as "extend[ing] the conventional understanding of citizenship as a legal-juridical category to include the qualitative and differential experiences of citizenship in everyday interactions and situations" (p. 9). This concept also allows for a consideration of the often partial, unequal, and stratified ways in which individuals and groups experience social belonging. In the case of Korean adoptees who may be presumed to be among the most privileged of transnational subjects, their mobility belies the limits of their cultural citizenship in both their adoptive countries and in South Korea—compromised by their racial difference in one context and by their lack of embodied cultural knowledge in the other. I employ "cultural citizenship" to describe the affective dimensions of identification with "Koreanness"—in other words, to use it as an analytic framework for talking about how Korean adoptees might "feel Korean."

A central ambiguity that is common to discourses about the Koreanness of overseas adoptees lies in conflicting notions of identity as either biologically given or culturally acquired. The OKF program, for instance, is geared toward cultural education and "aspire[s] to help Korean adoptees understand and appreciate their Korean identity" (Overseas Koreans Foundation, 2001). Here, Korean identity seems to be something that adopted Koreans already possess, implying that cultural identity is biologically given. But at the same time, it is something that requires "training" in order to be understood and appreciated, suggesting that Korean identity is something that must be culturally achieved. In a similar way, at the Gathering, an essentialized Koreanness was diversely articulated by government officials, adoption agency professionals, and adoptees, bringing out conflicting interpretations of whether or not Korean adoptees are Korean and, if they are, then *how* they are so.

Because of this central ambiguity, my research indicates that government attempts to grant Koreanness to adoptees inevitably produce awkward weddings of "culture" and "citizenship," generating unintended responses and resistances among adoptees, and therefore, I contend, open up alternative ways of understanding adopted Korean identity and belonging (E.J. Kim, 2003).

THE GLOBAL FAMILY OF KOREA

In August 2004, in a packed ballroom at a hotel near downtown Seoul, the South Korean Minister of Health and Welfare, Kim Geun Tae, addressed a group of 430 Korean-born adoptees with words uncommonly heard issuing from the lips of a government official. Although he expressed initial doubt and hesitation, wondering if he "had a right to say it," at the end of his speech, he intoned, *"saranghamnida,"* or "I love you." The occasion for this unusual pronouncement was the opening plenary of the third International Gathering of Korean Adoptees. The adoptees, ranging in age from their early twenties to their late fifties, had been raised in fifteen different countries across the Western world and converged on Seoul to participate in this four-day event. The rich symbolic potential of this "homecoming" was mined by organizers, journalists, and government officials, including Minister Kim, whose declaration of love was as much a pitch to the media as it was to the adoptees.

The following day, the major Korean dailies featured photos and articles about the conference's opening ceremony, some drawing causal connections between the pictures of tearful adoptees and the Minister's speech. From my observations at the opening plenary, however, many adoptees appeared to be either indifferent or perplexed by the Minister's words. Instead, the address given by Susan Soon-Keum Cox, adoptee and executive at Holt International Children's Services, seemed to provoke a more emotional response. Cox, who was adopted in 1956, had first thought up the idea of the Gathering conferences in the 1990s and was the principal organizer of the First Gathering in Washington, DC, in 1999. At the third Gathering, she spoke clearly and deliberately to her audience, as "a fellow adoptee":

> In spite of our differences . . . the commonalities shared among us as Korean adoptees is undeniable, and it is unspoken, and it is powerful. It connects us to one another through our shared history and the experience with our beginnings and it extends to who we are now. As Korean adoptees, we are now citizens of our adopted nationalities, but we are forever emotional citizens of Korea, of our birth country and our culture. We are also citizens of a unique world community of Korean adoptees.

Cox herself is not a figure free from controversy, in part because of her role as spokesperson for other "fellow adoptees," a significant position that allows her to give voice to what she calls their "unspoken" commonalities.

Nevertheless, these commonalities to which she referred have proven to be deeply affective. In social spaces such as the Gathering conferences, these commonalities have been discovered, reproduced, and maintained over the past several years by adoptees in cities throughout the world, in cyberspace, and through a range of practices, from artistic to social to activist. Thus, a radically dispersed and deterritorialized group of people is articulating a new diasporic Korean identity, through *re*territorializations of transnational space.

The roots of this diaspora can be found in a common experience of loss. As with other diasporic or exiled groups, adoptees often project a nostalgic yearning on a mythic homeland, and this search for roots can also lead to new social formations and cultural practices. Their shared social spaces and discourses are part of a process of recuperation and re-membering—in the sense of recalling but also, of reconstituting—individual and collective histories and memories. Recovering and producing memory through narrative is key to the production of the Korean adoptee subculture. Korea, as place of origin and of actual return, is central to this remembering process, which is, in turn, delimited by available modes and technologies. Indeed, the ability of adopted Koreans to think of themselves as Koreans has only recently been made possible by the rise of multiculturalism, global flows of communication and media, Korea's rapid modernization, and through the direct intervention of the Korean state, which now welcomes adoptees as overseas Koreans, to join the global Korean "family."

South Korea's legislative and political recognition of adoptees in the late 1990s was credited in part to the advocacy and encouragement of First Lady Lee. It was also closely tied to the cultural and economic "globalization" *(segyehwa)* policy nominally inaugurated under President Kim Young Sam and expanded under President Kim Dae Jung (S.S. Kim, 2000). OKF, which was established in 1997, is the prime government agency for incorporating overseas Koreans who are welcomed back as part of a global economic consolidation project and also to participate in Korea's international reputation. The government's interest in the overseas Korean population is focused on developing economic linkages with the diaspora and also with producing a sense of unified Korean identity *(hanminjok)* and personhood among Koreans around the globe.

At both the first and third Gatherings, the presiding first ladies of Korea conveyed official welcoming addresses to the adoptee participants. This fact strongly suggests how adoption is framed as a domestic, or "feminine" issue best handled by the president's wife, rather than the president himself. At the 1999 Gathering, for instance, First Lady Lee Hee-ho provided a matronly face for the symbolic motherland via video, embracing adoptees as a source of pride for adoptive parents, Korean culture, and the South Korean state. She emphasized the ethnic roots of Korean adoptees, exhorting them to "forget your difficult past and renew your relations with your native country in order to work together toward common goals based on the blood ties that cannot be severed." She underscored the role of adoptees in the future of South Korea, which, as she stated, is "developing day by day to become a first-rated nation in the twenty-first century. It will be a warm and reliable support for all of you."

Likewise, First Lady Kwon Yang-suk, the wife of President Roh Moo-hyun, sent a welcoming speech to the third Gathering in which she articulated a similar message:

> Korea is now the twelfth largest economy in the world and its system of democracy has come of age. We will continue to do our best to ensure that you and your children can live with a sense of pride and dignity in this nation. Always remember that your roots are here . . . Rest assured that your motherland, the Republic of Korea, will never forget you and we will stand by you.

Both of these messages draw upon a globalization ideology, coupled awkwardly with metaphors of nurturance. Embedded in an economic discourse in which the South Korean nation continues to aspire to first world status, these messages reflect the acute sensitivity of the Korean state to its position in the global hierarchy of nations. In this narrative, South Korea, which may have been unable to take care of her own in the past, is now capable of incorporating, "supporting," and "standing by" her abandoned children. Rather than economic or material support, however, the Korean state, by becoming fully modern, can offer symbolic and moral support by promising to be a source of ethnic "pride." As Madame Kwon stated, "We owe it to you to build a country that inspires pride. A dignified nation that stands tall in the community of nations."

Hence, similar to the Minister of Health and Welfare's hesitant "I love you," official messages from the government present maternalistic or paternalistic desires to embrace adoptees as "family," but these expressions are shot through with ambivalence about who adoptees are (Korean or Western, children or adults, tragic or lucky), and if they will be able to forgive and forget enough to accept their role as ambassadors and bridges connecting Korea to the West. As one adoptee asserted, regarding Koreans' reactions to adoptees in Korea, "They don't know what to *do* with us."

I interpret these expressions of the Koreanness of adopted Koreans in the context of a broader discourse that constructs certain overseas Koreans as productive "bridges" between South Korea and the global economy, writing them into a narrative of neoliberal capitalism, even as it excludes "other" Koreans—women, biracial Koreans, and non-affluent diasporic Koreans in the global South (Park, 1996). Some Koreans may believe that adoptees have fared well, having entered into a privileged Western world, with all the opportunities for education and advancement it can afford. This crude calculation, however, discounts the pain and loss of family, belonging, and history that adoptees must often grapple with. Moreover, the histories of adoptees are intimately linked to those who were left behind by Korea's economic rise and those left out of the official story of Korean modernity. Returning adoptees thus bring the darker stories behind the so-called "miracle on the Han"—stories of poverty, divorce, rape, abandonment, and teenage pregnancy—into view.

At the first Gathering, the Korean ambassador to the United States noted, "You demonstrate the capacity to transform oneself from humble beginnings to success." And many of the speeches in the opening plenary of the conference emphasized the "success" of the "crazy 'social experiment'" of international transracial adoption, as symbolized by the adoptees in attendance (Gathering of the First Generation of Korean Adoptees, 1999, p. 6). Around the third Gathering, educational achievement was an important indicator of this success, as the results of the survey from the first Gathering were cited frequently by the media; 70 percent had graduated college, 24 percent had graduate degrees, and 15 percent were enrolled in university or postgraduate work. The trajectory of adoptees thus reflects the progress and development model offered by the narrative of South Korea's phenomenal modernization—its meteoric rise out of a tragic colonial past, through the devastation of war, to its ascendance as a newly industrialized "Asian Tiger," boasting the world's eleventh largest economy by 1996.

The testimonies of attendees at the first Gathering, however, complicated the meanings of that success, and suggested how, in contrast to familial and nationalist rhetoric of the South Korean state, adoptees experience cultural citizenship with respect to Korea and Koreanness. In the workshops they shared intimate and painful memories of Korea, their childhoods in America, and the negative experiences of living in a white culture—with a "white" name and family but an Asian physiognomy. In fact, I argue, what constituted their ties to South Korea are precisely those memories of the "difficult past," which First Lady Lee exhorted the adoptees to "forget." Unearthing those memories is part of the process of return, search, and reunion for many of these adoptees. As Lisa Lowe (1996) points out, "'political emancipation' through citizenship is never an operation confined to the negation of individual 'private' particulars; it requires the negation of a history of social relations" (pp. 26-27). The "forgetting" of personal and national trauma is encouraged in not only American multicultural ideologies but also in the attempts by the South Korean government to produce a homogeneously "Korean" yet heterogeneously dispersed "family" based on shared ancestors or "blood."

The experiences of adoptees in South Korea, as expressed at the Gathering and in other contexts, reflected a sense of disappointment, the failure of the fantasy of "home" to exist in reality. For some it was a very painful time, as they faced their pasts, confronted their feelings about being adopted, and worked out complicated issues about race, ethnicity, and culture. Many expressed amazement at finally being in a place where they looked like everyone else, but also the difficulty of not "relating" to Koreans or Korean culture. The primacy of blood in South Korean cultural understandings of individual disposition and national character has been rejected by adoptees who cannot accept the essentializing and ethnocentric assumptions of South Koreans who subscribe to a strong ethnic nationalism. Others had more positive experiences, with one attendee insisting that one or two trips would not be enough but, rather, having himself been back to Korea six times, that "you have to go several times to understand your relationship to [Korea]."

Yet overwhelmingly, across all age sets, the adoptees expressed feelings of discrimination from Americans and feelings of rejection from both South Koreans and Korean Americans. For adoptees who grew up isolated from each other and who primarily identified culturally as Americans, racial discrimination posed a particularly difficult form of double-consciousness. Even the most empathetic parents were perceived as unable to fully relate to the experience of racism, thereby intensifying feelings of alienation and racial difference. Many agreed with one attendee's sense that "Koreans reject the American side, Americans reject the Korean side," adding that "Koreans reject the adoption side. For them, I ha[ve] no family, no history."

At the same time, adoptees who were encouraged to make connections to their Koreanness by their adoptive parents also stated that they rejected those attempts as adolescents, with some feeling that pushing culture on them was "over-determined" as if they were "the only ones with an ethnic identity." Many agreed that "kids just want to fit in and be normal" and that they felt most comfortable in "mainstream" white culture. But recognition of a historical and cultural shift was palpable. As one adoptee stated, an "international identity is emerging," and another informed his cohort, "Don't you know? Asian people are 'in' now."

What characterized these perspectives on the Koreanness of adopted Koreans, however, is a discourse that doubly orientalizes Korea, whether in claiming or disclaiming "Koreanness." Adoptees who feel alienated from Korea, as well as from "traditional" Korean or Korean diaspora communities, often consider Korea and Koreans to be the Other, at the same time that they attempt to understand what it means "to be Korean." Adoptees have used the metaphor of a pendulum to describe the experience of swinging between Korean and American "sides," yet there is also a tendency to speak of being Korean in ethnicized and essentializing ways.

The alienation that is expressed through "otherizing" or orientalizing has the potential to produce more complex and nuanced models of and for "Korean culture." Andrea Louie (2000) writes about Chinese-American youth on "roots tours" to China, arguing that the tours raise "tensions . . . between historically rooted assumptions about Chineseness as a racial category and changing ways of being culturally, racially and politically Chinese (in China and the diaspora)" (p. 655). Adoptees, occupying an ambiguous and troubled place in the Korean social imaginary, raise similar tensions and similar possibilities for opening up a space for adoptee cultural citizenship in the diaspora and in Korea.

WEDDING CITIZENSHIP AND CULTURE

The difficulties of negotiating the cultural citizenship of adopted Koreans became even more clear to me during the course of the 2001 OKF program that I accompanied as a "counselor." There were six counselors on the tour, which brought together thirty adoptees, ranging in age from sixteen to thirty-four, who had been raised in North America, Australia, and eight European countries. This motherland tour was perhaps atypical in the degree to which conflicts and contestations flared, but these clashes offer productive ways of examining the underlying sources of tension between native Korean organizers and overseas adoptees.

The ten-day tour was, in many ways, an attempt to wed Korean adoptees to an idea of Korea, an invitation to the motherland so that they might, as offered by the president of OKF, "begin to feel the breath of Korea's rich culture." The program occupied the participants with activities that included trips to ancient palaces and courses on Korean "traditional" food and customs, thereby introducing them to a Korea of the past, rather than of the present. Attendees were largely discouraged from experiencing contemporary urban South Korean life, aside from one afternoon of sightseeing in Seoul, several hours at Korea's largest amusement park, and a presentation of the ROK's military prowess at the Demilitarized Zone (DMZ). GOA'L cosponsored the OKF program, and one day of the tour was devoted to the third annual GOA'L conference.

For most of the participants, the OKF program was an opportunity to come to South Korea, to meet other adoptees, and to share their stories. For some of them, it was a chance to try to find out more about their birth families or to try to meet their foster parents. The program, however, was geared toward "cultural training" and constructed the adoptees as tourists, with an emphasis on their lack of cultural competence, over an acknowledgment of their intimate and embodied ties to Korea. In addition, the program became an opportunity for the Korean media to dramatize adoptee stories, spectacularize their lack of cultural knowledge, and to highlight the efforts of the Korean government to welcome the adoptees back to their motherland. The media became a problematic presence, underscoring for many adoptees the instrumentalizing logic behind the program itself. Indeed, the "adoption problem" in Korea is one that the major broadcasting stations have exploited in recent years. Adopted Koreans returning to South Korea every year, many to search for birth family, are particularly vulnerable to the media's appetite for melodramatic content, especially issues surrounding family separation, cultural loss, and cathartic reunion.

The OKF tour illustrates the difficulties inherent in imbuing adopted Koreans with cultural citizenship. One afternoon of the tour was spent at the administrative offices of Kangdong-gu, a district on the eastern edge of metropolitan Seoul. The mayor of the district has been a strong supporter of GOA'L and has often bestowed upon visiting adoptees "honorary citizenship" *(myôngyekungmin)* to his district. The participants of the OKF program had been invited for their own group citizenship ceremony. The mayor welcomed the adoptees, and in his ardently delivered speech went so far as to suggest that each adoptee consider Kangdong-gu to be his or her "hometown" *(kohyang)*. "If you get lost, you can tell people that you are from Kangdong-gu." They should, he said, feel free to contact the district office if they had any problems while in Korea. Each adoptee was ceremoniously given a certificate and an ID card with his or her picture and Korean name—neither of them were official documents but, rather, symbolic artifacts intended as a gesture of welcome to the adoptees.

A volunteer representative for the adoptees, a college student from Massachusetts, then rose and gave words of appreciation to the mayor on behalf of the group. She was overwhelmed with the show of generosity and broke down in tears. Afterward I asked two American adoptees what they thought of the ceremony. One of them, echoing the sentiments of the woman from Massachusetts, said in earnest, "It was so nice of them. I can't believe it.

They really didn't have to do this." Two European adoptees offered starkly different impressions. They were deeply offended and compared the ID cards to toys, agreeing with each other that "they are treating us like children."

The differing responses to the Kangdong-gu ceremony are related to the differing needs of returning adoptees. The aforementioned European adoptees were longtime sojourners in Korea, and had been struggling to find work so they could remain; they were both near fluent in English, but preference at English language institutes is given to native-speakers, and there is little demand for instructors of European languages. The gesture of welcome from Kangdong-gu's mayor, therefore, seemed trivial and infantilizing. For most of the other adoptees, this trip to Korea was their first, and their plans were to remain for only a short time. For them, the gesture was symbolically meaningful and sincerely appreciated—the card was received as a memento that they could cherish rather than as a fake ID that had no practical purposes.

This divergence of opinion over the ID cards that was rooted in the differences of the adoptees' respective circumstances evaporated over the next several days. And so, too, did the symbolic power of the Kangdong-gu ID cards, which, as laminated pieces of cardboard with passport-size photos pasted on, started to come apart within a couple of days. By the end of the trip, the adoptees, despite differences in age, nationality, personal histories, and individual concerns, expressed collective outrage at the camp organizers and the Korean government. Although not entirely unanimous, the majority felt that the tour experience had been co-opted and abused by the Korean government, primarily through the media. They demanded to have a meeting with the president of OKF to present their concerns about the program. Many felt that they had been misinformed about the program, which had initially indicated on its Web site that assistance would be provided for birth-family searches. This had not been offered, despite repeated requests by adoptees who had rested their hopes on leaving Korea with some clues or information about their pasts. They were thoroughly cynical, believing that "it's all about money." More than one adoptee said, "This is about the media and the World Cup. They're using us to show how great adoption is."

There was a strong sense of solidarity among the group, overcoming latent rifts due to cultural and linguistic barriers between the English-speaking and French-speaking adoptees. Yet, some did exhibit ambivalence, expressing their gratitude to the Korean government for hosting the trip and to the director and counselors for their friendship, whereas others were incensed enough to threaten to leave the group altogether. One adoptee from Chicago told me that the program was the first time he had felt like he "fit" in among a group of people, and for many of the adoptees on the trip, for whom this was the first time they had met other adoptees like themselves, it seemed to be a very memorable, if not a transformative, experience.

As the breakdown of the tour shows, gestures of welcome by the South Korean government may be unwittingly misguided and may provoke alienation rather than identification and, sometimes, active resistance. One reason may be that the welcoming embrace of Korean adoptees offered by the South Korean government can also be a stifling one, one that encourages "forgetting" of the specific historical and biological connections adoptees have to Korea. From another perspective, the program's "breakdown" might also be considered a demonstration of its success—based on the powerful bonds that formed among a very diverse group of individuals over a very short period of time. For, it was not only the desire to see and experience Korea but also to meet other adoptees that motivated many participants to join the program. In this way, the OKF tour, like other Korean adoptee social spaces, became an opportunity for the building of social ties and emotional bonds founded on a shared Korean identity—as Koreans who are adopted.

The third Gathering in Seoul in 2004 provoked new discussions of the "unique world community" that Susan Cox described, and demonstrated the community's increasing coherence as a social formation. With more and more adoptees sharing information about birth-family search, living and working in Korea, and language and cultural programs, a common storehouse of knowledge is being assembled in person and online. As adopted Koreans gain cultural competence in Korea, they are also conducting their own research into tours to Korea, organizing their own programs, or petitioning for adoptee involvement in postadoption services at the organizational level. In addition, they are asserting the necessity of having adoptee-centered programs that take adoptees' needs and desires seriously, and that provide a view of culture and history as it is lived, rather than as pristine and prepackaged.

CONCLUSION

Lisa Lowe (1996) employs the concept of "disidentification" in her discussion of minority cultural politics in the United States that applies equally well to the experiences of overseas adopted Koreans in a transnational context. "Disidentification," she writes, "expresses a space in which alienations, in the cultural, political and economic senses, can be rearticulated in oppositional forms . . . it allows for the exploration of alternative political and cultural subjectivities that emerge within the continuing effects of displacement" (1996, pp. 103-104). I draw upon Lowe's work in my contention that adopted Koreans' alienation from the official discourses of the South Korean state lay the ground for the construction of an alternate Korean adoptee subjectivity. Encounters between adoptees and Korea—as place, people, nation, state, culture, and history—also need to be considered in the context of other adult adopted Korean social practices, and as part of a larger process of re-membering a collective Korean adoptee identity and community.

Certainly, overseas adoptees experience "disidentification" from the hegemonic racial and cultural scripts in the countries where they were raised, and this alienation contributes to the desire to connect to Korea, to locate an "authentic" identity (Meier, 1998). Adopted Koreans in Korea have made impressive strides in their struggle for recognition and support, and they have won many advocates, such as the mayor of Kangdong-gu and a member of the National Assembly. Other adoptees, however, are more skeptical of the government's interest in adoptees and argue that more needs to be done to finally end international adoption from Korea, such as greater promotion of domestic adoption and reform of the social welfare system.

Against the attempted enrollment of adoptees into the nationalistic myth of progress and development, or into an ahistorical spectacle of "tradition," the self-representation of Korean adoptees through creative work and social practice provides the means for connecting individual and group visibility. I interpret these practices as parts of an unofficial history of adoption from South Korea, providing stories of dislocation and displacement that create alternative ways of imagining and constructing adopted Korean identity. It is through these practices taking place in a range of locations—in cyberspace, at conferences, through artistic production, and on trips to South Korea—that Korean adoptees are constructing their own "roots" (E. J. Kim, 2001). In addition, the South Korean state's policies regarding overseas Koreans will continue to adapt to changing circumstances within and without its borders, with greater acknowledgment of the diversity among the Korean population abroad and at home.

Therefore, my research suggests that the relationship between adoptees and Korea is not only diverse across axes of nationality, age, and gender, but it is also a constantly evolving one. As "Korean adopteeness" is increasingly articulated by a collective, global, and spatially dispersed group of adoptees, they are being recognized as such within their adoptive countries as well as in Korea. Moreover, they are also self-identifying and claiming their status as part of the Korean diaspora. Adoptee cultural citizenship is thus connected to Korea, as a nation-state and ethnic-cultural paradigm, but more important, it is also produced out of a disidentification from "Korea." The social memory of Korean adoptees is necessarily fractured, diverse, and deterritorialized. Their shared storytelling, as a gathering and writing of collective histories, is a kind of disidentificatory practice out of which Korean *adoptee* identity and cultural citizenship emerges.

REFERENCES

Gathering of the First Generation of Korean Adoptees (1999). [Brochure] The Gathering Conference, September 10-12, 1999, Washington, DC.

Kim, E. J. (2001). Korean adoptee autoethnography: Refashioning self, family, and finding community. *Visual Anthropology Review, 16*(1), 43-70.

Kim, E. J. (2003). Wedding citizenship and culture: Korean adoptees and the global family of Korea. *Social Text, 74*(1), 57-80.

Kim, S. S. (2000). *East Asia and globalization.* Lanham, MD: Rowman and Littlefield.

Louie, A. (2000). Re-territorializing transnationalism: Chinese Americans and the Chinese motherland. *American Ethnologist, 27*(3), 645-669.

Lowe, L. (1996). *Immigrant acts: Asian American cultural politics.* Durham, NC: Duke University.

Meier, D. (1998). *Loss and reclaimed lives: Cultural identity and place in Korean American intercountry adoptees.* Unpublished doctoral dissertation, University of Minnesota, Minneapolis.

Overseas Koreans Foundation (OFK) (2001). *Summer cultural awareness training program guide.* Seoul, Korea: Overseas Koreans Foundation.

Park, H. O. (1996). Segyehwa: Globalization and nationalism in Korea. *The Journal of the International Institute, 4*(1). [Retrieved on March 7, 2005, from http://www.umich.edu/~iinet/journal/vol4no1/segyeh.html.]

Siu, L. (2001). Diasporic cultural citizenship: Chineseness and belonging in Central America and Panama. *Social Text, 69,* 7-28.

Chapter 8

Mothers Without Mothering: Birth Mothers from South Korea Since the Korean War

Hosu Kim

Over the past fifty years, approximately 200,000 Korean children have been placed into foreign adoption; 150,000 of them were sent to the United States (G. Kim, 2005). Until adult adoptees began visiting Korea and demanding recognition for themselves and their birth mothers, no one there discussed this history of intercountry adoption, or spoke of their birth mothers. Both figures were erased from Korean history and pushed into the shadows, eclipsed by the nationalistic prerogative of the country's quest for economic development.

This chapter focuses on the figure of the birth mother, who too often has been overlooked in the discourse of intercountry adoption. The terms *intercountry* and *foreign* adoption were selected over *transnational* or *international* adoption because this research focuses specifically on the historical, geopolitical, cultural, and socioeconomic circumstances, as well as the ramifications of adoption practices between Korea (the sending country) and the United States (the receiving country). In Korea, the term *birth mothers* usually denotes women, whatever their marital status, whose babies were placed for adoption. Circumstances of relinquishment are often due to social constraints such as economic hardship, domestic abuse, prejudice, and the stigmatization of single motherhood. Due to a high correlation between unwed mothers and birth mothers in Korean adoption, people often confuse the terms and use them interchangeably. However, it is important to remember that not all unwed mothers are birth mothers, nor are all

International Korean Adoption
© 2007 by The Haworth Press, Inc. All rights reserved.
doi:10.1300/5734_08

birth mothers unmarried. In particular, the recent but growing attention to the figure of the birth mother on reality television shows suggests a stark contrast with predominant findings in earlier Korean adoption literature.

The figure of the birth mother, both present and absent in the adoption process, has recently become not only visible but more importantly treated as a central, significant figure of Korean adoption discourse. Since the 1980s when the first cohort of Korean adoptees entered adulthood, Korean adoptees have started to become more visible through various cultural formats such as films, videos, artworks, memoirs, and television search shows both in the United States and Korea. Since then, the number of Korean-born adoptees who visit Korea annually has been increasing. This unexpected phenomenon has garnered unprecedented attention after the morally charged accusation by the Western media against Korea's unscrupulous adoption activity in the late 1980s. Over the past fifteen years, Korea's adoption discourse has developed in terms of Korean adoptees' search and their reunion with their birth families, especially their birth mothers. Furthermore, recent studies (Anagnost, 2000; Eng, 2003; Hübinette, 2004; E. Kim, 2003; Yngvesson, 2002) have made invaluable contributions by introducing the perspectives of adoptees and by suggesting a framework that allows for the inclusion of birth mothers' stories and recognition of their re/productive labor in a transnational circuit of human capital.

The growing visibility of Korean adoptees unsettled the "amnesia" of the Korean government and its people. Korean adoptees have raised morally and ethically charged questions such as: "Why couldn't my parents bring me up?" and "Why was I sent away to a foreign country?" Through their presence, the returning adoptees, the ghostly children of Korean history, have demanded that Koreans, including their numerous, unknown birth mothers, remember this traumatic past once erased from the official national history. The astonishing number of Korean children involved in foreign adoption and their ghostly double—birth mothers—bear the mark of a repressed national trauma.

There is very little information about the Korean birth mothers who gave life to the more than 200,000 children placed in foreign adoption. We do not know for sure how many women have been birth mothers in the past fifty years. The overwhelming emotional and social costs, due to the pervasive social stigma faced by these women, have led to their erasure. Consequently, the very impossibility of grasping the figure of the birth mother has led me to engage in interpretive analysis, instead of relying on an empirical set of data, and to explore, instead, a different mode of knowing the birth mother. Drawing both on psychoanalytic accounts of trauma and a new analysis of affective labor in the contemporary service economy, I employ feminist modes of knowing and ethics of memory, involving conceptual tools, such as responsive listening and responsible telling. Responsive listening, as Hirsch and Smith (2002) argue, equips me to be "conscious of granting . . . the irretrievability of the past, the irreducibility of the other, and the untranslatability of the story of trauma" (p. 13). A responsible telling, meanwhile, radicalizes the human capacity for remembering or rendering the past by critically interrogating the historical, geopolitical, and socioeconomic circumstances surrounding these women and their re/productive labor.

This chapter attempts to rethink the premise and ramification of foreign adoption through a critical lens on the figure of the birth mother changing over time. Although it often has been understood historically as a humanitarian effort on the part of private citizens in the Western world, I argue the practice of intercountry adoption is a radical example of global inequality played out at the site of actual women's bodies and often pits two women—the birth mother and the adoptive mother—against each other in a struggle to claim a legitimate motherhood. This chapter critically engages traditional notions of the family, motherhood, and citizenship, on the part of both sending and receiving parties. Therefore, in the following section, I discuss the three historical stages of Korean adoption, focusing on the changing demographics of adoptees, which hints at a figure of the birth mother overlaid in Korea's nationalistic agenda at each period. Hence, my research offers a different analysis from other adoption narratives typically dominated by adoptive parents and adoption professionals' perspectives. The re/productive labor of birth mothers will be examined (1) in the nexus of South Korea's economic development plans and U.S. hegemony in the country, as well as (2) via engaging a new analysis of affective labor, as it relates to the transnational service economy. Through a cross-examination of the major figures of the birth mother that loomed in earlier adoption literature and critical feminist literature, I will reveal how a military prostitute and a woman factory worker served to secure Korea's national agenda at each period. Second, a critical overview of the ways in which the figure of the birth mother is constructed in television documentaries will examine the process by which the motherhood of birth mothers is reclaimed and negotiated, especially in relation to the rhetoric surrounding the American dream and the concept of adoption as a gift. This chapter also suggests the long-term ramifications of intercountry adoption from Korea to the United States, which unilaterally reinforces a moral hierarchy between the two countries, as far as the transnational circulation of human capital is concerned.

I will combine two concerns—nationalist discourse and the political economy of affective labor—to examine how the rhetoric surrounding the

American dream, citizenship, and motherhood is deployed in intercountry adoption. More specifically, my focus is on what David Eng (2003) described as "specific to pre- and post–World War II histories of imperialism, immigration, racialized exploitation, and gendered commodification" (p. 9).

TRAUMA AND THE FIGURE
OF THE BIRTH MOTHER

Cathy Caruth (1996) argues that a traumatic event involves an experience that the subject witnesses but cannot easily remember at all. In turn, the trauma repeats itself, thus demanding the subject to belatedly reexperience the event. The birth mother's relinquishment of her child suggests a traumatic event. Following the separation from the child, the birth mother never has the opportunity to mourn properly, but is affected for the rest of her life (Baik, 1995; Reyman, 2001). The loss of the child may not be directly claimed or consciously experienced by the birth mother, because of the traumatic nature of the parting. However, with the return of adult adoptees, birth mothers, regardless of their knowledge of their children's fate, are made to reexperience the departure of their babies. At the least, they are made to relive the trauma of the experience.

Therefore, the figure of the birth mother, at first excluded from Korean history and often from her own life story, later enters the discourse and materializes as a cultural icon of personal and national trauma; thus, her figure becomes a part of social reality. As Avery Gordon (1997) points out, social reality involves a constant negotiation between what can be seen and what is in the shadows. I propose that the figure of the birth mother haunts the adoption narrative, and thereby I wish to engage what Gordon (1997) describes as "the paradox of tracking through time and across all those forces which make its mark by being there and not there at the same time" (p. 6). The erasure is inseparable from what remains, for what is lost is known only by what remains of it and by how these remains are produced and maintained (Eng & Kazanjian, 2002). This chapter aims to configure birth mothers as a nodal point by which their remains are produced and maintained in the realm of a new affective economy. The figure of the birth mother, erased from adoption narratives but emergent as trauma, is selectively visible through the demographic and cultural shifts that have led to an acknowledgment of the adoptees' cultural and racial identity as foreign adoptees in adoption discourses. Understanding of this trauma forms the theoretical and methodological framework of this project. The next section will review the history of intercountry adoption in terms of how U.S. military and humanitarian actions and Korea's economic development plans interlock two sovereign countries into a kinship system transcending the boundaries of race, class, and citizenships.

INTERCOUNTRY ADOPTION AND KOREA

The history of intercountry adoption is best understood in relation to the Korean War (1950-1953). Prior to the war, Korea had been colonized by Japan for thirty-six years (1909-1945); then, it was "liberated" by the United States and its allies at the end of World War II. Following its liberation from Japan, Korea was divided along the thirty-eighth parallel by the United States and USSR. Each nation installed an occupation government in the region it controlled. This division set the stage for a Cold War face-off on the Korean peninsula and resulted in a devastating war. Even today, fifty years later, the war and its legacy bleeds its consequences into the daily fabric of Korean society.

After the war, the devastated southern part of Korea was rehabilitated with foreign aid from "free world" countries, primarily the United States. For instance, Moon (1997) states that the U.S. military and economic assistance amounted to one-tenth of Korea's GNP until 1970. The United States was seen as a symbol of wealth, democracy, and philanthropy, as well as a big brother. This U.S.-aid-based reconstruction of South Korean society after the Korean War fostered "American fever," which can translate into an absolute belief that "whoever goes to America, his or her life will be better off." The United States was also considered Korea's closest ally despite growing criticism toward the United States' role in the war on the Korean peninsula.[1] According to Chungmoo Choi (1995), "South Korea's economic, political and, most of all, military dependency on the United States allowed for further American intervention into South Korean affairs and firmly situated the nation at the edges of the American empire" (p. 242). This particular geopolitical and cultural background of the U.S. influence in Korea for the past fifty years provides a deeper understanding for the scales and the continuity of intercountry adoption between Korea and the United States.

Since the inception of intercountry adoption, more than 150,000 children, representing more than 75 percent of all adoptees from Korea, have been placed in U.S. families. Thus, Korean adoptees form the majority of all foreign-born children adopted by U.S. citizens (Evan B. Donaldson Adoption Institute, 2001; Kane, 1993). Korean adoptees make up about 10 percent of the entire Korean-American population, though their presence was rarely acknowledged until recently (Hübinette, 2004). Given the dearth of domestic adoption in Korea, the high proportion of children adopted by U.S. families, and the strong military and cultural presence of the United States, adoption in Korea has become synonymous with foreign adoption, particularly in the United States.

I will trace the footprints of the erased birth mothers over the three historical stages of intercountry adoption in terms of the demographics of Korean adoptees. Each stage is rendered in a context that comprehensively analyzes geopolitical and socioeconomic accounts of Korea and the United States. This approach allows me to highlight the Korean government's economic development plan and various discourses over time regarding intercountry adoption, especially to the United States, thereby offering a possibility for a critical interpretation of the erased figure of the birth mother.

The First Stage (Early 1950s to Mid-1960s): Cold War and Adoption

Since the Korean War, the South Korean government has continued to emphasize the importance of national (military) security by holding to the tenet of anticommunism. This bloody war left numerous casualties including more than 100,000 war orphans. After the cessation of the Korean War, instead of establishing domestic social services to deal with orphaned children, the South Korean government, driven by a national agenda of military security and economic development, relied on foreign resources and private humanitarian initiatives (W. Choi, 1996). In addition, the country's massive poverty and the traditional, cultural emphasis of familial blood lineage further discouraged the creation of homes in Korea for orphaned children.

Of the many needy children, mixed-race children were most likely to be considered for homes abroad by the Korean government and private adoption agencies. Most mixed-raced children were born to Korean women and U.S. soldiers stationed at U.S. bases in Korea during and after the war. The women who gave birth to mixed-race children were regarded as military prostitutes.[2] Thus, those children bearing a stigma of their mothers' occupation are identified as a group of children who needed homes outside of Korea. In 1954, the South Korean government established the Child Placement Service *(Adongyanghohoe)* to place biracial children in foreign adoption, particularly to their fathers' country, the United States (Chun, 1989; Hurh, 1967). The Holt Adoption Program, Inc., alone had processed more than 50 percent of adoption placements during this time. As part of a humanitarian response to the war's devastation, adopting children from South Korea was initiated mostly by private citizens in the United States and numerous U.S. servicemen who were at that time stationed in Korea. From the cessation of the war to the mid-1960s, approximately 8,000 children, many of whom were biracial, were placed in Christian families in the United States (Hurh, 1967; Sarri, Baek, & Bombyk, 1998; Weil, 1984). However, Hurh (1967) argues that there is a clear pattern of preference in terms of a child's race and gender. The order of preference is (1) Caucasoid-Korean female, (2) Caucasoid-Korean male, (3) Korean female, (4) Korean male, (5) Negroid-Korean female, and (6) Negroid-Korean male. Despite the soaring number of children who were in need of homes, this was not the time when the number of Korean children placed in intercountry adoption reached its highest annual figure.

The move to place war orphans and biracial children into foreign adoption was done not only to save them from poverty, orphanhood, and stigmatization but also, as Klein (2003) points out, the adoption of Asian babies was part of U.S. foreign policy actively carried out and promoted by Christian missionaries and private agencies by "containing the region" from the threat of communism. According to the prevailing Cold War ideology, the United States was portrayed as the savior of Korea and its children from the threat of communism. Klein (2003) argues that, after World War II, the adoption of Asian babies was aligned with the foreign policy interests of the United States. It is critical to acknowledge that, from the start, humanitarian aid and a political agenda were embedded into the concept and practice of intercountry adoption.

The Second Stage (Mid-1970s to Late 1980s): Development and Adoption

Another national agenda along with Korea's military security was its long-term economic development plan. As part of their development plan, the Korean government implemented a Family Planning Program under the slogan "Raise only two children well" (둘만 낳아 잘 기르자) in order to control the population increase. In addition, the Korean government encouraged the emigration and foreign adoption of financially burdensome children (Chun, 1989; Hurh & Reid, 2000; I. Park, 1994; S. Park, 1994; Sarri, Baik, & Bombyk, 1998). As a result, the number of adopted children increased substantially from the mid-1970s to the 1980s, reaching over 8,000 children at its apex (Chun, 1989; Kane, 1993; Ministry of Health and Social Welfare, 2001; Sarri, Baek, & Bombyk, 1998).

Full-blooded Korean children, mostly born into extreme poverty, provided nearly the entire supply of adoptees during this second stage. At its

peak, in the mid-1980s, Korean babies involved in foreign adoption represented 0.1 percent of all live births in Korea and 20 to 30 percent of all children involved in intercountry adoptions worldwide (Kane, 1993). During
the 1970s and 1980s, young female factory workers formed the largest pool
of birth mothers (Chun, 1989; Hwang & Yoon, 1996; J. Kim, 1974; S. Kim,
1997; Koh, Hong, & Kim, 1989). Also, this is the time when unwed mothers were identified as the source of a social problem, and the leading cause
for foreign adoption.

Since the 1970s, due to the scarcity of healthy white babies available for
adoption in the United States, the number of children in intercountry adoption from Asia has been increasing. Of all Asian children adopted in U.S.
homes since the 1970s, two-thirds were born in Korea (Evan B. Donaldson
Adoption Institute, 2001).

The Third Stage (1988 to the Present): Globalization and Adoption

This period can be characterized by a substantial decrease in the number
of Korean children being placed in foreign adoption, as well as a shift in focus from the children adopted out of Korea to the "returning" Korean-born
adoptees. In 1988, when South Korea prepared to host the Seoul Olympics,
the Western mass media accused Koreans of "baby selling" (Rothschild,
1988). This embarrassing charge led the South Korean government to halt
all foreign adoption that year and actively brought about programs that
worked to decrease the number of children sent out of the country for adoption. Since the adoption scandal in 1988, the Korean government implemented a program to end all overseas adoptions, yet failed to deliver a
reliable and consistent government policy through a national campaign promoting domestic adoption[3] (E. Kim, 2003; Sarri, Baek, & Bombyk, 1998).
The international criticism against South Korea's unscrupulous adoption
activity broke the silence in this shameful part of Korea's history. A myriad
of news articles, television documentaries, and soap operas, as well as feature films, have dealt with foreign adoption from Korea and the figure of the
adoptee as well as his or her birth mother. However, this growing interest in
Korean-born adoptees casts another shadow on the young women who become birth mothers, as they continue to be overlooked.

Today, the number of Korean children in foreign adoption has decreased
to approximately 2,200 children each year. But it still exceeds the number
of Korean children in domestic adoption. A significant percentage of the
children in foreign adoption have been reported to have special needs
(C. Kim, 2000). Almost all these babies were born to unwed mothers, rang-

ing mostly from their late teens to early twenties (Ministry of Health and Social Welfare, 2003). Since the late 1990s, the Korean government has begun acknowledging the overseas adoptee community as part of the Korean diaspora under the rhetoric of globalization *(se-gye-wha)*. In 1998, President Kim Dae Jung gave a historical public apology to all adoptees, further asserting that they were overseas Koreans who would carry on the significant role of bridging East and West, and in advancing Korea's global interests (Hübinette, 2002; E. Kim, 2003). Adoptees reared in Western countries are seen as potentially useful for enhancing Korea's economic development and competition in a world market.

There is a lack of accurate documents concerning birth mothers, and what social work literature does exist is filled with stereotypes and overgeneralization of birth mothers in Korea. Based on the three different categories of women identified in earlier literature, I wish to offer a subversive view of the figure of the birth mothers in order to illuminate the underlying forces that lock them in undesirable and even dangerous categories of women. Further, I wish to illustrate how the figure of the birth mother served to secure Korea's national development, which was closely tied with U.S.-led world hegemony.

THREE COHORTS OF BIRTH MOTHERS' CHARACTERISTICS IN KOREA

The Korean adoption literature identifies three categories of women as potential birth mothers: women who are engaged in the sex industry, women working in low-paying factory jobs, and runaway teenagers (Hurh, 1967; Hwang & Yoon, 1996; J. Kim, 1974). I offer an examination of these three populations, and consider how the re/productive labors of birth mothers have been contingent on different historical stages of adoption, particularly in relation to Korea's economic development plan, which is closely associated with U.S. military dominance, as well as a birth mother's role in the U.S.-led world economy.

Birth mothers who formed the first cohort (1950s and 1960s) were said to have "undesirable occupational statuses" as *yang sekshi* or military prostitutes (Hurh, 1967, p. 11), a considerable number of whose children were of mixed race. The existence of military prostitutes was often missing in the official foreign relations' discourse between Korea and the United States. Yet, they were well-known as "unofficial ambassadors," responsible for taking care of the emotional and personal needs of U.S. soldiers in their mission to keep the Korean peninsula safe (Enloe, 1990; Moon, 1997; Yuh,

2002). Thus, the first birth mothers, military prostitutes, served as indirect agents for national security, while the South Korean government and adoption agencies encouraged them to place their *twi-gi* (biracial) children in adoption (Higginson & Kearly, 2003; Hurh, 1967; Meier, 1999). The biracial children represented their mothers' illegitimate sexual behaviors with foreigners, thus carrying over a mother's shame and Korea's shame. A difficult life in Korea was anticipated for these children, and so they were of the first to be placed on the waiting list for intercountry adoption.

The second cohort of women was identified as young factory workers. In the 1970s and 1980s they played a major role in "the miracle of the Han," i.e., South Korea's rapid industrialization and corresponding explosion in Gross National Product. The state-led industrial sector recruited young women from rural regions in Korea to work in factories set up in free-trade zones. These factories predominantly manufactured textile and shoes, and sought to exploit the Asian women's labor (Mohanty, 1991; Ong, 1987). A rapid industrialization accompanied with urbanization led to a disruption of traditional family reflected in a changing notion of women's productive labor and their independent living arrangements. These female factory workers resuscitated and secured Korea's economic future by enduring unbearable work conditions and harassment (S. Kim, 1997). The majority of female workers whose average income was far below a livable wage arranged a particular residence to make ends meet by sharing a room with multiple fellow factory workers, which contributed to their unplanned pregnancies. In turn, factory women workers' bodies have been employed to produce commodities, from famous designer athletic footwear to babies.

The third cohort of birth mothers (from the late 1980s to the present) is characterized as troubled teenage girls—high school dropouts or runaways from dysfunctional families saddled with poverty, domestic violence, or sexual abuse from stepfamily or single-parent households. The way in which a pregnant high school student becomes a dropout is noteworthy for the following reason. The Korean educational system does not commonly allow pregnant girls to continue in school. In most cases, a girl gets pregnant first and then "chooses" to drop out voluntarily before school authorities kick her out. Birth mothers are characterized as troubled teenagers who are not ready to be mothers, and therefore are undeserving of public assistance to rear their children.

However, my research on birth mothers' Web sites in 2005 suggests that most women in their early twenties were engaged in a relationship when they conceived a baby. Today, one out of four women wants to keep her baby, reflected in my findings (G. Kim, 2005). Due to social stigma of the single mothers and double standard, these young women are not supported by their very own families and friends, which leaves them no other option except adoption. In other words, contemporary Korean birth mothers place their own babies up for adoption; thus they maintain an ideal of heterosexual and middle-class family formation.

This examination of birth mothers and their stigmatized positions as workers and as troubled girls suggests the roles that women's bodies have played in South Korea's economic development and its engagement in global capitalism. These adoption practices have evolved at the expense of the women's re/productive labors. Thus, intercountry adoption further reinstates South Korean nationalist discourse, reinforcing a sexualized and gendered relationship to the United States, as (fore)shadowed in the figure of the birth mother (Kim & Choi, 1998).

Numerous studies show a high correlation between unwed mothers and birth mothers who give up their children for adoption (Chun, 1989; Hwang & Yoon, 1996; J. Kim, 1974; S. Kim, 1997; Park, Cho, & Chae, 1993). This finding reflects a trend in the social scientific literature to attribute the source of foreign adoption to the illegitimate sexual conduct of women. In light of such studies, policy analysts argued strongly for preventive programs focusing on sex education for vulnerable young women. The emphasis on single unwed mothers neglects the significant number of women in common-law or legal marriages who gave up their children for adoption because of extreme poverty, which recent adoption discourse identifies as a sole cause for foreign adoption in Korea. This analytical trend reflects a double standard and social prejudice against poor, unmarried women, and thus reinforces heterosexual, middle-class, male-centered family formations in Korea through the regulation of women's sexuality. While Korean unwed mothers are accused of being "a source of foreign adoption," there is no discussion of their male counterparts, unwed fathers, thus reflecting the sexual double standard that rules the lives of men and women (Chun, 1989; J. Kim, 1974; Park, Cho, & Chae, 1993). It is within this historical context that the narratives of the birth mothers have been silenced. Over the years, the figure of the birth mother has all but disappeared from Korea's domestic discussion about adoption. With Korean-born adoptees' return and search for their birth families, the figure of the birth mother on television search shows illustrates a stark contrast with the figure once identified as its shadow and creates a cleavage of the figure of the birth mother in adoption discourse.

AFFECT ECONOMY AND THE FIGURE
OF THE BIRTH MOTHER

To adoptive parents, the presence of birth mothers can be discomfiting (Brodzinsky & Brodzinsky, 1998; Rush, 2002; Wegar, 1997; Yngvesson, 1997). One of the most prevalent reasons for adopting foreign-born babies is the idea that transnational adoptions are closed transactions (Berry, Barth, & Needell, 1996). The adoptee's past is sealed with institutional support, i.e., the legal and social mechanisms of adoption are based on confidentiality or secrecy (Wegar, 1997). For example, when a child is adopted, the adoptive parents' names replace the birth parents' on the new birth certificate (Bartholet, 1999; Wegar, 1997; Yngvesson, 1997). Therefore, a child is technically *born* to adoptive parents. However, since transnational adoption often involves obvious physical differences between the parents and child, it requires a constant and deliberate effort from the adoptee, as well as the adoptive parents, to construct a middle-class, white American family. Such constructions often neglect the differences imbricated in the child's past. Thus, the "present absence" of the birth mother is culturally, psychologically, and racially always within an adoptive family.

Throughout the 1970s and 1980s organizations, such as Concerned United Birthparents (CUB) in the United States, advocated on behalf of adoptees for the rights of birth parents. They fought for adoptees' rights to gain access to their birth records and to seek reunions with their birth families (Wegar, 1997). In 1972, the National Association of Black Social Workers (NABSW) expressed concerns about transracial adoptions, arguing that white parents were not equipped to help black children deal with racism. The heated debates over transracial adoptions and the rights of adoptees to access their birth records generated considerable interest in the racial and cultural identity formation of transnational adoptees. This development enabled a new understanding of birth mothers and of the adoptees' pasts (Anagnost, 2000; Wegar, 1997; Yngvesson, 1997). The rebuilding of the adoptees' cultural and racial identity, as Anagnost (2000) discussed, involves affective labor, which generally is understood to be the feminine labor of caring and nurturing. It often belongs to the realm of adoptive mothers' labor.

The adoption economy can be characterized in terms of contemporary service economy, what Michael Hardt (1999) described as a system in which "information, communication, knowledge, and affect come to play a foundational role in the production process" (p. 92). All involved activities in adoption are to ensure the children's well-being. Long before adoptive mothers engage in their maternal labor, there has been a division of affective labor conducted by various participants, including foster mothers, orphanage workers, social workers at adoption agencies, and birth mothers. These components construct a global system of stratified reproduction. The current practices of adoption, I might argue, emphasize the presence of birth mothers and their caring labor more than ever before. This foregrounding convinces adoptive parents that their adopted child has the potential to be successful and thus worthy of their emotional and material investment. The presence of other (birth) mothers, and their losses at one end of adoption, as Anagnost (2000) states, offers the reassurance that "there was a bond, [and] affect, at the origin, that the child will be capable of delivering fully on its promise of love" (p. 400). As a result, birth mothers serve as significant figures that provide "affectively necessary labor" that ensures a successful adoption (Hardt, 1999, p. 100). They also are treated as a primal bond to the adoptees' racial/cultural identity in the growing, postadoption, and service economy, i.e., annual cultural festivals, culture camps, and trips to the *motherland*.

Since the late 1980s, the number of Korean adoptees from the United States and Europe who visit Korea has been rising, approximately 2,000 to 3,000 each year. Corresponding to the rise in returning adoptees, a myriad of television shows has covered adoptees' experiences and their search for their biological Korean families. Since the 1980s television search shows have not only broadcast reunions between Korean adoptees and their birth families but also have assisted in searches for birth families and have filmed reunions with birth mothers. As a result, television shows have become a primary source of public discourse about Korean adoptees and their birth mothers. On these television shows, birth mothers, who had previously been erased from the adoption narrative, emerge as significant figures that appear to reconcile the pains and losses of foreign adoption through meeting their children and reclaiming their motherhood. The returning adoptees and their birth mothers are often brought together through a communication apparatus (television) that can deploy this production of affects. Here, I argue that birth mothers are made the affective figure, encapsulated in a dominant narrative of adoptees as *successful citizens* and of foreign adoption as being unfortunate, but inevitably necessary. The nation's shame and guilt over relinquishing its children is interlaced with foreign adoptions from Korea, and has led to the embracing of Korean adoptees with the rhetoric of motherland.

The dominant narrative surrounding returning adoptees today in Korea tends to celebrate their resilience and their successes. The adoptee's return to Korea is interpreted as an inevitable homecoming, a manifestation of irrevocable Korean identity in the old saying that "blood is thicker than water," thus reinforcing the significance of a blood lineage that underlies the heterosexual patriarchal family. Ironically, this patriarchal bias was a major social order that disapproves of single mothers. The return of adoptees is presented as a premise to reclaim the motherhood for the birth mother, who is made to incorporate the adoptees' successful stories into their motherly investment in adoption, a dominant narrative that parallels Korea's own development. Thus, the adoptees' losses and pains, the dark side of their success, have never been fully recognized or understood. Instead, their pains are subsumed in their reunion stories with their birth mothers, thus playing out a popular genre of Korean television.

According to the search and reunion narrative that is popular on television, the circumstances around the adoptee's birth and adoption often involve extreme poverty or undesirable living conditions due to a separation from the birth mother's husband. These separations can be caused by natural deaths, divorce, or domestic abuse. These all suggest the circumstances of their birth were within a marriage and that the figure of the birth mother was already a legitimate mother who is different from the figure of the unwed mother characterized by her immoral sexual behavior. Thus, this figure of the birth mother is ready to deliver, in front of adoptees and on television, *immortal motherly love* and a public apology for her original lack of mothering. The ambivalence and other unresolved feelings felt by adoptees and/or birth mothers surrounding their reunion often are glossed over by the media's depiction of adoptees as successful adults. Most television shows present the personal traumatic experiences of both adoptees and birth families as completely resolved, merely by virtue of their meeting. Furthermore, they quickly jump to an assumption of "living happily ever after" following the reunion. Such narratives contrast with the reality of many postreunion cases. In reality, adoptees and birth mothers often have trouble rebuilding a relationship, owing to the lack of a shared language, history, and cultural background, as well as the disparities in geographic and socioeconomic locations (M. Park, 2001).

These television shows perform "important cultural work in constituting and consolidating group identities" in terms of carving out personal and collective memories (Hirsch & Smith, 2002, p. 8). Korean adoptees are the objects of a sentimental economy, i.e., foreign adoption. These returning adoptees attest to the personal trauma, as well as the national trauma of the devastating Korean War and the extreme poverty that followed. In addition, their presence asks the South Korean government and its citizens to reflect on their own moral responsibilities in regard to placing children into foreign adoptions. As a circuit of affect creation and manipulation in the entertainment industry, these television shows produce "collective subjectivities and sociality" around foreign adoption (Hardt, 1999, p. 92). Laden with strong emotions, they package the pain and losses of adoptees and birth mothers as temporally and spatially contained, and invoke television viewers to redeem the trauma through "feelings of ease, well-being, satisfaction, excitement, and passion; [there is] even a sense of connectedness or community as a result of affect creation and manipulation by the entertainment industry" (Hardt, 1999, p. 96). The figure of the birth mother is deployed as a site of reconciliation upon their reunion with their children for personal as well as national trauma in Korea.

To sum up, the affect economy connects the traumatic losses of birth mothers with the adoptive parents' desire for a child (often thwarted due to infertility). Increasingly, the figure of the birth mother is deployed as an affective pull, producing the adoptee's desire to return to the motherland in search of the mother; all these narratives are scripted into the discourse of South Korea as motherland. Thus, the figure of the birth mother generates a certain kind of affect consolidation, both in the national discourse and in the global affect economy. In the following section, I illustrate how this emerging figure of the televised birth mother slips into the intersection of two discourses: (1) the gift rhetoric of adoption discourse; and (2) the American dream, as embodied in the success of returning adoptees.

THE CHILD AS GIFT OR ADOPTION AS GIFT?

In U.S. adoption discourse, the gift rhetoric views the child not as an object of the marketplace but rather as a gift of birth mothers. Stemming from a discomfort with the commodification of children, this narrative became popular in U.S. cultural discourses of adoption, despite its limited analysis[4] of race and class (Rothman, 2000; Solinger, 2001). The rhetoric of gift emphasized particular qualities of gift giving, such as love, generosity, reciprocity, and permanent connections between the parties; it developed along with an increasing rate of open adoptions that gave some leverage to U.S. birth mothers of "desirable babies," usually meaning healthy, white babies (Modell, 1999). This shift from viewing the adoptee as a child salvaged by adoptive parents to the child seen as a gift from birth mothers is manifested in intercountry adoption practices. However, the ways in which the gift rhetoric is understood in intercountry adoption may not promise a quality, ongoing relationship between the U.S. parents and the Korean birth mother. This is due to the closed nature of adoption practices, as well as the wide disparity in the two parties' geographical, cultural, national, and socioeconomic locations.

The idea of adoption being a gift for the child is used both by U.S. adoptive parents and Korean birth mothers. However, the ways in which gift rhetoric has played out suggests that adoption itself, and not the child, is the gift being given. For example, from Dorow's (1999) edited collection of Korean birth mothers' letters to their own babies, "Adoption was my gift to you. I wished for you to have many opportunities. I believe you have those opportunities now" (p. 37). An adoptive mother's letter to her son's birth mother stated ". . . one day your son will be able to thank you himself for being so selfless and loving to him" (Holt International Inc., 2003, p. 7). These sentiments suggest that adoption guarantees a better life for the child. Often, the better life that adoption offers is premised only in terms of material conditions; such an ideation ignores the multiple set of losses to the child, as well as to the birth family, loss that often resonates as an ongoing trauma for the rest of their lives. Considering the geopolitical, cultural, historical, and economic contexts in which Korea and the United States were embedded after the war, this gift rhetoric informs and is informed by the affective relationship between the United States and Korea, especially in terms of the American dream.

The term *American dream,* coined by Horatio Alger, refers to the idea that living in America is a vast opportunity in which anyone can become successful and wealthy through honesty, hard work, and fixed determination. This notion of "American dream" is contextualized in postwar Korea as a cultural reality of "American fever" *(miguk byong)*. American fever, borrowing from Yuh's elaboration (2002), is "the desire to escape crowded, tiny, repressive Korea for expansive, freedom-filled America, to escape the ordinariness and the poverty and seek one's fortune in a land of opportunity" (p. 66). The American dream is a key motivation for many Korean immigrants seeking a better life in the United States. Given this as a cultural background and the high rate of children in foreign adoption who have been sent to U.S. families, the gift rhetoric of adoption suggests that the child will receive maximum opportunities if given up for adoption in the United States. The birth mother's loss is translated as absolute love for the child, and I might argue, is read as a maternal sacrifice on behalf of better mothering. The birth mother's relinquishment of her child is interpreted as the sacrificing of an incompetent motherhood for a dutiful motherhood (Park, Cho, & Chae, 1993; Reyman, 2001).

Whereas the gift rhetoric in the U.S. adoption discourse demands adoptive parents show gratitude toward birth mothers who have given up their precious babies, Korean birth mothers must show gratitude toward U.S. adoptive parents for rearing their Korean children with the best of opportunities. The Korean birth mother who is reunited with her child on television often expresses her gratitude toward the adoptive parents and country. One birth mother who met her child's adoptive parents said, "Thank you for raising [my] child so well" (B. Park, 2001). Thus, in the midst of the media's overwhelming emphasis on the "returning" adoptees' successes, the figure of the Korean birth mother plays into the gift rhetoric, intertwined with the American dream, and forming a moralistic indictment inherent in the practice of intercountry adoption and transnational capitalism.

The American dream, with its promise of a better life for the adopted child, is not limited to Korea; it is widely circulated in intercountry adoption sites where the United States has been the dominant receiving country (Escobar, 1995; Ortiz & Briggs, 2003; Rush, 2002). Many Americans conceive of transnational adoption as morally compelling "because they believe America offers the 'best' place of refuge to needy children" (Rush, 2002, p. 118). The American dream is also at work in stereotyping Asians in the United States in terms of the "model minority myth"; such stereotypes produce the desire for Asian children, when healthy, white babies are unavailable for adoption. Asian children, seen as obedient and high achieving, are presented as evidence of the benefits of being raised in the United States, thereby intensifying the preference for Asian children in transnational adoption (Eng, 2003). While Asian-Americans are thought of as a "model minority" living out the "American dream," they are nonetheless denied full integration or assimilation into U.S. society (Eng & Han, 2000; Lowe, 1996). The adoptees' unassimilable Asian features constantly haunt adoptees, unwittingly pointing to birth mothers, the "ghostly doubles" that give adoptees the status of "perpetual foreigners" (Anagnost, 2000; Eng & Han, 2000). The birth mothers again become a mark of trauma; accordingly, it might be more accurate to say, as Cheng (2001) declared, that "the origins of the American dream [for Korean adoptees] in the U.S. are built on the structure of loss, grief, and entombment [of birth mothers]" (p. 9).

ACTIVATING THE MEMORY OF BIRTH MOTHERS

It has taken fifty years for the figure of Korean adoptees and their birth mothers to appear in Korean history. As Bal (1999) argues, "[T]o enter memory [means] the traumatic past needs to be made narratable" (p. iv). This chapter as part of a larger project on Korean birth mothers attempts to provide a critical framework in which the traumatic pasts interlaced in the intercountry adoption between Korea and the United States can be acknowledged, thereby offering a critical interpretation to the figure of birth mothers who *are there and are not there, at the same time,* over the past fifty years.

The figure of birth mothers, once erased in adoption discourses, has become visible through the acknowledgment of their affective labor—virtual, caring labor. Thus, the emerging birth mother is manifested in the rapidly growing postadoption service economy, as well as the entertainment industry. Within this economy, the rhetoric surrounding Korean patriarchal family formation, which had long denied motherhood to single women, now interprets the Korean adoptees' returns as an inevitable homecoming. Their returns appear as "returns to the investment" that birth mothers have made by placing their children into foreign adoption, thereby nominally granting motherhood to these women. The narrative of birth mothers on television rewrites the birth mother's loss as the birth mother's sacrifice; their (incompetent) mothering is relinquished, and adoption to the United States is seen as their best gift, thus repetitively corroborating the success of the American dream embodied in the returning adoptees. The selectively visible figure of birth mothers also can be read as a site of the "collectivization of affectivity," where the birth mothers' pains and losses are defined as an unfortunate, but inevitable, part of a shared Korean national history. The site also produces a value in the affective economy of adoption by its pull, drawing adoptees and their adoptive parents to the motherland. But this selectively visible figure of the birth mother revolving around search and reunion narratives also informs that not all birth mothers are unwed mothers.

This chapter engages a subversive reading of birth mothers as in/visible figures in terms of their re/productive labors in order to challenge dominant adoption narratives about saving children and of children being gifts. Through this cross-cultural examination of the adoption literature in the United States and Korea, it is clear that the adoption narrative of intercountry adoption has always been constituted as an affective relationship between sending and adoptive parents, as well as between sending and adoptive countries (Choi, 1998; Rush, 2002; Yngvesson, 2002). In other words, senders are obliged to feel ashamed of sending off children and, in turn, to be indebted to adopters who will give care and nurturance to their offspring. Given Korea's tenacious and vigorous activities in intercountry adoption over the past fifty years, the adoption narrative, particularly with its emphasis on a "better life" through adoption, has unwittingly functioned to reassert the United States' benevolence and moral superiority over an irresponsible Korea, signified as an irresponsible birth mother.

Following a feminist methodology, as Hirsch and Smith (2002) suggested, I have employed a "responsive listening" to the silences of birth mothers in adoption discourses and a responsible telling by contextualizing the bodies of birth mothers in intricate webs of geopolitical, socioeconomic, and cultural specificities that surround intercountry adoption between South Korea and the United States. My strategy aims to reorganize the narrative of intercountry adoption with the figure of the birth mother as the center of analysis, thus fostering an ethical and political scholarship on Korean birth mothers.

Today, the "reclaimed" motherhood for birth mothers is being juxtaposed with the Korean government's efforts to reconcile this shameful history. Meanwhile, about 2,000 women are newly becoming birth mothers each year. In order for Korea to reconcile its shame and guilt, I believe it is crucial for women who want to keep their babies to be socially and materially allowed to raise their children on their own. This chapter challenges the narrow, prevailing definition of a legitimate family formation; often it is restricted to a heterosexual, patrilineal, middle-class family formation. I hope this chapter prompts a critical dialogue, engaging and activating the incipient bodies of the birth mothers in transnational adoption.

NOTES

1. The official rhetoric has been contested widely since two junior high school girls were killed by a U.S. armory vehicle around the U.S. bases in 2002 in South Korea. Koreans demanded that the GIs and their supervisors be brought to the Korean courts for justice, while the U.S. government did not offer a public apology. Thus, even the general public in South Korea realized the unequal relationship between the United States and South Korea and demanded the revision of the SOFA (Statue of Forces Agreement) between the United States and Korea. This incident played a key role in raising the consciousness of the Korean general public's awareness of the crimes against civilians by U.S. military personnel since the Korean War and in shifting the perspective of Korean people toward the United States and in helping them to question the nature of a "brotherly" diplomatic relationship.

2. K. Moon (1997) and Yuh (2002) argue that approximately 1 million Korean women have engaged in military prostitution as institutionalized industry around the U.S. foreign bases in South Korea since 1945.

3. The South Korean government's attempt to terminate foreign adoption has been repetitively revoked since its initial plan in 1960, mostly in response to North Korea's accusation of South Korea selling babies to foreign countries. It is clearly illustrated in a recent interview with Kim, Geun Tae, a minister of health and welfare in Korea: "Foreign adoption is not the best, nor the second to best solution even (to children in need of home). Maybe it is a fire exit. It will be stopped. But *not right now*. I am *not* considering to propose a bill or make a legislature to stop foreign adoption from Korea" (aired on *KBS,* May 25, 2005; italics added).

4. Rothman (2000) and Solinger (2001) questioned how freely birth mothers can exercise their "choice" on the grounds that they have limited resources or lack of

subsistence. Yngvesson (2002) also argued that the gift rhetoric obscures "the dependencies and inequalities that compel some of us to give birth to and give up our children while constituting others as 'free' to adopt them" (p. 230).

REFERENCES

Anagnost, A. (2000). Scenes of misrecognition: Maternal citizenship in the age of transnational adoption. *Positions, 8*(2), 389-421.

Baik, Y. (1995). A study on mental health issues of birth mothers who relinquish their children. *Chongshin Boghun kwa Sah Hwo Sahyop, 2,* 121-140.

Bal, M. (1999). Introduction. In Bal, M., Crewe, J., & Spitzer, L. (Eds.), *Acts of memory: Cultural recall in the present* (pp. vii-xvii). Hanover, NH: Dartmouth College.

Bartholet, E. (1999). *Family bonds: Adoption, infertility, and the new world of child production.* New York: Beacon Press.

Berry, M., Barth, R. P., & Needell, B. (1996). Preparation, support, and satisfaction of adoptive families in agency and independent adoptions. *Child and Adolescent Social Work Journal, 13*(2), 157-183.

Brodzinsky, D., Smith, D.W., & Brodzinsky, A. B. (1998). *Children's adjustment to adoption: Developmental and clinical issues.* Thousand Oaks, CA: Sage Publications.

Caruth, C. (1996). *Unclaimed experience: Trauma, narrative, history.* New York: Johns Hopkins University Press.

Cheng, A. A. (2001). *Melancholy of race: Psychoanalysis, assimilation, and hidden grief.* Cary, NC: Oxford University Press.

Choi, C. (1995). Transcapitalism, national imaginary, and the protest theater in South Korea. *Boundary 2, 22*(1), 235-261.

Choi, C. (1998). Nationalism and construction of gender in Korea in dangerous women. In E. Kim & C. Choi (Eds.), *Dangerous women: Gender & Korean nationalism* (pp. 9-32). New York: Routledge.

Choi, W. (1996). *Oeguk' minganwonjodanch' eui hwaldongwoa hanguksahoesaon paljone mich'in yonghyang* [Activities of foreign voluntary agencies and their influences upon social work development in Korea]. Unpublished doctoral dissertation, Seoul National University, Korea.

Chun, B. (1989). Adoption and Korea. *Child Welfare, 68*(2), 255-260.

Dorow, S. (1999). *I wish for you a beautiful life.* St. Paul, MN: Yeong & Yeong Book Company.

Eng, D. (2003). Transnational adoption and queer diasporas. *Social Text, 21*(3), 1-37.

Eng, D., & Han, S. (2000). A dialogue on racial melancholia. *Psychoanalytic Dialogues, 10*(4), 667-700.

Eng, D., & Kazanjian, D. (2002). *Loss: The politics of mourning.* Berkeley: University of California Press.

Enloe, C. (1990). *Bananas, beaches, bases: Making feminist sense of international politics.* Berkeley: University of California Press.

Escobar, A. (1995). *Encountering development: The making and unmaking of the Third World.* Princeton, NJ: Princeton University Press.

Evan B. Donaldson Adoption Institute (2001). *Annual Report.* New York: Evan B. Donaldson Adoption Institute.

Gordon, A. (1997). *Ghostly matters: Haunting and the sociological imagination.* Minneapolis: University of Minnesota Press.

Hardt, M. (1999). Affective labor. *Boundary 2, 26*(2), 89-100.

Higginson, J., & Kearly, P. (2003). *Unlocking the past.* Flat Rock, MI: A.N.Y.O. Publishing Company.

Hirsch, M., & Smith, V. (2002). Feminism and cultural memory: An introduction. *Signs, 28*(1), 1-19.

Holt International Inc. (December 2003). Letter from an adoptive mother. *Together with Holt, 3,* 6-7.

Hübinette, T. (2002). *The adopted Koreans–diaspora politics and the construction of an ethnic identity.* Proceedings at the First World Conference of Korean Studies, Academy of Korean studies, SeongNam, Korea.

Hübinette, T. (2004). Adopted Koreans and the development of identity in the "third space." *Adoption & Fostering, 28*(1), 16-24.

Hurh, N. S., & Reid, W. J. (2000). Intercountry, transnational adoption, and ethnic identity. *International Social Work, 43*(1), 75-87.

Hurh, W. (1967). *Marginal children of war: An exploratory study of American-Korean children.* Proceedings at the Joint Meeting of Midwest and Ohio Valley Sociological Societies.

Hwang, O., & Yoon, M. (1996). The study of the development of the characteristics of unwed mothers in Korea. *Dongguk Journal: Humanities & Social Sciences, 35,* 219-247.

Kane, S. (1993). The movement of children for international adoption: An epistemological perspective. *The Social Science Journal, 31*(4), 323-339.

Kim, C. (May 2000). In search of Korean children sent for the U.S. [Electronic version]. *Monthly Chosun.* Retrieved February 24, 2003, from http://www.monthly.chosun.com/html/200004/200004220003_21.html.

Kim, E., & Choi, C. (1998). *Dangerous women: Gender & Korean nationalism.* New York: Routledge.

Kim, E. (2003). Wedding, citizenship, and culture: Korean adoptees and the global family of Korea. *Social Text, 21*(1), 57-81.

Kim, G. (Executive Producer). (May 25, 2005). The country exporting babies: The double faces of foreign adoption. [Television series]. In *In-Depth 60 Minutes.* Seoul, Korea: KBS.

Kim, J. (1974). Mee-hon-mo ui daehahn Yeonku [A study of unwed mothers]. Unpublished master's thesis, Ewha Women's University, Seoul, Korea.

Kim, S. (1997). *Class struggle or family struggle? The lives of women factory workers in South Korea.* New York: Cambridge University Press.

Klein, C. (2003). *Cold War orientalism.* Berkeley: University of California Press.

Koh, J., Hong, S., & Kim, S. (Executive Producers). (September 1989). Jee-ghum woorinen–Haewoeipyangah [Now what? Korea born foreign adoptees] [Television broadcast]. Seoul, Korea: MBC.

Lowe, L. (1996). *Immigrant acts: On Asian American cultural politics.* Durham, NC: Duke University Press.

Meier, D. (1999). *Loss and reclaimed lives: Cultural identity and place in Korean-American intercountry adoptees.* Unpublished doctoral dissertation, University of Minnesota, Minneapolis.

Ministry of Health and Social Welfare (2001). *Statistics of children who were in foreign adoption.* Seoul, Korea.

Ministry of Health and Social Welfare (2003). *Statistics of children who were in foreign adoption.* Seoul, Korea.

Modell, J. (1999). Freely given: Open adoption and the rhetoric of the gift. In L. Layne, (Ed.), *Transformative motherhood* (pp. 29-64). New York: New York University Press.

Mohanty, C. (1991). Under Western eyes. In C. T. Mohanty, A. Russo, & L. Torres (Eds.), *Third World women and the politics of feminism* (pp. 51-80). Bloomington: Indiana University Press.

Moon, K. (1997). *Sex among allies.* New York: Columbia University Press.

Ong, A. (1987). *Spirits of resistance and capitalist discipline: Factory women in Malaysia.* Albany: State University of New York Press.

Ortiz, A. T., & Briggs, L. (2003). The culture of poverty, crack babies, and welfare cheats: The making of the "healthy White baby crisis." *Social Text, 21*(3), 39-57.

Overseas Koreans Foundation (2004). *Community 2004: Guide to Korea for overseas adopted Koreans.* Seoul, Korea.

Park, B. (Executive Producer). (September 9, 2001). Hyunduk Sebastian's Special Homecoming [Television series episode]. In *KBS Sunday Special.* Seoul, Korea: KBS.

Park, H., Cho, Y., & Chae. M. (1993). Mee-hon-mo cheongchak eo dae han yosonghak jok bee pahn [A feminist critique on social policy of unwed mothers]. *Ehwa Women's University Graduate Studies Seminar, 25,* 268-302.

Park, I. (1994). *A study on search of Korean young Adult adopted persons in the USA.* Unpublished doctoral dissertation, Ewha Women's University, Seoul, Korea.

Park, M. (2001). *An Exploratory Study on Reunion after Adoption–From the Viewpoint of the Birth Mothers.* Unpublished master's thesis, Ewha Women's University, Seoul, Korea.

Park, S. (1994). *Forced child migration: Korean-born intercountry adoptees in the United States.* Unpublished doctoral dissertation, University of Hawaii.

Reyman, L. (2001). *Musings of a ghost mother.* Kearny, NE: I&L Publishing.

Rothman, B. (2000). *Re-creating motherhood* (2nd ed.). New Brunswick: Rutgers University Press.

Rothschild, M. (January 1988). Baby for sale. South Koreans make them, Americans buy them. *Progressive 52*(1), 18-23.

Rush, S. E. (2002). Domestic and international adoptions: Heroes? Villains? or Loving parents? The race and nationality precepts as explanations for international adoptions. In B. E. Hernandez-Truyol (Ed.), *Moral imperialism: A critical anthology* (pp. 116-132). New York: New York University Press.

Sarri, R. C., Baek, Y., & Bombyk, M. (1998). Goal displacement and dependency in South Korean–United States intercountry adoption. *Children and Youth Review, 20*, 87-114.

Shiao, J., Tuan, M., & Rienzi, E. (2004). Shifting the spotlight: Exploring race and culture in Korean-White adoptive families. *Race & Society, 6*(1).

Solinger, R. (2001). *Beggars and choosers: How the politics of choice shapes adoption, abortion, & welfare in the US.* New York: Hill and Wang, Inc.

Takagi, J. T., & Park, H. (1995). *Women outside* [Documentary Film]. New York: Third World Newsreels.

Wegar, K. (1997). *Adoption, identity, and kinship: The debate over sealed birth records.* New Haven, CT: Yale University Press.

Weil, R. (1984). International adoptions: The quiet migration. *International Migration Review, 18*(2), 276-293.

Yngvesson, B. (1997). Negotiating motherhood: Identity and difference in "open" adoptions. *Law & Society Review, 31*(1), 31-68.

Yngvesson, B. (2002). Placing the "gift child" in transnational adoption. *Law & Society Review, 36*(2), 227-256.

Yuh, J. (2002). *Beyond the shadow of Camptown.* New York: New York University Press.

Chapter 9

A Sociological Approach to Race, Identity, and Asian Adoption

Jiannbin L. Shiao
Mia H. Tuan

INTRODUCTION

Since 1948, more than 140,000 Asian adoptees have been raised in the United States, primarily by parents and kin who are white (Figure 9.1). Coming mainly from Korea, but more recently from China, Asian adoptees constitute the bulk of what Weil (1984) has referred to as the "quiet migration" of international adoptees. As a group whose existence challenges traditional rules for racial engagement and intimacy, Asian adoptees provide a significant case for extending sociological theories on race, identity, and the Asian-American experience. In this chapter, we link the study of Asian adoption to broader sociological concerns. As an alternative to the dominant psychosocial approach in the adoption literature, we offer an approach viewing racial/ethnic identity as a dynamic formation in relation to wider social contexts that can change over the life course. To illustrate, we draw from data collected for our study, titled "Asian Immigrants in White Families: Korean Adoptees in America," and offer preliminary analyses.

THE ASIAN ADOPTION PHENOMENON

In 1955, Harry and Bertha Holt revolutionized adoption practices by adopting eight Korean children orphaned by the Korean War. While they were not the first to adopt foreign-born children, the Holts' decision received major media attention and spurred other, mostly white, American families

International Korean Adoption
© 2007 by The Haworth Press, Inc. All rights reserved.
doi:10.1300/5734_09

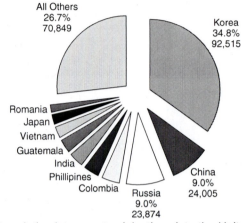

FIGURE 9.1. Cumulative Intercountry Adoptions into the United States, 1948–2000. *Note:* Data sources are Altstein and Simon 1991 and U.S. State Department 1998. Total children adopted 1948-1987: 137,437. Total orphan visas FY1989-2000: 128,087; 1988 data is unavailable. State Department data for "All Others" include only the top 20+ source countries.

to follow suit. Their actions contributed to a shift in the culture of adoption. Prior to this, adoptions typically took place under a shroud of secrecy as families sought to conceal any evidence of parental infertility (Simon, 1994). Efforts were made to match children on the bases of ethnicity, race, religion, and social background. The Holts' actions publicly legitimized transracial and cross-cultural adoptions on humanitarian grounds. In response to overwhelming inquiries from prospective parents, the Holts founded one of the first and largest international adoption agencies, thus eventually institutionalizing the practice of adopting from abroad.

While exact figures are hard to come by, in 2001 nearly one out of every three children adopted in the United States was an international adoptee (Kinder, 2003). In recent years eastern Europe and Latin America, most notably Russia and Colombia, have become major sources for adoptable children. However, neither region compares to Asia in terms of sheer numbers. Asian countries account for 55.8 percent of all international adoptions that have taken place since 1948; Korea alone accounts for 34.8 percent of all children adopted from abroad. China currently accounts for the majority of Asian adoptees coming annually to the United States.

The majority of international adoptions are therefore also transracial adoptions, adoptions involving the placement of children who are of a different race from their parents. While a black child adopted by an Asian family (or any other combination) constitutes a transracial adoption, the present discourse almost always presumes a more restricted cast of characters. We suggest that the typicality of the usual suspects in the discourse arises not from their numerical preponderance but rather from their association with the central discourses of transracial adoption and international adoption: racial difference and national difference, respectively. Blacks and whites dominate U.S. discourse about racial differences. The reality, however, is that white adoptions of Asian children far outnumber any other combination.

THE DESIRABILITY OF ASIAN ADOPTEES

Asian adoption has long been viewed favorably by prospective white parents willing to adopt across racial lines (W. J. Kim, 1995; Silverman, 1980). It is generally understood that Asian countries are reliable sources for healthy children, are more lenient in terms of age and marital status requirements, and offer a speedy and efficient adoption process. But equally important is the fact that adopting an Asian child is generally seen as a humanitarian act without all of the potential landmines associated with adopting from other racial groups. While adopting a domestic child-of-color may trigger criticism and charges of "stealing" a minority community's most precious resource, adopting a child from Asia is likely to elicit social praise for adoptive parents "saving" a homeless or abandoned child (Freundlich, Child Welfare League of America, & Evan B. Donaldson Adoption Institute, 2000; D. S. Kim, 1978). Adopting an Asian child is seen as far less controversial and complicated, particularly in comparison with adopting a black child. Since part of the reason behind the "attractiveness" of Asian adoptees to prospective parents comes from implicit comparisons with black adoptees, we provide a brief overview of the black-white adoption controversy that erupted in the 1970s but continues to be a highly charged topic today.

CONTROVERSY OVER BLACK-WHITE ADOPTION PLACEMENTS

In 1972 the National Association of Black Social Workers (NABSW) sent shock waves throughout the adoption community by issuing a biting statement denouncing the placement of black children with white families. Referring to the practice as "cultural genocide," NABSW questioned the ability of white parents to foster healthy racial identities for children-of-color and to prepare them for "survival in a racist society." Critics charged that transracial placements left children in a racial and cultural "no man's land," without full acceptance by either the white majority society or the cultural/racial community from which the adoptees originally came (Ladner, 1977; Neal, 1996). Critics further charged that the child welfare system systematically undermined black families by putting little effort into rehabilitating black parents estranged from their children, working with extended families, or encouraging prospective parents to adopt. Attention was also called to the fact that the majority of adoption workers and supervisors in public as well as private adoption agencies were whites with little cultural competency working with black clientele (Gilles & Kroll, 1993).

The ensuing controversy received major scholarly and media attention despite the fact that the number of black children being placed into white families has always comprised a tiny fraction of all adoptions. Nevertheless, even these small numbers dropped precipitously in the wake of the statement as placement agencies actively sought to match black adoptees with prospective black parents, and prospective white parents backed away from the controversy.

Another effect of NABSW's statement was to trigger a serious reexamination of transracial placements involving other racial minority groups. The passage of the Indian Child Welfare Act of 1978, for example, which effectively limited placements of Native American children with white parents, came in the wake of the ensuing controversy. While not nearly as heated as the controversy over black-white adoption, debates were also waged over the practice of international adoption, with opponents equating such placements with colonial exploitation and the commodification of children (Freundlich et al., 2000; Ngabonziza, 1988). Curiously, however, Asian-white adoption drew little public scrutiny despite comprising the largest category of transracial and international adoptees in America. In fact, placements of Asian children with white families not only continued but increased dramatically after the controversy.

How this came to be despite the serious concerns raised by NABSW, and how Asian adoptees raised in white families have fared in developing "healthy" racial identities, are issues that have not generated much scholarly attention. Cast as model minorities and honorary whites by scholars and the media alike, Asians are often portrayed as having overcome social acceptance problems today (Lee, 1996). Consequently, an underlying assumption held by many adoption professionals and white adoptive parents has been that Asian children face few difficulties being raised in white families because of their race and, further, that racial identity issues are not salient for them (W. J. Kim, 1995). Unlike the black and native communities, the Asian-American community has not challenged transracial placements, perhaps because it remains heavily foreign-born and thus oriented toward adjustment and acculturation rather than challenging the practices of the racial majority.

ASIAN ADOPTION AS AN AREA OF SOCIOLOGICAL INVESTIGATION

The fields of psychology and social work dominate available research on Asian adoption and are primarily concerned with family social adjustment and other developmental issues (physical, language, cognitive, self-esteem, and psychosocial) as a way to assess placements. This is an important point to keep in mind since it shapes how researchers in the field approach race, ethnicity, and identity. In effect, researchers tend to operationalize racial and ethnic identity as an adoptee's relative comfort with being racially different from her or his parents and family.

With the exception of a handful of scholars (Dorow, 2002; Feigelman & Silverman, 1983; Simon, 1994; Simon & Altstein, 1977, 2000; Tessler, Gamache, & Liu, 1999), the topic of Asian adoption has not generated much research from sociologists. And work that exists lacks clear connection to current trends in the sociological literatures on race, identity, and the Asian-American experience. Usually, when Asian-white adoptions have been studied, they have been included as a point of comparison to black-white adoptions and the controversy surrounding the practice. As Silverman (1980) notes, the available research is "concerned less with basic questions of sociological interest, than with the policy debate over transracial adoption" (p. 3).

Yet current research in the sociology of race, identity, and the Asian-American experience raises significant questions for the study of Asian adoptees, especially for the concern with whether they achieve "healthy" identities. Putting aside this psychosocial concern, sociological approaches create problems for the concept of an essentialist identity, a consciousness natural, primordial, or necessary for members of a group. Instead, racial identity is understood as an ongoing process whose meaning and content changes over the life course. In effect, the focus shifts from examining whether an adoptee's racial identity is disrupted by being raised within a white family to researching its dynamic formation in relation to wider social and political forces that change over time.

RESEARCH

The Asian-American Experience

First, throughout U.S. history, the "Asian" has long been a symbol for "foreignness" (Lowe, 1996; Said, 1979). It should therefore not be surprising that Asian-white adoptions have been noted more commonly as international adoptions, those taking place across international lines, than as transracial adoptions. This deflection of race into a discourse of national and cultural difference has meant that issues raised by transracial adoption scholars have remained largely focused on blacks and whites, while studies of international adoption have largely evaded the concerns of transracial discourse and other race discourses in general.

Consequently, many white parents of Asian adoptees see less of a need to encourage them to associate with coethnic peers and adults, compared with white parents of black children (Feigelman & Silverman, 1983; D. S. Kim, 1978). Instead of focusing on healthy racial identity development, interacting with the wider Asian-American community, or developing coping strategies for addressing racism, white parents are more likely to put their energies toward cultural and heritage preservation, if anything at all. While valuable, such efforts address only half the equation since they rest upon a past point of reference rooted in the country of origin while downplaying their children's current lives in America. This emphasis runs the risk of essentializing cultural practices, which, even in the homeland, are subject to revision and discarding. Furthermore, it assumes that their children will not need to be familiar with emergent Asian-American cultural forms or address how race and racism might affect their lives. Because white adoptive parents view Asian adoption through an international lens, they may assume that they and their children can simply sidestep the racial identity politics typified by the transracial adoption controversy.

In sum, sociological research on Asian-Americans brings into question assumptions of problem-free identity development (Kibria, 1993, 2000; Song, 2003; Tuan, 1998; Zhou & Bankston, 1998). Evidence of rising anti-Asian sentiment, coupled with the perception that all Asians, irrespective of generational status, are "forever foreigners," are only a few of the challenges Asian-Americans currently face in developing a healthy racial identity in the United States. How these challenges might be exacerbated or mitigated because an Asian-American has white parents has not been adequately addressed. Nor is it known how Asian adoptees differ from Asian-Americans raised by their biological parents in terms of racial and ethnic identity development or how they deal with racially charged incidents. Because of immigration history, most Asians in the contemporary United States are foreign-born (Lai, Arguelles, Organization of Chinese Americans, & National Coalition for Asian Pacific American Community Development, 2003); consequently, Asian-American parents are a heavily immigrant population whose experiences and understandings of what it means to be a racial minority are actually quite limited. Thus, the applicability of one key assumption made by NABSW, that same-race parents, adoptive or biological, are better prepared to teach black youth how to cope with racism is not clear in the case of most Asian parents.

"New" Ethnicity Research

Second, recent developments in ethnicity theory have shown that youth experience their parents as more than simply "repositories" of cultural traditions. New perspectives on ethnic identity (Kibria, 1993; Portes & Zhou, 1993) focus on post-1965 immigrants and refugees and complicate earlier assimilation perspectives with more serious consideration of how immigrant parents orient their children toward the larger society. Even within the family, immigrant parents take the outside world into account, encouraging their children to accommodate societal rules without assimilating the perceived shortcomings of the host society (Gibson, 1988). However, how white adoptive parents compare in socializing their technically immigrant Asian children is not known. We suggest that scholars view white adoptive parents as more than just "lacking culture" relative to Asian parents, and instead as cultural selectors (Gibson, 1988), resource carriers (Zhou & Bankston, 1998), and models for racial/ethnic etiquette (Ogbu, 1978) through their actual practices, if not also their expressed beliefs.

For example, adoptees play in racial and ethnic neighborhoods and schools, which present different challenges for achieving acceptance. Scholars have identified significant geographic effects on how individuals become aware of and learn the meaning of racial and ethnic differences (Frankenberg, 1993; Tuan, 1998). As they get older, they will have to navigate locally arbitrary, yet often highly salient, hierarchies for social belonging—a process that may involve racial strategies (Perry, 2002). These studies suggest the importance of understanding how white families facilitate or complicate social acceptance for Asian adoptees. Since the majority of Asian adoptees are reared in predominantly white neighborhoods, in what ways does having white parents and siblings facilitate their social acceptance amongst white neighbors and peers? In what ways does having white parents hinder their social acceptance amongst Asian peers and other communities of color? What advice, if any, do white parents offer their Asian children in developing racial strategies?

As another example, in the study of the "new second generation," assimilation is now understood to be *segmented* so that the path to economic success depends on where immigrant children grow up and the social and material resources available to them (Gans, 1992; Zhou & Bankston, 1998). Through the lens of segmented assimilation theory, how the experiences of Asian adoptees, many of whom are technically members of the new second generation, might compare with others in terms of social mobility, resources, and attitudes toward the majority society remain areas in need of exploration. For example, do white families take into account their racial/ethnic heterogeneity while transmitting advice for social advancement? How do adoptees compare their own "life chances" with those of their white parents and siblings?

Race As a Social Construction

Third, research falling within the framework known as racial formation theory or, more broadly social constructionism, places emphasis on not only the *what* of identity and culture construction but also the *how* and *when* (Omi & Winant, 1994). As Nagel (1994) states, "(T)he process of cultural construction is at least as powerful a force in ethnic identity, organization, and renewal as the contents or structure of the culture itself" (p. 44). Instead of viewing racial and ethnic identity as static inheritances from family and kin, these studies demonstrate

1. how the very categories available for identification are historically dynamic (Omi & Winant, 1994);
2. how groups reconstruct collective identities in nontraditional forms (Kibria, 2000; Nagel, 1994, 1996; Song, 2003; Tuan, 1998; Vo, 1996);
3. how individuals negotiate their identity in relation to broader stereotypes, discourses, and collective identities (Frankenberg, 1993; Lee, 1996; Waters, 1999);
4. how individual identities "develop" in interactions with coethnics and racial others (Nagel, 1996).

Thus, whether Asian adoptees develop an identity as American, white, Korean, Asian, or Asian-American becomes more an issue of broader social and political conditions, social networks, and stage of life than of psychological health. Rather than focusing on the relative identification with a taken-for-granted category or participation in a static and distant foreign culture, emphasis is placed on how these and other categories and social practices are chosen, discarded, and/or revised over time and the factors triggering those shifts. These areas of research point to new ways of thinking about Asian adoption, effectively shifting the focus from what race/ethnicity means within the family to the broader contexts in which adoptees and their families encounter racial/ethnic constructs. For example, when do adoptees identify with white culture, other Korean-Americans, or Asian-American concerns? How does identity shift between interactions with whites, blacks, Korean-Americans, Asian immigrants, Asian ethnics, and other adoptees? How do adoptees negotiate stereotypes of adoptees, Asians, and Asian adoptees in U.S. culture?

CLUES FROM THE "ASIAN IMMIGRANTS IN WHITE FAMILIES: KOREAN ADOPTEES IN AMERICA" STUDY

With these questions and considerations in mind, we designed a qualitative and comparative study of adult Korean adoptees raised in white families. In the broadest sense, our study examines the strategic roles Asians play vis-à-vis whites and blacks in American race relations and the effects this positioning has on the lives and identity formations of Asian adoptees. In the narrower sense, we examine the processes by which adoptees negotiate their racial/ethnic identity in their public and private lives over time and compare these with Asian-Americans more broadly.

Funded by the Russell Sage Foundation, we conducted in-depth interviews with sixty adult Korean adoptees invited from a gender-stratified random sample of placement records. The Holt International Children Services, the organization first responsible for placing Korean adoptees with American families, provided confidential access to their placement records. Prior to sampling and invitation, we restricted the population to the placements with families then residing in the West Coast states of either Washington, Oregon, or California. Age was also an important criteria for us since we wanted to interview adoptees (twenty-five years of age or older at the time of the interview) who could reflect upon their childhoods and other stages of life. Our interviews inquired into four major aspects of adoptees' life experiences: (1) childhood through their secondary years, (2) young adulthood, (3) current ethnic practices and lifestyle, and (4) reflections on identity and society.

Are Asian adoptees able to develop meaningful racial identities despite having been raised in white families?

While a complete data analysis remains in progress, we have conducted a preliminary examination of twenty-two adoptee interviews. These initial findings allow us to examine one of the primary concerns raised by the NABSW and its relevance to Asian adoptees. One way we approach the question of whether Asian adoptees are able to develop "healthy" racial identities while raised in white families is by exploring an adoptee's level of comfort in interacting and identifying with other Asians and Asian-Americans. We inductively placed the adoptees into one of four categories of interactional comfort.

Adoptees who feel comfortable and identify with other Asians share similar characteristics. Group 1 adoptees either grew up in communities with significant Asian populations or in adulthood moved into communities with many Asians. Their high level of exposure to and familiarity in interacting with a wide cross-section of Asians and Asian-Americans allows them to put their own experiences into greater perspective. Far from essentializing what it means to be a "real" Asian/Asian-American, Group 1 adoptees consider their own experiences as Asians raised within white families to be a legitimate part of the Asian-American experience. Furthermore, they are equally comfortable around Asian coethnics as they are with whites. Group 1 adoptees provide the most serious challenge to transracial adoption critics. Despite being reared in white families, they have developed comprehensive racial identities that are not only personally meaningful but also actively engaged with other Asians/Asian-Americans.

Group 2 adoptees are similar to Group 1 adoptees, but lack some of their confidence because they have had less experience interacting with Asian coethnics, typically only since adulthood. In effect, Group 2 adoptees appear to be on their way to becoming Group 1 adoptees. By and large their comfort zone consists of white people, but they are taking active steps to expand the circle to include Asians. Consider this quote from Sheri, a Group 2 adoptee, as she discusses the early stages of her friendship with several Asian co-workers:

A: It was the first time I started hanging around, Asians . . . So I remember, I absolutely remember to this day the first time I went to a movie. We walked into the Garden Theater and I felt like I was in a gang. I was so uncomfortable.

Q: Uh huh. Because you felt as though you stood out or something?

A: No. I don't know. I just felt uncomfortable. Because my husband and I, we went to Seattle once to go visit my friends and, all Asians, you know . . . and we're talking, you know, they speak the language, they have the accents. You know, I don't have any of that . . . I'd never been around Asians like that.

As Sheri's experience conveys, Group 2 adoptees are still wrestling with expectations (their own and others) of who and what a "real" Asian is and whether they identify with that image. While very interested in befriending other Asians and exploring their own Asian/Asian-American identity, Group 2 adoptees still experience some ambivalence over their own authenticity as "real" Asians. For them, a "real" Asian is somebody who speaks an Asian language fluently, grew up with Asian parents, and is intimately familiar with Asian cultural traditions. Since none of these criteria apply to them, they feel unsure regarding their right to and the appropriateness of identifying as Asian. However, Group 2 adoptees seem to be moving away from such a rigid and essentialist definition of who or what is an Asian. The more they are exposed to a broad cross-section of Asians/Asian-Americans, the more they move toward becoming Group 1 adoptees.

In response to NABSW's question, then, Asian adoptees are indeed able to feel comfortable and identify positively with other Asians and Asian-Americans. To put an important twist into the discussion, however, the process of developing a healthy racial identity may not occur while they live with or, for that matter, even involve their white parents. Instead, the process may not occur until they move out on their own and opportunities for interacting with other Asians become more plentiful. College, for example, was cited by some as the first time they were exposed to significant numbers of Asians and Asian-Americans. Others talked about moving to regions of the country with sizable Asian populations as key to their developing an Asian or Asian-American identity.

Equally important to note is that, if these same adoptees were asked whether they felt comfortable interacting and identifying with Asian co-ethnics at earlier stages in their lives, the majority would have responded negatively. Except for the handful of adoptees who grew up in areas with significant numbers of Asians/Asian-Americans, the majority had very little contact growing up and little opportunity to develop a sense of comfort and identification. While some parents made efforts to expose their children to other Asian adoptees through Holt-sponsored gatherings or informal networks, very few made the effort to expose their children to nonadopted Asians. As a result, these adoptees felt comfortable around other Asian adoptees but not other Asian coethnics. In short, it has taken time, greater maturity, and opportunity for most Group 1 and 2 adoptees to develop healthy identities as Asians/Asian-Americans.

Opportunities for interaction, however, were a necessary but not sufficient condition for developing a positive Asian/Asian-American identity. Adoptees in Groups 3 and 4, regardless of opportunity, were not comfortable associating with other Asians and did not personally identify as Asian/Asian-American. Group 4 adoptees, in particular, identified as white; Group 3 adoptees were more likely to identify as American. Both groups feel uncomfortable interacting with Asians, particularly those who are foreign-born, because they do not identify with them. As Diane, a Group 3 adoptee, put it:

A: I feel most comfortable with whites or other minorities. The least comfortable with [pause] other Asians. Not Asian-Americans but Asians.

Q: Foreign.

A: Foreign Asians, yeah.

Q: And what makes them more or less comfortable for you?

A: Um, maybe [pause] because there is a connection with them, but not so. It kind of makes me uncomfortable like we're both Asian, but yet um, you know, I don't speak their language, I don't, you know, each their [pause] you, I don't do the daily things that they do. Like with their families and their, you know, cultural differences I guess. And sometimes there's assumptions that I do, you know, like if I'm not, you know, if I didn't say anything to them, there is sometimes that assumption that I understand them, but I don't.

Both groups' views of Asians are largely based on popular racial stereotypes (i.e., quiet, poor English, clannish, nerdy, and studious), and their own identities were often described as contrary to these stereotypes. While similar in many ways, Group 4 adoptees' attitudes are more hardened than Group 3 adoptees. Both describe their comfort zone as resting squarely among whites, but Group 3 adoptees express a willingness to befriend Asians/Asian-Americans should the opportunity arise. The effort, however, would have to come from others since they have no interest in seeking opportunities out. Group 4 adoptees, in contrast, have even less interest in getting to know other Asians and, in fact, have an aversion to doing so. Consider the following quote from Andy, a Group 4 adoptee:

You put me in a room full of Asians, my hands would sweat. Yeah, I'd get nervous. You know, like, I can feel myself getting really nervous. And I try to keep it under control. I don't think the common person would know that I'm nervous. They'd only know because I'm telling them.

In sum, Groups 3 and 4 adoptees have troubling views of Asian coethnics. As critics of transracial placements predicted, these adoptees have ambivalent relationships with the cultural and racial communities from which they originally came. In effect, they have internalized many of the racist stereotypes that exist about Asian people despite being Asian themselves. As many a Group 4 adoptee said to us, "I'm not like your average Asian person." When pressed to elaborate, a litany of antistereotypes were offered: "I speak my mind"; "I'm super social"; "I wasn't very good in school." Rather than seeing how their own experiences might actually be part of the Asian-American experience, they see themselves as exceptions to that experience.

CONCLUSION: FROM FAMILY ADJUSTMENT TO DIVERSE MEANING AND CONTEXTS

As even our very preliminary analysis suggests, the concerns raised by NABSW defy simplistic yes/no responses. In the case of Asian adoptees, we must consider a multitude of factors other than simply their parents' race in shaping whether they develop positive racial identities. Taking our cue from recent developments in the sociologies of race, identity, and the Asian-American experience, we have argued against viewing racial and ethnic identity as a static inheritance from family and kin, which may or may not be disrupted when parents and other family are of a different race. Instead, we have advocated for an approach that views racial/ethnic identity development as an ongoing process that unfolds over the life course and against the backdrop of broader social contexts.

Beyond one's family and kin are the extrafamilial institutions and influences such as the social geography in which one is raised including residential neighborhoods, schools, and friendship networks. These extrafamilial factors vary with "place" (Meier, 1999)—the region of the country and type of locale into which adoptees place themselves as adults. Other environmental factors yet to be explored include organizational affiliations, leisure activities, career and employment contexts, political participation, and personal experiences with racism and discrimination (Frankenberg, 1993; Nagel, 1996; Tuan, 1998; Waters, 1990, 1999).

Together, this approach allows scholars to contextualize Asian adoption within broader racial relations in the post–civil rights era. We thus suggest

that Asian adoptee research shift its major question from "How well adjusted are adoptees (transracial, international, and/or Asian)?" to "How do
race and ethnicity come to have personal meaning for individuals?" In sum,
we invite international adoption scholars to take seriously the issues engaged by transracial adoption scholars, to become the latter in name and not
simply fact.

REFERENCES

Dorow, S. (2002). "China r us?": Care, consumption, and transnationally adopted
    children. In D. T. Cook (Ed.), *Symbolic childhood* (pp. 149-168). New York:
    Peter Lang.
Feigelman, W., & Silverman, A. R. (1983). *Chosen children: New patterns of adop-
    tive relationships.* New York: Praeger.
Frankenberg, R. (1993). *White women, race matters: The social construction of
    whiteness.* Minneapolis: University of Minnesota Press.
Freundlich, M., Child Welfare League of America, & Evan B. Donaldson Adoption
    Institute (2000). *The role of race, culture, and national origin in adoption.* Wash-
    ington, DC: Child Welfare League of America: Evan B. Donaldson Adoption
    Institute.
Gans, H. J. (1992). Second-generation decline: Scenarios for the economic and
    ethnic futures of the post-1965 American immigrants. *Ethnic and Racial Stud-
    ies, 41*(1), 173-192.
Gibson, M. A. (1988). *Accommodation without assimilation: Sikh immigrants in an
    American high school.* Ithaca, NY: Cornell University Press.
Gilles, T., & Kroll, J. (1993). *Barriers to same race placement.* St. Paul, MN: North
    American Council on Adoptable Children.
Kibria, N. (1993). *Family tightrope: The changing lives of Vietnamese Americans.*
    Princeton, NJ: Princeton University Press.
Kibria, N. (2000). Race, ethnic options, and ethnic binds: Identity negotiations of
    second-generation Chinese and Korean Americans. *Sociological Perspectives,
    48*(5), 77-95.
Kim, D. S. (1978). Issues in transracial and transcultural adoption. *Social Case-
    work, 2*(2), 477-486.
Kim, W. J. (1995). International adoption: A case review of Korean children. *Child
    Psychiatry & Human Development, 43*(4), 141-154.
Kinder, N. (2003). *International adoption: Trends and issues* (issue brief). Wash-
    ington, DC: Child Welfare League of America.
Ladner, J. A. (1977). *Mixed families: Adopting across racial boundaries* (1st ed.).
    Garden City, NY: Anchor Press/Doubleday.
Lai, E. Y. P., Arguelles, D., Organization of Chinese Americans, & National Coali-
    tion for Asian Pacific American Community Development (2003). *The new face*

of Asian Pacific America: Numbers, diversity, & change in the 21st century. San Francisco, CA: Asian Week with UCLA's Asian American Studies Center Press.

Lee, S. J. (1996). *Unraveling the "model minority" stereotype: Listening to Asian American youth.* New York: Teachers College Press.

Lowe, L. (1996). *Immigrant acts: On Asian American cultural politics.* Durham, NC: Duke University Press.

Meier, D. I. (1999). Cultural identity and place in adult Korean-American inter-country adoptees. *Adoption Quarterly, 48*(3), 15-48.

Nagel, J. (1994). Constructing ethnicity: Creating and recreating ethnic identity and culture. *Social Problems, 42*(4), 152-176.

Nagel, J. (1996). *American Indian ethnic renewal: Red power and the resurgence of identity and culture.* New York: Oxford University Press.

Neal, L. (1996). The case against transracial adoption. *Focus Point, 10*(1), 18-28.

Ngabonziza, D. (1988). Intercountry adoption: In whose best interest? *Adoption and Fostering, 12,* 35-40.

Ogbu, J. U. (1978). *Minority education and caste: The American system in cross-cultural perspective.* New York: Academic Press.

Omi, M., & Winant, H. (1994). *Racial formation in the United States: From the 1960s to the 1990s* (2nd ed.). New York: Routledge.

Perry, P. (2002). *Shades of white: White kids and racial identities in high school.* Durham, NC: Duke University Press.

Portes, A., & Zhou, M. (1993). The new second generation: Segmented assimilation and its variants. *The Annals of the American Academy of Political and Social Science, 42*(2), 74-96.

Said, E. W. (1979). *Orientalism* (1st Vintage Books ed.). New York: Vintage Books.

Silverman, A. R. (1980). *Transracial adoption in the United States: A study of assimilation and adjustment.* Ann Arbor, MI: University of Michigan.

Simon, R. J. (1994). Transracial adoption: The American experience. In I. Gabor & J. Aldridge (Eds.), *Culture, identity, and transracial adoption* (pp. 136-150). London: Free Association Books.

Simon, R. J., & Altstein, H. (1977). *Transracial adoption.* New York: Wiley.

Simon, R. J., & Altstein, H. (2000). *Adoption across borders: Serving the children in transracial and intercountry adoptions.* Lanham, MD: Rowman & Littlefield.

Song, M. (2003). *Choosing ethnic identity.* Cambridge, UK; Malden, MA: Polity Press.

Tessler, R. C., Gamache, G., & Liu, L. (1999). *West meets east: Americans adopt Chinese children.* Westport, CT: Bergin & Garvey.

Tuan, M. (1998). *Forever foreigners or honorary whites: The Asian ethnic experience today.* New Brunswick, NJ: Rutgers University Press.

U.S. State Department (2001). Immigrant Visas Issued to Orphans Coming to the U.S.: Top Countries of Origin, http:/travel.state.gov/orphan_numbers.html.

Vo, L. T. (1996). Asian immigrants, Asian-Americans, and the politics of economic mobilization in San Diego. *Amerasia Journal, 22*(2), 89-108.

Waters, M. C. (1990). *Ethnic options: Choosing identities in America.* Berkeley: University of California Press.

Waters, M. C. (1999). *Black identities: West Indian immigrant dreams and American realities.* New York: Russell Sage Foundation; Cambridge, MA: Harvard University Press.

Weil, R. H. (1984). International adoptions: The quiet migration. *International Migration Review, 33*(2), 276-293.

Zhou, M., & Bankston, C. L. (1998). *Growing up American: How Vietnamese children adapt to life in the United States.* New York: Russell Sage Foundation.

Chapter 10

Lifting the Shroud of Silence:
A Korean Adoptee's Search
for Truth, Legitimacy, and Justice

Rebecca Hurdis

PROLOGUE

I am walking down the streets of Seoul, and with each woman I pass I ask myself, "Is she my mother?" I search through the blank expressions, the smiles, the sorrows, the stern and the serious, looking for something familiar amid the sea of faces, hoping that some forgotten instinct will rise from the depths of my memory and at last guide me back home, to her. She is my shadow—always close enough to see but unable to capture. I am haunted.

To be haunted is to trigger a memory—to trigger something that lacks full comprehension. It is an awareness of what is not seen but felt. It ties us back to a history that dwells uncomfortably in our memory and consciousness. It is the space that is absent and invisible. It is precisely what we wish we knew and simultaneously what we hope to forget. It runs deeper than just the personal because its invisibility simultaneously is forever present as it creates our social memory.

Avery Gordon's (1997) text, *Ghostly Matters,* explores the way in which "ghosts" and "haunting" serve as a catalyst for a different way of knowledge and alternative site for history. Haunting has three primary characteristics: "(1) the ghost imports a charged strangeness in the place of sphere it is haunting, (2) the ghost is primarily a symptom of what is missing, and (3) the ghost is alive" (p. 63). The most important aspect of the ghost is its concern is for justice above all. Our society is created through what it

International Korean Adoption
© 2007 by The Haworth Press, Inc. All rights reserved.
doi:10.1300/5734_10

chooses to remember and what it hopes to forget, and yet the location of denial is the site where we must begin to excavate the experiences and stories of the forgotten people, the ghosts. By locating and uncovering the voices of yesterday, not only can we have a deeper and more inclusive attempt at history but also "we as a society can be transformed" (p. 63).

We don't have power over the ghosts. We do not find them; they find us. They come to remind us to not forget and to push us to remember the pursuit of justice. I walk down the streets of Seoul, of Connecticut, of California, of anywhere, and she appears. My ghost. My mother. Her presence begs forgiveness while demanding attention, demanding that I remember her not only as my biological mother but also as a woman living in Korea without enough resources, unable to keep her daughter, a woman who lives in the remnants of the Korean War, a woman who lives in a country that exports more "unwanted" babies than any other Asian country. She reminds me that we, she and I, are part of something larger. Our stories reside not only in ghostly experiences of regret but also in a history that is often neglected. As Gordon eloquently concludes, "[U]ltimately haughtiness is about how to transform a shadow of a life into an undiminished life whose shadows touch softly in the spirit of a peaceful reconciliation" (p. 60). This is the beginning of my truth, my justice.

This chapter comes out of a personal and intellectual need to know more. I search to uncover a history and legacy that remains on the periphery of social knowledge. To be a transracial adoptee from Korea means that I search for answers anywhere and everywhere—history books, magazines, Web sites, memoirs, and emotions. This chapter is divided (united) into three sections. The first section discusses the transnational relationship between Korea and the United States and the role of Christianity. The second section examines the construction of gender in Korea through the exploitation of women and the commodification of children. It focuses on the way that birth mothers and their children became illegitimate subjects through the social and systematic process of international adoption. The third, and final, section explores the way Korean transracial adoptees negotiate their identities.

CHRISTIANITY AND THE KOREAN WAR

Let us begin with Christianity. In the late 1880s, there was a movement by Catholic Jesuits, and then by Protestant missionaries, to enlighten Asia with Christianity. It was a worldwide attempt to Christianize the world, and in Korea it found great success. Sucheng Chan (1990) remarks that Korea has been described as "the best mission field in Asia and perhaps in the world" (p. xxxii). Therefore, it is important to look at how Christianity influenced the social and political landscape of Korea helping to create Korea's modern nationalism.

In the 1880s, Catholic missionaries attempted to enter Korea. However, they were perceived as outsiders and their influence deemed unnecessary. As a result, the Korean government placed a ban on proselytizing. It was not until 1884 with the arrival of Horace N. Allen that Protestantism became acceptable. Allen was not only a missionary but also a doctor and was welcomed into Korea based on the latter. He gained the confidence of King Kojong and Queen Min after saving the life of one of their family members. His presence as a doctor helped to create a benevolent relationship between missionaries and Korea. Soon after his appointment to the King, many more Methodist and Presbyterian missionaries flocked to Korea, opening up the gates for the spread of Christianity. However, Korea's prolonged ban on proselytizing by missionaries was still in effect. Therefore, the work of Protestant missionaries mimicked social agencies rather than churches, assuming roles as teachers and doctors. The translation of the Bible into the Hangul dialect was also pivotal in the success of transmitting Christianity. The translated Bible was widely dispersed throughout the country. The ease of learning in Hangul promoted the simultaneous learning of Christianity with literacy (p. xxxv). The Protestant missionaries in Korea were not regarded with contempt, unlike those in many other Asian and African countries; instead, they were valued for the services and resources they offered. Christianity was further tolerated and accepted because Japan was viewed as the imminent colonizer and "Koreans did not equate Christianity with Western imperialism—a connection that hindered missionary efforts in other lands" (p. xxxii). Unlike European imperialistic projects that heavily involved the rhetoric of Christianity in establishing power, the relationship between colonialism and Christianity was absent in the case of Japan's occupation of Korea.

The presence of Christianity further gained validation during Japan's occupation from 1904 to 1945, with Koreans embracing Christianity as a form of resistance to Japan's imperialism. Christianity was viewed as a practice that refused and resisted assimilation. The missionaries also held an anti-imperialism, anti-Japanese sentiment that further encouraged Korean citizens to fight. Many of the American missionaries spoke out against the regime, sending eyewitness reports to their church headquarters in the United States, disclosing the atrocities they had witnessed (Chan, 1990). Christianity helped to fuse a Korean national identity by enabling Korean citizens to hold a higher vision of democracy. It altered Korean society by creating a sense of strength and self-determination. Christianity in Korea was seen as a political tool of resistance that was infused with notions of freedom.

With the defeat of Japan in War World II, Korea was liberated from Japanese rule on August 15, 1945. The southern half of Korea was occupied by the United States, while the northern half was protected by Soviet troops. It was divided by the thirty-eighth parallel, with hopes of reunification in the near future. The thirty-eighth parallel, although arbitrarily chosen, would mark the division between political ideologies, resulting in further mounting tensions. With no near vision of reunification, South Korea, with the support of the United Nations, declared itself as the Republic of Korea on August 15, 1948. On September 9, 1948, North Korean Communists established the Democratic People's Republic of Korea.

On June 25, 1950, the North Korean Army, with the assistance of Russian weapons, invaded the south, seizing Seoul in only three days. In a response, U.S. President Harry Truman ordered U.S. forces to help defend the Republic of Korea (Yonhap News Agency, 1982). The support by Russia and the United States emphasized the foreign interest in Korea and the influence of Cold War politics. The dissidence between the two Koreas clearly drew the political boundaries between democracy and communism. It neglected the priority for Korea's reunification and instead further deepened the dividing line between the two republics, locking in the involvement of the United States and Russia into their civil war. If one country withdrew their support, then the other would take complete control. The support of the United States was rooted in the firm belief that "any Communist gain anywhere was a serious setback everywhere" (Kaufman, 1997, p. 17). Russia was looking for expansion as well as security. Stalin gave his support to North Korea with the notion that the war would be won in three days. "In short, control of Korea by the Communists posed as much a threat to Japan and America's other Asian interest as domination of Korea by an unfriendly power threatened the Soviet Union's Asian interest" (p. 22).

After the Korean War, the country was left in shambles. The war left behind a wreckage of poverty, a lack of resources, and orphans. "Orphans were a product of lost parents, sexual encounters between American soldiers and native women, prostitution, rape, and poverty" (Cratty, 1998, p. 10). Many of the Korean War orphans were offsprings of U.S. soldiers and local women, further creating a sense of responsibility for the United States. The role of the media was heavily influential and instrumental in generating U.S. sympathy for the Korean War orphans. The images that were sent back to the United States helped to further formulate the victimization of these children while simultaneously creating a compassionate U.S. nation. "Children were used to 'dramatize the evils of godless' Asian communism to the American people, and demonstrate via television how communist regimes mistreat their own people" (p. 12). The media heavily relied on the image of the heartless communist to create the image of the benevolent democrat. The meanings behind these images were not just about communism versus democracy but also raised ethical questions. The U.S. sympathy tugged at the hearts and morality of Christian Americans and their desire to aid and protect the Christian culture of South Korea. This combination of politics and religion further upheld the U.S. involvement and identity in the Korean War as the providers and protectors of democracy while reifying communism. The message was clear: if there had been no communism, there would not have been a war, and if there was no war, then there would be no orphans. As the United States became more comfortable with their paternal role in Korea, international and transracial adoption became the response to the war orphan situation.

In 1953, the U.S. Congress passed the Refugee Relief Act that enabled 4,000 orphans to enter the United States in the span of three years (Altstein & Simon, 1992). In 1957, after finding the initial quotas too low to satiate American's need to adopt, Congress lifted the quota, allowing as many adoptions as possible to transpire. The Korean government also established an agency. It was called *Yangyenohwe* and was under the Ministry of Health and Social Affairs. Byong Chun (1989) states that it was created to "help Amerasian children to be adopted in their father's country" (p. 257). With the further assistance of U.S. missionaries situated in Korea, large-scale international and transracial adoption was able to begin.

Harry and Bertha Holt lived in Oregon. Like many U.S. citizens looking at the images of Korean War orphans, they became moved by the media's moral pleas. And as good Christians, they went to Korea and adopted eight children. Upon returning home, they were unable to forget the children left behind in Korean orphanages. They returned to Korea and established Holt International Children's Services in 1956. Bertha Holt postulates, "Holt's adoption work was stated by the Lord himself. He planned it in eternity, before time began. God knew there would be war in Korea and that Amerasian children would be left helpless and homeless" (Holt International Children's Services, n.d.). Her comment reflects the social and political use of Christianity in Korea while maintaining U.S. superiority. It reinforces the prominent attitude of the 1950s in relation to the Korean War orphans that the spoils of Communism were the political and ethical responsibilities of U.S. citizens. It also reveals how the foundation for aid in Korea by the United States was spawned from a moral and Christian perspective. Further supporting this marriage between religion and adoption, a Korean War adoptee asserts that his adoptive parents' generation was indisputably inspired and motivated out of a religious conviction to save the abandoned and poor children of the War (Hong, 1997). Holt became, and continues to be, the leading international adoption agency. They have provided more than 100,000 Korean children to families in the United States over the past thirty years (Holt International Children's Services, n.d.).

ILLEGITIMATE MOTHERHOOD

In the 1960s, as Korea became rapidly industrialized, the economic and political structures were rebuilt and reformed, also transforming the culture. Byong Chun (1989) remarks, "Industrialization, however, was followed by youth population shifts to big cities, changes in sexual mores, and a collapse of the traditional family system, creating social problems of unmarried mothers, out-of-wedlock children, and abandoned children" (p. 255). Despite the effects of modernization, Confucianism remained the cultural backdrop to socially acceptable behavior and attitudes. Confucian ideology is the foundation for Korea's national and cultural identity, dictating the gender assignment and expectations for Korean women. According to Cheri Register (1991), "Korean people trace their cultural origins to Confucius, and are infused with the Confucian values of male supremacy, filial obedience, and reverence for ancestral memory" (p. 11). In addition, Hyunah Yang (1998) explains that an aspect of this ideology is the expectation that women are chaste.

> Chastity as a notion circulates and works in powerful ways. By applying only to the women, and thus establishing a double standard of sexual conduct, the ideal of chastity plays a critical role in regulating women's sexuality. Chastity involves not virginity as such, but rather that there is always a proper place where female sexuality belongs. (p. 131)

Virtue, as well as social positioning, is derived from the relationship to men and their willingness to possess women. Female sexuality ceases to belong to the women, and thus they are forced to relinquish it to their men and their nation. It is through this exploitation of women's sexuality that men's respect and dignity are safeguarded. The women who did not adhere to ideologies of Confucianism were socially and politically rejected, oftentimes leaving behind a trail of shamed mothers and unwanted children.

Confucian ideology further impacted the idea of adoption within Korea. "The family culture of Korea, both systematically and substantially, has not allowed nonrelated adoptions, but has been sticking to adoptions within the paternal kinship" (Chun, 1989, p. 256). But even adoptions within the paternal kinship are not frequent, and when they do occur, there is an emphasis on matching physical characteristics so that the child will be able to "pass" as the adopted parents'. Furthermore, the demand and preference is for male infants. Because bloodlines and pure lineage are of such importance to Korean people, domestic adoption is stigmatized with the shame and illegitimacy of the mother. The Korean nation further supported unwed mothers' illegitimacy by not offering adequate or tangible social welfare structures. In 1981, only 2.9 percent of the budget was designated to social welfare, and of that only 32.5 percent went to child welfare (Altstein & Simon, 1992). Illegitimate children did not qualify for aid from the state, resulting in an absence of governmental financial support. The lack of state funding makes the government's position toward orphans clear. By not offering autonomy or economic assistance, these women and children were systematically denied social welfare, emphasizing their illegitimacy further. The support from the government was nonexistent, resulting in women seeking out aid from private and predominately Christian organizations. Many of these women found themselves confronted with few other alternatives to international adoption.

On the surface international adoption appears altruistic. Generic sentiments and statements such as "You are my child, and you are my greatest joy in life" or "You were not born in my belly but, rather, in my heart" glorify the tendency to simplify adoption. International adoption alleviates one nation's social problems by fulfilling another nation's need for children. It is protected by the intention of providing a "better life, a brighter possibility" for a child whose destiny in their birth country was doomed. Yet nothing is ever that simple, and we must look closer. International adoption undermines the social responsibility of a nation to its people. The receiving countries involved in international adoption are also complicit as there is little interest in providing aid to the birth countries and mothers, but rather the focus remains only on the extracted adopted child. Minimal attention is paid to the society where the child came from as the importance is placed on where the child is going. Kenneth J. Herrmann and Barbara Kasper (1992) write, "Although adoption may contribute to the well-being of tens of thousands of children, it may contribute to the continued oppression of tens of millions" (p. 50). International adoption works on a global system that continues to privilege First World nations through the exploitation of Second and Third World nations, specifically women and children. We must be critical of how children have become yet another resource that First World nations can afford to purchase. The transaction of adoption creates a dichotomy of legitimacy among women internationally by placing a price on motherhood. Second and Third World women lacking the financial resources to keep their children are encouraged or forced to place their children for adoption creating an identity of illegitimacy. Rooted in colonial histories and relationships, privileged First World women become the recipients of these children because they can afford to, designating them legitimate mothers. The question of international and transracial adoption has very little to do with a woman's inherent ability to be a good mother. Instead, it has everything to do with who can afford to be a mother at all. The rights of birth mothers are rarely discussed while women in First World countries celebrate their ability to obtain motherhood at any price. Herrmann and Kasper (1992) further explain, "The mere acceptance of international adoption overlooks the negative impact on children, birth mothers, adoptive parents, and the Third World countries from which the children are removed" (p. 47). Access to social, economic, and political resources remain central issues for international adoption. The subjectivities of birth and adoptive mothers are tangled and steeped in histories of colonialism and privilege.

It is apparent that Korean society operates in a manner that privileges maleness. The stigmatization of an unwanted pregnancy lies on the mother's shoulders. She is solely responsible, while the father is not legally or culturally bound. As the father is alleviated of responsibility, the mother becomes an illegitimate subject. Through her perceived disloyalty to the state and culture, she has become marked. If she keeps her child, she will face scorn and social ostracism; therefore, her only redemption is in relinquishing her child for adoption. The state offers her options through international adoption, but these options only benefit the state. Their political and social disenfranchisement marks them as illegitimate subjects, and illegitimate mothers pass this illegitimacy to their daughters and sons.

DAUGHTERS OF THE GHOST

I have inherited not only the black hair, round face, small hands, and full lips of my birth mother, but I also have inherited the lineage of illegitimacy. My birth mother's illegitimacy flows through my consciousness just as her blood does. First and foremost, my existence lies in the exploitation of my birth mother. I am a product of the transnational relationship between Korea and the United States because I am their creation and their capitalist commodity. But despite my initial location in Korea and my relocation to the United States, I am destined to remain an illegitimate subject. As an international transracial adoptee, I will forever remain on the outskirts of society—eternally regarded as an orphan. In Korea, our status as orphans becomes our definitive illegitimate subjectivity. We become wards of the state and missionaries as we wait to be adopted. And yet, once in the United States, we still remain illegitimate despite our newfound class and world status. Our illegitimacy is directly linked to being orphans and a memory of war. It is further marked by the racial difference that we find in our new Caucasian families.

As a transracial Korean adoptee, my existence is divided into two worlds. I have traveled thousands of miles to this land that my birth mother must have imagined, as a refuge, to be a sanctuary. I have traveled over many borders, both real and imagined, to be where I am today. History and experience compound the layers to my identity, and it is the intention of this section to begin to uncover the sediments of my mind. It is necessary for me to situate myself in this topic because I believe that there is an importance in disclosing my role. It helps the reader as well as the writer to locate the space in which she is speaking. This portion of the chapter is extremely subjective. It is my own analysis of what it means to be a transracial and international Korean adoptee.

Through the transference from Korea to the United States, transracial and international adoptees transform from the undesirable orphans to the wanted adoptees. As we cross the vast ocean on 747 airplanes, the details of our previous lives in Korea slip away into generic folklore. There seem to be two dominant narratives explaining our existence, both equally sad and yet mystical. One is that we were left, with our birth dates pinned to our blanket, on a doorstep of some man who was affiliated with an orphanage or missionary. The second popular story is that we were abandoned—the place is insignificant and the time unknown. We are reassured by these dismal tales because we are told that we have made it to this land of opportunity. We are told that it shouldn't matter that we were left; all that matters is that we were brought to a family that did want us and, in the reconfiguration of an American family, were saved.

As we walk through the pearly white gates of the United States, we also transform into U.S. national subjects. As we are forced to relinquish our Korean nationalism, we are taught to embrace U.S. patriotism. For many adoptees, including myself, one of the first memories I have is the day that I was naturalized. I stood with my mother and many other adoptees before a judge in a courtroom in Baltimore, Maryland. I remember being dressed in my Sunday best. The excitement generated all around me was reassuring although I had no idea of its implications or meaning. All I knew was what I had been told: I was becoming an American citizen. All I had to do was answer the judge's questions and say the Pledge of Allegiance. And then with one swoop of his magic wand, or actually it was his gavel, I became an American. On top of receiving a small little flag, I was also rewarded with a bag of M&Ms that I didn't even have to share with my brothers. This story depicts the connection between patriotism and validation. Our exposure begins very early encouraging the creation of our U.S. national identity. It is a given, not a choice.

Fast-forward twenty years. There is a whole generation that is now coming of age. We are beginning to analyze and understand the complexity of our existences as we search for our identities. One of the first moves in negotiating our identities is breaking the silences of our childhood. Difference in all of its complexities becomes the foundation of our identities. It is learned from the very beginning yet long before memory. Rebecca Smith (1997) expresses, "I always knew I was adopted. I don't recall the exact moment my parents told me. But I knew it made me different from others, almost as if I was born with a handicap" (p. 106). We begin to deconstruct the way we have internalized adoption and the inherent notions of difference. I believe that one of the reasons we hesitate to speak about our experiences and feelings of differences is because we fear that we are betraying our parents. Another Korean adoptee, Mi Ok Song Bruining (1997) articulates, "I was told that I was abandoned, rejected, and unwanted. My parents told me I should feel grateful and lucky to be adopted and should not feel sad about anything" (p. 64). Kari Ruth (1997) writes, "We allay our parents' fears by internalizing our own" (p. 144). Our voices become a perceived threat and are understood to undermine the benevolence of our parents. Yet it is not the character of our adoptive parents that we are challenging, but the compounded messages we were given as children as we look for a way to unravel the confusion in grappling for an identity. In addition, our voices reflect the inability to discuss the implications of being racialized within a white norm. It poignantly describes the lack of discussion between parents and children about race. Lark Cratty (1998) further supports this: "Nobody taught me how to talk about my identity or race, my heartache for a woman I never knew, nor the racism that was inflicted upon me" (p. 2). Therefore, it is from within this absence of space that we begin to speak.

Connected to our notions of difference, many Korean adoptees strive for authenticity either as an "American" or as a "Korean." But it is an impossible search because our internalized differences speak our fears. Mi Ok Bruining (1997) writes, "I was convinced I was going insane because I felt so inauthentic. I did not feel white, as I had been raised. I did not feel Asian, as I clearly looked and was" (p. 66). YoungHee (1997) describes her self-perception:

I used to believe I was white. At least I was completely emotionally invested in this belief. Theoretically I was white, my family is white, the community I grew up in was white, and I could not point out Korea on a map, nor did I care about such a place. The only thing I heard about Korea was that they ate dogs. I denied that I was Korean to everyone, most painfully, I denied it to myself. (p. 86)

These writings indicate the difficult process for finding a complete identity. Furthermore, they reflect the conflict and dichotomy of having to choose to be either an American (read as white) identity or a Korean identity. What is so crucial in comprehending these statements is that, even though an identity split occurs between being American or being Asian, there really is no choice at all. These women are situating themselves within an American narrative creating the "other" to be Korean/Asian. The perception of Korean/ Asian culture as being the "other" is engrained in negative stereotypes about Asia and Korea. The refusal of understanding Asian culture or the ability to identify Korea on the map reasserts the intention of identifying as American or white. These accounts show how being too Asian was unacceptable in the culture and environment in which we were raised.

As adults, we now begin to deconstruct and decolonize our minds. We begin to understand how our racial subjectivity was created to be white and now we are able to reject it. As young adults, many adoptees resist whiteness by discovering and defining their Asian and Korean roots. This discovery allows for another part of our identity to emerge—the Korean/Asian persona. Su Niles (1997) espouses,

Through the years of understanding the impact of intercountry adoption on myself and other adoptees, I have finally come to accept these things: I am Korean. I will always be Korean. I can no more alter that than I can my gender. And I am going forward to the goal I've set before me: To attain the best of my ability the culture that by birth, truly belongs to me. (p. 154)

Incorporating an Asian identity is a crucial step in the quests of many adoptees. They fill the void, alienation, and rejection of whiteness by replacing it with an Asian community. Many adoptees begin to identify with Korean culture, embarking in learning about language, food, and society through trips back to Korea. This journey attempts to recuperate the knowledge of culture and society to find a place where the adoptee fits into Korea. It provides agency to move out of a white world that is associated with pain into an Asian world that feels empowering, validating, and celebratory. Jo

Rankin articulates, "I have totally embraced the Korean culture. Most of my friends are Korean adoptees, and those who are not, are Asian-Americans" (Hong, 1997, p. 38).

Simultaneously, many adoptees continue to accept their U.S. social construction of whiteness. They do not have an interest in Korean/Asian cultures and adamantly defend their position by claims like, "I am not Korean; I am American." These attitudes invoke positive ideas about the possibilities of assimilation and the belief that inhabiting the familiar culture of whiteness supersedes any valued notion of racial difference. Rebecca Smith (1997) writes, "I wasn't some poor, illiterate from Asia. I was American. And I wanted to achieve what I thought that meant" (p. 106). This resonates in the idea that America is a melting pot and that, regardless of your race, you can become an American. The declarations made by these transracial adoptees further support "model minority" myths and immigrant success stories. It also elevates American (white) culture by condemning anything Asian, anything un-American. To identify solely as an American embraces an identity that is rooted in our U.S. white cultural background. Any identification with Korea remains purely as a phenotypic adjective rather than a sense of being.

The third response in formulating an identity is an understanding and compassion for the previous two and a rejection of the American versus Asian dichotomy. This is the space with which I identify. The first two identities seem nationalistic. Their loyalties lie within a lie. It feels as though their desire for inclusion results in romanticism and nostalgia both denying our inclusive existence as adoptees. For adoptees, the embracing of Korean culture and the creation of a Korean nationalist identity seem contradictory. Adoptees look to embrace a culture and country that has created their illegitimacy and their removal. But I think that it is problematic to believe that reclaiming a Korean name, or learning Korean food and dance, leads an adoptee to fulfillment. It is an exchange of race and cultures, not an absolution. However, I also believe that having an understanding of what it means to be Korean-American or Asian-American is extremely important. I agree that we cannot deny our history and our ties with Korea, but I also believe that there are places where we can belong in the United States. Korean adoptees intensely understand the subtlety and nuances of race and racism in the United States. Most adoptees easily remember the taunts of schoolchildren or the lifelong effects of gendered stereotypes. Many adoptees possessing these experiences, and the knowledge that accompanies them, identify with a pan-ethnic Asian-American identity that moves beyond being just an adjective of ethnicity. Our histories as Korean adoptees living in America can be contextualized within a larger Asian-American history and culture. We as adoptees cannot deny that we come from two worlds and that we live in multiple worlds. We can't deny that our growth and privileges are inheritances from our U.S. parents just as we can't deny that we are Korean-Americans.

Instead of looking to identify with one or the other, I look for a deeper understanding and a balance between the two. It is more honest to question identity as being open-ended than to solidify myself in something that is exclusive. I strive for peace and reconciliation in this adopted life. As Su Niles (1997) writes, "My journey is two-fold: To lay to rest the past and create for myself a future" (p. 152). It is too simple to say that I am American or that I am Korean just as it is too simple to say I am pro-adoption or anti-adoption. There are too many complexities that have shaped our experiences as adoptees, making it impossible to create a single homogenous identity. Niles further expresses:

> I walk in this skin. And in this skin, I have found another world. Not in America, not in Korea . . . but where? I cannot wholly accept one and wholly reject the other. It is painful to embrace two worlds, to tie the laces of the insides of me. Closely resembling a war within where there is neither victor nor vanquished, I understand—perhaps too late—this may be destiny. To sit forever by the impenetrable wall. (p. 153)

Instead of attempting to create an identity out of already foreclosed spaces of nationalism, I seek to manifest an identity that embraces hybridity and multiplicity where complexities and contradictions can thrive. Although the challenge is difficult in a society that favors homogeneity, I am committed to creating a third space where our voices and multiple identities can begin to grow. I dismiss the quest for an authentic identity while embracing an agenda of multiplicity.

Today, and every day, we confront the ghosts of our past. It is a past that began long before our births and adoptions but which weaves throughout our lives. It intertwines our birth mothers' stories with ours. We feel the weight of Korea's civil war as it bears down its influence onto our lives and identities—the effects of war. We feel the tie of Christianity since we were brought to this country through the work of missionaries and find ourselves in Protestant homes—the effects of God. We are born out of political, social, and economic disruption. The legacy of adoption.

The experiences of international transracial adoptees are plagued with illegitimacy. Our illegitimacy haunts us as our double identity continues to be in a perpetual state of conflict and negotiation. Our lives are built on a hidden history, but it is a history that we can never distance ourselves from because the pain is always a reminder. We search for something tangible, something whole, and something legitimate. We beg to know our complete stories, to know our past. There will always be a sense of disconnection as we will always remain fragmented. We struggle to move out of our trauma into a space of justice where we uncover our silences, our voices, our histories, and our existences. Illegitimacy breaks our hearts again and again, yet we still search for peace—peace of mind, peace of the past, and peace of heart.

The voice of today's Korean adoptees is one of frustration and pain, but it is also one of resolution and justice. As we begin to speak our stories, we become reflexive exposing our experiences and our realities. Through each other we create a lineage. It is one that runs horizontally instead of vertically. We stand side by side sharing a similar history. We look behind us and see the past we were situated in—a historical wink in time. We look toward each other and see common experiences and perceptions of our lives, but we also see the differences that make us each who we are. We look toward the future and see hopes of peace, potential, and a lineage that moves forward, moving us out of limbo.

REFERENCES

Altstein, H., & Simon, R. J. (1992). *Adoption, race, and identity.* New York: Praeger Publishers.

Bruining, M. O. (1997). A few words from another left-handed adopted Korean lesbian. In T. Bishoff & J. Rankin (Eds.), *Seeds from a silent tree: An anthology by Korean adoptees* (pp. 64-72). Glendale, CA: Pandal Press.

Chan, S. (1990). Introduction. In M. Paik Lee (Ed.), *A quiet odyssey: A pioneer Korean woman in America* (pp. xxi-lx). Seattle: University of Washington Press.

Chun, B. H. (1989). Adoption and Korea. *Child Welfare, LXXIII*(2), 255-260.

Cratty, L. (1998). *Transracial/international adoption: The oral history of Ju Ein Yoo a.k.a. Rebecca Lynne Hurdis.* Unpublished undergraduate thesis, University of California, Santa Cruz. Used with permission.

Gordon, A. (1997). *Ghostly matters: Haunting and the sociological imagination.* Minneapolis: University of Minnesota Press.

Herrmann, K. Jr., & Kasper, B. (1992). International adoption: The exploitation of women and children. *Affillia, 7*(1), 45-58.

Holt International Children's Services (n.d.). Retrieved May 15, 1997, from www.holtintl.org.

Hong, T. (1997). Beyond biology. *A Magazine (June/July),* 34-41.

Kaufman, B. (1997). *The Korean War: Challenges in crisis, credibility, and command.* New York: McGraw-Hill.

Niles, S. (1997). My story . . . thus far. In T. Bishoff & J. Rankin (Eds.), *Seeds from a silent tree: An anthology by Korean adoptees* (pp. 145-148). Glendale, CA: Pandal Press.

Register, C. (1991). *Are those kids yours?* New York: Free Press.

Ruth, K. (1997). Dear Luuk. In T. Bishoff & J. Rankin (Eds.), *Seeds from a silent tree: An anthology by Korean adoptees* (pp. 143-144). Glendale, CA: Pandal Press.

Smith, R. (1997). Unconventional Seoul. In T. Bishoff & J. Rankin (Eds.), *Seeds from a silent tree: An anthology by Korean adoptees* (p. 106). Glendale, CA: Pandal Press.

Yang, H. (1998). Re-membering the Korean military comfort women: Nationalism, sexuality, and silencing. In E. Kim & C. Chungmoo (Eds.), *Dangerous women: Gender and Korean nationalism* (pp. 123-140). New York: Routledge.

Yonhap News Agency (1982). General information. *Korean Annual 1982, 268.*

YoungHee, (1997). Laurel. In T. Bishoff & J. Rankin (Eds.), *Seeds from a silent tree: An anthology by Korean adoptees* (pp. 86-88). Glendale, CA: Pandal Press.

PART IV:
BIRTH-COUNTRY PERSPECTIVES

Narratives offering a birth-country perspective on Korean international adoption are virtually absent in the literature, paralleling the lack of representation of birth-parent experiences or voices. The Korean ethos of canonizing patrilineal bloodlines serves to marginalize and silence birth mothers and to impede discourse about adoption. Nonetheless, international adoption is firmly embedded in child welfare practice and within the psyche of the Korean people. Lee discusses recent trends in the child welfare system and adoption, identifying some of the key issues facing adoption policy and practice in Korea, while Bai provides a critical look at international adoption as a child welfare practice and the increasing role of domestic adoption in Korea, and Hübinette examines the popular culture's representations of adoption through film, television, and music, and the role that the media has played in bringing international adoption into the arena of public consumption and awareness. The chapters by Lee and Bai contribute uniquely to the understanding of Korea's somewhat tenuous response to this borderless child welfare practice.

Chapter 11

Recent Trends in Child Welfare and Adoption in Korea: Challenges and Future Directions

Bong Joo Lee

INTRODUCTION

An overriding principle of modern child welfare policy and practice is that every child deserves a family that provides love, nurturing, and protection. For most children, biological parents provide an adequate family life. When biological parents cannot or are unwilling to provide such an adequate family life, society must assume responsibility for providing alternative forms of care. Over the years, this substitute care system has been developed in broad categories of residential care, foster care, and adoption. Among these alternative forms of care, adoption has been regarded as the most desirable option because it provides a child stability, security, and a psychological sense of belonging (Schulman & Behrman, 1993). Adoption is a legal process that creates a parent-child relationship between individuals who are not biological parent and child, and thus provides a permanent home for a child who cannot be cared for by biological parents (Hollinger, 1991).

Although there is a consensus in the current child welfare literature and thinking that adoption is a more desirable option for children who need permanent homes, adoption is a complicated matter in practice. From a legal perspective, it means that the birth parents' rights are terminated and the rights and responsibilities of parenting are bestowed on the adoptive parents.

This chapter has been previously published as "Adoption in Korea: Current Status and Future Prospects," *International Journal of Social Welfare,* 16: 75-83.

International Korean Adoption

doi:10.1300/5734_11

From a moral perspective, a society has to come to agreement to decide whether and when birth parents should be judged incapable or unwilling to provide care for their children so that adoption can be considered. Adoption is a social matter where the best interests of the child are collectively sought for the future of the society. Adoption is also a cultural matter because family-forming and parenting practices are all deeply rooted in the cultural tradition of every society.

Korea's modern history of adoption started with an effort to provide permanent homes for Korean Civil War orphans during the mid-1950s. Since then, there have been more than 210,000 adoptions. Approximately 150,000 children found new homes in other countries through international adoptions, and another 60,000 children were adopted within the country. During the same period, Korea has gone through tremendous changes economically, socially, and culturally. The period represents unprecedented economic development in Korea, in which Korean society finally made an escape from the absolute destitution it suffered since the time of modernization. Per capita gross national income increased almost forty times from below $300 in the early 1970s to about $10,000 in recent years (Korea National Statistical Office, 2005). From a mainly agricultural society fifty years ago, Korea has developed into one of the world's leading industrial countries.

Family norms too have changed significantly during the period. If extended families based on agricultural economy were the norm fifty years ago, nuclear families in major urban settings are the norm now. Fertility patterns have changed dramatically. The crude birthrates, which measure the number of births per 1,000 individuals, decreased almost 60 percent from 31.2 births per 1,000 in 1970 to about 11.6 births per 1,000 in 2001. Historically, divorce has been a very rare event in Korea because of the stigma associated with broken families. However, family dissolution through divorce has become much more common in Korea in recent years. Crude divorce rates increased by almost 200 percent, from 1 per 1,000 to 2.8 per 1,000 in the past ten years (Korea National Statistical Office, 2005).

With such dramatic changes in Korean society in the past fifty years, the purpose of adoption has also had to change. If early modern adoption history were about finding and providing permanent homes for war orphans and children abandoned due to destitution, recent history has seen increasing demand for adoption to function as a key component of the continuum of child welfare services providing care for children who need protection and care outside of their families' homes.

Redefining the purpose of adoption has been a challenge over the years. The purpose of this chapter is to examine the current status of adoption in

Korea and to shed some light on the issues that must be addressed for future development. The chapter is organized as follows: The next section provides a brief history of adoption in Korea, followed by a section discussing recent trends of the Korean child welfare system and adoption in Korea. In the final section, I outline some key issues facing adoption policy and practice in Korea and offer suggestions for future development.

A BRIEF HISTORY OF ADOPTION IN KOREA

Adoption has existed from ancient days in every culture (Kadushin, 1980). Before modern times, the main purpose of adoption usually was to provide male heirs to childless couples in order to maintain family lines (Sokoloff, 1993). The primary beneficiary was thought to be the adopting parent, who was able to avoid the extinction of the family line by adopting a child (Hollinger, 1991).

According to Kim (1986), the history of adoption in Korea goes back to ancient times. It appears that ancient Korean adoption laws also were designed to maintain and achieve "the best interests of the family" by providing means to maintain family lines and estates (Woo, 2002). This tradition of "the best interests of the (adopting) family" is still manifest in current adoption laws (Woo, 2002). This strong influence of "the best interests of the family" principle can be traced back to the cultural tradition that places a strong emphasis on family cohesion, family lines, and fulfilling the requirement of ancestor worship. Confucianism has been the dominant philosophy affecting individual behaviors and family processes in Korean society for several hundred years. The core value of Confucianism evolves around the family. According to Confucianism, the family takes precedence over its individual members. Within the family, a strict hierarchy specifying the order and status between family members is considered very important. Strict obedience by children of adult family members is regarded as a virtue. Keeping the dignity and honor of a family has traditionally been regarded as far more important than seeking an individual family member's well-being. Within such a cultural context, providing male heirs to childless families to maintain family lines has been emphasized as the primary purpose of adoption.

Confucianism also places a strong emphasis on the importance of blood-relatedness in keeping a family's continuity and cohesion. Thus, there is a very significant stigma associated with adopting someone as a family member when he or she is not related by blood. Bai (1995), for example, points to this cultural belief about the importance of family as a main reason adoption has been so rare among Korean families and is done in secrecy when it happens. Although Confucianism's strong emphasis on blood-relatedness in keeping family's continuity seems to be a major factor related to the low level of interest in adoption in Korea, it is interesting to find that a similar concern about *bad blood* has been a main reason for the low level of interest in adoption for many years in other cultures. For example, reading of the U.S. adoption history indicates that it has been only since the 1920s that the level of interest in adoption increased. Sokoloff (1993) summarizes the situation in United States prior to the 1920s as follows:

> Prior to the 1920s very few legal adoptions of children actually took place when compared with the numbers of children in institutions, in foster care, or in situations created by informal transfers. Many child-less couples and, indeed, many child-placing workers, had serious doubts about the future potential of poor, abandoned, and particularly, illegitimate children. Concerns about inheritance of "bad blood" were widespread, and even families who were motivated to take homeless children in foster care were often unwilling to establish a permanent relationship through legal adoption. (p. 22)

Indeed, he further points out that a major reason for the increased interest in adoption, especially infant adoption, among childless couples in United States since the 1920s is the changed perception that environment, not heredity, is the major determinant of child development. In Korea, however, confounded by the strong influence of Confucianism's emphasis on "blood-relatedness," the general perception still seems to be that heredity, not environment, is the major determinant of child development. And, in turn, this general belief is a major factor explaining the low level of interest in adoption.

The contemporary legal process of adoption in Korea is regulated by two main laws: the Korean Family Law and the Special Adoption Assistance Act. The Family Law, first enacted in 1958, adopted the tradition of "the best interests of the family" principle by specifying that the primary purpose of adoption was providing means to maintain family lines and estates (Woo, 2002). With this intent, the law recognized adoption mainly as a private family matter, and judicial supervision over adoption was minimal. As long as a few provisions of the law were satisfied and there was written consent from the child's biological parents or legal guardian, finalization of adoption was approved by the court. The interests of the child were not expressly emphasized in the legislation. There were no provisions for investigation of the adoptive homes before placement or follow-up of the children after the placement.

Since the passage of the Family Law of 1958, child welfare reformers pressed the law to recognize the "best interests of the child" (Bai, 1996, 1998; Kwon, 1997). Through several revisions of the law, most recently in 1990, the Family Law has moved slowly to incorporate the "best interests of the child" principle as the basis for adoption. The 1990 revision eliminated several provisions that had the sole purpose of adoption as maintaining family lines (Kwon, 1997).

The first major national legislation influencing the adoption of homeless children was the Special Adoption Assistance Act of 1961. Its primary goal was to promote international adoption in order to find permanent homes for Korean Civil War orphans and children abandoned out of destitution. Because Korean society was struggling to recover from the catastrophes created by the Civil War and weaknesses in economy, the Act was considered a temporary measure in response to the large number of homeless war orphans and refugees who needed permanent homes. Until the mid-1970s, Korean adoption policy had been regulated by two separate law systems: the Family Law, which stipulated that the traditional goal of adoption of providing means to maintain family lines governed domestic adoption, and the Special Adoption Assistance Act of 1961, which maintained that the specific goal finding permanent homes for Korean Civil War orphans and children abandoned out of destitution governed international adoptions.

By the mid-1970s, however, there was increased criticism for sending Korean children to foreign countries. With economic development and rising nationalism, it was seen increasingly as national embarrassment to send thousands of children abroad for adoption. As a result, a number of measures have been put in place to reduce international adoption. Today, there is a government policy goal to reduce international adoption by 5 percent each year. With the goal of reducing and ultimately ending international adoption, there has been a continued effort to increase domestic adoption. Revision of the Special Adoption Assistance Act in 1994 represented such an effort.

The 1994 revision of the law expressly emphasized the interests of the child. It recognized that providing a legal mechanism to maintain family lines is not the sole purpose of adoption, and for the first time emphasized adoption as a key component of the continuum of child welfare services providing care for children who need protection and care outside of homes (Kwon, 1994). According to Kwon, it contained the following major provisions:

1. All adoptive placements must be preceded by a licensed adoption agency approval, and independent (nonagency) adoption placements are prohibited.
2. Adequate investigation of the adoptive homes before placements had to be performed by a licensed adoption agency.
3. Supervision and follow-up of the children had to be provided after placement.
4. Postadoption services were to be provided by a licensed adoption agency.
5. Adoption subsidies were to be provided to adoptive parents.

The Child Welfare Law first enacted in 1961 also has significant implications for adoption policy and practice, and its revision in 2000 is a particularly important piece of legislation that specified abuse and neglect as a condition requiring protection through government intervention. Before this legislation, there was no law mandating the reporting of suspected child abuse and neglect. Only some selected services were provided by private agencies and advocacy groups to abused children and their families on a voluntary basis. With several cases of severe abuse and neglect reported in mass media in the late 1990s, advocacy groups and child welfare experts pushed the revision of the law to include mandatory reporting clauses. Their efforts ultimately led to the revision in 2000 that added clauses mandating the child abuse and neglect reporting and services in the law. As a result, the law provided the definitions of child abuse and neglect, mandated reporting systems including establishment of a twenty-four-hour hotline, instituted regional child abuse/ neglect prevention centers, and provided legal basis for the government's intervention in case of suspected child abuse and neglect.

This law could have had the effect of enlarging the pool of children coming to the attention of public authorities as in need of care because of abuse and neglect. In the three years since the revision of the law, the mandated reporting has not resulted in large increases in the number of children who need care in out-of-home settings—largely because the implementation of the law has been problematic for various reasons. Despite the fact that the law had clauses requiring mandatory reporting, it failed to specify the procedures and legal authority for intervention, especially when an out-of-home placement is required. As a result, there have been very few out-of-home placements, even for those reported and substantiated cases of abuse and neglect (Chang, 2003). The revision was also ambiguous about resources and guidelines necessary to enable the newly established abuse/neglect prevention centers to deal more effectively with the abused/neglected children and their families.

Along with the difficulties encountered in the process of implementing the revised law, another key barrier has been the cultural tradition that places a strong emphasis on family cohesion and autonomy in Korean society. The core value of Confucianism revolves around the family. Thus, a matter such as an allegation of child abuse has been strictly regarded as a family matter, leaving no room for intervention from the society. *Saving face* is a very important concept with regard to keeping family matters within the family. This cultural tradition explains why Korean families generally have a tendency not to seek help outside of the family, from social service agencies for example. Because of this cultural tradition, neighbors suspecting child abuse have been very reluctant to report it, fearing that they are violating the suspected family's dignity, and the family members themselves prefer solving the "family problem" by themselves instead of going outside of the family for help.

Nevertheless, the long-term effect of this law and its revision may still be significant. As more program measures are being implemented to improve the intervention side of child protective services in coming years, it is expected that the pool of children needing out-of-home placements will increase.

TRENDS IN ADOPTION

Before we turn our attention to recent adoption trends in Korea, it is necessary to understand the relative status of adoption in the context of the overall child welfare service system in Korea. Table 11.1 shows the number of children who came to the attention of public authorities as needing protection each year from 1990 to 2000, and how they were cared for across different child welfare service settings. The number of children who needed protection had been stable at around 5,000 during the first half of the 1990s and then increased to more than 7,000 by the end of 2000. The increases in the later half of the 1990s reflect the new demand caused by increased poverty rates due to the Asian financial crisis during the period. During the entire period, the majority of children removed from their homes were placed in residential care. By comparison, family foster care and adoption accounted for only a small proportion of the children. Throughout the decade, 10 to 17 percent of the children who needed out-of-home protection were adopted.

TABLE 11.1. Number of Children Needing Protection by Type of Care in Korea, 1990-2000

		Status			
Year	Total*	Residential Care (%)	Family Foster Care (%)	Adoption (%)	Child-Headed Households (%)
1990	5,721	65	20	15	0
1991	5,095	67	20	13	0
1992	5,020	62	24	14	0
1993	4,451	66	21	13	0
1994	5,023	59	18	15	8
1995	4,576	62	11	10	17
1996	4,951	64	15	10	12
1997	6,734	58	18	13	11
1998	9,292	55	25	14	6
1999	7,693	61	16	15	8
2000	7,760	57	18	17	7

Source: Ministry of Health and Welfare, 1990-2000, Yearly Report.

*The numbers represent children needing protection who come to the attention of the government each year.

Table 11.2 shows the overall trend in the number of adoptions in Korea.[1] An examination of national estimates of the number of formal adoptions reveals that there were a total of 213,322 adoptions during the period of 1958 to 2002. The number of adoptions steadily increased during the 1960s and 1970s, hitting a peak yearly average of more than 9,000 adoptions during the 1980s, and then declined to a yearly average of fewer than 3,500 adoptions in the 1990s. The number of adoptions has increased to slightly more than 4,000 per year since 1999.

For a more complete picture of adoption in Korea, the number of total formal adoptions must be divided into two categories: domestic adoptions and international adoptions. Table 11.2 shows that the majority of adoptions during the period were adoptions to foreign countries. During the entire period, 62,941 (29.5 percent) were domestic adoptions and 150,381 (70.5 percent) were adoptions to foreign countries. With an effort to increase domestic adoptions and discourage international adoptions since the mid-1990s, however, the proportion of domestic adoptions increased to a level of about 40 percent in the recent period.

TABLE 11.2. Number of Adoptions in Korea, 1958-2002

Year	Total	Domestic	International	Percentage of Domestic
		Type of Adoption		
1958-1960	2,700	168	2,532	6.2
1961-1970	11,481	4,206	7,275	36.6
1971-1980	63,551	15,304	48,247	24.1
1981-1985	50,502	15,424	35,078	30.5
1986-1990	41,322	11,079	30,243	26.8
1991-1995	16,791	5,817	10,974	34.6
1996	3,309	1,229	2,080	37.1
1997	3,469	1,412	2,057	40.7
1998	3,675	1,426	2,249	38.8
1999	4,135	1,726	2,409	41.7
2000	4,122	1,686	2,436	40.9
2001	4,206	1,770	2,436	42.1
2002	4,059	1,694	2,365	41.7
Total	213,322	62,941	150,381	29.5

Source: The data from 1958 to 1998 are from Park and Seo (2000). The data from 1999 to 2002 are from Seo, Cho, Park, and Ahn (2004).

The data on the number of adoptions by disability status of children are shown in Table 11.3. There is a stark difference between domestic adoption and international adoption in terms of the proportion of children with disabilities who are adopted. Throughout the period, children with disabilities accounted for about 23 percent of all international adoptions. By comparison, less than 0.5 percent of all domestic adoptions involved children with disabilities. Even in the more recent period when there has been increased emphasis on domestic adoption, the proportion of children with disabilities among domestic adoptions has not increased, staying at a little below the 1 percent level.

Children come into adoption placements for different reasons. Table 11.4 shows the number of adoptions according to the reasons for entry into substitute care from 1958 to 1998. Examination of the number of formal adoptions by reasons for placement reveals that the characteristics of the children placed for adoption changed dramatically during the period. In the early period (up to 1970), the vast majority of children placed for adoption

TABLE 11.3. Number of Adoptions by Disability Status, 1958-2002

| | Number of Children | | | | | |
| | Domestic Adoptions | | | International Adoptions | | |
Year	Total	Disabled	Percentage	Total	Disabled	Percentage
1958-1960	168	0	0.0	2,532	1,588	62.7
1961-1970	4,206	0	0.0	7,275	2,064	28.4
1971-1980	15,304	1	0.0	48,247	4,598	9.5
1981-1985	15,424	3	0.0	35,078	7,058	20.1
1986-1990	11,079	9	0.1	30,243	9,320	30.8
1991-1995	5,817	100	1.7	10,974	4,892	44.6
1996	1,229	17	1.4	2,080	935	45.0
1997	1,412	12	0.8	2,057	784	38.1
1998	1,426	6	0.4	2,249	846	37.6
1999	1,726	14	0.8	2,409	825	34.2
2000	1,686	18	1.1	2,436	634	26.0
2001	1,770	14	0.8	2,436	743	30.5
2002	1,694	16	0.9	2,365	827	35.0
Total	62,941	210	0.3	150,381	35,114	23.4

Source: The data from 1958 to 1998 are from Park and Seo (2000). The data from 1999 to 2002 are from Seo, Cho, Park, and Ahn (2004).

were abandoned children—Korean Civil War orphans and children abandoned out of destitution. During the 1961 to 1970 period, about 61 percent of all adopted children were abandoned children. Since 1970, however, the proportion of abandoned children decreased significantly. By 1998, abandoned children represented only about 8 percent of all children placed for adoption. During the same period, the proportion of adopted children of premarital births increased significantly. During the 1961 to 1970 period, the proportion of premarital births accounted for about one-fifth of all children placed for adoption. The proportion increased steadily during the 1970s and 1980s, reaching over 80 percent toward the end of the 1980s. At present, about 90 percent of all children placed for adoption are premarital births.

The changing trends from abandonment to premarital births as the main reason for adoption suggest that the nature of the problem causing parents to relinquish their children for adoption has shifted from deep poverty-related issues to unwanted pregnancies among unmarried women. The in-

TABLE 11.4. Number of Adoptions by Reasons for Entry into Substitute Care, 1958-1998

Year	Total	Premarital Births (%)	Abandoned (%)	Broken Families[a] (%)
1958-1960	2,700	10.7	65.0	24.3
1961-1970	11,481	21.5	60.8	17.8
1971-1980	63,551	42.0	35.0	23.0
1981-1985	50,502	65.4	17.3	17.2
1986-1990	41,322	81.8	6.6	11.6
1991-1995	16,791	83.8	8.1	8.1
1996	3,309	85.3	9.0	5.7
1997	3,469	88.8	7.7	3.5
1998	3,675	89.6	8.1	2.4
Total	196,800	60.8	22.7	16.6

Source: The data from 1958 to 1998 are from Park and Seo (2000).

[a]The term "broken families" generally refers to the situation of family dissolution due to divorce, separation, and/or death of parents.

crease in the number of unmarried mothers coupled with the strong stigma of unwed motherhood is the primary reason for adoption placement in recent years in Korea.

CHALLENGES AND FUTURE DIRECTIONS OF ADOPTION IN KOREA

Over the years, adoption has come to be accepted as the most desirable solution for children who need out-of-home placements. However, there are significant barriers in the path to improving adoption, especially domestic adoption, so that it can be considered a realistic placement option for children who need protection and care in Korea. The purpose of this section is to identify major areas where significant barriers exist in adoption and to offer suggestions for improvement.

Expanding Family Foster Care

In order to improve domestic adoption, it is critical to expand and strengthen the family foster care system in Korea. It is well documented that foster care placements can serve as an important pathway to adoption, especially for those children with special needs (such as older children or children with disabilities). For example, recent data indicate that children adopted by foster parents comprise approximately two-thirds of all older-child adoptions in the United States (Pecora, Whittaker, Maluccio, & Barth, 2000).

Because of its cultural orientation emphasizing the importance of blood-relatedness in keeping the family's continuity and cohesion, it could in fact be a very foreign idea to take care of children of "strangers" by becoming an adoptive parent in Korean society. Within such a cultural context, however, starting with being a foster parent first could serve as a learning experience to ease the anxiety and responsibility of taking care of nonrelated children. By experiencing the foster parent role, parents can be encouraged to explore the possibility of becoming adoptive parents.

Historically, family foster care has been used only as a temporary placement option, in limited scope, in the form of preadoption services. Even though Korea has no officially stated policy favoring foster care over residential care, in recent years policymakers and the general public have begun to recognize that long-term residential care may be detrimental to children and that more "family-like" care should be considered as a policy option. As a result, sixteen Family Foster Care Support Centers that provide programs of recruiting and institutionalizing foster care families were established in 2003 (Seo, Cho, Park, & Ahn, 2004). However, more active policy measures need to be put in place to strengthen and improve the family foster care system in Korea.

Currently, only about 5,600 children are being cared for in family foster care placements, and the vast majority of them (about 61 percent) are placed with relatives, most likely with grandparents with limited financial resources (Seo et al., 2004). In that regard, the current monthly foster care payment of about $50 per child needs to be raised significantly to be a realistic measure to help foster families meet the financial necessities of raising a child. More active outreach and recruitment efforts to expand the pool of foster care parents are also needed. Along with such efforts to expand the foster care system, there needs to be a more concerted effort to link the foster care system and the adoption world. For example, combining recruitment and preparation for foster parenting and adoption can be an effective method to link the two.

Adoption of Children with Special Needs

The term *special needs* is generally used to describe those children for whom it is particularly difficult to find permanent homes because of the presence of certain characteristics and conditions (McKenzie, 1993). Those characteristics generally regarded as hard to place include older age at adoption (older than four years), emotional and behavioral problems, part of a sibling group, and disabilities (Rosenthal, 1993). These children also often need specialized postplacement services once adopted.

Unfortunately, prospects for the adoption of children with special needs in Korea are particularly alarming. Because most domestic adoption still involves healthy infants primarily adopted by childless couples to maintain family lines, children with special needs who need care out of homes are most likely placed in institutions. Lack of systematic data on special needs adoption speaks for the general lack of commitment to improve the situation. There are no national-level systematic data available on children adopted by age or by sibling group status. One can only make some inferences by looking at the data on adoption of children with disabilities. As shown before, fewer than 0.5 percent of all domestic adoptions involved children with disabilities over the past fifty years. Even in the more recent period when there has been increased emphasis on domestic adoption, the proportion of children with disabilities among domestic adoptions has not increased, staying at a little below 1 percent.

There needs to be a strong commitment to the development of adoption opportunities for children with special needs. The current policy measures for supporting adoption of children with special needs include a special adoption subsidy of about $420 per month and reimbursement up to $2,000 per year for the related health care cost (Seo et al., 2004). However, these subsidies are only available for adoptions involving children with disabilities.

There are two problems with the current policy measures. First, these subsidies are simply not adequate to improve the rate of adoption of children with disabilities. Second, the definition of children with special needs should be broadened. Currently, it only includes children with disabilities; the definition should be broadened to include all children who are hard to place, such as older children and children with emotional and/or behavioral problems.

I suggest launching a special needs adoption initiative. Some concrete measures include the development of special needs units at adoption agencies. The government can initiate training, research, and development programs for adoption of special needs children. A purchase-of-service program that reimburses participating adoption agencies for placing a special needs child for adoption should be considered as a measure to improve domestic adoption. Postadoption services also need to be strengthened to support children with special needs and their adoptive parents.

International Adoption

Over the years, there has been a great deal of controversy about the pros and cons of international adoption. Facing vast numbers of children in need of homes because of the Korean Civil War and economic deprivation during the 1950s and 1960s, international adoption was regarded as the only realistic option to find permanent homes. As the need to place war orphans diminished and economic development ensued in the 1970s, there was increasing concern about not being able to take care of the nation's own children in its birth country. To some, international adoption is seen as separating children not only from their birth parents but from their racial, cultural, and national communities as well (Bartholet, 1993). To others, international adoption is still regarded as the only available realistic option to find permanent homes for many children, especially children with special needs. Government policy toward international adoption has been swayed by the tensions between these two different views over the years. International adoption was promoted during the 1960s, followed by an effort in the 1970s to control international adoption. Then, during the 1980s, there were efforts to promote international adoption as a way of encouraging migration to foreign countries in order to control the domestic population growth problem (Park & Seo, 2000). During the same period, there was also a strong push for emigration from Korea to the same Western countries where the internationally adopted children were sent (Yoo, 2001). Since the early 1990s, the position is again back to discouraging international adoption with intent to ultimately stop it completely in the near future.

Although both approaches to international adoption certainly have their own merits, one has to ask how much of the debate and the actual policy changes over the years have been based on the best interests of children. Unfortunately, it seems that the debate often has been based on emotionally charged arguments, ideologies, and ad hoc evidence. The general sentiment against international adoption and the government's response to it also seems to have been swayed mainly by perceived embarrassment at an inability to take care of our own children. What has been missing is sincerely questioning what is best for the welfare of children and a systematic effort to search for an answer. Is international adoption preferable to domestic institutional care from the perspective of the child's welfare? If so, under what circumstances? What are the options domestically available if international adoption is to be discouraged? What are the ways to strengthen those options? Is the outcome of international adoption different from that of domestic adoption? If so, in what ways and under what circumstances? These are some of the questions that need to be answered based on evidence. Unfortunately, there are no evidence-based answers to these fundamental questions to guide our thinking and policy at the present time. The starting point should be agreement that the guiding principle be for the best interests of the child. Starting from there, we need to reexamine international adoption policy and practice.

Open Adoption

Berry (1993) provides the following definition of open adoption: "Open adoption refers to the sharing of information and/or contracts between the adoptive and biological parents of an adopted child, before and/or after the placement of the child, and perhaps continuing for the life of the child" (p. 126). Since the beginning of modern adoption history, closed adoption based on the principle of secrecy, anonymity, and the sealing of records has been the standard adoption practice in Korea. This is not surprising because the development of Korea's early adoption practice was heavily influenced by the U.S. practice, and the U.S. practice at that time (during the 1950s and 1960s) was dominated by the closed adoption principle. The origin of such a practice in the United States is traced back to the Minnesota Act of 1917, in which the statutory requirements that adoption be confidential and that the original birth certificate and adoption records be sealed were established to shield adoption procedures from public scrutiny (Sokoloff, 1993).

Under the closed adoption system, adopted children grow up and reach adulthood without any way of finding their biological parents. It has been postulated that such secrecy attached to information about the past and the origin of one's own life contributes to identity confusion and is a major factor leading to barriers of healthy development of adopted children (Bai, 1996, 1998; Baran & Pannor, 1993; McRoy & Grotevant, 1988). By comparison, the benefits of open adoption are thought to be (1) that open adoption may improve adoptive parents' empathy toward the birth parents of the adopted child and reduce denial of the child's biological heritage; (2) open adoption may diminish birth mothers' separation grief; and (3) open adoption may prevent the adoptees' identity confusion (Berry, 1993).

In recent years, there has been a strong push for open records and adoptees' rights to information in United States, and it is reported that adoption professionals are generally supportive of giving adoptees access to the records (Berry, 1993). Similar to the recent trend in United States, there have been strong arguments put forth to move to a more open adoption practice in Korea[2] (see, for example, Bai, 1996, 1998). Similar to the current situation of the United States, open adoption has strong critics and supporters in Korea. Critics worry that open adoption might lead to prolonging separation grief and to interfering with bonding between adoptive parents and child.

Given that most adoption practice is still based on the closed adoption principle in Korea, there needs to be more exploration of open adoption practice for the benefits of children and families. However, the lack of empirical evidence in Korea makes it difficult to weigh possible benefits and risks of open adoption. Most of the criticism and support is based on the philosophical, ideological, and emotionally charged arguments, and/or on ad hoc evidence. Clearly, more rigorous research is needed to understand the effects of open adoption on children and families.

Better Information on Adoption

There clearly is a need for a more systematic data collection effort for adoption. To the best of my knowledge at the time of this writing, there is no national-level comprehensive data on adoption. More systematic information on characteristics of adoptions, adopted children, birth parents, adoption seekers, adoptive parents, and adoption outcomes is needed for developing informed policy and practice. It should be a top priority for the Korean government to encourage and support such data-gathering and research efforts.

CONCLUSION

The nature of adoption has changed dramatically in the past fifty years, and continues to change in Korea. If the first half of modern adoption history were about finding and providing permanent homes for war orphans and children abandoned out of destitution, the second half saw increasing demand for adoption to function as a key component of the continuum of child welfare services providing care for children who need protection and care outside of homes. However, responding to this change has been a challenge over the years. Although the number of children needing protection increased in recent years, the majority of children in out-of-home placements are still placed in residential care. Despite the recent emphasis on increasing domestic adoption, more than half of all children placed for adoption find their homes in foreign countries. Most domestic adoptions are still primarily for healthy infants for the purpose of maintaining family lines as indicated by very few children with disabilities finding permanent homes through domestic adoption and premarital births being the primary reason for placement for adoption.

Now, reform of adoption policy and practice is clearly needed in Korea. The starting point for such reform should be agreement that the guiding principle be for the best interests of the child. The philosophy guiding our future direction should be the belief that adoption is a service to the child and that the goal of adoption is to find parents for children, not children for parents. Adoption should be thought of as a key component of the continuum of child welfare services providing care for children who need protection and care outside of their birth homes.

NOTES

1. The data presented here deal only with formal adoption practiced in Korea. There is no systematic data on informal adoptions that occur without obtaining legal approval.

2. At present time, the term of "open adoption" in Korea is used to describe simply the situation where there is a public acknowledgment that a child is adopted. Because "secret" adoption is so prevalent in Korea, the supporters of open adoption practice are pushing first just to achieve the goal of making adoption acknowledged publicly.

REFERENCES

Bai, T. S. (1995). Toward improving adoption services in Korea: Challenges and efforts. *Journal of the Korean Society of Child Welfare, 3,* 107-126.

Bai, T. S. (1996). Significant factors that will help adoption to be a successful experience for the adoptive parents in a modern society. *Yonsei Social Welfare Review, 3,* 103-120.

Bai, T. S. (1998). Suggested revisions on adoption laws and program development for adoption in Korea. *Journal of the Korean Society of Child Welfare, 7,* 127-155.

Baran, A., & Pannor, R. (1993). Perspectives on open adoption. *Future of Children, 3*(1), 119-124.

Bartholet, E. (1993). International adoption: Current status and future prospects. *Future of Children, 3*(1), 89-103.

Berry, M. (1993). Risks and benefits of open adoption. *Future of Children, 3*(1), 125-138.

Chang, W. J. (May 21, 2003). *Analysis of current situation of child protective services and their challenges.* A discussion paper presented at The Public Discussion of Improving the CPS System. Seoul, Korea.

Hollinger, J. H. (1991). Introduction to adoption law and practice. In J. H. Hollinger (Ed.), *Adoption law and practice.* New York: Matthew Bender & Co., Inc.

Kadushin, A. (1980). *Child welfare services.* New York: Macmillan Publishing Co.

Kim, C. H. (1986). *A study of adoption system.* Unpublished doctoral dissertation, Chungang University, Seoul, Korea.

Korea National Statistical Office (2005). Korean Information Statistical System. Retrieved June 21, 2005, from http://kosis.nso.go.kr/.

Kwon, J. H. (1994). The content and the future of family-related law for child welfare. *Korean Journal of Family Law, 8,* 120-121.

Kwon, J. H. (1997). Child welfare and Korea's adoption laws. *Korean Journal of Family Law, 11,* 683-696.

McKenzie, J. K. (1993). Adoption of children with special needs. *The Future of Children, 3*(1), 62-76.

McRoy, R. G., & Grotevant, H. D. (1988). *Openness in adoption: New practices, new issues.* New York: Praeger.

Ministry of Health and Welfare (1990-2000). *Yearly statistical report.*

Park, J. R., & Seo, H. R. (2000). *Child welfare.* Yang Seo Won: Seoul, Korea.

Pecora, P. J., Whittaker, J. K., Maluccio, A. N., & Barth, R. P. (2000). *The child welfare challenge.* New York: Aldine de Gruyter.

Rosenthal, J. A. (1993). Outcomes of adoption of children with special needs. *Future of Children, 3*(1), 77-88.

Schulman, I., & Behrman, R. E. (1993). Adoption: Overview and major recommendations. *The Future of Children, 3*(1), 4-15.

Seo, M. H., Cho, A. J., Park, S. K., & Ahn, H. A. (2004). An evaluation of comprehensive child protection and development planning and a study of feasibility of child indicators report. Korea Institute for Health and Social Affairs: Seoul, Korea.

Sokoloff, B. Z. (1993). Antecedents of American adoption. *The Future of Children, 3*(1), 17-25. A publication of the David and Lucile Packard Foundation.

Woo, B. C. (2002). A study on the adoption system in Korean family law. *Korean Journal of Family Law, 16*(2), 169-202.

Yoo, I. J. (2001). Korean-American experience: Ethnic mobilisation as a mode of incorporation. *Review of Korean Studies, 4*(2), 11-54.

Chapter 12

Korea's Overseas Adoption and Its Positive Impact on Domestic Adoption and Child Welfare in Korea

Tai Soon Bai

INTRODUCTION

Korea's international adoption program began after the Korean War (1950-1953). Harry Holt traveled to Korea from Oregon in 1955 and brought twelve war orphans home to the United States to provide them with permanent adoptive families (Holt Children's Services, 2002). Since then, more than 150,000 children have found adoptive homes overseas. Korea continues to place its homeless children internationally for adoption, long after the end of the War, because few permanent homes can be found domestically (Bai, 2000b).

At the onset of international adoption, there was little awareness of the difficulties these children might face while growing up in a totally different culture as an ethnic minority, whether in the United States or Europe. Little consideration was given to the emotional and psychological stress overseas adoptees might go through in adjusting to life in a foreign environment, away from their homeland, and having conspicuously different physical features. Rather, it was assumed that, if children could find loving permanent homes overseas, it would be preferable to remaining in Korea, where future prospects might be bleak. Homeless children in Korea at that time usually ended up in residential institutions with as many as seventy other children, where they would remain until they aged out of the system at eighteen years old.

International Korean Adoption
© 2007 by The Haworth Press, Inc. All rights reserved.
doi:10.1300/5734_12

Until the early 1990s, when many overseas adoptees were beginning to come back to Korea to search for their birth families and their roots, Korea gave little thought to how important it might be for these children to reconnect with their homeland (Bai, 1998b). Many heartfelt stories about adoptees being separated from their birth families and longing to be reunited began to appear on television and be featured in daily newspapers. Almost everyone who read or heard these stories felt empathy for those tearful young adults who would solicit assistance in locating birth relatives. The flood of overseas adoptees returning to find their roots seems to have made a significant impact on domestic adoption and child welfare in Korea (Bai, 1998b, 2002).

Korea has made great economic achievements over the past fifty years, as evidenced by its entry into the Organisation for Economic Cooperation and Development (OECD) in 1996. Yet, children are still sent overseas to adoptive homes. In recent years, the average annual number of overseas adoptions has been around 2,400 (Table 12.1). Many outsiders may wonder why Korea has been unable to find enough adoptive homes domestically for children.

This chapter will first look at domestic adoption practice. Then, it will examine how Korea's international adoption may have contributed to the development of domestic adoption practices and overall child welfare.

TABLE 12.1. Statistics on Korea's Domestic and Overseas Adoption

Year	Domestic Adoptions	Overseas Adoptions	Total
1988	2,324	6,463	8,787
1989	1,872	4,191	6,063
1990	1,647	2,962	4,609
1992	1,190	2,045	3,235
1994	1,207	2,262	3,469
1996	1,229	2,180	3,309
1997	1,412	2,057	3,469
1998	1,426	2,249	3,675
1999	1,726	2,409	4,135
2000	1,686	2,360	4,046
2001	1,770	2,436	4,206
2002	1,694	2,365	4,059
2003	1,564	2,287	3,851

Source: Ministry of Health & Welfare (2004).

DOMESTIC ADOPTION PRACTICE IN KOREA

Adoptees' Need for Continuity and Successful Adoption

Parenthood through adoption is by nature different from that by birth (Kirk, 1984; Bai, 1997). From a family system's perspective, a person is born into a family system that includes birth parents, genetic background, and extended family (Bradbury & Marsh, 1988). In contrast, adoption often necessitates that the child be completely removed from the birth family system in order to enter the adoptive family system. However, the adoptive child brings with her or him all of her or his genetic identity to the adoptive home. The adoptee's genetic identity is something that cannot be changed or altered by adoption, but will always be an integral part of who she or he is (Bai, 1997; Bradbury & Marsh, 1988; McRoy et al., 1988; Reitz & Watson, 1992).

Consequently, adoptees' past identities are not something that should be denied in their new homes (Brodzinsky et al., 1992). Rather, adopters must facilitate their children's understanding of their preplacement history to include recognition of the existence of birth parents (Hartman & Laird, 1990; Kirk, 1984). Adopted children need to be able to mourn the loss of birth parents and to feel comfortable with their genetic heredity in order to form a positive self-identity (Brodzinsky et al., 1992; Hoopes, 1990; McRoy et al., 1988). Knowledge of where one is located in a generational continuum supports the development of a positive self-identity and self-esteem (Carter & McGoldrick, 1980; Rosenberg, 1989).

Self-identity refers to one's concept or sense of who he or she is as an adult (Reitz & Watson, 1992). Erikson's theory of psychosocial development of one's life cycle says that, when a child approaches adolescence, the child has a task of autonomy from his or her parents to form his or her ego identity: The adolescent needs to achieve independence and form his or her self-identity before he or she moves to the critical tasks of adult stages of the life cycle (Lidz, 1983). The identity formation needs to be achieved in adolescent years for the life cycle's important tasks, which are capacities for intimacy with another person, for productivity, and for integrity for one's own and only life cycle (Lidz, 1983).

However, for the case of the adopted child, the task of forming identity can be a lot more complicated than the nonadopted child, in that the former has two sets of parents to separate himself from. And further, it can be far more difficult for him if he has little or no knowledge of his biological family to have identified with first: It can be very hard to separate oneself from something that one doesn't really know about (Brodzinsky et al., 1992). For this reason, the adopted child has to know about his or her genealogical background to link himself or herself with for self-identity. And for this reason, open adoption, where adoptive parents keep contacts with their child's birth family, should be in practice for the well-being of the child (Grotevant & McRoy, 1998). And open communication style about adoption within the family was shown to result in higher identity scores among adoptees than the closed one (Hoopes, 1990). When adoption is openly confronted and dealt with, it's more likely to be integrated into the adoptee's self-concept, whereas the suppression of questions and emotions related to adoption can lead to symptom development (Reitz & Watson, 1992; Brodzinsky et al., 1992). Because of this complexity in forming the adoptee's self-identity, adoptive parents must provide their adopted child with any information regarding his birth parents and circumstances around the adoption.

For an adoptee to feel connected to her roots and to develop a positive self-identity, stories about her adoption should be told repeatedly by adoptive parents (Hartman & Laird, 1990). The child should feel free to talk about her birth parents and about being adopted with her adoptive parents. When communication is open and discussions about adoption are welcomed, the child is less likely to be confused and encounter behavioral problems in adolescence (Bai, 1997; Hartman & Laird, 1990). Thus, secrecy in adoption has not shown to positively support the child's well-being (Bai, 1997, 1998a, 2000a; Grotevant & McRoy, 1998).

Secretive Adoption in Korea

Likelihood of Keeping Adoption Secrecy in Korea

In Korea, most parents wish to keep their children's adoptive status a secret because of the high value placed on blood lineage. Thus, healthy infants are more likely to be adopted than a child with conspicuous physical characteristics, such as an older child or a child with a physical handicap (Bai, 1997, 1998a; Social Welfare Society, 1999). Approximately 95 percent of prospective adoptive parents wish to adopt a healthy child under six months of age. Children with special needs have difficulty finding adoptive homes in Korea, and are therefore more likely to be placed overseas (Table 12.2) (Bai, 1995, 1997, 2003; Social Welfare Society, 1999).

Most Korean adoptive parents wish to keep adoption a secret from others in society, so much so that they choose not to tell the child or extended family members. Confidential and secretive adoption is possible for several reasons. First, unlike in the United States, Korean parents are not required to petition the court for adoption. They can simply register the child's name

TABLE 12.2. Domestic and Overseas Adoption of Handicapped Children

	Domestic Adoptions			Overseas Adoptions		
Year	Special Needs Children	Total	Percentage of Total	Special Needs Children	Total	Percentage of Total
1994	44	1,207	3.7	987	2,262	43.6
1995	28	1,025	2.7	1,045	2,180	48.0
1996	17	1,229	1.4	935	2,080	45.0
1997	12	1,412	0.9	784	2,057	38.0
2001	14	1,770	0.8	743	2,436	30.5
2002	16	1,694	1.0	827	2,365	35.0
2003	20	1,544	1.3	649	2,287	28.4
Total	151	9,881	15.3	5,970	15,667	38.1

Source: Ministry of Health & Welfare (2004).

in their family registry. Only proof of birth issued by a hospital is required to place the name of a newborn child in the family registry. However, if a baby is not born in a hospital, parents can merely report that he was born elsewhere and present two adults who will validate their claim (Bai, 1995, 1997, 1998a). Second, postadoption supervision is not mandatory, so adoptive families can move and have no further contact with adoption agencies (Bai, 1995, 1998a). Third, the four major private adoption agencies that facilitate 75 percent of adoptions in Korea have historically been supportive of parents' efforts to maintain secrecy, reportedly on behalf of the adoptees' well-being in a blood-tied society (Bai, 1995, 1998a). For example, adoption workers would bring newborn babies to hospitals to unite them with adoptive mothers who faked pregnancy in order to stage a supposedly natural birth (Bai, 1995, 1997). For these reasons, in Korea, it has been very possible for parents to keep adoption a secret, even from their adopted children.

Highly Valued Blood Lineage in Korean Society

Korean society's traditional emphasis on blood-relatedness in the family undermines the role and rights of a non-blood-related heir. Parents in Korea fear that if their child's adoption is known to others, the adoptee would be less respected because of social prejudice (Bai, 1995, 1998a). This could jeopardize the child's well-being in society and is the major reason most parents wish to keep adoption a secret. Another reason for secrecy may be concern with society's prejudice against infertile couples. More than 90 percent of adoptive parents are infertile (Bai, 1995, 1997). Reproductive loss is significant to infertile couples in that it is associated with subsequent multiple losses, such as the loss of genetic continuity, the loss of self-image as a fertile person, the loss of pregnancy, and the loss of parenting experience. Infertility is truly a wound to the mind and body of those desiring to parent (Bai, 1997; Conway & Valentine, 1988). Infertile couples therefore need to properly mourn this loss of an imagined biological child and successfully achieve a healthy adjustment to infertility before they apply for adoption (Bai, 1997; Mahlstedt & Johnson, 1988). Those who have not resolved these conflicts over infertility are more likely to deny that adoption is different than birth and wish to keep it a secret, and for some parents that may include simulating a natural birth (Bai, 1997; Kirk, 1984). In Korea, infertile parents have more to overcome before adoption. Infertility was traditionally considered as a serious handicap and a shame to the couple and to the family. Prejudice against it still remains strong, so adoptive parents would not want to make their infertility public by telling others about their adoption. This is why infertile parents are more likely to keep adoption a secret in Korea (Bai, 1995, 1997).

While Korean parents are preoccupied with the idea of protecting their children from social prejudice, they forget another very significant factor for the adoptee's well-being—the need to know of their birth origins and to feel connected to their roots. Most adoptive parents have no contact with adoption agencies after the child's placement, so they have had no opportunities to be educated about how to help their adopted children develop a positive self-identity (Bai, 1998b, 2003). Korean adoptive parents did not think about the needs of adoptees in that context until the 1990s, when many overseas adoptees began returning to search for their birth families (Bai, 1998b, 2003).

Domestic Adoptees in Korea

Most adoptees in Korea have not been free to talk about their adoptions while growing up, since their parents were intent on secrecy. Though they may suspect the truth, they tend to avoid asking questions about their adoption for fear of hurting their parents, who they know do not want to discuss it (Bai, 1998b; Rosenberg, 1989). Consequently, adoptees in Korea often feel confused and unhappy. This confusion with regard to self-identity may make it hard for them to develop stable relationships with their adoptive parents (Bai, 1997, 1998b).

IMPACT OF INTERNATIONAL ADOPTION
ON THE DEVELOPMENT OF DOMESTIC ADOPTION
AND CHILD WELFARE PRACTICES

The Adoptee's Need for Roots

Starting in the early 1990s, Korean adoptees who went overseas as young children have been returning to Korea to search for their birth families and their roots. Their efforts have been widely publicized by the mass media (Bai, 1995, 1998b). Thanks to returning overseas adoptees, many more Koreans are beginning to understand adoptees' basic needs to know about their genetic origins and their birth parents, regardless of their love and loyalty for their adoptive parents (Bai, 2000b; Grotevant & McRoy, 1998).

Adoptive parents in Korea have seen that returning adoptees are often accompanied by their overseas adoptive parents. These adoptive parents who assist in their children's search for birth parents have shown Koreans and Korean adoptive parents positive models of adoptive parenting (Bai, 1998b, 2003). This has been a new learning experience, particularly for current and prospective adoptive parents. Now, many are beginning to fully understand that adoptees need to know about their roots and that these needs are completely separate from their love for adoptive parents and need not threaten the relationship they have with their adopted children (Bai, 2000b, 2003; Grotevant & McRoy, 1998).

Korean Adoptive Parents' First Self-Help Group

Due to the secretive nature of adoption, Korean adoptive parents did not seek out support from each other, nor organize as a group until 1999 (Bai, 1995, 2000b; MPAK, 2000). Seeing overseas adoptees returning to their homeland helped some parents to confirm their belief that children could not thrive if secrecy surrounded adoption (Bai, 2003; Grotevant & McRoy, 1998). They also became aware that more problems were likely in secretive adoptions than in openly discussed ones (Kirk, 1984; MPAK, 2000).

The self-help group Mission to Promote Adoption in Korea (MPAK) held its first historic annual conference in 2000 (Bai, 2003; MPAK, 2000). It has provided superb role models for prospective adoptive parents and invaluable support for new adoptive families, including postplacement services that Korean adoption agencies could not provide because of personnel shortages (Bai, 2003; Winkler et al., 1988). Members of the self-help group have been presenting their adoptions in an open manner and discussing adoption with their children, creating a new and better adoption practice among Korean adoptive parents (Bai, 2003; MPAK, 2001). Its members throughout the country share their adoption stories through the MPAK Web site, writing about raising children and communicating with each other. Their diaries can be read by any interested person. They share the difficulties they encounter in raising an adopted child in a blood-tied society, as well as the great joy and happiness they find in becoming parents (Bai, 2003; MPAK, 2004).

The influence of Korea's first self-help group for parents appears evident in the increased number of domestic adoptions and a shift toward more open attitudes about adoption. The group's existence and its members as role models have encouraged many prospective parents who otherwise might be hesitant to go through with adoptions (MPAK, 2001). The number of annual domestic adoptions has increased by 400 to 500 after 1999. The increase is believed to be attributed in large part to the birth of the self-help group and its members' active role models shown through mass media and its Web site (Bai, 2003; MPAK, 2004).

Children's Needs for Continuity Are Recognized

Revision of Korea's Adoption Law

Korea's Adoption Law was completely revised in 1995 to reflect adoptees' need for roots, recognizing the importance of such knowledge for their well-being (Bai, 1995, 1998a, 2002). In the revised Adoption Law, openness about adoption is emphasized as essential for adoptees' well-being. In Korea, openness about adoption simply means that adoptive parents reveal the truth of adoption to the adopted child and to others, rather than keeping adoption a secret. It does not necessarily mean that there is communication or contact between the birth and adoptive families, as in the United States. For the first time, the law provides for postadoption supervision, preadoption education for prospective adoptive parents, adoption subsidies for children with a handicap, and financial support for family foster care, and requires adoption agencies to support Korean overseas adoptees' visits to Korea (Bai, 1995, 1998a).

However, the law has its shortcomings. For example, postadoption supervision is at the discretion of the adoption agency director and is not mandated for all families. Also, family foster care services are provided only to infant children who are to be adopted overseas within two years. Nevertheless, the expense and support of family foster care is included for the first time in Korean law as the government's financial responsibility (Bai, 1998a, 2000b, 2002).

The 1995 Adoption Law revision reflects the needs of adoptees rather than those of adoptive parents (Bai, 1998a). Adoption subsidies were further expanded in 2004 to include financial support for counseling services for adoptees with behavioral or emotional needs (Ministry of Health & Welfare, 2004).

Revision of Korea's Child Welfare Law

The child welfare network was started as a way of coping with the overwhelming number of children orphaned following the Korean War. Goodwilled private citizens established orphanages to take care of children left alone on the streets. These private institutions, which were funded by the government, housed groups of fifty to seventy children mostly under the age of eighteen years. These institutions have played a very important role in child welfare for more than fifty years. Unlike in the United States, residential care for children is the least expensive option in Korea (Bai, 2000a).

There were no provisions for government-funded family foster care services for nonadoptive children in their care before the 2000 Child Welfare Law revision (Bai, 2000b, 2002). Overall, the emotional needs of children in the child welfare system were not given much consideration because of a lack of understanding and financial shortages (Bai, 2000b). For example, parents' visits to their children in residential care were discouraged because of shortages in trained personnel who could appropriately respond to the children's emotional needs, which often resulted in acting out behaviors after the parents would leave (Bai, 2000a; Usher et al., 1999).

Children's needs, beyond food and shelter, have not been given much consideration (Bai, 1996, 2000a). However, seeing returning overseas adoptees looking for their birth parents has helped Koreans to rethink the importance of helping children in residential institutions to keep family relationships when they have been separated from their parents because of unemployment and economic difficulties, divorce, parents' alcohol problems, imprisonment, etc. (Bai, 2000a,b; Table 12.3).

In the revised Child Welfare Law, family foster care is, for the first time, stated as the preferred type of child care for children who are separated from their parents (Bai, 2000b, 2002). In 2003, the government established agencies for family foster care with financial supports in sixteen different regions across the country, and more regional agencies have since been added to expand services to more children (Ministry of Health & Welfare, 2004; Table 12.4).

TABLE 12.3. Reasons Children Enter the Care System in Korea

Year	Abandoned	Unwed Mothers	Lost Children	Economic Shortage, Abuse, etc.	Total
1994	1,386	1,781	192	1,644	5,023
1996	1,276	1,379	189	2,107	4,951
1997	1,372	1,833	342	3,187	6,734
1998	1,654	4,120	277	3,241	9,292
1999	1,432	3,058	216	2,987	7,693
2000	1,276	2,938	144	3,363	7,760
2001	717	4,897	98	6,374	12,086
2002	1,634	4,337	–	5,012	10,057
2003	628	4,457	–	5,058	10,222

Source: Ministry of Health & Welfare (2004).

TABLE 12.4. How Children in the System Are Cared for in Korea

Year	Total	Residential Group Care	Family Foster Care	Adoption	Youth-Headed Families, etc.
1995	4,576 (100%)	2,819 (62%)	505 (11%)	472 (10%)	780 (17%)
1996	4,951 (100%)	3,161 (64%)	727 (15%)	479 (10%)	584 (11%)
1997	6,734 (100%)	3,917 (58%)	1,209 (18%)	898 (13%)	710 (11%)
1998	9,292 (100%)	5,112 (55%)	2,353 (25%)	1,283 (14%)	544 (6%)
1999	7,693 (100%)	4,683 (61%)	1,249 (16%)	1,181 (15%)	572 (8%)
2000	7,760 (100%)	4,453 (58%)	1,406 (18%)	1,337 (17%)	564 (7%)
2001	12,086 (100%)	6,274 (52%)	3,090 (26%)	1,848 (15%)	874 (7%)
2002	10,057 (100%)	4,663 (46%)	2,177 (22%)	2,544 (25%)	673 (7%)
2003	10,222 (100%)	4,824 (49%)	2,392 (23%)	2,506 (24%)	500 (4%)

Source: Ministry of Health & Welfare (2004).

CONCLUSION

When Korea abruptly started international adoption to deal with war orphans, children's needs to be connected with their roots were not recognized in child welfare (Bai, 2000b, 2002). Since then, approximately 150,000 Korean children have gone to adoptive homes abroad, mostly in the United States and Europe (Bai, 2000a). Not until many overseas adoptees were seen coming back to their motherland to search for their birth parents did Korea begin to understand and to provide what children need when they are separated from birth families (Bai, 1998b, 2002, 2003).

Many Korean adoptive parents learned about the importance of ethnic and cultural bonds from returning overseas adoptees, and this has promoted a more open attitude toward adoption (Bai, 2003; MPAK, 2000). Korea's first adoptive parents' self-help group has helped to change the social climate, making adoption more accepted (MPAK, 2000, 2001, 2004). This seems to have contributed to the annual increase by 400 to 500 in the number of domestic adoptions in recent years in Korea (Bai, 2003; Ministry of Health & Welfare, 2004; MPAK, 2004).

Children's emotional needs upon separation from their birth parents are also reflected in the revised Child Welfare Law in Korea. Child welfare services like family foster care and child protective services are for the first time clearly stated as the government's responsibility (Bai, 2000b, 2002).

Returning Korean overseas adoptees have helped Korea and its people to understand that society should take care of all of its children, beyond blood ties, because the family can be very easily dissolved in a modern society (Bai, 2000b). Overseas adoptees had to leave their birth country when they were young, because there were no permanent homes for them in Korea. The tragedy and the pain of many of these Korean children are being felt strongly by Korea and its people. Their experience is no longer unnoticed, but will continue to reshape the practice of domestic adoption and child welfare in Korea.

REFERENCES

Bai, T. S. (1995). Ways to improve Korean adoption practice through changes in its adoption law and other adoption related measures. *Journal of the Korean Society of Child Welfare, 3,* 107-126.

Bai, T. S. (1996). Ways to improve the quality of services provided for children residing in residential institutions in Korea. *Journal of the Korean Society of Child Welfare, 4,* 109-134.

Bai, T. S. (1997). The difference in adoption practice for child welfare between Korea and the United States. *The Journal of Humanistic Studies, 7,* 188-203.

Bai, T. S. (1998a). Suggested revisions on adoption law and program development for adoption in Korea. *Journal of the Korean Society of Child Welfare, 7,* 127-155.

Bai, T. S. (1998b). *Understanding adoption and its success in a modern society.* Kyungnam, Korea: Kyungnam University Press.

Bai, T. S. (2000a). How children of disintegrated families in Korea are cared for by the society. *Journal of the Korean Society of Child Welfare, 9,* 227-246.

Bai, T. S. (2000b). The future of Korea's child welfare and its service direction in the 21st century. Conference Proceedings from the 13th International Conference of the Korean Society of Child Welfare, Seoul, Korea, 57-86.

Bai, T. S. (2002). Korea's domestic adoption and its law, and Korea's child welfare law. *Laws on Korea's child welfare* (pp. 189-234). Seoul: Sowha Press.

Bai, T. S. (2003). Adoptive parents' self-help group and its influence for domestic adoption development in Korea. *The Journal of Humanistic Studies, 16,* 188-203.

Bradbury, S., & Marsh, N. (1988). Linking families in preadoption counseling: A family system model. *Child Welfare, 67*(4), 327-335.

Brodzinsky, D. M., Schechter, N. D., & Henig, R. M. (1992). *Being adopted: The life-long search for self.* New York: Doubleday.

Carter, E., & McGoldrick, M. (1980). *The family life cycle: A framework for family therapy.* New York: Gardner.

Conway, P., & Valentine, D. (1988). Reproductive loss and grieving. In Valentine. D. (Ed.), *Infertility and adoption: A guide for social work practice* (pp. 43-64). New York: Haworth Press.

Grotevant, H. D., & McRoy, R. G. (1998). *Openness in adoption: Exploring family connections.* Thousand Oaks, CA: Sage Publications.

Hartman, A., & Laird, J. (1990). Family treatment after adoption: Common themes. In D. Brodzinsky & M. Schechter (Eds.), *Psychology of adoption* (pp. 221-238). New York: Oxford University Press.

Holt Children's Services (2002). *Holt 2002 since 1955.* Seoul, Korea: Holt Children's Services.

Hoopes, J. L. (1990). Adoption and identity formation. In D. Brodzinsky & M. Schechter (Eds.), *Psychology of adoption* (pp. 144-166). New York: Oxford University Press.

Kirk, D. H. (1984). *Shared fate: A theory and method of adoptive relationship* (2nd ed.). Port Angeles, WA: Ben-Simon Publications.

Lidz, T. (1983). *The person: His and her development throughout the life cycle.* New York: Basic Books.

Mahlstedt, P., & Johnson, T. (1988). Support to person experiencing infertility: Family and fiends can help. In D. Valentine (Ed.), *Infertility and adoption: A guide for social work practice* (pp. 43-64). New York: Haworth Press.

McRoy, R. G., Grotevant, H. D., & White, K. L. (1988). *Openness in adoption: New practice, new issues.* New York: Praeger.

Ministry of Health & Welfare (2004). *Child welfare plan for the year.* Republic of Korea: Ministry of Health & Welfare.

MPAK (Mission to Promote Adoption in Korea) (2000). Conference proceedings from the first national conference for Korean adoptive families. Seoul, Korea.

MPAK. (2001). *Adoptive families' adoption diaries: Story about love for children born in the heart.* Seoul, Korea: Moonwhain Publications.

MPAK (2004). Conference proceedings from the fifth national conference for Korean adoptive families. Seoul, Korea.

Reitz, M., & Watson, K. W. (1992). *Adoption and the family system strategies for treatment.* New York: The Guilford Press.

Rosenberg, M. B. (1989). *Growing up adopted.* New York: Bradbury Press.

Social Welfare Society (1999). Conference proceedings from the conference for adoptive parents to change adoption attitudes and improve domestic adoption in Korea. Seoul, Korea: Social Welfare Society.

Usher, C. L., Randolph, K. A., & Gogan, H. C. (1999). Placement patterns in foster care. *Social Service Review, 73*(1), 22-36.

Winkler, R. C., Brown, D. W., Keppel, M. V., & Blanchard, A. (1988). *Clinical practice in adoption.* Elmsford, NY: Pergamon Press.

Chapter 13

The Korean Adoption Issue and Representations of Adopted Koreans in Korean Popular Culture

Tobias Hübinette

Korea is the country in the world that so far in modern history has sent away the largest number of its citizens for international adoption. Since 1953, at the end of the Korean War, 160,000 children have been dispatched to fifteen main host countries in the West on the continents of Europe, North America, Australia, and New Zealand (Ministry of Health and Welfare, 1999). The demographic scope, time span, and the geographical spread are absolutely unique in the history of child migration, and still, more than 2,000 children leave Korea annually for international adoption. This intercontinental transfer and circulation of Korean children on a mass scale was for many years silently taking place in the shadow of Korea's rapid, but nonetheless brutal, path to modernity and nation-building.

However, from around 1970, the subject of international adoption and overseas adopted Koreans, henceforth known as the Korean adoption issue, has played a part in Korea's public culture turning up now and then in the political discussion, in media, and in popular culture. The purpose of this chapter is to examine the Korean adoption issue by focusing primarily on various popular cultural representations of adopted Koreans, mainly in feature films and popular songs. After a short introduction to media representation according to British cultural studies and the development of the Korean adoption issue, I will go through some of the main popular cultural works taking up the adoption issue from 1988 up until today. At the end, these representations are conceptualized as a way of creating a discourse on

International Korean Adoption
doi:10.1300/5734_13

adopted Koreans and linked to ongoing processes of globalization, reconciliation, and reunification within the Korean society, as I argue that the
Korean adoption issue can be seen as a struggle to accommodate and overcome a national trauma.

THE IMPORTANCE OF POPULAR CULTURE

Media has an enormous capacity in shaping a nation's values and norms,
and has historically played a major role in spreading the gospel of nationalism (Anderson, 1983). The power of the media in establishing and affirming imagined bonds among its patrons has also been shown by several
studies among different ethnic groups (Gillespie, 1995; Morley, 2000).
Cultural studies, sometimes known as the Birmingham school, evolving in
Britain from the 1960s, are concerned with the relationship between identity and media in late modernity with its constant flow of multiple identities
(Mulhern, 2000; Storey, 2001). In cultural studies, media is seen as a social
force with the logic of its own instead of merely being a device for transmitting information. Print media and audiovisual products are not just commodities made for profit, as they consciously select and interpret "facts"
and "events," and frame and direct them in a specific grammar recognizable
to the audience. In this way, the media becomes a crucial agent in the construction and reproduction of nationalist ideology as mediated images and
representations produce meanings and establish individual as well as collective identities.

The media's aspect of producing and reproducing ideologies and realities is even more apparent in popular culture with its fluid mobility and
widely spread and easily consumed character, unfettered by time and space.
Popular culture is here defined as mass-produced commodities associated
with mass communication, spurred by commercial interests, and intended
for mass consumption. The critical importance of the Korean cinema and
music industry in constructing and spreading images of adopted Koreans
among the general public cannot therefore be underestimated. In this chapter, I apply the British cultural theorist Stuart Hall's (1997) understanding
of how representational practice works in my examination of representations of adopted Koreans in Korean popular culture. I adhere to a
poststructuralist and social constructionist approach where meaning is produced within language by the work of representation. The privileged medium of popular culture is arguably one of the most important and
influential representational systems in modern societies in its mass production and circulation of images of the world.

The genres I will be dealing with are feature films and popular songs, and the study is underpinned by the conviction of the influential role of cinema and popular music in categorizing and stereotyping through representation, and how these mediated images easily become accepted as "common knowledge." The popular cultural productions examined in this chapter have been selected for their representations of adopted Koreans in a wholly Western setting, and the titles have been found by means of reviews in Korean newspapers and by the help of Korean Film Database (http://www.koreafilm.or.kr).

THE DEVELOPMENT OF THE KOREAN ADOPTION ISSUE

In the first two decades of international adoption from Korea, there are few traces of any media coverage of overseas adopted Koreans, and it seems fair to assume that issues concerning adoption were treated as an integrated part of the problem of mixed-race children. This situation changed overnight in 1970, when North Korea suddenly and unexpectedly accused its southern neighbor of selling Korean children to Westerners as an appalling example of so-called flunkeyism (Penner, 1996; Sarri, Baik, & Bombyk, 1998). The accusation led to panic-stricken temporary stops, and the entire adoption program being classified and transformed into something close to a state secret. However, from then on the adoption issue was there to stay as an uncomfortable subject turning up now and then in political discussions, and it is no coincidence that the Korean feature films containing overseas adopted Koreans date from this period.

The earliest of cinematic work depicting an overseas adopted Korean is probably Cheong Jin Woo's *When April Goes By* (1967) where Mun, a Korean woman adopted by a French family at the time of the Korean War, returns to Korea as an adult and gets to know Seong-hun, a Korean man working for the French embassy in Seoul (Cha & Cheong, 1967). Two other early adoption films are Lee Du Yong's *A Guilty Woman* (1971) depicting a male adoptee from the United States, Young-Hun, who returns to Korea after his American adoptive father passed away to marry his childhood friend, and Kwon Young Sun's *Between Love* (1972), telling the story of the American adoptee Michie Brown who amazingly is readopted to a Japanese family (Lee & Lee, 1971; Park & Kwon, 1972).

The second half of the 1970s also saw the first generation of adult adopted Koreans visiting Korea as participators in the first organized visiting programs and being interviewed in Korean newspapers and magazines.

Already from the beginning, a clear tendency to portray "lucky" and "successful" adoptees and express a strong gratitude toward the adoptive parents and the host countries was established, and this way of portraying overseas adopted Koreans has come to stay in Korean mainstream media, contradicting, as we soon will see, the popular cultural representations.

In 1988, the Seoul Olympic Games showcased a proud and newly democratized and industrialized Korea to the world. However, all of a sudden, Western journalists started to write about the adoption program, and portrayed the proud host country as the leading global exporter of children (Park, 1994). The unexpected attention was painful and humiliating, and as a result of this negative foreign media coverage of the Korean society, the adoption issue from then on has become more or less institutionalized in the country's public sphere. The adoption issue was particularly accentuated during the time of Kim Dae Jung's presidency between 1998 and 2002. In 1998 President Kim delivered an official apology to the adopted Koreans for having sent them abroad for international adoption.

Up until 1988 adopted Koreans had played a part in the plot in a dozen or so Korean feature films, but from the year of the Olympics, overseas adoptees have also figured in genres such as novels and short stories, comics and children's books, musicals and plays, television dramas and serials, and popular songs. A milestone in this development was Chang Kil-su's *Susanne Brink's Arirang* from 1991, after which the presence of adopted Koreans in Korean popular culture literally exploded (Kim & Chang, 1991).

SUSANNE BRINK'S ARIRANG

In 1991, Chang Kil-su's film *Susanne Brink's Arirang* (Kim & Chang, 1991) was widely seen at Korean cinemas and played a crucial role in establishing the adoption issue among the general public. The film tells the story of Susanne Brink from her departure from Korea as Yu-suk Sin at the age of three, through her hardships as an adopted Korean in Sweden, and to her return and reunion with her birth mother twenty years later. The real Susanne Brink had been portrayed in a documentary from 1989 through which she found her birth mother, and her life was made into a novel that became the base of the film script. Through the film, Susanne Brink became Korea's most well-known adopted Korean, and several follow-up documentaries have been made about her.

The film starts with short interviews with adopted Koreans in Sweden who aggressively spit out bitter phrases of having been sent away to such a distant and foreign country as Sweden. The story itself begins in a poor neighborhood in Seoul where a mother of three children lives a difficult life. The mother decides to relinquish Yu-suk, the youngest daughter, for international adoption. She buys her new clothes and prepares a last meal. During mealtime, Yu-suk instinctively understands what is going on and starts to cry. After a final farewell to siblings and neighbors, the mother takes Yu-suk on her back for one last time and walks to Kimpo Airport, where a social worker from an adoption agency waits impatiently with two other children who have other countries as destinations. The mother signs the necessary documents and buys Yu-suk a doll as a last memory from Korea. In a heartbreaking scene the mother suddenly regrets her decision, but forces herself to part from Yu-suk as the plane is about to leave.

At Arlanda Airport in Stockholm, a Swedish couple with their biological son eagerly awaits their adoptive daughter. Yu-suk is welcomed as Susanne in a language she does not understand and by people whose strange appearance frightens her. She clings desperately to the Korean flight attendant who will be her last contact with another ethnic Korean for many years. After a car trip to Norrköping, a city south of Stockholm, Susanne enters her new home, a typical suburban middle-class villa. She meets her Swedish relatives who have arranged a welcoming dinner, and during her first day in her new country Susanne falls asleep at the dinner table.

The film now continues in a wholly Swedish setting, in Swedish with Korean subtitles and with Swedish actors except for Susanne herself, who is played by the famous Jin-sil Choe. During adolescence Susanne is terribly abused by her adoptive family. Her Swedish brother calls her a "gook," and her adoptive mother beats her and forces her to do housework. After a severe beating, Susanne tries to commit suicide. On entering high school, Susanne leaves her adoptive family and moves to a boarding house in Stockholm to start her own life. She meets a Swedish man, and becomes a single mother to a daughter, since the father does not want to have a biracial child. A couple of years later she meets another Swedish man, but this time her best friend from high school manages to steal him from her. Now abandoned by everyone—her Korean family, her Swedish family, her daughter's father, her boyfriend, and her best friend—Susanne again tries to commit suicide and ends up at a mental hospital. After being discharged, she moves to another town where she continues to live alone with her daughter.

One day a Korean TV team doing a documentary on adopted Koreans in Europe visits Susanne. While crying, Susanne plays the famous Korean folk song "Arirang" on the piano in front of the camera and asks her biological mother why she sent her away to a country so far from Korea. After some time Susanne receives a phone call from Korea, informing her that her biological mother has been found through the documentary. Susanne travels to Korea together with her daughter for the first time after more than twenty years. After the reunion with her Korean mother, the film ends with Susanne giving a speech directed to the audience and the Korean people. Susanne tells about the tens of thousands of Koreans sent away for adoption to foreign countries and that many of them are treated poorly and feel unhappy. Finally she demands that Korea has to stop its international adoption program. This highly political message of the film was also what critics focused on in their reviews.

FROM THE SPECTACULAR TO THE NATURAL

The adoption issue had turned up in Korean films before *Susanne Brink's Arirang* (Kim & Chang, 1991), but never before had the subject been dealt with in such a conscious and open way. In 1990, there were stories in the media that the Korean director So-yong Kim had plans to make a film called *American Dream,* in which an American couple adopts a Korean child with the sole and cynical purpose of serving as an organ donor to their biological child who is in need of a new heart. However, this film came to nothing as a result of strong criticism from the U.S. Embassy as well as from adoption agencies. During the same year, Pak Ch'ôl-su's *Oseam Hermitage* was released, a film in which international adoption plays a minor part (Lee & Pak, 1990). Two biological siblings, Kil-son and Kam-i, run away from a Catholic orphanage after having been informed that the boy Kil-son will be sent away for adoption to the Netherlands. The siblings try to find their home and their mother, but finally end up at a Buddhist hermitage after a dramatic odyssey through a rapidly changing 1970s Korea filled with hardships.

In 1991, *Berlin Report,* another film dealing with the adoption issue as its main theme, was released, with celebrated Park Kwang-su as director (Seo & Park, 1991). Compared with *Susanne Brink's Arirang* (Kim & Chang, 1991), the film received less attention, possibly because it dealt with too many issues at the same time. *Berlin Report* is a psychological thriller with strong political undertones, making use of the division of both Korea and Germany in the plot. Director Park actually pointed out himself in an interview that the film might be too complicated for the ordinary filmgoer. The leading character in *Berlin Report* is Sông-min, a Korean foreign correspondent based in Paris, who starts to investigate a mysterious murder case of an adoptive father to a Korean daughter, Marie-Ellen. The correspondent and Marie-Ellen fall in love with each other, and in the course of their unusual relationship, her family history is exposed. The adoptive father turns out to have been a former Russian military officer who, during the war, had been tortured by the Nazis. He adopts Marie-Ellen as a single parent and abuses her sexually. But Marie-Ellen has a biological brother, Yông-ch'ôl, who was placed in a family in Germany, where he as an adult is a political activist on the extreme Left. Together, Sông-min and Marie-Ellen search for Yông-ch'ôl in West Berlin, and in the end it turns out that it is the brother who had killed Marie-Ellen's adoptive father. In the film, the two siblings are depicted as confused adopted Koreans who are living destructive and rootless lives, desperately longing for each other and their lost Korean heritage.

In an even more experimental film from 1995, Pae Yong-gyun's *The People in White,* an adult adopted Korean man from the United States mysteriously known as H returns to Korea and arrives to a dreamlike place called Haech'ôn, where the past and the present coexist (Pae & Pae, 1995). In the company of restless spirits, H experiences Korea's troubled and tortured past. Two years later, the legendary cult director Kim Ki-duk dealt with both the adoption and unification issues in *Wild Animals* (Kwon & Kim, 1997). Like *Berlin Report* (Seo & Park, 1991), *Wild Animals* is also set in Paris and deals with the division of Korea seen through the fates of three ethnic Koreans who happen to meet one another in the French capital: Ch'ông-hae, a South Korean painter, Hong-san, a North Korean defector, and Lola, an adopted Korean woman working as a semiprostitute. Lola is a striptease dancer, and has been abused by both her adoptive father and her French boyfriend. The trio becomes a symbol of a divided and dispersed nation, and in a final spectacular scene Lola kills her South and North Korean compatriots, an act that can be interpreted as the impossibility of overcoming the country's division.

At the end of the 1990s, the adoption issue occurred as a minor part of the plot in several films. One example is *Push! Push!,* a comedy about the daily routines at a maternity ward in Seoul, made by the director behind *Oseam Hermitage,* Pak Ch'ôl-su (Kim & Pak, 1997). The film contains a scene in which a high school student delivers a child. The ward sister calls an adoption agency and makes an agreement to relinquish the child for international adoption. The student refuses to see her own child after birth, but when parting she starts to scream that she wishes her child to be adopted domestically, not to be sent away to a far-off country. An example of a Korean film in which an adopted Korean turns up without making too much fuss is Jin Won-Seok's *Too Tired to Die* from 1998, where an aged Anglo-American artist in New York is living together with Anouk, a young and strongly orientalized and sexualized adopted Korean woman from France (Hwang & Jin, 1998).

November 1999 opened up with Lee Jang-soo's highly popular *Love,* a romantic melodrama set in Los Angeles' Koreatown (Lee & Lee, 1999). *Love* is a story about the relationship between Myông-su, a Korean marathon runner, and Jenny, an adopted Korean. Myông-su visits Los Angeles for a track race, and meets Jenny, who at an early age had run away from her adoptive parents and had grown up as a foster child of Myông-su's relatives in Koreatown. This film is nothing else but an ordinary love story, and what was spectacular with films like *Susanne Brink's Arirang* (Kim & Chang, 1991) and *Berlin Report* (Seo & Park, 1991), i.e., the fact that an adopted Korean plays a major role in a Korean film, can be said to have turned into something natural with *Love.*

SAD SONGS ABOUT ADOPTION

In 1997 the rock band Sinawe released its sixth album, *Haerangsa,* containing the song "Motherland" (Sheen & Sinawe, 1997). The lyrics vividly portray an adopted Korean who feels himself to be physically different, "another skin colour, other eyes and hair," and who "forever will be alone." The song ends with a desperate cry for help: "I call for the Motherland!" Another early adoption song is the jazz musician Chung Won Young's "Yông-mi Robinson" from 1998, describing the melancholic feelings of an adopted Korean woman in the United States who is longing for love (Chung & Chung, 1998).

On June 11, 1999, Clon, Korea's then leading hip-hop band, invited all adopted Koreans who were visiting Korea to a free concert called *Be Strong* at Seoul Arts Centre. At this extraordinary event, the group performed songs from their new album *Funky Together,* including "Abandoned Child," explicitly dedicated to all adopted Koreans overseas (Kim & Clon, 1999). The song describes, according to a review, "the pain and sorrow of an adoptee." "Abandoned Child" portrays an adopted Korean who cries alone and longs for the Korean mother and Korea, and as the refrain asks over and over again: "Why was I abandoned, why am I crying alone?" and "I know nothing about my name, my country, and my language."

The most famous song about adoption performed by a Korean pop group is Sky's "Eternity" from the 1999 debut album *Final Fantasy* (Kang & Sky, 1999). The video version of the song, which was elected as Korea's best music video of the year, uses the form of an action film to tell the dramatic story of how two brothers are adopted by two different families in Canada and how their lives are fatally intertwined twenty years later. As adults, one brother has become a depressed criminal played by the famous actor Cha

In-pyo and the other an aspiring police agent. In a dramatic shooting, the police brother kills his own sibling, and the music video ends with the surviving brother about to leave for Korea from the same airport the siblings arrived at as adoptive children. Critics considered the music video as an outspoken contribution to the political debate on international adoption.

The extremely popular group H.O.T. included a song touching upon the adoption issue in their last album, *They Are Nothing Different with Us* (Lee & H.O.T., 2000). The song "Abandoned Children" depicts family problems as a reason for adoption, while the adoptees ask themselves "Why were we abandoned?" in the refrain. In October 2001, H.O.T.'s former singer Moon Hee Jun released his solo album *Alone,* which in a few days sold 400,000 copies and reached the top position on Korea's selling list (Lee & Moon, 2001). The title song "Alone" is, according to an interview with Moon Hee Jun himself, a song about an adoptee's "sorrow and misfortune": "The overseas adoptees live miserable lives," according to the singer. Moon Hee Jun states that he received inspiration for the song while studying the contents of adopted Koreans' home pages on the Internet. The text tells about confusion and resignation: "If I had been sent away out of love, I would have understood everything."

THE CONSTRUCTION OF A DISCOURSE
ON ADOPTED KOREANS

So, how can we interpret all these references to the adoption issue that have been around in Korean popular culture for the past fifteen years? Can they be seen as spurred by commercial sentimentality or as authentic expressions of sympathy? Can they be seen as plain art for art's sake or as political statements? On a superficial level, many would say that Korean cinema and music industry use adopted Koreans in films and songs because they sell. However, as the media expert John Fiske (1989) points out, popular culture always creates its own discourses beyond cynical commerciality. Or put another way, when Korean producers of films and pop music use the adoption issue in commodities created for a mass attendance, it is not just that money comes in, but a discourse comes out. The adoption issue has figured in the political debate since the end of the 1980s, but it is through popular culture that the discourse on adopted Koreans has been created and gained a mass spreading.

This discourse on adopted Koreans, which contradicts mainstream media's preoccupation with "successful" adoptees, centers on their being unhappy in their adoptive country, on their being abused by their adoptive parents, and on their longing for their Korean mother and Korean culture. That is exactly the connecting thought from *Susanne Brink's Arirang* (Kim & Chang, 1991), in which adopted Koreans are abused by their adoptive families, to *Berlin Report* (Seo & Park, 1991) and *Wild Animals* (Kwon & Kim, 1997), in which adopted Koreans live rootless and destructive lives, and to *Love,* in which adopted Koreans long for contact with other Koreans. The same goes for songs like Clon's "Abandoned Child" (Kim & Clon, 1999), in which adopted Koreans long for their Korean mother, Sinawe's "Motherland" (Sheen & Sinawe, 1997), in which adopted Koreans long for Korean culture, and to Sky's "Eternity," which again reiterates that adopted Koreans live rootless lives. This homogenizing, stereotypical, and standardized discourse, most probably an expression of guilt, is also what confronts adopted Koreans when visiting Korea or meeting Koreans. Coming from Sweden, I have, for example, often been asked whether I had the same experience as Susanne Brink.

Furthermore, I interpret the appearance of adopted Koreans in popular culture as a reflection of the existence of Appadurai's (1996) *global ethnoscape,* the shifting and translocal landscape of migrants having become building blocks of imagined worlds, as national identities and cultures nowadays are constructed and organized on a worldwide level in the age of globalization. As mediums of communication, cinema and popular music offer us dreams and fantasies of the world, showing us who we are and from whom we are different. The interest in adopted Koreans can also be linked to ongoing processes of reconciliation and reunification. With democratization and especially during the tenure of President Kim Dae Jung (1998-2002), the issue of settling with the past *(kwagô ch'ôngsan)* and finding the truth *(ûimunsa)* has come to the forefront (Ahn, 2002). This reconciliation process includes the discovery of previously hidden and forgotten moments of modern Korean history such as the adopted Koreans who, for many years, were made invisible by nationalist feelings of shame and humiliation. Collective remembering and mourning are not unique to Korea, but are classical features of any postcolonial nation (Ahluwalia, 2002; Whelan, 2003).

Finally, it seems that the South Koreans have come to understand the shared fate with millions of ethnic Koreans in North Korea and around the world of experiencing exile and homelessness, parting and separation after a brutal century of colonialism, division and war, and emigration and adoption (Lee, 1985). The problem of separated families *(isan kajok)* is considered to be the most important aspect of reunification and has also become a powerful metaphor of the Korean nation itself epitomized in the bittersweet cult of *Han* (Freda, 1999; Grinker, 1998). The concept of all ethnic Koreans, seen as one dispersed family, is also acknowledged by the Republic of Korea National Red Cross (1977) in its report on the problem of separated families, which starts by accounting displacements under Japanese rule, continues with population movements before and during the Korean War, and ends with modern emigration and international adoption.

However, sometimes things are not as solemn as they seem, for a discourse has its own exaggerations and weaknesses. I remember watching an episode of the TV program *Non-Invited Guests* on MBC in December 1998 (Munhwa Broadcasting Corporation, 1998). The participants were supposed to play a scene where an adopted Korean girl returns to her hometown and meets her biological mother for the first time. In spite of the obvious gravity of the situation, both the participants and the studio spectators had trouble not giggling or even laughing. I understand from the merry situation that one of the most effective ways to deal with a national trauma, as the adoption issue indeed is in Korea, is through catharsis-like humor.

REFERENCES

Ahluwalia, P. (2002). Toward (re)conciliation: The postcolonial economy of giving. In D. T. Goldberg & A. Quayson (Eds.), *Relocating postcolonialism* (pp. 184-204). Oxford: Blackwell.

Ahn, B.-O. (2002). The significance of settling the past in modern Korean history. *Korea Journal, 42*(3), 7-17.

Anderson, B. (1983). *Imagined communities. Reflections on the origin and spread of nationalism.* London: Verso.

Appadurai, A. (1996). *Modernity at large: Cultural dimensions of globalization.* Minneapolis: University of Minnesota Press.

Cha, T.-J. (Producer), & Cheong, J. W. (Director) (1967). *When April Goes By* [Motion picture]. Korea: Keuk Dong Entertainment.

Chung, W. Y. (Producer), & Chung, W. Y. (Artist). (1998). *Yŏng-mi Robinson* [Music album]. Korea: Universal Records.

Fiske, J. (1989). *Understanding popular culture.* Boston: Unwin Hyman.

Freda, J. K. (1999). Discourse on *Han* in postcolonial Korea: Absent suffering and industrialist dreams. *Jouvert, 3,* 1-2. Retrieved September 25, 2003, from http://social.chass.ncsu.edu/jouvert/v3i12/freda.htm.

Gillespie, M. (1995). *Television, ethnicity, and cultural change.* London: Routledge.

Grinker, R. R. (1998). *Korea and its futures. Unification and the unfinished war.* New York: St. Martin's Press.

Hall, S. (1997). The work of representation. In S. Hall (Ed.), *Representation: Cultural representations and signifying practices* (pp. 13-74). London: Sage.

Hwang, C.-U. (Producer), & Jin, W.-S. (Director) (1998). *Too tired to die* [Motion picture]. Korea: Dream Search.

Kang, M. (Producer), & Sky (Artist) (1999). *Final fantasy* [Music album]. Korea: Doremi Record.

Kim, J. H. (Producer), & Pak, C.-s. (Director) (1997). *Push! Push!* [Motion picture]. Korea: J Com.

Kim, K.-S. (Producer), & Chang, K.-S. (Director) (1991). *Susanne Brink's Arirang* [Motion picture]. Korea: Sewon Films.

Kim, Y. S. (Producer), & Clon. (Artist) (1999). *Funky together* [Music album]. Korea: Woofer Entertainment.

Kwon, K.-Y. (Producer), & Kim, K.-D. (Director) (1997). *Wild animals* [Motion picture]. Korea: Dream Cinema.

Lee, H.-J. (1985). National division and family problems. *Korea Journal, 25*(8), 4-18.

Lee, M.-D. (Producer), & Lee, D. Y. (Director) (1971). *A guilty woman* [Motion picture]. Korea: Deok Yung Films.

Lee, S. M. (Producer), & H.O.T. (Artist) (2000). *They are nothing different with us* [Music album]. Korea: SM Town.

Lee, S. M. (Producer), & Moon, H. J. (Artist) (2001). *Alone* [Music album]. Korea: SM Town.

Lee, T. W. (Producer), & Pak, C.-s. (Director) (1990). *Oseam hermitage* [Motion picture]. Korea: Tae Heung Films.

Lee, W.-S. (Producer), & Lee, J.-S. (Director) (1999). *Love* [Motion picture]. Korea: Dong-A Export Corporation.

Ministry of Health and Welfare (1999). *Statistics from Ministry of Health and Welfare*. Seoul: Ministry of Health and Welfare.

Morley, D. (2000). *Home territories: Media, mobility, and identity*. London: Routledge.

Mulhern, F. (2000). *Culture/metaculture*. London: Routledge.

Munhwa Broadcasting Corporation (1998). *Non-invited guests*. Seoul: Munhwa Broadcasting Corporation.

Pae Y.-G. (Producer), & Pae Y.-G (Director) (1995). *The people in white* [Motion picture]. Korea: Pae Yong Gyun Production.

Park, S. H. (1994). *Forced child migration: Korea-born intercountry adoptees in the United States*. Unpublished doctoral dissertation, University of Hawaii, Manoa.

Park, W. S. (Producer), & Kwon, Y. S. (Director) (1972). *Between love* [Motion picture]. Korea: Korea Art Movie.

Penner, E. E. (1996). *Comparative analysis of international child adoption practices and policies in Korea and China*. Unpublished master's thesis, McGill University, Montreal, Quebec, Canada.

Republic of Korea National Red Cross (1977). *The dispersed families in Korea*. Seoul: Republic of Korea National Red Cross.

Sarri, R. C., Baik, Y., & Bombyk, M. (1998). Goal displacement and dependency in South Korean-United States intercountry adoption. *Children and Youth Services Review, 20*(1-2), 87-114.

Seo, B.-K. (Producer), & Park, K.-S. (Director) (1991). *Berlin report* [Motion picture]. Korea: Mokad Korea.

Sheen, D. C. (Producer), & Sinawe (Artist) (1997). *Haerangsa* [Music album]. Korea: Doremi Record.

Storey, J. (2001). *Cultural theory and popular culture: An introduction* (3rd ed.). London: Prentice Hall.

Whelan, K. (2003). Between filiation and affiliation: The politics of postcolonial memory. In C. Carroll & P. King (Eds.), *Ireland and postcolonial theory* (pp. 92-108). Cork, Ireland.

PART V:
GLOBAL PERSPECTIVES

Korean children have been placed into homes throughout the United States, Canada, Europe, and Australia. Their experiences vary greatly, as do the environments in which they find themselves. Notably, the United States' and Canada's heterogeneity reflect their individual immigration policies, with many of the European countries such as Denmark, Sweden, and the Netherlands being more homogeneous. It is, therefore, important to include contributions from other receiving countries when considering Korean international adoption.

Australia's history of international adoption from Asia contrasts with the United States' in that the placement of Vietnamese children preceded that of Korean children. Gray offers a comparison of these two groups, with the experiences of Korean adoptees juxtaposed against that of the older Vietnamese adoptees. Juffer's longitudinal study followed adoptees in the Netherlands from infancy to school age, measuring attachment, IQ, behavior, and psychosocial well-being. Individually both study findings have implications for policy and practice in their respective countries; and within the context of this collection, they further underscore the complexity and enormity of placing children in the diaspora as a matter of child welfare practice.

Chapter 14

Identity and International Adoptees: A Comparison of the Vietnamese and Korean Adoptee Experience in Australia

Kim Gray

BRIEF BACKGROUND ON INTERNATIONAL ADOPTION IN AUSTRALIA

International adoption is a relatively recent phenomenon in Australian history. Unlike the United States, where adoption of children who were victims of war became popular after the Second World War, international adoption in Australia did not commence in any systematic way until the Vietnam airlift in 1975. Adoption of children from South Korea commenced in the mid-1970s, and since the early 1990s, 30 percent of the total number of international children adopted has come from South Korea. During the 1990s, while the number of international adoptions in other Western nations, particularly in the United States, continued to increase, in Australia the number of international adoption placements decreased from 338 in 1991 to 289 in 2001 (Australian Institute of Health and Welfare, 2000-2001). However, the opening of an international adoption program with China in 2000 has contributed to the number of placements rising steadily each year. Australian Institute of Health and Welfare report that a total of 421 international placements were made in 2005-2006, including 103 from South Korea and 116 from China (Australian Institute of Health and Welfare, 2005-2006).

International adoption is regulated and strictly controlled by individual State and Territory governments in Australia under the relevant Adoption Act and by the Commonwealth Government under the Immigration (Guardianship of Children) Act 1946. Earlier, welfare departments showed reluctance to encourage and support families wishing to arrange international placement, and recent research shows this reluctance continues to pervade

International Korean Adoption
© 2007 by The Haworth Press, Inc. All rights reserved.
doi:10.1300/5734_14

adoption departments throughout Australia (Standing Committee on Family and Human Services, Parliament of the Commonwealth of Australia, 2005; Gray, 1999).

The reasons why Australia has so few international placements are complex. Brennan (1993) suggests that the reasons include what he sees as a "natural bureaucratic fear of scandal" and also that "there clearly is a kind of ideology in the social-welfare bureaucracy, and possibly more widely, that sees foreign adoptions as something to be discouraged and if possible prevented" (p. 166). Explanations for official reluctance to encourage international adoptive families in Australia go beyond bureaucratic inadequacies and needs to be understood within particular historical, social, and cultural contexts. Australia's adoption policy and practice in recent decades has been significantly influenced by past domestic adoption practices including issues such as secrecy in adoption, the "Stolen Generation,"[1] and by ideas expressed by the National Association of Black Social Workers in Britain and the United States such as the importance of *racial matching* in adoption and issues relating to "loss of identity" and "loss of culture" associated with international adoption. It is a highly politicized arena as it is in other Western countries; however, unlike countries such as the United States, where adoptive families receive financial support to adopt, in Australia, adoptive parents receive no financial government assistance to adopt a child from an overseas country and minimal ongoing support once the child has entered the country (Standing Committee on Family and Human Services, Parliament of the Commonwealth of Australia, 2005; Gray, 1999).

AIM

This chapter forms part of a wider doctoral project on issues of *race, culture,* and *identity* in relation to international adoptees in Australia. *Race,* in this context, is about having a historically and socially constructed identity that is imposed by others and also about the self-identity process of an individual "being" or claiming a particular identity. The scientific theory of race consisted of a system of racial supremacy and a hierarchy of various peoples based on racial determinants. The system of categorization is closely linked with the rise of nationalism in Europe and other Western nations (Castles, 1996; Goldberg, 1993). *Culture,* in this context, refers to the idea of culture as a way of life, dynamic or constantly changing. The word *culture* is now often used as a more politically acceptable alternative to the use of the word *race* in discussions about identity. In this way, the meaning of *cultural identity* is reduced to essentialist notions about origins and roots rather than being seen as a dynamic (as opposed to static) process.

The aim of this study is to compare the life histories of a number of adult adoptees born in Vietnam with the life histories of a younger group of Korean adoptees, in an effort to place the development and articulation of their hybrid identities in the context of Australia's adoption policies and immigration policy and its history of race relations. The first international adoptees to arrive in Australia came from Vietnam. Their experiences of growing up in Australia during a time when assimilation policies were still evident in everyday social practices are compared to the experiences of the Korean adoptees who arrived in Australia a decade later. The Korean adoptees in this study are experiencing their adolescent years in "multicultural" Australia, where policy emphasis has changed from assimilating and silencing cultural difference to an emphasis on celebrating cultural difference.

This study attempts to address some questions about how adoptees have experienced growing up in a predominantly white culture. How have societal perceptions and government policy impacted the way they see themselves? Are there differences in the experiences of the first international adoptees and those who arrived in Australia more than a decade later? What can we learn from the experiences of the adolescent and adult adoptees in this study?

It is hoped that, by gaining an understanding of the similarities and differences between the Korean and Vietnamese adoptees' life experiences, this chapter may make some contribution toward a better understanding of the contemporary adoptee experience in Australia. This is an area that has been little researched to date, and a greater understanding is needed to inform future international adoption policy, welfare workers, social workers, the adoption community, and the broader Australian and international community.

METHODOLOGY

The project uses a number of strategies to collect data and to confirm validity and data quality. Triangulation (Denzin, 1970a,b; 1978) is established by combining different methods (including in-depth interviews, participant observation, and analysis of various documentary data) and a number of theoretical perspectives and placing the life experiences of Australian adoptees within the broader context of the historical, social, political, and cultural construction of international adoption in Australia.

Although the study uses data from a number of different sources including adoptee anthologies and other documentary data (as described in the following text), it is based on a case study of twelve international adoptees—

six adolescent Korean adoptees (between fourteen and twenty years old) and six adult Vietnamese adoptees (between twenty-eight and thirty-four years old) living in various states of Australia.

RECRUITMENT OF PARTICIPANTS
AND DATA COLLECTION

Participants were recruited by contacting key organizers of ICASN (Intercountry Adoptee Support Network), an online support service for Australian international adoptees, and other nongovernment adoptive family support services across Australia. The organizations wrote to their membership requesting those who were interested in participating in the project to contact the researcher.

Qualitative data were collected primarily by the use of semistructured, in-depth interviews via e-mail correspondence, face-to-face interviews, and phone interviews over a period of twelve months from the end of 2001 until the end of 2002. Interviews were also conducted with some of the Korean adoptees' parents. A number of the adoptees provided their personal documents such as diary entries, poetry, speeches on adoption given at public gatherings, and recollections of traveling to their birth country. These firsthand accounts provided an additional rich source of data. Participant observation techniques were used at a number of adoptee gatherings such as an Adolescent Korean Adoptee seminar and the Saet Byol Korean Adoptive Families culture camp held each year in Sydney. The adoptee gatherings also allowed collection of additional data in the form of interviews with key organizers of adoptee activities and representatives from adoptive family support groups.

Another source of adoptee experiences was found in documentary data such as newspaper articles, adoption support group magazines and newsletters, adoptee Web sites, television documentaries, and in *The Colour of Difference: Journeys in Transracial Adoption* (Armstrong & Slaytor, 2001), a collection of stories by Australian-born transracial adoptees and international adoptees. In the United States, Korean and Vietnamese adoptee stories were sourced from Web sites and Korean adoption experiences from anthologies such as *Voices from Another Place: A Collection of Works from A Generation Born in Korea and Adopted to Other Countries* (S. Cox, 1999).

The interviews focused on adoptees' recollections of growing up in an interracial family in multicultural Australia, school and community experiences of racism, issues of cultural identity, how adoptees negotiated and resisted others' attempts to categorize them, and how their complex identities are continually changing. While both the Vietnamese and Korean adoptees shared some similar experiences in relation to issues of adoption and issues of racial and cultural difference, key differences also emerged from the narrative accounts of Vietnamese adoptees describing their early years when compared with the experiences of the adolescent Korean adoptees.

It is important to note that the Vietnamese adoptees are now mature adults looking back on their adolescent years with the benefit of hindsight unlike the Korean adolescents in this study. However, the majority of Vietnamese adoptees recollected memories of racial isolation living in predominantly white neighborhoods with little access to information about their country of birth and birth circumstances and little opportunity to explore such issues. Their experiences contrast with the majority of the Korean adoptees who speak of attendance at Korean classes, culture camps, adoptee seminars, exposure to cultural diversity, and experiences of traveling to their birth country. The differences in social policy and differences in cultural and political contexts is the main focus of this study as is the impact of social change on the lives of international adoptees.

DATA ANALYSIS

Data analysis commenced in the collection phase when the researcher clarified her understanding and interpretation of the responses by continually checking with the participants throughout the lengthy interview process. Analysis was completed by the researcher; however, two supervisors/mentors were consulted for discussions regarding data interpretation.

The narrative accounts of adoptees were analyzed and compared using qualitative coding and sampling techniques described by Glaser and Strauss (1967) and further developed by Strauss and Corbin (1990). The study also considers postmodern, postcolonial, feminist, and critical race theory in conjunction with the empirical data to gain an understanding of how adoptees define themselves and their everyday experiences as part of a minority group in a predominantly white society.

SOCIOPOLITICAL CONTEXT

The Vietnamese adoptees in this study arrived in Australia in the early to mid-1970s during a time when Australia's assimilation policies were still evident in everyday social practices and perceptions.

The Immigration Restriction Act of 1901 established a racial distinction between whites and nonwhites, those who were deemed capable of assimilation and those who were not based on Social Darwinian racial theories of the time. "Inferior" races were believed to lower the quality of life, and there was also the concern that the emerging Asian nations of the region may be a political threat to Australia (Kivisto, 2002; Murphy, 1993). This White Australia policy restricted non-Europeans from entering Australia and had been in place since 1901. It was the dominant immigration policy until 1966 and not entirely extinguished until 1975. Following Australia's involvement in World War II, a decision was made to promote an immigration program to encourage white immigrants. There were a number of reasons for this immigration policy: encouraging *New Australians* (as recent immigrants were called at the time), who could effectively assimilate, was seen as a way to counter the falling birthrate, as a way for Australia to effectively defend itself following the Japanese attack on Northern Australia in World War II, and to provide a workforce for the expanding industrial sector. D. R. Cox (1987) notes an ethnic preference hierarchy that saw British and northern European immigrants being eligible for assistance under assisted passage schemes, while southern Europeans were usually required to meet their own passage costs.

However, the arrival of Indochinese refugees from Vietnam following the fall of Saigon in 1975 began a highly controversial period in Australia's political history. As Viviani (1996) suggests, the White Australia policy had been officially abolished just two years before the fall of Saigon, and this policy had symbolized "a deep-seated threat mentality among Australians of all political persuasions—the fear that a significant change in the racial composition of the Australian people would inevitably mean the erosion of deeply held political and social values" (p. 7).

The Whitlam Federal Labor Government (1972-1975) effectively brought to an end the discriminatory immigration policy by embracing multiculturalism and introducing the Race Discrimination Act of 1975 in an effort to protect minority groups and combat racism (D. R. Cox, 1987; Kivisto, 2002). International adoption in Australia effectively commenced at this time with the arrival of 292 Vietnamese children as part of Operation Babylift. Harvey (1981) reports that the New South Wales government welfare department "showed a marked reluctance to encourage and support families wishing to arrange . . . intercountry placements" (p. 38). However, a number of individual Australian families made arrangements directly with orphanages in Vietnam to adopt children, and the end of the Vietnam War saw a change in official attitudes.

The Vietnamese adoptees in this study spent their adolescent years amidst controversy about the appropriateness of a policy of multiculturalism. While a bipartisan policy on Asian immigration largely supported a nondiscriminatory policy, other outspoken people played their part in influencing public opinion. I refer here to the debate about Asian immigration in the 1980s where historian Geoffrey Blainey and the then Opposition Leader, John Howard, espoused views about the *degree of tolerance* that the public has toward Asian immigrants and their lifestyle, which was seen as incompatible with the Australian one (Kapferer, 1988; Viviani, 1996). Given the political controversy over Vietnamese boat people and assimilationist views expressed in the public domain, as well as the policy of adoption secrecy, there was little space, opportunity, or resources for Vietnamese adoptees to explore any identity other than their position in predominantly white, middle-class families. The effects of these policies on Australia's early adoptees will be discussed further on in the chapter.

The experiences of Vietnamese adoptees growing up in Australia are compared with those of a younger group of Korean adolescent adoptees who arrived more than a decade later in the late 1980s. While the Korean adoptees arrived when the policy of multiculturalism was being debated in public discourse, their adolescent years are in a different sociopolitical context. There has been a shift in public attitudes about multiculturalism as the face of the nation changes.

South Korea is now one of Australia's major trading partners and a significant number of South Korean people now come to Australia for work and education opportunities. While in recent years there has still been opposition to nonwhite immigrants by right-wing extremists, such as Pauline Hanson, who hark back to the "good old days" and Prime Minister John Howard continues to use boat people as scapegoats in his political campaigns, it appears that the majority have accepted the move from assimilation to multiculturalism (Kivisto, 2002). Kivisto cites the work of Jeremy Beckett (1995) and Robert Ho (1990) on community attitudes to multiculturalism in Australia and suggests that "while many Australians are critical of illegal immigrants and concerned in various ways about adjustment problems that members of some groups experience, the majority of the public rejects this politics of the rear-guard and embraces in principle the idea of multiculturalism" (p. 112). Australia's national identity is changing and international adoptees' identities need to be considered within the context of these dynamic changes.

INTERNATIONAL ADOPTEES AND CULTURAL IDENTITY

Much of the literature on international adoption from the different perspectives of adoption workers, adoptive support groups, researchers in the field, academics, and, more important, adoptees themselves focuses on the importance of cultural identity in the lives of adoptees. So, how can cultural identity be understood in this context, and what is its significance for international adoptees?

Issues about cultural identity are linked to the uncertainty of the times in which we live. Postmodern theorists have illustrated how the breakdown in traditional values in contemporary times has contributed to a general feeling of uncertainty and fear (Bauman, 1997; Hall, 1990, 1992). Melucci (1997) sees the multiple choices and experiences of the individual as causing a crisis of identity. Whereas in the past "the meaning of individual behavior was always sought on some plane of reality lying above or below the individual—nature, the kinship system, the state, class, or Society . . . in contemporary systems the construction of the meaning of action shifts to the individual" (p. 64). Melucci sees one way out of the confusion that comes with the "multiple experience of the self" is to "once again attach ourselves to a stable nucleus in a desperate attempt to reconstitute an essence—for example, by reviving primary bonds of belonging, like kinship or local and geographical ties" (p. 65).

In other words, in order to escape the confusion and alienation that life brings, we seek some form of group or community belonging where we can rediscover the historical and other ties that unite us. It is the idea of discovering common historical and cultural links, of "reconstituting an essence," of uncovering "who we really are" that is particularly relevant to understanding cultural identity as it relates to international adoptees.

The effects of colonialism and Western imperialism can be seen through a history of transportation, slavery, invasion, and migration resulting in many displaced, fragmented, and marginalized communities of the world. Hall (1990) draws on the work of Frantz Fanon to illustrate how, in postcolonial societies, the process of rediscovering some form of essential identity has been used as a way to resist the debilitating effects of colonialism. Hall describes two different ways of thinking about cultural identity. The first position can be explained as "one shared culture," the idea that people who share a history, ancestry, and certain cultural codes are "one people." In this way, their shared culture is fixed at a certain point in history and as such does not change. He uses the Afro-Caribbean experience to illustrate how this understanding of cultural identity provides "continuous frames of reference and meaning beneath the shifting divisions and vicissitudes of our actual history. This 'oneness'. . . is the truth, the essence, of 'Caribbeanness,' of the black experience" (p. 223). Hall sees this idea of cultural identity as playing a crucial role in all postcolonial struggles.

In the Australian context, the history of white dominance over Aborigines is a racist history of colonization, oppression, and forcible removal of children based on religious and scientific notions about the inferiority of indigenous people. A major part of their struggle has been to rediscover a shared history and culture and to have that cultural "essence" recognized in the wider community. However, as Holland, who identifies as a *murri,* states

> while it is important to recognize that essentialist positions do have strategic political value at times, essentialist notions of Aboriginality often restrict us from acknowledging and celebrating the diversity within our own families and communities. It also denies the differences that many of us embody within ourselves. (Holland, 1996, p. 98)

Hall and Holland's ideas on essentialism and the complexities involved in identity construction need to be considered during this discussion on the Vietnamese and Korean adoptee "communities" in Australia.

"DIFFERENCE" AND DIVERSITY IN ADOPTEE EXPERIENCES

Listening to the stories of Vietnamese and Korean adoptees, it becomes clear that another view of "cultural identity," a more complex dynamic view, needs to be considered. Until very recently, international adoptees in Australia had not striven to establish a common voice. However, like members of other postcolonial movements who have united around geographical, historical, and cultural ties and experiences of marginalization and "difference," some international adoptees in Australia are now coming together with adoptees in the United States, Canada, Europe, and Scandinavia (through Internet discussion groups, Web sites, international adoptee conferences, adoptee anthologies, etc.) to reflect on issues of identity, on feelings of difference, and on experiences of racism.

The first international adoptees to come to Australia are now in their late twenties and early thirties, so it would be easy to suggest that their interest in searching for "who they really are" is related to their age and the fact that they are now living independently of their white parents and are in a better position to explore issues of identity. But this does not explain why some of the younger Korean adolescent adoptees in this study are also choosing to explore issues of cultural identity and race as well as knowledge about their birth families and birth culture at a different stage in their life compared with the Vietnamese adoptees. It also does not explain why there are varying levels of interest in exploration of birth culture within the Vietnamese adoptee group and also within the younger group of Korean adoptees. It would appear that exploration of cultural identity and birth history is far more complex than being the "right age" or level of maturity (although it is obviously a contributing factor in some cases), and has much to do with the interplay of individual experiences with Australia's adoption policies, with the policy of multiculturalism, and the politics of ethnic identities.

It is worthwhile at this point to mention Hall's (1990) second position in relation to cultural identity. This position recognizes that, along with the significant similarities in experience, cultural identity is about the recognition of differences that, when explored, tell a more complex story about "what we have become." So, rather than only seeing cultural identity as some "essence of being," which is stuck in some type of time warp and has only to be discovered to give meaning to the postcolonial experience, the second position speaks not only about "being" something but rather about "becoming."

RESULTS

I will use some examples from Vietnamese and Korean participants in the study and Korean adoptee contributions in other documentary data to better illustrate this position. Their narratives provide us with an insight into the different circumstances of adoptees who arrived in Australia at particular points in time where particular political and social factors were at play. Williams, a Vietnamese war orphan writing on the adopted Vietnamese diaspora, says:

> The desire of a homeland is the something that unites the adopted Vietnamese community. Many adopted Vietnamese have visited their birth country in recent times and many others express a desire to go back and explore their heritage and also to search for any surviving relatives. (Williams, 2001)

In the chaos to airlift babies from Saigon's orphanages prior to the Vietcong invasion from the north, children left the country with little identifying documentation or documentation that contained incorrect information. Williams, a Vietnamese war orphan who was one of the first adoptees to arrive in Australia as part of Operation Babylift, says:

My own search starts with my birth documents—a birth certificate etc., but when I was in Vietnam, I didn't even bother looking for my orphanage. I didn't feel I wanted to see Vietnam for the first time and stress over lost paper trails etc. I think Ty Andre can sum up a bit of why I didn't go at it tooth and nails.

Williams goes on to quote Ty Andre, a Vietnam War orphan who writes:

Among the thousands of babies who passed through Sancta Maria, only a handful had birth certificates. There were no papers for the children who'd been abandoned, or whose parents had been killed. Every birth certificate had its price . . . a Western official would tell (the orphanage owner) how many birth certificates he needed and the owner would negotiate a price. (Ty, 1997)

Williams' concerns are also voiced by other Vietnamese adoptees:

I fully realize that I may not find her (my birth mother), that my document I have are not mine but those belonging to a deceased infant, purchased as an identity when I had none to allow me to leave Vietnam. I know too that she may not want to be found, and that she could be anywhere in the world now. And of course (it is possible) that she is dead. All these are still hypothetical pragmatic outcomes that I am trying not to get emotionally attached to.

Most of the Vietnamese adoptees in this study speak of feelings of alienation and isolation, particularly in their adolescent years. Their experiences, of growing up in a white family and in a predominantly Caucasian community, mirror many of the experiences of Korean adoptees in other Western countries at that particular time in history (Meier, 1998). The narratives of the Vietnamese adoptees, then, need to be considered within the historical context of Australia's assimilation policy and policy of adoption secrecy. Although the White Australia policy was abolished in the 1970s, racist societal perceptions about "Asians" remained firmly embedded in everyday language and social practices. In addition, the Vietnamese adoptees in Australia, like the Korean adoptees who arrived in the United States and other Western nations after the Korean War, had either very little, or no, access to information about their birth family and birth culture.

Williams writing on Vietnamese orphans in America and Australia says:

> Placed in mainly white homes, the Asian children would grow up the subject of social debate and speculation that there might be difficulties. However, there was a lack of services to fully prepare parents on the need to ensure cultural heritage, language and identity was a part of their children's education. Emphasis was on assimilation and "'fitting in" with their family and the mainstream society they were located in, often far from Vietnamese-American communities and Asian-American in general. (p. 3)

The effects of the policy of assimilation on some of Australia's earliest international adoptees are poignantly articulated by adoptees such as Anne, whose story is by no means unique:

> As a teenager and adolescent I felt truly ugly. I rarely looked in the mirror and when I did, it was never with pride. I struggled to accept my own reflection because my inner feelings were in conflict with my exterior or my perceived exterior. I sound Australian. But I look Asian. I feel white. But I look Asian.
>
> I spent all of my primary school years in this small town. I think I was the only adopted person there, and the only Asian kid in town. It's hard to remember when my whole world consisted only of my house, my family, school and school friends. At school I was teased for looking Asian. Kids tease other kids for whatever reasons are visible; because I looked different that was the vice they used against me. I can't recall there being any Asian families in the town. I'm not even sure if there was an Asian restaurant. (Anne, Vietnamese adoptee, age twenty-nine years)

However, Anne's ambivalence in relation to racial identity sharply contrasts with another Vietnamese adoptee, Sophie, who was raised in a more "multicultural" area by parents who resisted the assimilationist tendencies of the broader community and incorporated cultural diversity into their everyday life. Sophie states:

> Mum and Dad have traveled the world so our house was unusually multicultural in the music, ornaments, food, activities, religion. Vietnamese culture was by no means thrown at me, in fact we never really did much at all Vietnamese. Though in hindsight it is probably just as well as it may have ended up feeling like a bit of token effort, or a bur-

den that my presence in the family was brought into it. The easygoing acceptance of all cultures in a sincere and searching way was far more important I believe in giving me the tools to explore my own cultural roots in my own personal time in different ways as I grew up, not family pressured time.

The family friends that were made by my parents through work and local groups were very diverse in their cultural background. Malaysian, Ukrainian, Dutch. My mother's career headed into teaching adult migrants and so our house was often filled with people of many cultures. Even though this occurred my parents did not push me to belong to them in any way, they in turn did not try to "take me on" in a cultural sense of teaching me things, even the Vietnamese migrants. In the suburb, and reflected at primary school, there was always a variety of cultures present. (Sophie, Vietnamese adoptee, age twenty-nine years)

Sophie's reflections on her parents' ability to provide her with "the tools to explore (her) own cultural roots in (her) own personal time" and her feelings about not being pressured to "fit" into imposed categories offers wonderful insights for younger adoptive families and adoption workers. It also resonates with particular meaning when we consider the experiences of the younger Korean adoptees in this study, a little further on in the chapter.

THE IMPACT OF MULTICULTURALISM AND THE CONSTRUCTION OF "DIFFERENCE"

Multiculturalism gradually started to emerge in the 1970s, following the failure of Australia's assimilationist policies and as a response to political mobilization of "ethnic" minorities (Vasta, 1996). In the early stages of the policy there was a concentration on recognizing "the significance of ethnic communities" and on legitimizing the importance of "cultural maintenance." However, following the 1989 Federal Government policy statement, *National Agenda for a Multicultural Australia,* "the emphasis has been on the social and cultural rights of citizens, and the need for the state to pursue active policies to combat discriminations and to achieve social justice" (Vasta, 1996, p. 47).

However, government policy in relation to multiculturalism remains primarily concerned with the management of cultural difference. As Vasta (1996) suggests, despite access and equity strategies aimed to improve services and resources to groups with differing needs, the strategies "have had little measurable effect on the way government relates to minorities"

(p. 59). This means that indigenous Australians and migrant groups remain in their position of "other" in relation to the dominant white culture, have effectively been kept "in their place," and racism remains in institutional and interpersonal interactions on an everyday level. It is important to be aware that those who are labeled as "other," in relation to white normality, such as international adoptees, are finding ways to redefine themselves and to resist racism. This will be discussed in greater depth further on in the chapter.

Government emphasis on categorizing people on the basis of ethnicity assumes sameness within groups based on a common biological essence or birthplace or on shared physical characteristics, language, or customs. In an effort to celebrate and recognize cultural differences, ethnic minorities have also used similar criteria to gain access to their share of resources. Ethnicity and culture have become the major site of political struggle for minority groups, and in recent times some older international adoptees have also entered the domain of identity politics. An example of international adoptees becoming involved in identity politics can be seen in recent discussions on an international adoptee LISTSERV (i.e., Korean Adoptees Worldwide) where some members discussed ways to reclaim their lost cultural heritage by the creation of a "new ethnic group" united around common experiences of loss. In Australia, following the publishing of *The Colour of Difference: Journeys in Transracial Adoption* (Armstrong & Slaytor, 2001), some adult adoptees have formed online support networks and have been successful in influencing adoption policy on issues relating to cultural identity and international adoption. It is important to be aware that the use of racial characteristics or shared cultural differences, in order to construct well-defined boundaries around particular groups in society, is used by individuals, communities, and nations for particular political purposes. But we need to go beyond the tendency to reduce questions of identity to simplistic discussions about *ethnicity* and consider the complexities and life choices involved in identity construction, the way identities are continually changing, and how people position themselves and live through the constraints imposed by the dominant culture.

KOREAN-AUSTRALIAN IDENTITIES

When we talk about cultural identity, we assume there is a split. And we waste our time trying to mend it. We talk about resolving a dichotomy, finding balance between two worlds, creating space for two cultures or building bridges. I don't think those things are achievable or realistic. They are confining concepts rooted in dualism. Their resolutions lead you to separate, pick and choose or sort and categorize. What I'd really like to do is push "puree," from *Kimchee on White Bread* by Kari Ruth, Korean/American adoptee. (Ruth, 1999, p. 80)

International adoptees, like other "hybrid" groups who do not fit comfortably in any one racial or cultural category, are often portrayed in adoption literature and autobiographical texts as stuck "between two cultures" (Armstrong & Slaytor, 2001). However, as Luke and Luke (1999) suggest in their analysis of Australian interracial families, "the assumption that cultures, ethnicities, and, indeed races are homogeneous, unified and singular phenomena may—however unintentionally—silence and marginalize complex local differences" (p. 228). Indeed, the reality of the international adoptees' experiences in this study does not support the idea that they are doomed to a life in "no man's land" or that recovering some form of cultural "essence" is the key to understanding "who they are" or more importantly "who they have become." It is far more complex and dynamic than that.

Adoption policy in Australia, as in other Western countries, has been significantly influenced by identity issues resulting in major changes in adoption legislation to incorporate more open adoption arrangements and to facilitate reunions of adoptive children with their "natural" families. The campaign for the "right to know" has established a new form of identity politics in social work, and in some sectors there has been the tendency to make generalist assumptions about all adoptees being destined to a life of identity confusion as a result of the severance of their genetic and historical connections. There is also the suggestion that all adoptees have an "innate" need to reconnect with their birthplace and birth family. But there are significant differences in the way individual adoptees choose to respond to their adopted status and to their experiences of racial difference, and their choices will continue to change throughout their lives. A look at the narratives from some of the younger adoptees will illustrate the diversity and differences of their lived experiences. The quotes included are taken directly from e-mail interviews conducted with the participants and are therefore expressed in their own individual style.

Min Kyung (seventeen years old) lives with her Korean adopted sister (thirteen years old) and her parents in Sydney's Western suburbs. She speaks here about her relationship with her parents and about her adopted status:

> I guess I am lucky to have parents who aren't always reminding me that I am adopted like a lot of other parents; they don't force me to go to Saet Byol (Korean school in Sydney) or anything, they just treat me

as normal and I respect them, like normal parents. My parents play a big role in why I have no problem with being adopted; they teach me about Korean culture, they take me and my sister to eat Korean at a Korean restaurant every now and then, my Mum teaches me to make Korean food, and she encourages me to learn the language and both support my choices about meeting my birth parents. They took me and my sister back to Korea to just explore and take in our culture, also just for a holiday. My friends are also a big help; none of them really ask about it. I guess I wouldn't mind if they did. They just treat me as normal. My other Korean friends help as well, I guess because I never feel out of place even with all my other friends, 'cause they are all Asian like me. (Min Kyung, Korean adoptee, age seventeen years)

Min used the word normal a number of times in her response, and this seems to suggest her preoccupation with wanting to fit into mainstream ideas about "natural" biological families. Not wanting to appear different to peers is a common response for any adolescent. However, in the context of her international adoptee status the pressure to "fit in" to the dominant white culture takes on a different meaning. Min seems to have found a sense of belonging within her peer group of Asian friends and within her family, who assist her in negotiating her position of difference. Min Kyung's adopted sister has traced her birth parents, and Min explains why her feelings about a reunion with her own birth mother are different to her sister's feeling:

Even though my sister found her birth parents, I don't think that I want to, well at least not for the time being. Both my parents are very encouraging for me to find them, and the agency kept asking me if I wanted to, because I think that my birth mother is looking for me. However, I don't think I want to. Sometimes I feel a bit selfish because I have no interest in finding my biological parents. I just think that my parents now are very important to me and to me they are basically my only parents. (Min Kyung, Korean adoptee, age seventeen years)

Amy spoke about attending Korean culture camps and other Korean-related activities and how they contributed to her feelings of difference:

My parents took me to a few (Korean camps) when I was younger . . . I didn't really like them. (My sister) and I just kept to ourselves . . . they were just people I didn't really want to meet. I don't really think that they really achieve much. We talk about everyone being the same, yet these camps or picnics divide us. I guess to some people it gives them peace of mind that they are not alone being adopted and Asian and the older ones can help the younger ones with racism and being adopted. Personally I prefer not to go to them. My parents like them more than I do. They went to one a couple of months ago without me, mind you, and loved it. I guess it's good for them too. To talk to the other parents and find out about their kids. My parents are so funny. . . . (Amy, Korean adoptee, age seventeen years)

Jon, another Korean adoptee, has different experiences in relation to Korean culture camps and searching. Jon (fourteen) was adopted into a large Australian family consisting of nonadopted siblings and internationally adopted siblings from a number of other countries. He lives in an Australian city and has enjoyed incorporating Korean culture into his life from a very early age. Jon has traveled to Korea twice, the second time he and another Korean adoptee were able to visit their birth country through sponsorship from a Korean company.

I tried to meet with my birth mother when I was in Korea in April 2000. The social workers found her and she didn't want to meet me. The social workers didn't know why. I felt disappointed because of her reaction but I am glad I tried to meet her . . . My birth mother had given false information to ESWS and I do not know why she had relinquished me. I do not feel bad about this though because I can understand the position she was in. (Jon, Korean adoptee, age fourteen years)

Jon also talks about what he likes about "being Australian" after his trips to Korea and how he incorporates Korean culture into his life:

When I was young, before I was a teenager, I went to Korean camps up in Sydney and places with Korean adoptive families in the Kimchi Club. I have always been interested in Korean culture. When I was little I liked to be involved in picnics and things like that. As I got older I wanted to have more involvement. That really changed after my first trip to Korea when I was eleven. My interest has grown stronger over the years and my parents have encouraged me to learn Korean a lot. I'm really glad that they did encourage me and I am glad that I agreed to it.

What I like about living here and being Australian is you have more free time. In Australia we have more freedom. We don't have soldiers walking around the place. I wouldn't mind maybe a month in the Army but I'm glad I don't have to join for three years like I would in Korea. Australia isn't as polluted. I noticed that a lot in Korea this time. There is a lot more space here because there are less people. I like both countries equally and both cultures are great. . . . (Jon, Korean adoptee, age fourteen years)

Josie lives with her parents in a culturally diverse suburb. Like Jon, Josie also considers what she sees are the advantages to living in Australia:

> I get the best of both worlds . . . a Western, contemporary attitude with fair ideals like women not being oppressed, or my parents having a big thing about me marrying an Asian guy or any other Asian culture downfalls like say, living in a house with my grandparents or various other relatives. On the other hand with those morals and my capacity to fully understand English I feel equipped to retaliate against racism. And I suppose with my Asian body I wouldn't get as fat as a Caucasian person, with the huge amount of food I eat. LOL (laugh out loud). . . . (Josie, Korean adoptee, age seventeen years)

It is interesting to consider Jon and Josie's reflections about the differences between Korean and Australian culture. They, like the other Korean adoptees mentioned in this study, are obviously assessing life in Korea through a Westerner's viewpoint. However, they have been able to form opinions about their birthplace based on educational resources and travel opportunities that were largely unavailable to many of the earlier adoptees. Access to knowledge about their birth circumstances and their birth culture firsthand allows them to determine their own life choices about issues such as searching. It also allows them to consider their adoption in a broader global sense, that is, to consider such things as gender inequalities, power imbalances, and the social, political, and economic factors that have contributed to their relinquishment. "Korea," then, is not some unknown place to be fantasized about or to be feared but rather as just one part of their hybrid identity; Korea continues to influence what they will become.

DEALING WITH RACISM

Most of the adoptees in this study spoke about incidents of racism in their daily lives. The separation and distinction of social groupings on the basis of race remains a social reality in Australian popular and social discourse, although the word *race* is now often substituted with more politically acceptable terminology such as *ethnicity* and *cultural heritage*. Although multiculturalism in Australia has seen strategies of access and equity implemented to reduce incidents of discrimination, those who are visibly different from the dominant white population are still subject to racisms in the wider community. However, there are significant variations in the level of racism that individual international adoptees are subject to, as well as key differences in the way they negotiate and resist such discourse.

Two Korean adoptees in this study live in predominantly monocultural areas, and both have suffered more severe forms of discrimination than the other adoptees. David (sixteen years old) lives with his adoptive parents and has three older nonadopted sisters. He traveled to Korea with his adoptive parents when he was fourteen years old, and hopes to meet members of his birth family when he travels again to Korea this year. He spoke about his attendance at an Adolescent Adoptee Seminar, where he told other adolescent adoptees about his experiences of racism. He says:

> . . . it was really funny because I told them the stories about me being bashed up a lot as a kid and they didn't think I was telling the truth . . . maybe because it was too upsetting, some of the stories I have. . . . (David, Korean adoptee, age sixteen years)

Other adoptees spoke about how they negotiate racism:

> I don't want to sound mean nor rude. Yet if people are racist or rude toward myself or my friends or family, I will simply tell them what I think. I hang around different groups now. Wogs,[2] surfies, whatever 'cos I believe it doesn't matter what you look like on the outside but what is inside. All my experiences I have come across in my life have only made me stronger and a better person. I love my life, SIMPLE!!! (Amy, Korean adoptee, age seventeen years)

Amy spoke about how she identifies with other adolescents through their common interest in popular music, which appears to be an experience shared by all the other adolescent adoptees:

> The first question I was asked on my first day at primary school was "what's your top ten and which guy do you want to go out wit?" They didn't seem to notice me being Asian and my sister being Fijian. (Amy, Korean adoptee, age seventeen years)

Josie discusses her friends and their common music interests. She also talks about how she plans to help others at her school who are experiencing racism:

I like all kinds of music; mainly dance and pop, but I listen to grunge and R&B too. It just depends, 'cos my friends have very specific tastes, so I leave myself open to all kinds of music. Most of my friends have multicultural backgrounds. . . . (Josie, Korean adoptee, age seventeen years)

I don't personally get any racist comments because first I don't hang around people who aren't my friends, and my friends are like my protectors. And also, making a racist comment is considered really low and people who do that are bagged out anyway . . . I feel lucky that I live in a place where racism is not very common. It is most often Caucasian people, or in my age area—vain, opinionated Caucasian girls . . . There have been quite a few cases, however, of racism in my school, only just recently. It annoyed me so much I have taken the liberty of starting up the school's antiracism team, which broke up a few years ago, I think . . . I was thinking . . . instead of just complaining all the time and watching as others get harassed, I might as well do something for myself and help others in the same boat in the process. I was quite proud of myself actually. . . . (Josie, Korean adoptee, age seventeen years)

Josie points to how some of her experiences of racism and feelings of difference are shared by other nonadopted adolescents:

I have a friend (who is) Chinese and, like me, understands what it's like to have both the Asian and Australian cultures clash. She's not adopted, and prefers to be "Australianized" with her grunge/alternative clothes and heavy music and so on. . . . (Josie, Korean adoptee, age seventeen years)

Indeed international adoptees share many experiences with other marginalized groups in society. However, the diversity within their position of "difference" suggests that responses to marginalization can take many forms and is played out in a multitude of ways. Most of the adolescents in this study have found a sense of "belonging" through their membership in peer groups who share a common interest in music and other forms of popular culture. Some of the older Vietnamese and Korean adoptees are also finding cultural expression through theater, documentary film, poetry, anthologies, and public speaking about adoption issues.

Stephen, a Vietnamese adoptee, twenty-eight years old, is an arts worker in Melbourne. Stephen's projects include a theater production called *Vietboys,* where he addresses the diversity of Vietnamese experience in Melbourne exploring questions of identity, sexuality, violence, and depression in Vietnamese youth culture. He says ". . . I've become more Aussie-Vietnamese/Chinese (due to) degrees of popular culture."

Stacey is a Vietnamese adoptee who has struggled with issues of racism, her sexual identity, being different from her family, and peer pressure that saw her "caught up in the street scene" of crime and drugs. She spoke about her extreme loneliness and alienation from mainstream culture during her younger years. She found solace writing all her thoughts and feelings in the form of poetry. However, she does not want to be portrayed as a victim and resists suggestions that her adoptee status is to blame:

> Adoption was just a small part of my life . . . it wasn't because of my adoption that this has happened to me . . . some blamed their adoption for the way their life has gone . . . I guess I could go through my life and do that but I know it's not right . . . I realized that everyone is on their own journey . . . we are all adopted (and) we have our rights but I need to be recognized for who I am, not just as an "adoptee". . . the person gets lost in that focus. . . . (Stacey, Vietnamese adoptee, age twenty-eight years)

DISCUSSION AND CONCLUSIONS

The narratives of adolescent Korean adoptees and adult Vietnamese adoptees show significant differences in the way those in each group have experienced their early years. The differences need to be placed in the broader context of Australia's immigration policies, adoption policies, and its history of race relations. There are also significant differences within each group about issues of belonging, attitudes to searching, feelings about birth parents, responses to racial difference, and experiences of racism.

Within the Vietnamese group, Sophie's experiences of cultural diversity and her adoptive parents' openness to cultural difference despite the dominant assimilationist views of the time allowed her to explore adoption issues in her own time. Her experiences of growing up contrasted with the other Vietnamese adoptees, whose access to the resources and support to explore issues of racial difference and adoption were not available until they reached maturity.

The Korean adoptees, on the other hand, have the benefit of the current policy of openness in adoption, and this has allowed some younger adoptees to explore issues of adoption and racial difference at a much younger age than the first international adoptees. Unlike the Vietnamese adoptees whose birth records were destroyed in war, the younger Korean adoptees in this study have access to at least some birth information. They also have greater access to Korean language and culture classes, culture camps, Korean-Australian festivals, and seminars about issues such as dealing with racism, and they are living in a society where celebration of cultural diversity is now a part of mainstream urban culture. They have been exposed to different life choices at a much younger age than the first international adoptees and are exercising their right to choose when or if they wish to search for birth relatives and travel to their birth country.

This is not to say that all adoptees now have equal access to these resources. The two Korean adoptees mentioned in this study who have lived in less urban areas and who have suffered more extreme racism have sometimes struggled with issues of belonging and to find the support they need. While government-run compulsory seminars for prospective adoptive parents now routinely address issues of loss, racial difference, and racism that adoptees may suffer, postadoption support for adoptive families dealing with these issues is not always available.

Those Vietnamese adoptees who have moved into more cultural diverse areas as adults are now in a better position to explore different aspects of their complex changing identities through diverse forms of cultural expression, for example, through social networks with adoptees, theater, documentary film and other forms of artistic expression, various forms of work, academic pursuits, and travel to their place of birth and elsewhere. The narratives suggest that age and level of maturity are not the only factors that propel individuals into exploration of identity. The differences in adoptees' life experiences suggest that many factors including access to people with culturally diverse backgrounds, educational resources on adoption, social policy and social support, and community attitudes impact on an individual's life choices and their level of resilience in coping with the challenges of their situation.

It would appear that, while adoptees, adoptive parents, and adoption workers are now equipped with many more resources and educational tools, there is still a long way to go. Recent attempts by adult adoptees and adoption professionals to educate adoptive parents, adoptees, and the wider community about issues of racism and racial difference in the lives of international adoptees are to be applauded. However, there is a need for government departments to work in greater partnership with nongovernment adoption support organizations to provide appropriate postadoption services and to effectively disseminate information about available resources to assist those affected. This should not only include resources about search and reunion but should also include support for adoptive families in the very early years following the children's entry into their family.

Multiculturalism in Australia has both positive and negative effects. While it recognizes and celebrates cultural diversity in the public domain, it can also force minority individuals to choose a particular "ethnic" label as a way to gain a greater share of resources and recognition for their cause.

The stories of how adoptees see themselves in relation to issues of identity suggest that essentialist descriptions or conventional fixed categories describing *ethnicity, race,* or *adoptee* cannot adequately explain the complexity, ambivalence, and fluidity of international adoptee identities. One-dimensional labels effectively reduce complexity and differences to simplistic, generalist statements. As Hall (1990) suggests, cultural identity belongs to the future as much to the past and

> is a matter of "becoming" as well as "being" . . . Far from being grounded in a mere "recovery" of the past, which is waiting to be found, and which, when found, will secure our sense of ourselves into eternity, identities are the names we give to the different ways we are positioned by, and position ourselves within, the narratives of the past. (p. 225)

The stories in this chapter provide us with a rich account of overlapping experiences of difference, but above all show a glimpse of adoptee identity, not as a fixed, static entity, but rather of multiple identifications that are complex, contradictory, and continually changing. It suggests that theories that espouse international adoptees as forever floundering "between two cultures" needs reworking to incorporate the intricate, ambivalent, and dynamic nature of identity construction, which finds numerous positioning within the historical, social, cultural, and political constraints of the dominant culture.

We are yet to discover how the young international adoptees of today will experience their adulthood, but we do know that their youth and adolescence has been spent in a different sociopolitical context than Australia's first international adoptees. There is a clear need for ongoing research in this area. There is also a clear need to address the obvious power imbalances that exist between the adoption policymakers and the adoptees themselves. Adoptees need encouragement and opportunity to better articulate their own needs and to have a greater say in formulation and implementation of adoption policy. It is hoped that this chapter has contributed in some small measure to that goal.

NOTES

1. "Stolen Generation" refers to Australia's history of forcible removal of "mixed-race" Aboriginal children from their parents, extended families, and communities. See Human Rights and Equal Opportunities Commission Report, "Bringing Them Home: National Inquiry into the Separation of Aboriginal and Torres Strait Islander Children from their Families," April 1997.

2. "Wog" is a racist term given to southern European immigrants who arrived in the 1950s and 1960s. In contemporary times the word has been claimed by second-generation southern Europeans to describe themselves and their experiences, for example, the comical theatrical production *Wogs Out of Work* was produced and acted by second-generation Greek-Australians and contributed to the use of the word wog in everyday nonracist discourse.

REFERENCES

Armstrong, S., & Slaytor, P. (2001). *The colour of difference: Journeys in transracial adoption*. Sydney: The Federation Press.

Australian Institute of Health and Welfare (2000-2001). *Adoptions Australia* (AIWS Cat. No. CWS 15). Canberra: Australian Institute of Health and Welfare.

Australian Institute of Health and Welfare (2005-2006). *Adoptions Australia* (AIWS Cat. No. CWS 27). Canberra: Australian Institute of Health and Welfare.

Bauman, Z. (1997). The making and unmaking of strangers. In P. M. Werbner (Ed.), *Debating cultural hybridity: Multicultural identities and politics of anti-racism* (pp. 46-57). London and New Jersey: Zed Books.

Beckett, J. (1995). National and transnational perspectives on multiculturalism: The view from Australia. *Identities, 1*(4), 421-426.

Brennan, G. (1993). The baby trade: The political economy of intercountry adoption. In C. Kukathas (Ed.), *Multicultural citizens: The philosophy and politics of identity* (pp. 159-174). Canberra: Centre for Independent Studies, Australian Print Group.

"Bringing them home: National inquiry into the separation of Aboriginal and Torres Strait Islander children from their families" (April 1997). *Human rights and equal opportunities commission report*. Canberra, Australia: Sterling Press.

Castles, S. (1996). The Racisms of Globalisation. In E. Vasta & S. Castles (Eds.), *The teeth are smiling*. Sydney: Allen and Unwin.

Cox, D. R. (1987). *Migration and welfare: An Australian perspective*. Sydney: Prentice Hall.

Cox, S. (1999). *Voices from another place: A collection of works from a generation born in Korea and adopted to other countries*. St. Paul, MN: Yeong & Yeong Book Company.

Denzin, N. (1970a). *Sociological methods: A sourcebook*. London: Butterworths.

Denzin, N. (1970b). *The research act*. Chicago: Aldine.

Denzin, N. (1978). *Sociological methods: A sourcebook* (2nd ed.). London: McGraw Hill.

Glaser, B., & Strauss, A. (1967). *The discovery of grounded theory: Strategies for qualitative research.* New York: Aldine de Gruyter.

Goldberg, D. T. (1993). *Racist culture: Philosophy and the politics of meaning.* Oxford: Blackwell.

Gray, K. M. (1999). *In whose best interests: Adoptive families' experiences of the intercountry adoption process in Australia and the politics of "race," "culture," and "identity."* Unpublished Sociology Honours Thesis, University of Newcastle, Newcastle, New South Wales, Australia.

Hall, S. (1990). Cultural identity and diaspora. In J. Rutherford (Ed.), *Identity: Community, culture, difference* (pp. 222-237). London: Lawrence & Wishart.

Hall, S. (1992). The question of cultural identity. In S. Hall, D. Held, & T. McGrew (Eds.), *Modernity and its futures* (pp. 274-323). Buckingham and Philadelphia: Open University Polity Press.

Harvey, I. J. (1981). *Australian parents for Vietnamese children: A social and psychological study of inter-country adoption.* Sydney: New South Wales, Department of Youth and Community Services.

Ho, R. (1990). Multiculturalism in Australia: A survey of attitudes. *Human Relations, 4*(3), 259-272.

Holland, W. (1996). Mistaken identity. In E. Vasta & S. Castles (Eds.), *The teeth are smiling* (pp. 97-111). Sydney: Allen and Unwin.

House of Representatives Standing Committee on Family and Human Services (November 2005). *Overseas Adoption in Australia: Report on the inquiry into adoption of children from overseas.* The Parliament of the Commonwealth of Australia, Canberra.

Kapferer, B. (1988). *Legends of people, myths of state.* London: Smithsonian Institute.

Kivisto, P. (2002). *Multiculturalism in a global society.* Oxford, England: Blackwell Publishers.

Luke, C., & Luke, A. (1999). Theorizing interracial families and hybrid identity. *Educational Theory, 49*(2), 223-249.

Meier, D. (1998). *Loss and reclaimed lives: Cultural identity and place in Korean American intercountry adoptees.* Unpublished master's thesis, University of Minnesota, Minneapolis.

Melucci, A. (1997). Identity and difference in a globalised world. In P. Werbner & T. Modood (Eds.), *Debating cultural hybridity: Multicultural identities and politics of anti-racism* (pp. 58-69). London and New Jersey: Zed Books.

Murphy, B. (1993). *The other Australia: Experiences of migration.* Cambridge, England: Cambridge University Press.

Ruth, K. (1999). Kimchee on white bread. In S. Cox (Ed.), *Voices from another place: A collection of works from a generation born in Korea and adopted to other countries* (pp. 74-81). St. Paul, MN: Yeong & Yeong Book Company.

Strauss, A., & Corbin, J. (1990). *Basics of qualitative research: Grounded theory procedures and techniques.* Thousand Oaks, CA: Sage Publications.

Ty, A. (1997). *On my brother's shoulders*. Kent Town, South Australia: Wakefield Press.

Vasta, E. (1996). Dialectics of domination: Racism and multiculturalism. In E. C. Vasta & S. Castles (Eds.), *The teeth are smiling* (pp. 46-72). Sydney: Allen and Unwin.

Viviani, N. (1996). *The Indochinese in Australia 1975-1995: From burnt boats to barbeques*. Melbourne, Australia: Oxford University Press.

Williams, I. A. (2001). Diversity and diaspora: Vietnamese adopted as children by non-Asian families. *The review of Vietnamese studies, Internet resource centre, 1*(1). Retrieved April 28, 2005, from http://vstudies.learnabouthmong.org/revofvietstu.html. Used with permission.

Chapter 15

A Longitudinal Study of Korean Adoptees in the Netherlands: Infancy to Middle Childhood

Femmie Juffer
Marinus H. van IJzendoorn

INTRODUCTION

In this chapter we examine the development and adjustment of forty-eight children from South Korea adopted by Dutch families. All children were adopted in infancy, before the age of six months, and we followed them until they were seven years old as part of a larger study examining infant-parent attachment relationships and, later, child development. We start the chapter with a short introduction to international adoption in the Netherlands, with a special emphasis on Korean adoptees, and continue with an outline of our prospective, longitudinal study. For early childhood, we then focus on child and family characteristics, the Korean adoptees' competence and temperament, and the quality of the parent-child relationship. For middle childhood, we focus on the Korean adoptees' behavior problems, their social development and peer group popularity, and their IQ and cognitive development. In addition, Korean children's experiences with discrimination are examined.

ADOPTION IN THE NETHERLANDS

Since the 1970s, domestic adoptions in North America and Europe have drastically decreased, whereas, at the same time, the number of international adoptions has increased (Selman, 2002). In 2004, most international

International Korean Adoption
© 2007 by The Haworth Press, Inc. All rights reserved.
doi:10.1300/5734_15

adoptions in the United States (total: 22,884) were from China, Russia, Guatemala, South Korea, and Kazakhstan; whereas most international adoptions in Europe (15,847 in 2003) were from China, Russia, Colombia, Ukraine, and Bulgaria (Selman, 2005). In the Netherlands, adoption is predominantly international. Each year approximately 1,200 internationally adopted children arrive in the Netherlands, whereas only forty to sixty children are locally adopted within the country. The majority of the adoptive parents (80 to 90 percent) decide to adopt a child because they are involuntarily childless. To date, all prospective adoptive parents attend a compulsory preparation course before they can adopt, followed by a formal home study. Since the Netherlands ratified the Hague Convention on International Adoption in 1998, seven licensed adoption organizations are allowed to place children with adoptive families. In the period that our longitudinal study started (1986), the compulsory preparation course did not exist, so the adoptive parents of the Korean children described in this chapter were poorly informed of the consequences of adoption. Also, no specific adoption aftercare service existed for the families involved in our study.

In the Netherlands, approximately 4,200 adoptees originate from South Korea (Ministerie van Justitie, 2005). Many of them are adults now, as adoption from Korea started in the late 1960s. In fact, in our country the phenomenon of international adoption from outside Europe started with Korean adoptions. Until that time, adoptions were allowed from inside Europe only, for example, from Greece or Austria. In 1967, the Dutch writer Jan de Hartog, who lived and worked in the United States, was interviewed and filmed for a famous Dutch talk show. Jan de Hartog and his wife Marjorie had just adopted a Korean girl, and at the end of the interview some pictures of this child were shown on TV. That same night hundreds of people phoned the TV studio to apply for such an adoption, and in one month's time almost 1,000 parents were put on a provisory waiting list. A few years later Dutch law was changed, enabling adoptions from countries outside Europe. Jan de Hartog's (1968) book *De Kinderen* (The Children), describing his and his wife's experiences with their two adopted Korean daughters, became a best seller for prospective adoptive parents.

Large numbers of Korean children were adopted in the Netherlands in the 1970s and 1980s, but the number of Korean adoptions drastically declined in the 1990s. To date, only a few children are adopted from Korea. In 2000, sixty children arrived from Korea, in 2003 seventeen children, and in 2004 there were no adoptions from Korea (Ministerie van Justitie, 2005). Korean adoptees living in the Netherlands are united in an association of Korean adoptees, *Arierang* (named after "Arirang," a well-known Korean folk song; www.arierang.nl).

THE LONGITUDINAL ADOPTION STUDY

In 1986 we started a prospective, longitudinal study including 160 adoptive families (Juffer, 1993; Rosenboom, 1994). The families were randomly recruited through Dutch adoption organizations, and not selected on current or expected future problems. In this chapter we focus on the 146 adoptive families for whom longitudinal data from infancy to middle childhood were available (attrition rate 9 percent) and, in particular, the adoptive families with Korean adoptees. The adoptive parents were Caucasian, and in all families the adoptive mother was the primary caregiver. The families were predominantly from middle-class or upper-middle-class backgrounds. The children in the longitudinal study, sixty-five boys and eighty-one girls, were adopted from Sri Lanka ($n = 79$), South Korea ($n = 48$), and Colombia ($n = 19$). All children arrived in the Netherlands before the age of six months. The Korean and the Colombian children arrived in the Netherlands at a significantly older age (mean age: fifteen weeks) than the children from Sri Lanka (mean age: seven weeks).

Families were visited at home when the children were five, six, nine, and twelve months of age. Mother and child came to the university at twelve, eighteen, and thirty months. At age seven years, families were visited at home to observe mother-child interaction, to interview the mother, and to administer questionnaires to her. Also, the child's intelligence was tested in the home setting. The school was visited in order to interview classmates and to have questionnaires completed by the focal child's teacher.

The longitudinal study also included an experimental intervention trial, reported elsewhere (Juffer, Bakermans-Kranenburg, & van IJzendoorn, 2005; Juffer, Hoksbergen, Riksen-Walraven, & Kohnstamm, 1997). A short-term, attachment-based intervention was implemented in three sessions at home between the child's age of six and nine months in a randomly assigned experimental group. The intervention aimed at enhancing maternal sensitivity and infant attachment security (Juffer et al., 2005; Juffer, van IJzendoorn, & Bakermans-Kranenburg, in press). In this chapter, we will refer to the effects of this intervention in general terms only, as the number of Korean adoptees in this study does not permit separate analyses for Korean experimental and control children. This is also justified by the fact that differential effects for the three countries of origin (Sri Lanka, Korea, and Colombia) were never found.

In the following sections, the development and adjustment of the Korean adoptees is examined, first in early childhood and then in middle childhood. Only one out of forty-nine families with Korean adoptees enrolled in the study did not participate again in middle childhood (attrition rate 2 percent).

When possible, we compare the Korean adoptees with nonadopted children or with the other adopted children in our study, namely the adoptees from Sri Lanka and Colombia. We start with a description of child and family characteristics of the Korean group.

EARLY CHILDHOOD

Child and Family Characteristics

All forty-eight Korean children had lived in a children's home in South Korea before adoptive placement, and some of the children had lived in a Korean foster home for some time as well. The children were escorted from Korea to the Netherlands by professional caregivers and the children met their adoptive parents for the first time at Schiphol, the national airport near Amsterdam. In most cases, there was hardly any information about the preadoption socioemotional background of the children. Some of the children were relinquished by their birth mothers, whereas others were foundlings. Many birth mothers who relinquished the baby did so because they were unmarried mothers.

There were twenty-five male Korean adoptees (52 percent) and twenty-three female Korean adoptees. They were fifteen weeks old, on average, when they arrived in the Netherlands (range: ten to twenty-five weeks). The large majority of the Korean adoptees, forty-two (88 percent), had a normal health condition on arrival, and six children had health problems (such as malnutrition). About one-third of the Korean children, seventeen (35 percent), had a low birth weight (or first known weight, if the child was a foundling), i.e., less than 2500 g (5 lbs.). Also, fourteen children (29 percent) were born prematurely.

All parents who adopted a Korean child were Caucasian and married. The adoptive mothers' age ranged from twenty-six to forty-five years (mean age: thirty-four years) and the adoptive fathers' age ranged from thirty to forty-three years (mean age: thirty-six years). On a scale from 1 (low education) to 4 (high education), adoptive mothers appeared to have a moderate educational level (mean level: 2.50). This was comparable for the adoptive fathers (mean level: 2.81). About half of the Korean children were placed in a family with birth children (twenty-two Korean children, 46 percent), whereas the other twenty-six children were placed in families with adopted children only. Eighteen children (38 percent) were placed as the first child in the family, twenty children (42 percent) as second child, and the remaining ten children as third, fourth, or fifth child in the family. More than half of the parents (56 percent) had decided to adopt because they were involuntarily childless.

Child Temperament

At the child's age of twelve and eighteen months, temperament was measured with the Dutch Temperament Questionnaire, or DTQ (Kohnstamm, 1984), which is an adaptation of the Infant Characteristics Questionnaire (Bates, Freeland, & Lounsbury, 1979). The adoptive mothers completed this questionnaire on how they perceived their adopted child's negative mood, adaptability, and general difficultness (for more details, see Juffer, 1993). At twelve and eighteen months, there were no differences between the Korean children and the other adopted children in the study with respect to general difficultness. However, at twelve and eighteen months, the adoptive mothers perceived the Korean adoptees as having a less negative mood, compared with the adoptees from Sri Lanka and Colombia (Juffer, 1993) (twelve months: $p = .04$; eighteen months: $p = .01$). Also, at twelve months, the Korean adoptees were seen as more adaptable than the other adoptees ($p = .04$). Compared with nonadopted children, the Korean adoptees were not perceived as having a more difficult temperament (Juffer, 1993; Rosenboom, 1994).

Competence

At the age of twelve months, children were observed in two competence tasks to assess the quality of their exploration (play) behavior and to examine how quickly they mastered a contingency problem task (Juffer et al., 1997). During the exploration task, the child was presented with several toys, and the child's exploration behavior was ordered according to the level of exploration. At the low end of the scale, simple exploration behaviors, such as looking and mouthing, were placed. The high-quality end of the scale encompassed elaborate behaviors, such as pretend play (for a complete description, see Juffer et al., 1997). In the contingency analysis task, the baby was placed in front of an apparatus designed for this episode. The infant could see but not reach two stuffed animals behind a plexiglass screen. A red handle was within reach of the baby. As soon as the handle was manipulated, the stuffed animals moved and three lights turned on for two seconds. During the test it was scored how quickly the babies discovered this and learned to move the animals by themselves (Juffer et al., 1997).

The Korean adoptees scored significantly lower on the exploration quality task than the other adoptees ($p = .01$), but there were no differences between them and the other adoptees in how quickly they discovered how the contingency problem task worked. As adopted children's exploration quality may be hampered by a longer stay in the depriving setting of a children's home in the country of origin, we post hoc checked whether exploration quality of the Korean adoptees differed from the Colombian adoptees (who arrived at a similar age; see earlier text) as well as from the Sri Lankan adoptees. Post hoc tests indicated a significant difference between the exploration quality of Korean and Sri Lankan adoptees, but not between the Korean and Colombian adoptees. So, the Korean adoptees' lower scores on exploration quality may be a (temporary) consequence of a longer stay in a children's home.

Attachment Security

When the children were twelve months old, the Strange Situation Procedure (Ainsworth, Blehar, Waters, & Wall, 1978) was videotaped at the university. The Strange Situation activates the infant's attachment system as a response to the presence of a stranger and two brief separations from the mother. Infants were assigned into one of three patterns of attachment: secure (B), insecure avoidant (A), and insecure resistant (C). Moreover, every infant's behavior was coded on signs of insecure disorganized attachment (D) (Main & Solomon, 1990) (for more details, see Juffer et al., 1997, 2005; Juffer & Rosenboom, 1997). In particular, disorganized attachment is a serious risk factor for later child psychopathology (van IJzendoorn, Schuengel, & Bakermans-Kranenburg, 1999).

In the total sample, intervention effects were found on insecure, disorganized attachment: there were fewer disorganized attached children in those families who had received intervention compared to the families without intervention (Juffer et al., 2005).

At twelve and at eighteen months, 75 percent of the Korean adoptees were securely (B) attached to their adoptive mother, with no significant differences between Korean girls and Korean boys. There were no differences between the Korean adoptees and the other adoptees in the study, nor were the Korean children less often securely attached compared with normative groups (van IJzendoorn & Kroonenberg, 1988). Also, 10 percent (five out of forty-eight children) of the Korean adoptees showed insecure disorganized (D) attachment, which is comparable with the 15 percent for normative groups in the meta-analysis on disorganized attachment by van IJzendoorn and colleagues (1999). Again, there were no differences between Korean girls and boys.

Maternal Sensitive Responsiveness

Another aspect of the early parent-child relationship is parental sensitivity, the ability to accurately perceive the child's signals and to respond to them in a prompt and adequate way (Ainsworth et al., 1978). Parental sensitivity is significantly associated with children's attachment security, as has been empirically shown in a meta-analysis of correlational studies (De Wolff & van IJzendoorn, 1997) and a meta-analysis of intervention studies (Bakermans-Kranenburg, van IJzendoorn, & Juffer, 2003).

Sensitive responsiveness was observed in an eight-minute free-play situation, videotaped at home at six and at twelve months. While the baby was placed in an infant seat in front of a low table with the mother sitting next to him or her, the researcher presented a transparent box containing ten attractive toys. The mother was instructed to play with her child the way she usually played. Sensitive responsiveness was assessed with two rating scales for Sensitivity and Cooperation (Ainsworth, Bell, & Stayton, 1974) (for more details, see Juffer et al., 1997). In the total study, intervention effects were found on maternal sensitive responsiveness: mothers who had received intervention scored higher on these rating scales than the control mothers (Juffer et al., 2005).

At six and at twelve months, we found no differences on maternal sensitive responsiveness between the mothers of the Korean adoptees and the other adoptive mothers in the study. Also, their scores did not deviate from the scores of nonadoptive, biological mothers (Juffer & Rosenboom, 1997).

Maternal Instructive Behavior

Another aspect of maternal behavior, instructive behavior, relates to how the mother encourages and stimulates her child's accomplishments in a task situation. At eighteen months, maternal instructive behavior was assessed in the laboratory in three task situations (e.g., building a tower of blocks) during a total time of nine minutes. At thirty months, this was examined in the laboratory again in three task situations (e.g., playing an adapted game of table football) in a total time of fifteen minutes. We used the Erickson rating scales to assess maternal instructive behavior: emotional support, respect for the child's autonomy, structure and limit setting, hostility, and quality of instruction (for more details, see Stams, Juffer, & van IJzendoorn, 2002).

At eighteen and at thirty months, the adoptive mothers of the Korean adoptees showed significantly more optimal instructive behavior than the mothers of the other adoptees (eighteen months: $p < .01$; thirty months: $p = .03$).

MIDDLE CHILDHOOD

All families were visited again when the Korean adoptees were seven years of age. At this follow-up, most adopted children were eager to participate in the study, as many of them had seen themselves as babies on the videotape that we had offered the parents as a gift for their participation. Therefore, they appeared to be quite willing to participate in the intelligence assessment. We postponed the questioning of more intimate issues regarding the children's thoughts and feelings about their adoption and origin to a later follow-up at age fourteen years (Jaffari-Bimmel, Juffer, van IJzendoorn, Bakermans-Kranenburg, & Mooijaart, in press). In this section we focus on the Korean adoptees' behavior problems at home and at school, their social development and peer group popularity, their IQ and school performance, and their experiences with discrimination.

Behavior Problems

The Child Behavior Check List (CBCL) and Teacher's Report Form (TRF) were administered to the mother and teacher of the Korean adoptee involved. Both are standardized procedures to assess the child's behavior problems, such as aggressive or depressed behavior. The CBCL and the TRF both contain 118 problem items, which are scored on similar 3-point scales. Mothers and teachers indicated whether behavioral descriptions were (0) not at all true, (1) somewhat true, or (2) very true of their child. The CBCL and TRF provide criteria to determine percentages of children falling in the clinical range. The incidence of behavior problems in children exceeding the clinical cutoff criterion is likely to equal the incidence of behavior problems in children who have been referred to clinical settings. We used cutoff points that were based on a sample of 2,227 children between age four and eighteen years, drawn from the Dutch general population (for more details, see Stams, Juffer, Rispens, & Hoksbergen, 2000).

While in normative samples about 10 percent of the children fall in the clinical range, 15 percent of the Korean adoptees had problems in the clinical range of the CBCL, with no differences between Korean boys and girls. So, compared with nonadopted children, there were more children having serious behavior problems, as perceived by the adoptive mother. There were, however, significantly fewer Korean adoptees falling in the clinical range of the CBCL compared with the other adoptees from Sri Lanka and Colombia ($p < .01$). For the school setting, we also found that 15 percent of the Korean adoptees had behavior problems in the clinical range of the TRF, according to the teacher, with again no differences between Korean boys and girls. For the TRF, no differences were found between the Korean adoptees and the adoptees from the other countries.

Social Development and Peer Group Popularity

We first compared the Korean adoptees and the other adoptees on a composite score of social development (for a description, see Stams et al., 2002). Korean boys and girls appeared to have comparable scores on this measure. The Korean adoptees, however, had significantly higher, more optimal scores on this measure of social development ($p < .01$) than the other adoptees in the study.

Second, we examined peer group status and peer group popularity. Sociometric data were gathered in individual interviews at school. We interviewed a total of 3,744 school-aged children, i.e., all adopted children and their classmates. None of the children knew which child we were focusing on, i.e., the target adopted child. Each child could name three classmates as most liked and three classmates as most disliked. On the basis of these nominations, children were assigned to one of five sociometric status categories: popular, average, neglected, controversial, and rejected (for more details, see Juffer, Stams, & van IJzendoorn, 2004; Stams et al., 2000). For peer group status and popularity, we did not find gender differences, nor did we find differences between the Korean adoptees and the other adoptees in the study.

A large number of Korean adoptees were nominated by his or her classmates as popular (39 percent). In two large general population samples in the Netherlands (Stams et al., 2000), the percentage of popular children was thirteen, so the Korean adoptees were far more popular than their nonadopted counterparts. Thirty-three percent of the Korean adoptees were rated as average, and 28 percent were nominated as neglected, rejected, or controversial.

IQ and Cognitive Development

First, we compared the Korean adoptees and the other adoptees on a composite score of cognitive development (for a description, see Stams et al., 2002). We found no gender differences among the Korean adoptees, but we did find significant differences between the Korean adoptees and the other adoptees in the study. Korean adoptees had significantly higher, more optimal scores on cognitive development ($p < .01$).

Second, we examined the Korean adoptees' intelligence. Intelligence was measured with the Revised Amsterdam Child Intelligence Test (RACIT). Empirical evidence was found for convergent validity, as the RACIT correlated 0.86 with the Wechsler Intelligence Scale for Children-Revised (WISC-R). The raw scores were transformed to standardized intelligence scores with a mean of 100, and a standard deviation of 15 (for more details, see Stams et al., 2000).

The Korean adoptees had significantly higher IQs compared with the other adoptees in the study ($p < .01$). The mean IQ of the Korean adoptees was 114, with no significant differences between boys (mean IQ: 116) and girls (mean IQ: 111). Compared to the normative IQ of 100, Korean children had rather high IQs. However, the Flynn effect may partly be responsible for this difference. Flynn (1987) discovered that nowadays people score higher on intelligence tests than in the past, possibly because there are plenty of opportunities to gather information and knowledge that is relevant for testing.

Discrimination

In an interview with the adoptive mother, we asked whether the Korean adoptee was confronted with negative reactions from others (peers or adults) regarding his or her skin color, appearance, or origin (see Juffer, 2006; Juffer et al., 2004). Most children (63 percent) were not confronted with negative reactions on a regular basis; 35 percent did experience some negative reactions every now and then, and one adoptee was confronted with many negative reactions. For this variable, we did not find gender differences, nor did we find differences between the Korean adoptees and the other adoptees in the study.

DISCUSSION AND CONCLUSIONS

In our longitudinal study, we followed forty-eight Korean adoptees from infancy to middle childhood. Although all Korean adoptees experienced at least one major separation from their birth mother and spent some weeks or months in a children's home, their overall catch-up in the adoptive homes was impressive. In most domains of adjustment, early childhood attachment and temperament, and middle childhood social and cognitive development, they developed as well as normative, nonadopted children, or even better. Their competence (exploration behavior) seemed to lag behind in early childhood, but that may have been a result of a longer stay in a children's home, where they had less opportunities to play with toys. At the age of seven years, the Korean adoptees did not lag behind anymore with respect to cognitive development. On the contrary, their intelligence and general cognitive development was above average.

The positive catch-up of this group of Korean adoptees resembles the outcomes of our series of meta-analyses on adopted children's physical, socioemotional, and behavioral adjustment, and their cognitive development and IQ (Bimmel, Juffer, van IJzendoorn, & Bakermans-Kranenburg, 2003; Juffer & van IJzendoorn, 2005; van IJzendoorn & Juffer, in press; van IJzendoorn, Juffer, & Klein Poelhuis, 2005). The children who were adopted outperformed on IQ and school performance their peers or siblings who remained in the orphanage or burdened birth family (van IJzendoorn & Juffer, 2005; van IJzendoorn et al., 2005). Adoption seems to offer new opportunities for children who otherwise had to live in disadvantaged settings.

Some mechanisms may be responsible for the positive development of this group of Korean adoptees. First, the large majority of Korean adoptees (88 percent) had no health problems on arrival. Empirical research found that adoptees' later maladjustment is associated with health problems on arrival, reflecting inadequate preadoption (health) care (Verhulst, 2000). Second, some families had received an early childhood intervention resulting in positive short-term effects on maternal sensitivity and children's attachment security in early childhood and positive long-term effects on the reduction of problem behavior in middle childhood (Stams, Juffer, van IJzendoorn, & Hoksbergen, 2001). Third, the majority of the children were securely attached to their adoptive mothers, and their adoptive mothers showed sensitive behavior on the same level as did nonadoptive mothers. In a study reported elsewhere, we found that secure attachment and maternal sensitivity in the early childhood years predicted the adopted children's social and cognitive development at age seven years (Stams et al., 2002). Securely attached children and children who had sensitive mothers in early childhood showed more optimal social and cognitive behavior at age seven. Also, the mother's more optimal instructive behavior in early childhood, reported in this chapter, may have resulted in the Korean children's better cognitive development at age seven. In post hoc analyses we found that maternal instructive behavior in early childhood significantly predicted children's IQ at age seven.

This group of Korean adoptees showed more behavior problems compared with normative, nonadopted children, but the overrepresentation of problems was relatively modest. At this age, the behavior problems were not related to their experiences of (racial) discrimination (Juffer, 2006; Juffer et al., 2004). However, it should be noted as a possible limitation to our findings that the data was gathered from the mothers, who often are not aware of the extent or nature that their children experience discrimination and/or racialized teasing. It may be that adopted children start thinking, and sometimes worrying, more intensively about their adoptive status in middle childhood (Brodzinsky, Schechter, & Henig, 1992; Juffer, 2006; Juffer & van IJzendoorn, 2005), resulting in behavior problems at home and at school.

In sum, we found that Korean adoptees growing up in the Netherlands are well adjusted regarding most domains of child development in early childhood and in middle childhood, and this applied for the girls as well as for the boys. Their attachment security and later social development was comparable to nonadoptive children, or was even better, and the same applied for their cognitive development. In early childhood, their temperament as perceived by the adoptive mother did not deviate from nonadopted children, but in middle childhood the rate of behavior problems in the clinical range was somewhat higher than in nonadopted children. According to the mothers, most adoptees did not experience much (racial) discrimination from peers or adults. It will be very interesting to know how these Korean adoptees fare at the next follow-up, at age fourteen years, and to hear their personal experiences about their lives and about their adoption experiences.

REFERENCES

Ainsworth, M. D. S., Bell, S. M., & Stayton, D. J. (1974). Infant-mother attachment and social development: Socialization as a product of reciprocal responsiveness to signals. In M. P. M. Richards (Ed.), *The integration of a child into a social world* (pp. 99-135). London: Cambridge University Press.

Ainsworth, M. D. S., Blehar, M. C., Waters, E., & Wall, S. (1978). *Patterns of attachment:A psychological study of the strange situation.* Hillsdale, NJ: Erlbaum.

Bakermans-Kranenburg, M. J., van IJzendoorn, M. H., & Juffer, F. (2003). Less is more: Meta-analysis of sensitivity and attachment interventions in early childhood. *Psychological Bulletin, 129,* 195-215.

Bates, J. E., Freeland, C. A. B., & Lounsbury, M. L. (1979). Measurement of infant difficultness. *Child Development, 50,* 794-803.

Bimmel, N., Juffer, F., van IJzendoorn, M. H., & Bakermans-Kranenburg, M. J. (2003). Problem behavior of internationally adopted adolescents: A review and meta-analysis. *Harvard Review of Psychiatry, 11,* 64-77.

Brodzinsky, D. M., Schechter, M. D., & Henig, R. M. (1992). *Being adopted: The lifelong search for self.* New York: Anchor Books.

De Hartog, J. (1968). *De Kinderen* [The Children]. Baarn, the Netherlands: Prom.

De Wolff, M. S., & van IJzendoorn, M. H. (1997). Sensitivity and attachment: A meta-analysis on parental antecedents of infant attachment. *Child Development, 68*, 571-591.

Flynn, J. R. (1987). Massive IQ gains in 14 nations: What IQ tests really measure. *Psychological Bulletin, 101*, 171-191.

Jaffari-Bimmel, N., Juffer, F., van IJzendoorn, M. H., Bakermans-Kranenburg, M. J., & Mooijaart, A. (2006). Social development from infancy to adolescence: Longitudinal and concurrent factors in an adoption sample. *Developmental Psychology, 42*, 1143-1153.

Juffer, F. (1993). Verbonden door adoptie. Een experimenteel onderzoek naar hechting en ompetentie in gezinnen met een adoptiebaby. [Attached through adoption. An experimental study of attachment and competence in families with adopted babies.] Amersfoort, the Netherlands: Academische Uitgeverij.

Juffer, F. (2006). Children's awareness of adoption and their problem behavior in families with 7-year-old internationally adopted children. *Adoption Quarterly, 9* (2/3), 1-22.

Juffer, F., Bakermans-Kranenburg, M. J., & van IJzendoorn, M. H. (2005). The importance of parenting in the development of disorganized attachment: Evidence from a preventive intervention study in adoptive families. *Journal of Child Psychology and Psychiatry, 46*, 263-274.

Juffer, F., Hoksbergen, R. A. C., Riksen-Walraven, J. M. A., & Kohnstamm, G. A. (1997). Early intervention in adoptive families: Supporting maternal sensitive responsiveness, infant-mother attachment, and infant competence. *Journal of Child Psychology and Psychiatry, 38*, 1039-1050.

Juffer, F., & Rosenboom, L. G. (1997). Infant-mother attachment of internationally adopted children in the Netherlands. *International Journal of Behavioral Development, 20*, 93-107.

Juffer, F., Stams, G. J. J. M., & van IJzendoorn, M. H. (2004). Adopted children's problem behavior is significantly related to their ego resiliency, ego control, and sociometric status. *Journal of Child Psychology and Psychiatry, 45*, 697-706.

Juffer, F., & van IJzendoorn, M. H. (2005). Behavior problems and mental health referrals of international adoptees: A meta-analysis. *Journal of the American Medical Association, 293*, 2501-2515.

Juffer, F., van IJzendoorn, M. H., & Bakermans-Kranenburg, M. J. (in press). Supporting adoptive families with video-feedback intervention. In F. Juffer, M. J. Bakermans-Kranenburg, & M. H. van IJzendoorn (Eds.) (in press). *Promoting positive parenting: An attachment-based intervention*. Mahwah, NJ: Lawrence Erlbaum.

Kohnstamm, G. A. (April 1984). *Bates' Infant Characteristics Questionnaire (ICQ) in the Netherlands*. Paper presented at the Fourth Biennial International Conference on Infant Studies, New York.

Main, M., & Solomon, J. (1990). Procedures for identifying infants as disorganized/disoriented during the Ainsworth Strange Situation. In M. T. Greenberg, D. Cicchetti, & E. M. Cummings, *Attachment in the preschool years: Theory, research, and intervention* (pp. 121-182). Chicago: The University of Chicago Press.

Ministerie van Justitie (2005). Statistische gegevens betreffende de opneming in gezinnen in Nederland van buitenlandse adoptiekinderen in de jaren 2000-2004. The Hague, the Netherlands: Ministerie van Justitie (Ministry of Justice).

Rosenboom, L. G. (1994). Gemengde gezinnen, gemengde gevoelens? Hechting en competentie van adoptiebaby's in gezinnen met biologisch eigen kinderen. [Mixed families, mixed feelings? Attachment and competence of babies in adoptive families with birth children.] Unpublished doctoral dissertation, Utrecht University, Utrecht, the Netherlands.

Selman, P. (2002). Intercountry adoption in the new millennium; The "quiet migration" revisited *Population Resources Policy Review, 21,* 205-225.

Selman, P. (2005, September). *Trends in intercountry adoption 1998-2003: A demographic analysis.* Paper presented at the First Global Conference on Adoption Research, Copenhagen, Denmark.

Stams, G. J. J. M., Juffer, F., Rispens, J., & Hoksbergen, R. A. C. (2000). The development and adjustment of 7-year old children adopted in infancy. *Journal of Child Psychology and Psychiatry, 41,* 1025-1037.

Stams, G. J. J. M., Juffer, F., & van IJzendoorn, M. H. (2002). Maternal sensitivity, infant attachment, and temperament predict adjustment in middle childhood: The case of adopted children and their biologically unrelated parents. *Developmental Psychology, 38,* 806-821.

Stams, G. J. J. M., Juffer, F., van IJzendoorn, M. H., & Hoksbergen, R. A. C. (2001). Attachment-based intervention in adoptive families in infancy and children's development at age seven: Two follow-up studies. *British Journal of Developmental Psychology, 19,* 159-180.

van IJzendoorn, M. H., & Juffer, F. (2005). Adoption is a successful natural intervention enhancing adopted children's IQ and school performance. *Current Directions in Psychological Science, 14,* 326-330.

van IJzendoorn, M. H., & Juffer, F. (2006). Adoption as intervention. Meta-analytic evidence for massive catch-up and plasticity in physical, socio-emotional, and cognitive development. The Emanuel Miller Memorial Lecture 2006. *Journal of Child Psychology and Psychiatry, 47,* 1228-1245.

van IJzendoorn, M. H., Juffer, F., & Klein Poelhuis, C. W. (2005). Adoption and cognitive development: A meta-analytic comparison of adopted and non-adopted children's IQ and school performance. *Psychological Bulletin, 131,* 301-316.

van IJzendoorn, M. H., & Kroonenberg, P. M. (1988). Cross-cultural patterns of attachment: A meta-analysis of the strange situation. *Child Development, 59,* 147-156.

van IJzendoorn, M. H., Schuengel, C., & Bakermans-Kranenburg, M. J. (1999). Disorganized attachment in early childhood: Meta-analysis of precursors, concomitants, and sequelae. *Development and Psychopathology, 11,* 225-249.

Verhulst, F. C. (2000). Internationally adopted children: The Dutch longitudinal adoption study. *Adoption Quarterly, 4,* 27-44.

PART VI:
IMPLICATIONS FOR PRACTICE

Just as we have begun to accumulate research-based knowledge about the adjustment and identity issues common to many Korean and other international adoptees, our knowledge about practice with this unique group of families has also begun to develop. Adult Korean adoptees and their families have informed current practice both with the parents who adopt internationally and with the children themselves. Yoon's contribution speaks to practice with international adoptive parents. Yoon provides evidence of the need for parents to support their children's' ethnic socialization. Both Bergquist's focus on the practice of bibliotherapy and Lee's examination of a Korean "homeland" tour provide insight into practice with adoptees.

The three contributions in this section demonstrate that adoption practice with international adoptees has come a long way from the beginnings of advising parents to raise their children as "Americans." Yet, as the contributions here also illustrate, we are, in many ways, still in the beginning stages of accumulating support for effective practice in international adoption. As international adoption continues in increasing numbers from year to year, it is imperative that we continue to build knowledge about effective practice with families and adoptees.

Chapter 16

Utilization of Structural Equation Modeling to Predict Psychological Well-Being Among Adopted Korean Children

Dong Pil Yoon

International adoptions have been less politicized than domestic transracial adoptions in the United States, because many believe that issues such as ethnic identity and mental health of internationally adopted children are less important when one considers the consequences of remaining in an orphanage or an economically depressed country (Ressler, Boothby, & Steinbock, 1988). Furthermore, international adoptions have received less research attention than domestic transracial adoptions because it is difficult for researchers to extrapolate and transfer research findings from one ethnic group to another, given that social identity formation can be changed according to social, environmental, and historical processes. Thus, despite the potential significance of ethnic identity for transculturally adopted children, empirical attention to the subject has been limited. Furthermore, most research initiated during the 1970s and 1980s concentrated on a single factor such as the self-esteem or mental health of adopted children, thereby neglecting the complex relationship between adoptive parenting approaches and the children's ethnic identity formation processes.

The recognition of the complexity of different cultural and familial structures has stimulated broad definitions of ethnic identity and, in turn, generated complex methodological problems surrounding international

International Korean Adoption
© 2007 by The Haworth Press, Inc. All rights reserved.
doi:10.1300/5734_16

adoption studies. The absence of more valid measurement and sophisticated data analysis on international adoption has contributed to inconclusive findings (Feigelman & Silverman, 1983; D. S. Kim, 1978; Kirk, 1965; Smith, 1991; Sodowsky, Kwan, & Pannu, 1995). This situation has provided little understanding of the importance of the adoptive parent's role in the development of adoptees' ethnic identity and, in particular, a sense of ethnic pride. Thus, rigorous application of valid measurement and sophisticated statistical analyses is necessary to understand the complex interaction of cultural and familial structures in identity formation for children raised in either international or transracial adoptive families.

The purpose of this study is to test a proposed theoretical model examining the interaction of parent-child relationship, parental support of children's ethnic socialization, and collective self-esteem on psychological well-being of adopted Korean children. In order to raise the level of measurement and statistical data analysis typically reported in adoption literature, new measurement scales (parental support of adoptees' ethnic socialization and collective self-esteem) have been developed by Yoon (1997). In addition, Structural Equation Modeling (SEM) is used to explain more complex and comprehensive relationships between aspects of the adoptees' ethnic identity development process (the impact of parental support of ethnic socialization on adoptees' collective self-esteem), yielding more conclusive findings than those of previous studies.

LITERATURE REVIEW

For the past five decades, Korea has been the most frequent country of origin for Westerners, particularly U.S. citizens, seeking to adopt children from other countries. In particular, during the 1980s, more than 40,000 Korean-born children were adopted by North Americans, representing the largest number of all U.S. transculturally adopted children (C. I. Lee, 1996). From 1954 to June 2002, about 150,000 Korean-born children were internationally adopted, and in particular, about 96,000 Korean-born children were adopted by American families (J. Kim, 2002).

Theoretical Backgrounds and Previous Studies

The proposed theoretical model in this study is based on two theories: the self-concept theory (Erikson, 1968) and ethnic identity development theory (McGoldrick, 1982; Smith, 1991; Spencer & Markstrom-Adams, 1990). According to the self-concept theory, family support, including feelings of love and belonging, plays an important function in the lives of adolescents experiencing stress in their interpersonal environment. Bagley, Verma, Mallick, and Young (1979) and Coopersmith (1981), addressing issues of adjustment in the adopted children, found that love and the stability of the family structure led to positive self-esteem. In addition to the consistency and warmth of the family environment, previous studies have also shown that certain parental motivations for choosing to adopt a child with a different racial and ethnic background predict the child's healthy self-concept (D. S. Kim, 1978; Koh, 1988). Generally, findings have indicated that adoptive families did not have any serious problems with their adoptive children's initial and later adjustment (Falk, 1970; Feigelman, 2000; Singer, Brodzinsky, & Ramsay, 1985).

Ethnic identity is a process in which the ethnic person is constantly assessing the "fit" between the self and the different social systems in the environment (Spencer & Markstrom-Adams, 1990). The ethnic consciousness that arises from socialization experiences, not only within the family but also within a distinctive and strong community, will be translated into an integral part of one's self-definition (Grotevant, Dunbar, Kohler, & Lash, 2000). On the other hand, negative consequences of cultural conflict would be revealed by relatively poor psychological well-being, poor self-concept, problems with psychosocial development, and maladjustment.

Smith (1991) identified acceptance of one's ethnic group as leading to positive self-esteem and to preventing social alienation and self-estrangement; whereas, ethnic rejection leads to self-estrangement and maladaptive psychological behavior. Kirk (1965) points out that "accepting difference" is important for parents who adopt foreign-born children. McGoldrick (1982) theorized that it is through the family that culture is transmitted and that, as a result, ethnicity and family are strongly intertwined. As part of a larger study on self-esteem, Phinney and Chavira (1992) found that familial support might be an important prerequisite for minority youths to explore their cultures of origin. Rosenthal and Feldman (1992) indicated that feelings of ethnic pride were related to families marked by warmth and positive relationships. Wilkinson (1985) argued that specific features of internationally adopted children, in dynamic relationship with the larger American context, gave rise to a unique environment in which their parents and other significant people support and encourage them to facilitate the process of accepting their ethnic and cultural heritage. However, the process of cultural socialization is complicated by the apparent and immutable racial and ethnic differences between parents and children that form the basis of the international adoption paradox (Lee, 2003).

Despite the assumed significant relationship between ethnic identity, ethnic pride, and psychological adjustment of adopted children, studies examining these relationships have reported conflicting findings. With utilization of advanced statistical analyses, Feigelman and Silverman (1984) and Yoon (2001) found these factors to be of considerable importance in the psychological adjustment of Korean-born adolescent adoptees. In contrast, D. S. Kim (1978), Bagley and Young (1979), and Gill and Jackson (1983) found no significant association between ethnic identity and psychological adjustment. As those studies merely attempted to find the child's level of ethnic identity and self-esteem separately, there are critical limitations to understanding the dynamics of how these factors can impact on internationally adopted children's psychological adjustment. In particular, while measurements of racial identity and self-esteem can be accepted as reliable, their validity remains questionable.

Development of Theoretical Model

Reviewing previous international adoption studies clearly indicates that little attention has been made to examine whether or not adoptive parents' support of children's ethnic socialization is crucial for psychological well-being of adopted Korean children. Because the family is the primary social system through which culture is transmitted (McGoldrick, 1982), parental support for children's ethnic identity development is likely to be a significant factor for their psychological well-being. To fill in some gaps in previous research, based on the findings of Feigelman and Silverman (1983), Smith (1991), and Phinney and Chavira (1992), this study posits a theoretical model that a positive relationship between adoptive parents and children, along with sharing experiences of the children's ethnic socialization plus collective self-esteem, are fundamental in the children's identity development process. For this study, Yoon (1997) developed new measurement scales (parental support of ethnic socialization and collective self-esteem) to narrow the dimensions of ethnic identity. Thus, the proposed theoretical model was tested based on two hypotheses: (1) Adopted children who receive more parental support of ethnic socialization and have a more positive relationship with adoptive parents will have greater collective self-esteem; and (2) adopted children who have a more positive relationship with adoptive parents and have greater collective self-esteem acquired through parental support of ethnic socialization will have greater levels of psychological well-being.

METHOD

Sample and Data Collection

Between the early 1960s and mid-1980s, the majority of Korean-born children were adopted through the Holt International Children's Adoption Service, which has been the largest and oldest adoption agency of Korean children in the United States. Under professional supervision, the clerical staff of this agency went through their entire case records from 1980 to 1984, identifying names and addresses of qualified adoptive families. A total of 800 Korean-born adolescent adoptees were identified for the entire group between ages twelve and nineteen. With the nationwide mail survey in 1996, the original sample consisted of 800 adoptive families, with 241 including both adoptees and adoptive parents responding from twenty-eight states of the United States, giving a response rate of 30 percent, which is considered satisfactory in this type of survey method.

Among adoptees, males and females comprised approximately 43 percent and 57 percent of participants, respectively. Participants ranged in age from twelve to nineteen, with a mean age of 14.2 years (SD = 1.51). Adoptive parents were Caucasian (96 percent), had at least a college degree (61 percent), and had family incomes of greater than $60,000 yearly (61 percent). About 50 percent of the adoptive families had at least two Korean-born adopted children, and 77 percent lived in predominantly white communities. In terms of parents' ethnic identification of their child, 60 percent of the sample reported that they had raised their adopted children as Korean-Americans, 28 percent considered them as Americans, and 12 percent reported them as Asian-Americans.

Variables and Instruments

Parent-Child Relationship

To measure positive parent-child relationship, items were selected from the Parental Acceptance-Rejection Questionnaire (PARQ) (Barner & Olson, 1982) and the Parent-Adolescent Communication Scale (PACS). Subscales of the child version of PARQ (Rohner, 1986) assessed aspects of warmth in the parent-child relationship. The PARQ used a 6-point Likert-type response format (1 = strongly disagree, 6 = strongly agree). For this study, five items were selected from each dimension of acceptance and rejection according to the size of the factor loadings. The internal consistency reliabilities

(Cronbach's alpha) in this sample were 0.75 and 0.73 for acceptance and rejection, respectively.

The PACS was composed of two scales—one that measured the degree of openness in family communication, and one that assessed the extent of problems in family communication. For this study, the researcher selected five items from the Open Family Communication Scale and four items from the Problems in Family Communication Scale according to the size of the factor loadings reported. Thus, this scale was composed of nine items and used a 6-point Likert-type response format (1 = strongly disagree, 6 = strongly agree). Higher scores indicate a positive parent-child relationship. Cronbach's alpha for these two scales were 0.87 and 0.78, respectively.

Adoptive Parental Support of Adoptee's Ethnic Socialization (APSAES)

No existing instrument was found regarding adoptive parental support of adoptee's ethnic socialization, and thus the measurement was developed through literature review by the researcher in order to measure the extent to which adoptive parents help adoptees possess their own ethnic background (Yoon, 1997). The APSAES includes parents' direct and indirect support of the child's ethnic socialization (Yoon, 2004). The parents' direct support measures the degree of parents' support to help a child develop his or her ethnic background (i.e., "My parents want me to be proud of my ethnic background"; "My parents try to help me find out about my own ethnic group, such as its history, traditions, and customs"). The parent's indirect support measures the degree to which parents attempt to learn about and have contact with a child's ethnic background (i.e., "My parents would like to participate in cultural practice of my own group by eating food, listening to music, and/or learning language"; "My parents seldom try to find out about my own ethnic group, such as its history, traditions, and customs"). A two-item 6-point Likert scale to measure each dimension was used (1 = strongly disagree, 6 = strongly agree). Higher scores indicate greater parental support of adoptee's ethnic socialization. The internal consistency reliabilities of these two developed subscales were 0.76 and 0.73, respectively.

Collective Self-Esteem (CSE)

To measure collective self-esteem, an eight-item scale based on previously developed questionnaires was developed by Yoon (1997). In order to accurately specify and objectively measure sense of ethnic pride for the adoptees, the Collective Self-Esteem Scale (CSE) was composed of two subscales involving pride about ethnic origin and shame about ethnic origin (Yoon, 2004). Ethnic pride measures the degree to which a child has positive feelings about his or her ethnic background and a sense of belonging (e.g., "I am happy that I am a member of the ethnic group I belong to"; "I have a lot of pride in my ethnic group and its accomplishments"). Shame about ethnic origin measures the degree to which a child has negative feeling about his or her ethnic background and physical appearance (e.g., "I sometimes feel discomfort about my physical appearance"; "I am sometimes ashamed of my ethnic group"). Based on the factor analysis, five items were used for pride about ethnic origin and three items were used for shame about ethnic origin. The CSE used a 6-point Likert scale (1 = strongly disagree, 6 = strongly agree). Higher scores indicate greater collective self-esteem. Alpha reliability for these developed items was 0.85.

Psychological Well-Being

Psychological well-being was composed of two dimensions—one assessed the extent of positive well-being through positive affect and satisfaction with life and the other measured the degree of distress through anxiety and depression. To measure *positive well-being,* items were selected from the Affect Balance Scale (ABS) (Bradburn, 1969) and the Satisfaction with Life Scale (SWLS) (Diener, Emmons, Larsen, & Griffin, 1985). According to the size of the factor loadings, five items were selected from the ABS by selecting positive items and all five items from the SWLS. Higher scores indicate greater positive well-being. Cronbach's alpha for these two scales were 0.64 and 0.84, respectively.

To measure *distress,* items were selected from the State-Trait Anxiety Inventory (STAI) (Spielberger, 1979) and the Beck's Depression Inventory (BDI) (Beck, 1961). According to the size of the factor loadings, six items were selected from the STAI and six items from the BDI. Cronbach's alpha reliabilities for each subscale were 0.85 and 0.86, respectively. The STAI, BDI, and ABS used a 6-point Likert-type response format (1 = none of the time, 6 = all of the time), and the SL used a 6-point Likert-type response format (1 = strongly disagree, 6 = strongly agree). Higher scores indicate greater distress.

DATA ANALYSIS

Causal relationships among the four latent variables as well as the relationship between latent variables and observed variables were examined by Structural Equation Modeling (SEM-PROC-CALIS:LINEQS), using a maximum likelihood method for the estimation of parameters of the theoretical model. As the literature suggests that researchers should not rely solely on chi-square because it does not work equally well with various types of fit indexes, sample sizes, estimators, or distributions (Bollen, 1989; Hayduk, 1987; Joreskog & Sorbom, 1992), the alternative goodness-of-fit indices were also used, such as Goodness of Fit Index (GFI), Adjusted Goodness-of-Fit Index (AGFI), the Bentler's Comparative Fit Index (CFI), the Bentler & Bonett's Normed Fit Index (NFI), Non-Normed Fit Index (NNFI), and McDonald's Centrality Index (McDonald, 1989).

RESULTS

Descriptive Analyses

According to Table 16.1, parents' warmth scores ranged from 1 to 6 with a mean of 4.90 (SD = 0.70) and positive communication scores ranged from 1 to 6 with a mean of 4.40 (SD = 0.94), showing that adoptees moderately agreed to having a good relationship with parents. Adopted children reported experiencing a very slight level of both parental direct support for ethnic socialization (mean = 3.82, SD = 1.48) and parental indirect support for ethnic socialization (mean = 3.52, SD = 1.46), ranging from 1 to 6, respectively. In terms of sense of ethnic pride, adoptees reported having a moderate level of collective self-esteem (mean = 4.57, SD = 1.05), ranging from 1 to 6. Positive well-being scores ranged from 1 to 6 with a mean of 4.54 (SD = 0.81) and distress scores ranged from 1 to 6 with a mean of 2.72 (SD = 0.71), indicating that adoptees reported having a slight to moderate level of positive well-being and sometimes having emotionally distressful symptoms.

Table 16.1 also displays correlations among six variables. Parental direct support of ethnic socialization (0.26), parental indirect support of ethnic socialization (0.23), and positive communication (0.15) correlated significantly with collective self-esteem. Positive communication (0.61), parents' warmth (0.54), collective self-esteem (0.35), parental direct support of ethnic socialization (0.21), and parental indirect support of ethnic socialization (0.13) correlated significantly with positive well-being. Positive communication (−0.41), parents' warmth (−0.39), and collective self-esteem (−0.36) also correlated significantly and inversely with distress.

TABLE 16.1. Means, Standard Deviations, and Correlations Among Measured Variables

Variable	1	2	3	4	5	6	7
1. Parents' warmth							
2. Positive communication	0.72***						
3. Parental direct support of ethnic socialization	0.29**	0.27**					
4. Parental indirect support of ethnic socialization	0.20**	0.17*	0.79***				
5. Collective self-esteem	0.12	0.15*	0.26**	0.23**			
6. Positive well-being	0.54***	0.61***	0.21**	0.13*	0.35**		
7. Distress	−0.39**	−0.41**	−0.09	−0.08	−0.36**	−0.50***	
Mean	4.90	4.40	3.82	3.52	4.57	4.54	2.72
Standard deviation	0.70	0.94	1.48	1.46	1.05	0.81	0.71

Note: $N = 236$
*$p < .05$
**$p < .01$
***$p < .001$

Model Testing

The goodness of fit chi-square statistic for the theoretical model was nonsignificant ($p = 0.052$), indicating that the model is compatible with the observed data. Goodness-of-fit indices also showed that the proposed model displayed values of 0.94 on GFI, 0.90 on AGFI, 0.96 on CFI, 0.94 on NFI, 0.94 on NNFI, and 0.92 on MCI, indicating that values on all goodness-of-fit indices of the proposed model were well within the acceptable range (in excess of 0.90).

Measurement Evaluation

According to Figure 16.1, the path coefficients between parent-child relationship and its indicators were warmth, 0.82, and communication, 0.94. Direct support (0.79) and indirect support (0.98) showed significant paths to parental support of ethnic socialization. The path coefficients between psychological well-being and the measure for all indicators had high factor loadings: positive well-being, 0.82, and distress, −0.64. Distress had a negative path parameter with the endogenous latent variable, psychological well-being. In the study, one of its indicators of endogenous latent variables was fixed at 1.0 and variances of exogenous latent variables were standardized

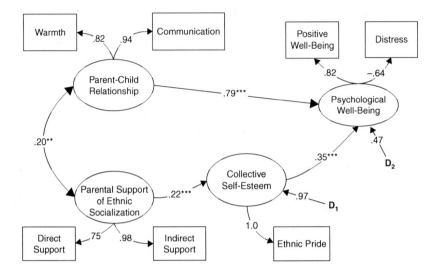

FIGURE 16.1. The Proposed Theoretical Model. *Notes: N* = 236; *p < .05, **p < .01, ***p < .001.

to 1.0 in order to set the scale of each latent variable. The t scores obtained for the coefficients ranged from -9.38 to 15.87, indicating that all factor loadings were significant ($p < .01$).

Structural Evaluation

Figure 16.1 shows that parents' support of the child's ethnic socialization had a direct positive impact on the child's collective self-esteem, indicating that coefficient between two factors is 0.22 ($t = 3.42, p < .001$). In this model, the parents' support of ethnic socialization can be a partial factor to increase the child's collective self-esteem, suggesting that a large portion of unexplained variances should be considered. The path coefficient between parent-child relationship and psychological well-being was highly significant ($\beta = 0.79, t = 12.51, p < .001$). The subsequent analysis supported that collective self-esteem as a mediator had a direct positive impact on the child's psychological well-being, indicating that path coefficient between two factors is 0.35 ($t = 6.59, p < .001$). In addition, the correlation between parental support of ethnic socialization and parent-child relationship was 0.20 ($p < .01$).

All path coefficients were statistically significant ($p < .01$), ranging from 4.18 to 9.20 (t value). Squared multiple correlation (R^2) for structural equation was 0.05 on collective self-esteem, indicating that about 5 percent of the variance of structural equation of collective self-esteem was explained by parents' support of the child's ethnic socialization; R^2 was 0.78 on psychological well-being, indicating that about 78 percent of the variance of structural equation of psychological well-being was explained by parent-child relationship and collective self-esteem (Table 16.2).

DISCUSSION

Consistent with previous research on adopted Korean children conducted by Kirk (1965), Smith (1991), and Yoon (2001), this study shows strong association between collective self-esteem and psychological well-being, suggesting that negative sense of ethnic identity may represent vulnerability for psychosocial adjustment. In contrast to findings that there is no significant relation between ethnic pride and general well-being involving mental and personal self-esteem (Bagley & Young, 1979; D. S. Kim, 1978), the results of this study demonstrate the salience of a positive sense

TABLE 16.2. Structural Parameter Estimates for the Proposed Theoretical Model

Path		Standardized Coefficient	Standard Error
Direct effect ($\rightarrow$.)			
Parent-child relationship	Psychological well-being	0.79	0.04
Parental support of ethnic socialization	Collective self-esteem	0.22	0.07
Collective self-esteem	Psychological well-being	0.35	0.03
Correlation between exogenous constructs ($\leftrightarrow$.)			
Parent-child relationship	Parental support of ethnic socialization	0.20	0.07
Indirect effect ($\rightarrow \rightarrow$.)			
Parental support of ethnic socialization	Collective self-esteem Psychological well-being	0.08	
Squared multiple correlations (R^2) for structural equations			
Psychological well-being		0.78	
Collective self-esteem		0.05	

of ethnic identity to adolescent adoptees' psychological well-being. In particular, the role of collective self-esteem as an intervening variable of parental support of ethnic socialization on psychological well-being of adopted Korean children has been found in this study. Korean-born adoptees who describe their parents as supporters of their involvement in ethnic socialization tend to feel more positive about their ethnic origins and background. Thus, adoptees who receive more parental support of ethnic socialization are more likely to have greater collective self-esteem and, therefore, have greater positive well-being and less psychological distress than those who do not.

In accordance with findings of previous studies (Bagley et al., 1979; Coopersmith, 1981; D. S. Kim, 1977), this study found that the parent-child relationship was significantly related to psychological well-being, suggesting that adoptees who receive family support providing feelings of love and belongingness are more likely to develop an adequate sense of self and have more positive well-being and less emotional distress than those who do not. Findings point to the family warmth and communication patterns as the primary source of psychological well-being for adoptees.

This study also found that a correlate of parental support of ethnic socialization was the parent-child relationship, which suggests that Korean-born adolescent adoptees who describe their parents as highly supportive in ethnic socialization report positive relationships with adoptive parents. The findings of the study are consistent with previous findings on identity development in which giving a child a positive emotional orientation and culture of origin produces the best outcomes of mental health (Sodowsky, Kwan, & Pannu, 1995). Perhaps adoptive parents who are actively involved in helping their child to develop ethnic identity have more open and close interactions with them. Alternatively, a positive family environment may lead adoptive parents to engage in the process of supporting the child's ethnic socialization.

This study was unique in that it attempted to capture the parental support of ethnic socialization as a significant factor to enhance collective self-esteem, which consequently increases psychological well-being of Korean-born children adopted by American families. By differentiating collective self-esteem from the broad concept of ethnic identity and utilizing Structural Equation Modeling (SEM), this study was able to find a causal relationship between collective self-esteem and psychological well-being, along with a moderate correlation between parental support of ethnic socialization and a positive parent-child relationship. Thus, the most significant finding of the study is that parental support of ethnic socialization enhanced by a positive parent-child relationship is very important for the adoptee's collective self-esteem and psychological well-being. The study also makes a significant contribution by improving on the methodology of cultural socialization research.

The limitations of the present study should be considered when interpreting these findings. First, although adoptive parents who participated in this study did not differ significantly from adoptive parents who did not participate in the study sociodemographically, the response rate of this study might limit the generalizability of study findings. A second limitation is the validity of the scales developed by the researcher. Although item development, involving relatively few items, was based on the ethnic identity scale using psychometrically sound measurement procedures with adequate internal consistency, the measure's validity in the study was not directly evaluated. Further studies on validity of measurement need to be expanded in the future.

Despite these limitations, findings of this study can provide significant implications for international adoption social workers. First, social workers need to help adoptive parents to be more sensitive and knowledgeable about potential problems with respect to ethnic identity. It is imperative that adoptive parents remain aware that the enhancement of collective self-esteem can increase their adopted children's psychological well-being and that sharing experiences of children's ethnic socialization can play a significant role in their children's unique process of self-concept development. The social workers need to help adoptive parents raise racial awareness and understand cultural competence (Vonk, 2001).

Secondly, in order to strengthen the functioning of adoptive families, social workers need to provide adoptive families with unique postadoption services and cultural awareness programs that can encourage adoptees to facilitate the process of accepting and maintaining their ethnic and cultural heritage. Adoption social workers need to increase their effort to reach out to adoptive families and link them to cultural resources, such as sharing information and utilizing ethnic resources targeted to this population. Even for adoptive parents with plentiful informal supports or resources, the continuum from early stages of adoption to later stages needs solid international adoption policies and programs to supplement both formal and informal support systems. Finally, adoption policymakers need to address the issues involved in ensuring that all adoptive parents and adopted Korean children can receive the ethnic/cultural awareness training that can help them remain psychosocially healthy while reducing conflicts associated with ethnic identity.

REFERENCES

Bagley, C., Verma, L., Mallick, M., & Young, L. (1979). *Personality, self-esteem, and prejudice.* Hampshire, England: Aldershot Gower.

Bagley, C., & Young, L. (1979). The identity, adjustment, and achievement of transracially adopted children: A review and empirical report. In G. Verma & C. Bagley (Eds.), *Race, education, and identity* (pp. 192-219). London: MacMillan.

Barner, H. L., & Olson, D. H. (1982). Parent-adolescent communication scale. In D. H. Olson & H. L. Barner (Eds.), *Family inventories: Inventories used in a national survey of families across the family life cycle* (pp. 33-48). St. Paul: Family Social Science, University of Minnesota.

Beck, A. T. (1961). An inventory for measuring depression. *Archives of General Psychiatry, 4,* 561-571.

Bollen, K. A. (1989). *Structural equations with latent variables.* New York: John Wiley & Sons.

Bradburn, N. M. (1969). *The structure of psychological well-being.* Chicago: Aldine.

Coopersmith, S. (1981). *The antecedents of self-esteem.* Palo Alto, CA: Consulting Psychologists Press.

Diener, E., Emmons, R. A., Larsen, R. J., & Griffin, S. (1985). The satisfaction with life scale: A measure of life satisfaction. *Journal of Personality Assessment, 49,* 71-75.

Erikson, E. H. (1968). *Identity: Youth and crisis.* New York: W. W. Norton.

Falk, L. L. (1970). A comparative study of transracial and inracial adoptions. *Child Welfare, 49,* 82-88.

Feigelman, W. (2000). Adjustments of transracially and inracially adopted young adults. *Child and Adolescent Social Work Journal, 17*(3), 165-183.

Feigelman, W., & Silverman, A. R. (1983). *Chosen children: New patterns of adoptive relationships.* New York: Praeger.

Feigelman, W., & Silverman, A. R. (1984). The long-term effects of transracial adoption. *Social Service Review, 36,* 588-602.

Gill, O., & Jackson, B. (1983). *Adoption and race: Black, Asian, and mixed race children in White families.* New York: St. Martin's Press, Inc.

Grotevant, H. D., Dunbar, N., Kohler, J. K., & Lash, A. M. (2000). Adoptive identity: How contexts within and beyond the family shape developmental pathways. *Family Relations, 49,* 379-387.

Hayduk, L. A. (1987). *Structural equation modeling with LISREL.* Baltimore: Johns Hopkins University.

Joreskog, K. G., & Sorbom, D. (1992). *LISREL VIII: A guide to the program and applications.* Chicago: SPSS.

Kim, D. S. (1977). How they fared in American homes: A follow-up study of adopted Korean children in the U.S. *Children Today, 6*(2), 2-6.

Kim, D. S. (1978). Issues in transracial and transcultural adoption. *Social Casework, 59,* 477-486.

Kim, J. (November 10, 2002). Intercountry adoption. *Dong A News, 11,* 9.

Kirk, H. D. (1965). *A theory of adoption and mental health.* New York: The Free Press.

Koh, F. M. (1988). *Oriental children in American homes: How do they adjust?* Minneapolis, MN: East West Press.

Lee, C. I. (December 15, 1996). Intercountry adoption: 40 years. *ChoSun IlBo, 12,* 29.

Lee, R. M. (2003). The transracial adoption paradox: History, research, and counseling implications for cultural socialization. *The Counseling Psychologist, 31*(6), 711-744.

McDonald, R. P. (1989). An index of goodness-of-fit based on noncentrality. *Journal of Classification, 6,* 97-103.

McGoldrick, M. (1982). Ethnicity and family therapy: An overview. In M. McGoldrick, J. K. Pearce, & J. Giordano (Eds.), *Ethnicity and family therapy* (pp. 3-30). New York: Guilford Press.

Phinney, J. S., & Chavira, V. (1992). Ethnic identity and self-esteem: An exploratory longitudinal study. *Journal of Adolescence, 15,* 271-281.

Ressler, E. M., Boothby, N., & Steinbock, D. J. (1988). *Unaccompanied children: Care and protection in wars, natural disasters, and refugee movements.* New York: Oxford Press.

Rohner, R. P. (1986). *The warmth dimension: Foundations of parental acceptance-rejection theory.* Beverly Hills, CA: Sage Publications.

Rosenthal, D. A., & Feldman, S. S. (1992). The nature and stability of ethnic identity in Chinese youth: Effects of residence in two cultural contexts. *Journal of Cross-Cultural Psychology, 23,* 214-227.

Singer, L., Brodzinsky, D., & Ramsay, D. (1985). Mother-infant attachment in adoptive families. *Child Development, 56,* 1453-1551.

Smith, E. J. (1991). Ethnic identity development: Toward the development of a theory within the context of majority/minority status. *Journal of Counseling and Development, 70,* 181-188.

Sodowsky, G. R., Kwan, K. K., & Pannu, R. (1995). Ethnic identity of Asians in the United States. In J. G. Ponterotto, J. M. Casas, L. A. Suzuki, & C. M. Alexander (Eds.), *Handbook of multicultural counseling* (pp. 123-154). London: Sage.

Spencer, M. B., & Markstrom-Adams, C. (1990). Identity processes among racial and ethnic minority children in America. *Child Development, 61,* 290-310.

Spielberger, C. D. (1979). *Understanding stress and anxiety.* New York: Nelson.

Vonk, M. E. (2001). Cultural competence for transracial adoptive parents. *Social Work, 46*(3), 246-255.

Wilkinson, S. H. P. (1985). *Birth is more than once: The inner world of adopted Korean children.* Detroit, MI: Harlo Press.

Yoon, D. P. (1997). *Psychological adjustment of Korean-born adolescents adopted by American families.* Unpublished doctoral dissertation, University of Illinois at Urbana-Champaign.

Yoon, D. P. (2001). Causal modeling predicting psychological adjustment of Korean-born adolescent adoptees. *Journal of Human Behavior in the Social Environment, 3*(3/4), 65-82.

Yoon, D. P. (2004). Intercountry adoption: The importance of ethnic socialization and subjective well-being for Korean-born adopted children. *Journal of Ethnic & Cultural Diversity in Social Work, 13*(2), 71-89.

Chapter 17

Once Upon a Time: A Critical Look at How Children's Literature Contextualizes Adoption for Asian Adoptees

Kathleen Ja Sook Bergquist

Multicultural children's literature and literature written to support children and families in the navigation of shifting definitions of family are relatively new. Adoption professionals and parents have sought out children's literature as a medium to facilitate discussion and to provide a language with which to navigate the socioemotional challenges of adoption. Literature written for Asian internationally adopted children began to appear in the 1970s, authored largely by adoptive parents out of a desire to develop a body of work that reflects their children's experiences.

This chapter presents a critical analysis of preadolescent adoption literature focusing on authenticity in the contextualization of sociopolitical factors of international adoption, and issues of identity, race, ethnicity, and marginalization. The analysis will explore and identify patterns in targeted readership (age, gender, parent, child, etc.), approaches (picture books, novels, first- and third-person narrative, etc.), and themes (identity, race, marginality, etc.). Current guidelines for evaluating and selecting children's literature in general and multicultural children's literature specifically will be used to evaluate how effectively books address adoption-related sociopolitical and psychosocial matters. I will explore the implications of these findings with regard to how effectively current children's literature negotiates

International Korean Adoption
© 2007 by The Haworth Press, Inc. All rights reserved.
doi:10.1300/5734_17

and supports the experiences of these, the youngest involuntary immigrants in the Asian diaspora.

To focus this study on adoption literature for preadolescent Asian international adoptees, it is necessary to review current research on multicultural and bibliotherapeutic children's literature and its use in postadoption strategies. Developmental theorists purport that the primary focus of children in elementary years is mastery through school and play. During this stage of *latency* and *industry* (Freud & Strachey, 1975), a child's world extends beyond the home to the school, and his or her social focus shifts from parents to peers. Upon entering school, adoptees leave the safety of their homes and must find their place among their peers and in a larger societal context. This transition is often marked by an awareness of their difference, and researchers have sought to understand the impact of adoption on these children's self-esteem, ethnic identity, racial identity, relationships to adoptive and birth families, and level of acculturation (e.g., Baden & Steward, 2000; Kim, 1978; Huh & Reid, 2000).

Similarly, adoption professionals and researchers have given much consideration to ways in which parents can support the development of their children's sense of self as adoptees and as racial and ethnic minorities. Elizabeth Vonk (2001) surveyed this body of literature and identified skills or criteria, which fell under three areas of competence: *racial awareness*—understanding the impact of race and ethnicity in the adoptee's life, an awareness of racism and discrimination, and an acknowledgment of one's own prejudices and biases; *multicultural planning*—providing opportunities for exposure to and participation in the adoptee's birth culture; and *survival skills*—preparing the child with the ability to navigate situations and individuals that may be racist or prejudiced. Books have been routinely used as a tool by parents, with the encouragement of adoption professionals, to build all three areas of competence. Adoption Web sites, trainings, and conferences regularly advertise and promote literature written for parents and adoptees.

Apart from the important work being realized by adoption professionals, I want to focus on how literature is used to help adoptees cope with the changing situations in which they find themselves. Specifically, I want to explore how strategies of *bibliotherapy* are incorporated, or not incorporated, into literature written for international adoptees. The term *bibliotherapy* was coined in a 1916 issue of *Atlantic Monthly* by Samuel Crothers and evolved out of the library practice of compiling reading lists of literature containing engaging characters and narratives that help people "make sense of their lives and give meaning to them" (Templeton, 1991, p. 372). The use of bibliotherapy with children began in the late 1940s and has been embraced by parents, teachers, and mental health professionals (Myracle, 1995).

There are two distinct applications of bibliotherapeutic practice: developmental and clinical (Rizza, 1997). Clinical use is employed by therapists and other mental health professionals as an adjunctive treatment with other therapeutic approaches (Pardeck, 1990, 1998). Parents and teachers often use developmental bibliotherapy in anticipation of normative life transitions or challenges; i.e., first-day-of-school anxiety, the arrival of a new sibling, bullying, or resisting peer pressure. Dietrich and Ralph (1995) propose that, by identifying with story characters, children are able to safely reflect on their own experiences and gain insight. In the context of adoption, the use of literature allows adoptees to vicariously examine their own experiences. Parents often make the incorrect assumption that, because their children do not talk to them about incidences of racialized teasing or questions about adoption and/or their feelings about being adopted, these are not concerns for their children. Adoptees frequently choose to avoid such conversations in an attempt to protect their parents or because they believe that their parents are unable to understand (Freundlich & Lieberthal, 2000). The bibliotherapeutic use of literature has the potential for opening lines of communication between parents and adoptees, providing a safer way to talk about and normalize the experiences of adoption.

The increase in multicultural children's literature shadows a trajectory of increasing diversity and a growing ethos of ethnic pluralism in the United States. Pataray-Ching and Ching (2001) argue that the importance of representation of diverse cultural/ethnic heritages is primary as children ". . . identify with characters that look like them, that participate in shared cultural traditions and daily experiences, and that know the struggles of their families' pasts" (p. 479). Similarly, Lu (1998) contends that the children's "identities live within these books" and that quality multicultural literature allows children to learn that others share their experiences, exposes the readers to positive coping strategies, and offers an opportunity for cultural identification. Pataray-Ching and Ching (2001) identified critical factors in reviewing multicultural literature, most important *authenticity* and *equitable representation* (p. 476). Determining authenticity involves recognizing embedded literary or illustrative stereotypes, misrepresentations, inconsistencies, or devaluing of culture. For instance, Asian-American children's literature tends to perpetuate the assumption that all Asians are either Chinese or Japanese and/ or all Asians are interchangeable based on these two groups' overrepresentation. Additional criteria for culturally relevant literature includes high literary quality, accuracy in historical and sociopolitical contexts, author's perspective, and credence given to the complexity of "tough issues" and presentation of multiple perspectives (Sims Bishop, 1992).

Pardeck (1990) identified four stages involved in bibliotherapy: identification, selection, presentation, and follow-up. He stresses particularly the importance of selecting a book with which the child is able to engage and gain insights into his or her own situation. Similarly, Dixey and D'Angelo (2000) identified three stages: identification, catharsis, and insight. They contend that, by relating to and connecting with the characters in a meaningful way, the reader then experiences an emotional or cathartic release through that identification. The literary metaphor allows the child to see positive ways of coping and presents options that may lead to behavioral changes in his or her own life. However, it has also been cautioned that the mere reading of a book does not constitute bibliotherapy (Rizza, 1997). Discussion or other creative expressions should be used to facilitate the child's deeper understanding and interaction with the story and resulting solutions to presented problems. Rizza advises to consider whether a book (1) lends itself to opening up dialogue between adult and child—or among other students in a classroom, (2) provides connections for the child to his or her own experiences, and (3) affirms the child's feelings and perspective. As Sharkey (1998) asserts, "Adoption is a complex, emotional topic often surrounded by myth, secrecy and media hype. Carefully selected books can help children—adopted and non-adopted—understand some basic truths about adoption" (p. 8).

SURVEY OF THE LITERATURE
ABOUT ASIAN ADOPTION

In order to examine the corpus of available adoption literature for Asian children of ages four to twelve years, I utilized Internet search engines, adoption reading lists, adoption Web sites, and Web-based booksellers. A total of thirty-five books were identified. I then categorized the books by targeted age of reader, as specified by either the publisher or point of purchase; and identified ethnic group of the adoptee. The books were analyzed for their treatment of the overarching themes of identity exploration, relationships to adoptive and birth families, and the sociopolitical context of relinquishment and adoption. After categorizing the available material, I divided the analysis into two parts: (1) a summary survey of the literature written for Asian adoptees in general; and (2) a more in-depth analysis of books targeting preadolescents.

In general, one notes a series of attributes that characterized the books. Three of the books are nonspecific and/or generalized Asian, meaning that the adoptee's country of origin is not identified, but illustrations and references to overseas adoption inferred that the child is of Asian descent. One of the picture books, *Allison,* features an adoptee that has a Japanese doll, and upon dressing up in a kimono realizes that she looks like her doll; however, there are no direct references to her country of origin (Say, 1997). The majority (43 percent) of the books are written about Korean adoptees, over one-third (37 percent) about Chinese adoptees, and three (10 percent) are about Vietnamese adoptees.

Although the literature written for Korean adoptees ranges fairly evenly between the two age groups, there are more than four times as many books written for younger Chinese adoptees than older. Also, two of the three books written for Vietnamese adoptees are written for older children. The availability of books in relation to age reflects the length of time that children have been adopted from their respective countries. Korean children have been adopted in the United States since the mid-1950s, while Chinese adoption began in the early 1990s. As a result, the majority of Chinese adoptees are under ten years of age. There are a total of ten books targeting preadolescents, almost two-thirds of which are written for or about Korean adoptees, and the remaining one-third are equally Chinese and Vietnamese.

TABLE 17.1. Literature for Preadolescent Asian Adoptees

Title	Author	Date	Point of View
Adopted from Asia	Koh	1993	
If It Hadn't Been for Yoon Jun	Lee	1993	
Kids Like Me in China[a]	Fry	2001	First-person adoptee
Mail-Order Kid	McDonald	1998	
Tall Boy's Journey	Halpert Kraus	1993	
We Don't Look Like Our Mom and Dad	Sobol	1984	
When You Were Born in China	Dorow	1997	Second-person adoptee
When You Were Born in Korea	Boyd	1993	
When You Were Born in Vietnam	Bartlett	2001	
Youn Hee and Me	Adler	1995	

[a]Picture book.

The subsample, surveyed in this study, listed in Table 17.1, consists of literature written for children between the ages of eight and twelve years, although the age designation is somewhat arbitrary because of varied age ratings from differing sources. Consequently, five of the selections are picture books that could be suitable for reading with younger children. The remaining five are middle-school or young adult novels. One book, *Story of Adoption: Why Do I Look Different?* (Lowe, 1987), was not included in the survey because it is currently out of print, and the author was unable to secure a copy.

All of the families portrayed in the stories are transracial, consisting of Caucasian parents with at least one adopted Asian child. Three of the families include biological children and one is a single-parent family. The narratives that clearly identify adoptees as central characters include five boys and three girls, two of which consist of related and nonrelated sibling groups.

It is interesting to note that the majority of the pieces were written, illustrated, and edited by adoptive parents or adoption professionals. The two exceptions, *Mail-Order Kid* and *If It Hadn't Been for Yoon Jun*, were authored by writers who do not have stated personal connections to international adoption. However, Marie Lee (1995), the author of the latter, is a Korean-American who has a stated identification with her main character's experience of growing up in a homogenously white Midwestern community: "I associated white with what was normal and Korea with everything that was weird, foreign, and embarrassing" (para. 10).

Although the overall context of each of these books is international adoption, the narrator and primary characters vary. *Adopted from Asia* (Koh, 1993), an anthology of personal essays, and *Kids Like Me in China*, an autobiographical account of an eight-year-old Chinese adoptee, are presented as first-person narratives of adoptees' perspectives. Three of the stories present adoptees' perspectives in third person; *Tall Boy's Journey* is described by the author as a composite of adoptees' experiences, *If It Hadn't Been for Yoon Jun* is fictional, and *We Don't Look Like Our Mom and Dad* is nonfiction. In addition, three of the books comprise a series, *When You Were Born,* about adoptees from Korea, China, and Vietnam. They are written in second person, purportedly offering adoptees a book that "has the sort of pictures that could have been in your photo album" (Boyd, 1993, p. 2). The authors of these three books attempt to provide adoptees with possibilities of what their preplacement experiences might have been like through the compilation of *normative* narratives. Older nonadopted siblings are the first- person narrators of the two remaining books, *Youn Hee and Me* and *Mail-Order Kid*.

THEMES IN LITERATURE ABOUT ASIAN ADOPTION

The multidimensional aspects of international transracial adoption are reflected in the children's literature, but with varying degrees of complexity, accurateness, and authenticity. The books were examined regarding their treatment of the following overarching themes: identity, relationships to adoptive and birth families, and sociopolitical context of relinquishment and adoption.

Identity

Preadolescence is described as a time of *latency* or *industry,* and adolescence as a period of transition from childhood to young adulthood with the accompanying tension of identity formation. However, parents and researchers are aware that transracial adoptees, by virtue of being visible minorities in their homes and communities, begin struggling with integrating their multiple identities in elementary and middle school years. When examining the books for their treatment of issues of identity four subthemes emerged: belonging, racialized teasing and rescue, embedded stereotypes, and cultural dissonance.

Issues of identity are addressed within the context of belonging—to the biological family, birth country, adoptive family, and as an *American.* Embroiled in an argument, Korean adopted brothers Eric and Joshua declare, "You're not my brother," to which their mother calmly explains, "In this family, you're brothers" (Sobol, 1984, p. 20). When five-year-old Simon is accused of not knowing that he is Korean, he responds "I'm not Korean, I'm American. See?" as he salutes an imaginary flag (Adler, 1995, p. 14). The *When You Were Born* series contains inviting images of "majestic mountains, rich river beds and land for farming" (Bartlett, 2001, p. 5) intended to help instill pride in adoptees for having been born in "such a magnificent country" (Dorow, 1997, p. 7). All three of the series editions close by encouraging adoptees to cherish their connection to birth parents and others who touched their preplacement lives: "You are forever in their hearts. May you keep them in your heart as you grow" (Bartlett, 2001, p. 42). Finding where one belongs can be a dynamic lifelong process. These stories, however, seem to foreclose that process by giving children the message that, by virtue of being adopted, their sense of belonging and perhaps loyalties are now firmly rooted in their adoptive families and country.

Any discussion about identity as it relates to being Asian-American necessarily includes, as Vonk (2001) points out, an understanding of the impact of race and ethnicity and an awareness of racism and discrimination. The two books, which are narrated from the perspective of the nonadopted sibling, address this only through scenes of racialized teasing or epithets wherein someone, usually the sibling, intervenes. Caitlin, in *Youn Hee and Me,* is admonished by a friend, "You can pretend all you want, but Simon doesn't look like your brother. He's got slant eyes and black hair, and you've got curly hair and blue eyes" (p. 15). Also, Alice Larsen, in *If It Hadn't Been for Yoon Jun,* is verbally assaulted by a classmate's father shouting, "You slanty-eyed gooks are taking over this goddamn town!" (p. 69), at which time her boyfriend comes to her defense. These incidents are often mediated by reassurances that adoptees are just like any other kids. The brothers in *We Don't Look Like Our Mom and Dad* struggle with defining their place within their family, but there is no real discussion about how they experience being Korean other than the physical differences. The narrator states, "Most of the time the boys don't think about being Korean. They are too busy . . ." (Sobol, 1984, p. 15). Where, then, does that leave children who do think about being Korean? Is the inference therefore that adoptees should not give thought to a deeply integral aspect of who they are?

Interestingly, the stories written and/or narrated by Asian-Americans address aspects of racial and ethnic identity more directly, and are more authentic in their balanced examination beyond incidents of racialized teasing. The teenagers and young adults in *Adopted from Asia* (Koh, 1993) speak candidly of their experiences as the *other,* relating both challenges and positive reference group identification. It is, however, often difficult to discern whether the adoptees enjoy their Koreanness simply because it makes them unique or because they have integrated their Korean-American identity into their sense of self. In *Kids Like Me in China,* eight-year-old Ying Ying is clearly reexamining her adopted identity as she returns to her orphanage in Changsha with her adoptive parents and makes friends with the children who welcome her as "one of them." The weight of leaving behind newfound friends who do not have "forever families" is palpable; however, it is striking that her desire is not to rescue them from their plight but to consider what it might be like to remain with them. As an adoptee she is able to conceive of an alternative to the rescue fantasy that Western imaginings assume as inevitable. The narrative and the texture of the illustrations present a more authentic representation of China than the soft-focused, slick photographs of the *When You Were Born* series. Images of peeling paint, overcrowded nurseries, and empty eyes provide a more accurate portrayal of institutional life. Through Ying Ying's telling, however, comes empathy and wonder at the enormity of it all. As she shares, "Sometimes I looked at all those babies in all those cribs and I didn't know what to think. Sometimes I just had to leave the room" (p. 17).

In addition, Marie Lee's development of seventh-grader Alice Larsen's character and her painful need to be *normal* and accepted provides a more complex and authentic examination. Alice insists that "I know I *look* Korean, but. . . . I feel totally American . . ." (p. 6). She idealizes a classmate who has "beautiful brown hair that was streaked blonde from the sun" (p. 7). Alice is horrified when there is a new Korean boy, Yoon Jun, in school, whom she describes as having "eyes like hers" (p. 15). The conflict his presence creates for her begins her struggle with coming to terms with who she is. The plot becomes riddled at times with contrived interactions between Alice and Yoon Jun, for instance, when the two are randomly selected to be partners on an international day project and when Alice is unexpectedly saved from injury by an oncoming vehicle by Yoon Jun. Lee's characterization of Alice as externalizing her conflict and scapegoating Yoon Jun, as well as her cautious progress toward accepting both herself and Yoon Jun, seem developmentally plausible. The author resists the temptation to conclude with Alice having a fully integrated sense of self, but rather characterized her as being tentative, yet active, in redefining who she is.

While incidents of stereotyping or racial epithets are tackled in the middle and young adult novels, there are also embedded images, language, and stereotypes in some of the books that present inauthentic or inaccurate representations. The overgeneralization of Asian cultural markers is evident. For example, Joanna Halpert Kraus (1993) describes Korean-born Kim Moo Young as "karate-kicking" a door. Similarly, eleven-year-old Caitlin, in *Youn Hee and Me,* explains that her five-year-old brother was affectionately nicknamed "her little samurai" by their mother because "Simon sure was at war here" (p. 8). The mother's generalization of a Japanese cultural reference to a Korean child, although perhaps plausible, is reflective of the assumed transferability of one Asian cultural context to another. Also, the author's fleeting reference to Simon or Si Won's tumultuous first-year transition into his new home until he became "fun to live with" minimizes the stress, isolation, cultural confusion, and loss that older adoptees experience. When Simon's older birth sister, Youn Hee, is adopted, Caitlin describes her as having "long straight hair and a cute kitten face . . . [she] was as delicate as one of those look-don't-touch costume dolls" (p. 19), reflecting Western orientalist imaginations of Asian girls as China dolls. Similarly, the commodification of Asian culture, artifacts, food, and language is literally personified in Joyce McDonald's *Mail-Order Kid.* When ten-year-old Flip orders a fox through the mail, he defends his actions to his mother by rationalizing "You got Todd [his six year old Korean adopted brother] through the mail! . . . Well maybe he didn't come in a cage . . ."

(p. 2). The mother's admonishment, "Your little brother did not come through the mail, Flip . . . I'm not going to stand here and argue with you" (p.13), does little to thoughtfully address the nonadopted child's genuine feelings of displacement and uncertainty about his new brother. Although the title and metaphor may be intended to be provocative and, presumably, to present teachable moments, the book lacks bibliotherapeutic value. The insensitivity to the complexity of adoption is problematic, but perhaps more troubling is the perpetuation of colonialist assumptions about human trade due to the juxtaposition of adoption of a child with the purchase of an animal.

In addition, several of the stories explore the cultural dissonance experienced by older adoptees as they are immersed in a different language, culture, and environment while simultaneously experiencing the trauma of loss and separation from birth country and all that is familiar. *Tall Boy's Journey, Youn Hee and Me,* and *Mail-Order Kid* feature older adoptees of ages five to eleven years and their adjustment to the United States. *Kids Like Me in China* offers a reverse perspective as Ying Ying Fry reimmerses herself in China for two weeks; however, the experiences are qualitatively different because Ying Ying is merely visiting and is traveling with her family.

Tall Boy's Journey is unique in its attempt to root the experience of adoption in the birth family. Joanna Halpert Kraus (1993) weaves the story of Kim Moo Young from a composite of several different adoptees' experiences. She gives life to his uncle and recently deceased *halmoni,* or grandmother, and infuses Korean cultural fables and superstitions into the plot. The anger, indignation, fear, and confusion of this eight-year-old boy are girded by his longing for his birth country, "He wanted his own straw mat on the floor of his grandmother's house. Even the poorest house had a floor heated by the kitchen fires below, an *ondul* floor. If this new country was so rich, why was the floor so cold?" In silent desperation he wonders "if he would ever see Korean faces again. The thought made him dizzy" (p. 17). Likewise, eleven-year-old Youn Hee is determined to return to Korea and is withdrawn, sullen, and resistant to her new sister's overtures (Adler, 1995). She runs into cultural clashes when she tries to discipline her brother by smacking him across the face, refusing to eat unfamiliar food, and preferring to sleep on the floor. Her sister's friends cannot understand how Youn Hee could be homesick for an orphanage until an empathic classmate points out, "She knew people there, didn't she?" (p. 76). Both *Tall Boy's Journey* and *Youn Hee and Me* invite the reader to explore the relationships between adoptee, birth country, birth culture, and birth parents. As the characters struggle with attachments to Korea, children and parents can vicariously examine issues of place and belonging and the adoptees' inextricable connection to preplacement history.

Relationships to Adoptive and Birth Families

Although relationships to adoptive and birth families are inherent to findings about belonging, a few of the books explored the experiences of biological siblings and the adjustment that adoptive families make. Ten-year-old Flip complains, "They thought he [his brother] should share a room with me so he'd feel more at home . . . But did anyone bother to ask me if I wanted company? No-o-o" (McDonald, 1998, p. 20). References to birth family are made, generally in vague romanticized terms, explaining that birth parents love their children but choose to make a plan for a better life for their babies. Kim Moo Young is sent to the United States by his uncle after the death of his parents and grandmother, explaining, "You will be tall, inside. You will be Tall Boy. I said it was a difficult mission. But it is a mission for Ooma, for Halmoni, and for me. Will you be my soldier across the sea?" (p. 13).

Ten-year-old Eric Levin wonders, "Why did she [his birth mother] give him up for adoption? What did she look like and why didn't she keep him? If she were to come to this country, would she recognize him? Would she talk to him?" (Sobol, 1984, p. 25). Although his questions go unanswered, the author concludes "Nevertheless they are a family because they choose to be one . . . Most important they share work and share love" (p. 32). The author's conclusion seems somewhat dismissive of Eric's earnest questions and poses some interesting assumptions about choice. Yoon Jun explains why he and his mother chose to immigrate to the United States: "'We come here, . . ., for better life. . . ., like you come here for better life.' Alice's chest tightened. 'But I didn't come here because I wanted to. My Korean parents gave me up—they abandoned me'" (M. G. Lee, 1993, p. 128). Marie Lee is the only author who uses the language of *abandonment*. Her positioning of that term is powerfully placed in Alice's voice, representing a real perception for adoptees. The neutralization of the event in the other books, through the use of vague references to children ending up in orphanages and such, minimizes the impact of relinquishment. Literature used for bibliotherapeutic purposes should reflect adoptees' realities, not merely be a vehicle for politically correct interpretations. Not addressing the loss and abandonment that is inherent in the adoptive experience leaves adoptees with no option but to internalize such feelings lest they make others uncomfortable.

Birth parents are virtually invisible, although two stories do include biological siblings and *Tall Boy's Journey* begins with his *halmoni*, or grandmother, and uncle in Korea. These fleeting and minimal representations provide clear messages to children about the importance of their preplacement histories. They also fuel adoptive parents' fantasies about the stork-like delivery of their children and relegate the birth mother to little more than a surrogate for the child that was intended to be theirs. Adoptive parents have romanticized this notion in their adaptation of a popular Chinese folk belief that couples are joined together at birth by a red string that forever connects them. Adoptees are likewise told that, even though they were born in China, they were predestined to become a part of their "forever" family. This romantic notion positions the birth mother's body as a commodity, a mere instrument in this fairy tale. This is disturbing at many levels, but most important is the impact of such hegemonic interpretations. Birth family and birth country are presented not as viable, authentic, and integral to the adoptee but rather as a historical footnote or a "made in China" imprint.

The Sociopolitical Context

Considerations about sociopolitical conditions surrounding adoption are contextualized almost exclusively in reference to birth country. Eric and Joshua's mother explains, "We needed to raise children, and you needed parents to raise you, we are a perfect match." "'But why did you want to adopt Korean children?' they often asked. 'There [were] a lot of children in Korea who needed parents, and the agency got us together'" (p. 12). Ying Ying Fry (2001) attempts to explain why the majority of children placed from China are girls: ". . . in China people love boys *and* girls. . . . But in China it's a boy's job to take care of his parents when they're really old and can't work anymore. Girls are supposed to take care of their husbands' parents" (p. 17). Both the *When You Were Born* series and *Kids Like Me in China* provide limited explanations of contributing factors to adoption. They discuss the impact of poverty, out-of-wedlock births, family planning policies, patriarchal lineage, and cultural factors. They also point out that some children are adopted within their birth countries; however, they fail to offer a clear explanation of why adoptees' birth countries facilitate more overseas than domestic adoptions and why their adoptive parents chose international versus domestic adoption. Ying Ying's words in *Kids Like Me in China* come with a disclaimer; much of the information provided about the history of Chinese adoption is drawn from research and presented in her voice. The language in the *When You Were Born* series is accessible to younger children, which broadens the market appeal. They can be read to younger children and also easily enjoyed by older children. However, the deliberately politically neutral and fairy-tale-like delivery of this very complex phenomenon is probably going to leave preadolescents with more questions than answers.

If It Hadn't Been for Yoon Jun is unique in that it touches on the moral imperative and charitable inclinations that motivate some parents to adopt; as Alice explains, "Sometimes, he [her father] even reminds me that if not for 'Christian kindness,' I would not be here. It makes me feel like I must have done something really bad when I was young, and that's why they sent me out of Korea!" (M. G. Lee, 1993, p.18). Marie Lee's work offers the only alternative other than the predictable "you needed a family and we needed a child" theory. It is also interesting to note that the author is not an adoptive parent, and therefore may feel more latitude to explore parental motivations.

The history of Korean international adoption is firmly rooted in Christian humanitarian responses, most notably through the early work of Harry and Bertha Holt, who "were inspired by their faith in Jesus Christ" to find families for war orphans in the United States (*Holt's philosophy,* n.d., para. 4). Reported parental reasons for wanting to adopt internationally include altruistic desires to provide a child a "better" life and wanting to help a child in need (Bergquist, Campbell, & Unrau, 2003). Inherent in such motivations are rescue fantasies and paternalistic First World assumptions about the moral responsibility of developed countries to deliver developing nations from their own social, economic, or political failings. These fantasies are fueled by images of Third World children playing in landfills, designed to galvanize the philanthropic impulses of Westerners. It may be argued whether it is important or even appropriate for children's books to explore the sociopolitical context of international adoption.

One of the criteria for bibliotherapeutic literature is to present authentic representations of the reader's experiences. The majority of the literature surveyed either essentializes the phenomenon to a simple supply-demand matching equation or contextualizes it solely within the sending country. The reality is that adoptees are very aware that they are perceived as benefactors of their parents' charity and of the pejorative assumptions that are made about their birth countries, which seemingly cannot take care of their own children. It is important, therefore, for bibliotherapeutic children's literature to offer frank and realistic explorations of parental motivations as well as the role that developed countries play in sustaining international adoption. Adopted children should understand that their adoption is not simply a symbol of their birth families and countries having failed them.

BIBLIOTHERAPY AND ASIAN-AMERICAN ADOPTEES

This study sought to survey the available literature for adolescent Asian adoptees, and reveals a range in the targeted readership and approaches. The books also varied in their authenticity and accurate representations of the identified themes of identity, relationships to adoptive and birth families, and sociopolitical context of relinquishment and adoption. The focus of the writing seemed to be correlated with the status of the author. In general, texts authored by adoptive parents focused largely on issues of adoption, i.e., the retelling of a child's "adoption story" and providing a historically accurate explanation of relinquishment, as in the *When You Were Born* series. In contrast, the writing by authors without a personal connection to adoption seemed to be more willing to explore the impact of transracial adoption, touching on issues of isolation, loss, incidents of racial teasing and epithets, and internalized racism. An exception to this is *Tall Boy,* written by an adoptive mother, which tackles the fear, loss, and cultural dissonance that older adoptees often feel. However, the story is limited to the retelling of Kim Moo Young's relinquishment, placement, and initial adjustment period—and does not examine the long-term implications of transracial adoption. Halpert Kraus's (1993) premature happy ending is overly simplistic and seemingly incongruent with the complexity of her main character and his preplacement history.

One of the major objectives of this study was to survey available adoption literature not just to critique its literary worth but to consider it within the context of bibliotherapy. Parents, with the encouragement of practitioners, regularly seek out resources that will support their children's understanding about adoption. Adoption literature is used to promote prosocial skills, offer coping strategies to deal with problems, and provide the young readers with language and images that reflect their experiences. Pardeck (1990, 1998) stresses the primary importance of book selection for bibliotherapeutic use and contends that books are not necessarily appropriate or relevant merely because they are about a particular subject matter. Although preadolescent children are independent readers and usually select their own reading material, it is usually the parents who seek out adoption literature for their children. Because of differing approaches and themes in the selected books, parents are cautioned to first read the piece to determine its appropriateness and also give serious consideration to the impact that the story will have on their child and what kind of insight they think might be gained. Table 17.2 may serve as a guide for selection of high-quality, bibliotherapeutic, multicultural literature for children. However, it is important to note that parents are not, merely by virtue of their status as adop-

TABLE 17.2. Bibliotherapeutic and Multicultural Children's Literature Criteria

Criteria	Application
High literary quality	Fully developed characters, plot, setting, themes, and style; originality of text and illustration, clarity and style of language; excellent illustration, design and format, subject matter of interest and value to children, and likelihood of acceptance by children
Affirms the child's feelings and perspective	Provides a literary metaphor by making connections for the child to his or her own experiences
Allows children to learn that others share their experiences	Normalizes adoptees' experiences
Exposes adoptees to positive coping strategies	Avoidance of rescue narratives and providing alternative responses to navigating racism, discrimination, and addressing adoption-related issues
Accurate/authentic representation of ethnic group	Avoidance of stereotypes, essentializing, and overgeneralization
Offers an opportunity for cultural identification	Validates adoptees' right to positively identify as Asian-Americans and with their community/culture of adoption
Accuracy in historical and sociopolitical contexts	Avoidance of oversimplification of the historical and sociopolitical context of adoption
Author's perspective	Provides a perspective that is unbiased by the author's personal experience and/or relationship to adoption
Credence given to the complexity of "tough issues"	Avoidance of minimization of adoption-related issues, and the complexity of identity for adoptees
Presentation of multiple perspectives	Providing more than just one perspective in order to facilitate the adoptee's critical consideration of options and alternatives
Lends itself to opening up dialogue	The value of bibliotherapeutic literature lies in its ability to engage readers in a discussion wherein shared learning and personal insights may be gained

tive parents, necessarily aware of the needs of their nonwhite adopted children. This raises a question about the role of adoption agencies in developing parents' multicultural awareness and competencies, and skills in addressing adoption-related issues with their children. Rather than just referring parents to the latest adoption-related children's book, agencies could offer annotated reading lists for parents that have been critically reviewed for their bibliotherapeutic value.

The use of the surveyed children's literature for bibliotherapeutic purposes with Asian adopted children raises several considerations with regard to the overall authenticity and accurateness in the treatment of the various themes. The level of authenticity and accurateness found within the stories varied widely. The books that tackled sociopolitical factors in relinquishment use accessible language for the targeted age group. The presentation of issues, however, is, for the most part, politically neutral. Despite the complexity of the subject matter, and the multiple perspectives inherent therein, all of the books had a tendency to oversimplify and minimize the presented themes, thereby giving them a fairy-tale-like quality. Given the target audience, this treatment underestimates the children's ability and desire to think critically about something that is so personal to them. Preadolescents are aware that adoption is not viewed by the majority as an alternative that is equally as viable as having birth children. They are also painfully aware that they are viewed as the *other,* even though they often wish to protect their parents by not telling them about incidents of racialized teasing or discrimination. Therefore, parents who wish to support their children in grappling with the challenges they face must seek tools that validate their experiences and what they know to be true rather than relying on happy endings that make the parents more comfortable. Literature that offers multiple perspectives and resists the temptation to use soft lenses will lend itself well to discussions that facilitate the children's consideration of how they feel about these issues.

What was probably most striking about the literature was not what was said but what was absent. There is an absence of authentic adoptees' voices, of discussion about parental motivations other than a desire to have children, of an acknowledgment that the children's status as Asian adoptees will continually shape who they are, and of the relationship between the birth and adoptive countries within a global context. The writings reflect the larger context in which they are authored, that is, a climate of managed care wherein acknowledgment or treatment of "problems" are time-limited, cultural sensitivity is given precedence over cultural relevancy or competency, and privilege is invisible to or denied by those who have it. Pardeck (1998) delineates adoptees' rights to grapple with what it means to be adopted and to develop a positive racial or ethnic identity and the role that bibliotherapy plays in this process.

It is difficult to conjecture whether the absence of critical consideration given to this very complex phenomenon is attributable to well-intended authors' desires to "protect" children or truly reflective of a lack of cultural relevance and invisible privilege. Much has been written about invisible privilege and its location in whiteness, arguing that white Americans are socialized not to recognize their own privilege even though they are able to acknowledge that nonwhites are disadvantaged (Johnson, 2001; McIntosh, 1988; Rothenberg, 2000). This denial or obliviousness to advantage often translates into "color-blind" or "we're all human" responses to race or other interlocking dimensions of difference, as evidenced by adoptive parents' common insistence that their children are "just like any other [white] kid." It is also important to recognize that there is an inherent aspect of privilege in adoption, involving an exchange between families of differing social classes and, in the case of transracial adoption, differing ethnic/racial communities from less advantaged to more advantaged. In order for literature to be culturally relevant it must accurately and authentically represent the experiences of its characters, something that may be less likely to happen if written from a position of invisible privilege.

Bibliotherapeutic convention specifies that parents should guide their children in a reflection process, i.e., journaling, discussion, or some other creative expression, to facilitate catharsis and insight (Abdullah, 2002; Dixey & D'Angelo, 2000; Pardeck, 1990, 1993, 1998; Rizza, 1997). Whether or not parents are willing or able to assume this responsibility could be addressed in postadoption trainings. This would ensure that agencies help parents in supporting their children explore adoption-related issues and could also facilitate a parallel process of bibliotherapy with parents.

In conclusion, it is important to acknowledge that the body of literature written for Asian adoptees is relatively new, and therefore the level of literary quality will undoubtedly increase over time. A cursory survey of the literature written for younger children, which is larger and more established, indicates a progression in relevance and authenticity. It is imperative that the literature accurately validates the complexity of Asian adoptees' experiences and that parents and adoption professionals give consideration to the bibliotherapeutic value of books selected for children.

REFERENCES

Abdullah, M. H. (2002). What is bibliotherapy? *ERIC Clearinghouse on Reading, English, and Communication Digest, 177*. [ED-99-CO-0028]. Retrieved April 26, 2005, from http://reading.indiana.edu/ieo/digests/d177.html.

Adler, C. S. (1995). *Youn Hee and me*. New York: Harcourt Brace and Company.

Baden, A. L., & Steward, R. J. (2000). A framework for use with racially and culturally integrated families: The cultural-racial identity model as applied to transracial adoption. *Journal of Social Distress and the Homeless, 9*, 309-337.

Bartlett, T. (2001). *When you were born in Vietnam*. St. Paul, MN: Yeong & Yeong.

Bergquist, K. J. S., Campbell, M. E., & Unrau, Y. A. (2003). Caucasian parents and Korean adoptees: A survey of parent's perceptions. *Adoption Quarterly, 6*(4), 41-58.

Boyd, B. (1993). *When you were born in Korea.* St. Paul, MN: Yeong & Yeong.

Crothers, S. M. (1916). A literary clinic. *Atlantic Monthly, 118,* 291-301.

Dietrich, D., & Ralph, K. S. (1995). Crossing borders: Multicultural literature in the classroom. *Journal of Educational Issue of Language Minority Students, 15.* Retrieved April 26, 2005, from http://www.ncela.gwu.edu/pubs/jeilms/vol15/crossing.htm.

Dixey, B., & D'Angelo, A. (2000). Using literature to build emotionally healthy adolescents. *Classroom on-line, 3*(6). Retrieved February 24, 2003, from http://www.ascd.org/readingroom/classlead/0003/1mar00.html.

Dorow, S. (1997). *When you were born in China.* St. Paul, MN: Yeong & Yeong.

Freud, S., & Strachey, J. (Eds.) (1975). *Three essays on the theory of sexuality.* New York: Basic Books.

Freundlich, M., & Lieberthal, J. K. (2000). *The gathering of the first generation of adult Korean adoptees: Adoptees' perceptions of international adoption.* Retrieved May 11, 2005, from http://www.adoptioninstitute.org/proed/korfindings.html.

Fry, Y. Y. (2001). *Kids like me in China.* St. Paul, MN: Yeong & Yeong.

Halpert Kraus, J. (1993). *Tall boy's journey.* Minneapolis, MN: First Avenue Editions.

Holt's philosophy. (n.d.). Retrieved April 27, 2005, from http://www.holtintl.org/media/holt.philosophy.shtml.

Huh, N. S., & Reid, W. J. (2000). Intercountry, transnational adoption and ethnic identity. *International Social Work, 43*(1), 75-87.

Johnson, A. G. (2001). *Power, privilege, and difference.* New York: McGraw-Hill.

Kim, D. S. (1978). Issues in transracial and transcultural adoption. *Social Casework, 59*(8), 477-486.

Koh, F. M. (1993). *Adopted from Asia.* Minneapolis, MN: EastWest Press.

Lee, M. (1995, Winter). How I grew up. *The Alan Review, 22*(2). Retrieved April 26, 2005, from http://scholar.lib.vt.edu/ejournals/ALAN/winter95/Lee.html.

Lee, M. G. (1993). *If it hadn't been for Yoon Jun.* New York: Houghton Mifflin Co.

Lowe, D. (1987). *Story of adoption, why do I look different?* Minneapolis, MN: East West Press.

Lu, M. Y. (1998). Multicultural children's literature in the elementary classroom. *ERIC Clearinghouse on Reading, English, and Communication Digest, 133.* [ED423552]. Retrieved April 26, 2005, from http://reading.indiana.edu/ieo/digests/d133.html.

McDonald, J. (1998). *Mail-order kid.* New York: G.P. Putnam's Sons.

McIntosh, P. (1988). *White privilege and male privilege: A personal account of coming to see correspondences through work in women's studies.* Wellesley, MA: Wellesley College Center for Research on Women.

Myracle, L. (1995). Molding the minds of the young: The history of bibliotherapy as applied to children and adolescents. *The Alan Review, 22*(2). Retrieved April 26, 2005, from http://scholar.lib.vt.edu/ejournals/ALAN/winter95/Myracle. html.

Pardeck, J. T. (1990). Using bibliotherapy in clinical practice with children. *Psychological Reports, 67,* 1043-1049.

Pardeck, J. T. (1993). Literature and adoptive children with disabilities. *Early Child Development and Care, 91,* 33-39.

Pardeck, J. T. (1998). *Using books in clinical social work practice: A guide to bibliotherapy.* Binghamton, NY: Haworth Press.

Pataray-Ching, J., & Ching, S. (2001). Talking about books: Supporting and questioning representation. *Language Arts, 78*(5), 476-484.

Rizza, M. (1997, Winter). A parent's guide to helping children: Using bibliotherapy at home. *The National Research Center on the Gifted and Talented Winter Newsletter.* Retrieved April 26, 2005, from http://www.sp.uconn.edu/~nrcgt/news/winter97/wintr972.html.

Rothenberg, P. (2000). *Invisible privilege: A memoir about race, class, and gender.* Lawrence: University Press of Kansas.

Say, A. (1997). *Allison.* New York: Houghton Mifflin Co.

Sharkey, P. M. B. (1998). Being adopted: Books to help children understand—update 3. *Emergency Librarian, 25*(4), 8-10.

Sims Bishop, R. (1992). Multicultural literature for children: Making informed choices. In V. J. Harris (Ed.), *Teaching Multicultural Literature in Grades K-8* (pp. 37-54). Norwood, MA: Christopher-Gordon Publishers, Inc.

Sobol, H. L. (1984). *We don't look like our mom and dad.* New York: Coward-McCann, Inc.

Templeton, S. (1991). *Teaching integrated language arts.* Boston: Houghton Mifflin.

Vonk, M. E. (2001). Cultural competence for transracial adoptive parents. *Social Work, 46*(3), 246-255.

Chapter 18

Reconstruction of the Psychosocial World of Korean Adoptees in the United States: A Search for New Meanings

Daniel B. Lee

Adoptive families who raise and accommodate children of diverse ethnic and racial backgrounds experience not only ordinal developmental demands for their adopted children including nurturing, educating, and socializing tasks but also the additional challenges of supporting their adopted children's acculturation and bicultural accommodation throughout different stages of the life cycle (W. J. Kim, 1995). Other salient emerging issues that concern adoptees, parents, and helping professionals include (1) psychosocial issues of ethnic identity; (2) resolution of intrapsychic trauma associated with losses and emotional cutoff; (3) cohort group networks; and (4) bridging interethnic boundaries (French, 1986; Smit, 2002). In previous studies on Korean adoptees' intellectual and adaptive performances, many authors have noted their relative satisfaction in comparison with other international adoptees in American settings (Clark & Hainisee, 1982; DiVirglio, 1956; D. S. Kim; 1977; W. J. Kim, 1995; Rathburn, McLaughlin, Bennet, & Garland, 1965) as well as in European countries (Hoksbergen, 1991), but more studies are needed to understand internal mental processes of adoptees' search for meaningful self-concept and ethnic identity integration (Liow, 1994).

One of the most salient sources of identity for international adoptees, aside from gender, age, and name, is racial characteristic. For them, race

International Korean Adoption
© 2007 by The Haworth Press, Inc. All rights reserved.
doi:10.1300/5734_18

and ethnicity pose added psychosocial complexity in achieving identity integration. Moreover, to achieve an optimal level of integration for self-identity, one cannot deny the importance of resolving the issues of discontinuity or loss associated with being uprooted from their country of birth and their ties to ethnic kinship. In the context of growing up and living in a monoracial environment, adopted Korean children may find themselves being different from their siblings and relatives in terms of racial traits and physical appearances, as well as from the predominantly white neighborhoods and schools in which they are situated. W. J. Kim (1995) and Tizard (1991) noted Feigelman and Silverman's (1983) findings that Korean adoptees were less comfortable with their appearance as compared with white adoptees. In school districts where there are Korean immigrant families, it may become further complicated for adoptees who neither speak their natal language nor bear Korean family names, thus making it uncomfortable to associate with other Korean-speaking immigrant children. Even when they are adopted after early childhood acquisition of their natal language, adoptees lose it fast in their acculturation process, as noted in the Swedish study of international adoption (Cederblad, 1982).

More comparative studies that capture the perspectives of international adoptees are needed in the areas of ethnic self-identity, mental health, and quest for meaningful connections to adoptees' roots and supportive social network (Deacon, 1997). The number of Korean overseas adoptions between 1953 and 2003 reached 154,573 in fifteen different countries including the United States (102,606), France (11,042), Sweden (8,830), Denmark (8,518), Norway (5,993), Netherlands (4,099), Belgium (3,697), Australia (3,039), Germany (2,352), Canada (1,739), Switzerland (1,111), New Zealand (559), Luxembourg (468), Italy (382), and England (72). Currently, more than 2,200 children are adopted overseas annually (Hübinette, 2003). Citing the U.S. Census Bureau report, Hübinette noted that Koreans accounted for 24 percent of internationally adopted children. The overall number of adoptees in the United States was around two million, with 257,792 being Asian-born. In Sweden, most overseas adoptees are from Korea, and the social and mental health indices are not encouraging as they have substantial difficulties in getting jobs and forming families. Hübinette (2003) reports:

> Sixty (60) percent of the overseas adoptees have jobs compared to 77 percent among ethnic Swedes, and half of the overseas adoptees belong to the lowest income category compared to 29 percent of the

Swedes. This means that there is widespread discrimination against Korean adoptees on the labor market, and when they get a job they are low-paid. Moreover, 29 percent of the overseas adoptees are married compared to 56 percent of Swedes, meaning that Korean adoptees are considered unattractive and have problems in finding a spouse. (n.p.)

The same report mentioned high levels of psychiatric illness, drug and alcohol addiction, criminality, and suicide. The suicide rate there is 500 percent higher among overseas adoptees than among ethnic Swedes (Hübinette, 2003). Problem behaviors among international adoptees were epidemiologically studied in Sweden by Verhulst and associates (1990). They found that effect of age at time of placement was critical: "Significantly more older children than younger children ($p < 0.05$) and more boys than girls ($p < 0.001$) scored above the 90th percentile of the frequency distribution of the Child Behavior Check List" (p. 106).

Adoptive parents may want to help their adopted children to explore their biological and ethnic backgrounds, thereby opening up new windows of opportunity for resolving adopted children's quest for their roots and integration of their ethnic identity. Liow (1994) elaborated a framework for exploring the meaning of heritage, birthright, ancestry, lineage, culture, behavioral traits, language, and religion for transracially adopted children. Tizard (1991) noted the lack of studies that examine the effect of racism on identity formation for these children. She further noted the impact of social and political factors on adoption described in Feigelman and Silverman's (1983) study. The factor of race and ethnicity is found to be undeniably important in the process of forming self-identity and group identity (Liow, 1994; Tizard, 1991). Thus, the adoptive parents need to become intentionally conscious about the inner struggles their adopted children are experiencing in searching and defining who they really are. The adopted children may often fantasize about their past with mixed feelings of doubt, fear, anger, guilt, and confusion.

The purpose of this chapter is to examine the meaning of homecoming, as well as the level of cultural integration and ethnic self-identity among adopted Korean youths and young adults through a narrative and social constructionist perspective. In addition, new meanings for reconstructing adoptees' psychosocial world are discussed. The following cases poignantly illustrate aspects of adoptees' search for ethnic identity.

THE MEANING OF HOMECOMING
FOR ADOPTED KOREAN YOUTHS
AND YOUNG ADULTS: CASE EXAMPLES

Case 1

Ms. V, a charming college student from Norway, came to study Korean culture at the Ewha Woman's University International School for Asian Studies in the summer of 1988. I went there as an instructor and had an occasion to hear her personal story. She was adopted into a Norwegian family in her early childhood, and it was not until her college years that she began to realize a sense of discontinuity from her culture of origin and the linkages to her own ethnic people. She, and the other ninety-seven students of Korean ancestry, had a similar quest to discover their sense of ethnic identity through acquiring Korean language skills and to experience their native country, people, and the ecology of their birth and early childhood. She was seeking to cultivate a linkage between the nearly 8,000 Korean adoptees in the Scandinavian countries, their natal culture, and their own ethnic people as a result of her homecoming experiences at Ewha. She was discovering a missing link she sought for a long time. When she returned to Norway, she wanted to work as a cultural mediator for other Korean *sisters* and *brothers* who would benefit from similar experiences.

Case 2

The second case involved a young commissioned U.S. Army medical service officer, Lt. S, who was adopted by a middle-class American family in southern California. Upon completion of his master's degree in psychology, Lt. S entered the Army as a way to explore the world, including his country of birth. I first met him at Fort Ord, California, and encountered him again a year later in the 8th U.S. Army Hospital in Seoul, Korea, where both of us were stationed. It was during the later period that I noticed his inner struggle with identity integration. He learned some basic Korean language while stationed in Korea during his thirteen-month tour of duty and met some Koreans inside and outside of the installation where he worked. Sometimes, he wandered around the nearby orphanages. He got frustrated with not being able to satisfy his fantasy of finding blood-related kin or making meaningful connections to the people and places of his early childhood. He became lost in the crowds of Korean people who did not recognize him as being Korean because of his American name and very limited native language skills. Without a mediatory agent to help him, his tour ended in disappointment. Lt. S did not accomplish what he initially wished to do. I met many individual youths and young adult Korean adoptees in the 1970s whose search, like that of Lt. S, ended unsatisfactorily without making meaningful contact because of a lack of mediatory support.

Case 3

Jennifer is a schoolteacher who grew up in the Midwest. She and her husband, who is a Caucasian adoptee, adopted a child from the same Korean orphanage in which she grew up. Unlike many other adopted children who were often abandoned, she knew her biological mother gave her up for adoption out of poverty in order to give her a better life in America. She was four years and eleven months old when she was adopted. However, she kept her biological mother's picture hidden under her pillow throughout her adolescent years. Later she discovered that her adopted mother was aware of the picture, but let her keep it, wishing to respect her space. She has kept that secret but not without having a sense of guilt. In tears, Jennifer told her story to an audience at a transcultural family conference at Ohio State University in 1984. Jennifer did not need to hide the picture of her biological mother once she was assured of her adopted parents' love and care and her sense of security grew. When she was thirteen years old she sought out therapy briefly to address identity issues. After she was married, she and her husband decided to visit her biological mother, the orphanage where she spent her early years, and the country of her ethnic roots. With the assistance of Holt Korea, Jennifer had a very positive reconnecting experience that was beneficial to both herself and her biological mother. She discovered that through the years her biological mother had kept a harmonica that was given to Jennifer as a gift from an American soldier. Both cried when her mother told her that after seeing Jennifer, who was healthy and accomplished, she no longer needed to keep the harmonica and gave it back to her biological daughter.

As illustrated in these three young adults' search for their ethnic roots and quest to construct new meanings, each pursued his or her own way, with or without help from others. Search for one's own identity involves a series of steps for transcultural adoptees, especially when doubt, mistrust, insecurity, fear of abandonment, anger, guilt, and grief still exist and impact their self-concept, ethnic identity integration, and interpersonal relationships. Much of their painful experiences or thoughts are often suppressed by the demands of immediacy for human survival. For those who are unprepared or ill-prepared for coping with harsh realities of racism, discrimination, and social distancing they may encounter in Korea, their early repressed feelings and psychological pain associated with abandonment, loss, and emotional cutoffs may reactivate, affecting their mental health.

SEARCH FOR CULTURAL ROOTS AND BIOLOGICAL KIN: HOMECOMING EXPERIENCES

As many adopted Korean-Americans are now adults, they are increasingly seeking to connect to their homeland to strengthen their ethnic identity and cultural linkages, in addition to searching for meaningful connections to their roots (Friedlander, 1999; Wilkinson, 1995). As noted by Wilkinson (1995), the search for one's identity can be a lifelong process and is a difficult task for international adoptees to complete. Based on both a review of the literature and the author's clinical and casual observations, participatory research was designed to observe and assess the significance of a homecoming group experience and its impact on ethnic self-identity and cultural connectivity. Outcome studies on the reunion between adoptees and biological parents are a relatively new phenomenon (Pacheco & Eme, 1993). As many adopted Korean-Americans are young adults, there is an increasing demand to search for the "forbidden," if not repressed, realm of integrating a whole sense of self by trying to discover or rediscover the missing link of ethnic identity and the more pressing and natural task of connecting to biological kin. To respond to these needs, several aftercare "homecoming" trip services have been initiated by adoption agencies including Holt International Children Services and Minnesota Children's Home Society (Winston, 2004). I organized a ten-day peace tour research project between July 16 and 25, 1994, under the sponsorship of the Korea Coalition of Peace Movement.

RESEARCH PROJECT

Sample Recruitment Procedure and Tour Sponsorship

A nonrandomized, purposive, convenience sample was used in this study. Tour participants were recruited through an advertisement in *OURS* (December 1994), a national newsmagazine for adoptive families with a circulation of approximately 20,000. The selection criteria included Korean adoptees between sixteen and thirty-two years, who had not visited Korea since their adoptive placement. A first-come-first-serve policy was used to select up to thirty participants who met the selection criteria. It is important to mention that the purpose, program and staff structure, tour guide, and resource organization were coherently synchronized to ensure the successful administration of the research project.

All participants were briefed, and all agreed to participate in the project. The host sponsoring organization was a voluntary civic group, the Korean Coalition for Peace Movement, located in Seoul. The sponsoring organization's pledge of support for this project encompassed the total in-country expenses, including hotel and host family accommodations, meals, bus transportation, tour guides, receptions, and sightseeing. The only cost incurred by the participants was approximately two-thirds of their round-trip air ticket expenses. This was initially one of the major attractive features for the project participants. The travel arrangements were handled through a Chicago-based travel agency. The tour advisory team members consisted of the tour leader (myself), one Korean-American tour coordinator, one adoptive parent (mother), and one Korean-American young adult as a counselor. They were involved from the first application screening to the tour terminal evaluation. While staying in Korea, the executive staff and board members of the sponsoring organization joined the advisory team to coordinate and manage the facilitation of services. Several civic and governmental organizations offered the participants many invaluable programs, cultural experiences, and services. The Chung-Ang University provided a two-day in-residence cultural education on Korean history, language, and culture while accommodating them at its dormitory facility in the countryside. One of the local high schools for girls provided twelve families to host participants over two nights. The Seo-cho District Council of the Metropolitan Seoul Government hosted an official welcome ceremony, and the tour bus transportation was provided by one of the sponsoring board member's church.

Project Purpose

The purpose of this study was to assess the nature of homecoming experiences gained through an organized group tour. The research assumptions inherent in this study were

1. that a carefully organized program with clearly stated goals, reliable program, and supportive structures would provide participants with a high degree of satisfaction in meeting their expectations and a low degree of risk in exploring searches for biological kin and cultural roots;
2. that the group tour experiences would enhance their appreciation of ethnic identity;
3. that the whole process of engaging themselves in search for biological kin, and/or learning more about their past would have a healing ef-

fect in reconstructing their past and integrating a newly discovered
sense of reality; and
4. that the tour experience, when positive, would produce a synergistic
   effect on the development of participants' peer support network, a renewed appreciation toward their adoptive parents, and a more elevated interest toward their own ethnic culture and history.

Participant Profile

As shown in Tables 18.1 and 18.2, the twenty-eight participants were
adopted between 1964 and 1991. The majority (82 percent) were adopted
during the 1970s. Except for one participant who was fathered by an unknown U.S. serviceman, the rest were racially Korean. All, except one who

TABLE 18.1. Survey Participants Profile by Subjects

Subject	Age	Sex	U.S. State	Adopted Year
1	15	F	MA	1979
2	16	F	NY	1979
3	16	M	MD	1986
4	17	F	MN	1977
5	17	M	NY	1980
6	18	F	CO	1976
7	18	F	WI	1977
8	19	F	CO	1986
9	19	M	MN	1976
10	19	M	FL	1991
11	19	M	VA	1975
12	20	M	CA	1974
13	20	F	MN	1975
14	21	F	WI	1979
15	21	F	MN	1975
16	22	F	CA	1976
17	23	M	MN	1974
18	23	F	IL	1973
19	23	F	MN	1975
20	23	F	HI	1973
21	23	F	MN	1975
22	25	F	HI	1973
23	25	F	PA	1979
24	27	M	MN	1970
25	30	F	NY	1975
26	32	M	MN	1970
27	32	M	MN	1964
28	35	M	MN	1973

TABLE 18.2. Demographic Data

Demographic Data	Mean	SD
Age	19.32	5.30
Years in United States	17.04	5.68
Years of Education	14.08	2.20

	Frequency	Percentage
Gender		
Male	12	42.9
Female	16	57.1
Marital status		
Single	23	82.1
Married	3	10.7
Divorced	1	3.6
Missing	1	3.6
Religion		
Christian	17	60.7
Catholic	5	17.8
No response	6	21.5
Birthplace		
Korea	27	78.6
Don't know	1	3.6
Father's birthplace		
United States	22	78.6
Korea	1	3.6
Don't know	3	10.7
Missing	2	7.1
Mother's birthplace		
United States	21	75.0
Korea	2	7.1
Don't know	3	10.7
Missing	2	7.1

did not know, were born in Korea. The mean age was 19.3 years with a range of between fifteen and thirty-two years. There were eleven males and seventeen females. The majority were single (82.1 percent), three were married, one divorced, and one did not report marital status. The participants predominantly reported that their adoptive parents were born in the United States; however, five participants indicated that they did not know where their parents were born. Seventeen were Christian (60.7 percent), five Catholic (17.8 percent), and six did not respond (21.5 percent). Geographically, they represented seventeen states: eleven from Minnesota, three from New York, two each from Wisconsin, California, Colorado, and

Hawaii, and one each from Massachusetts, Montana, Florida, Virginia, Illinois, and Pennsylvania.

Methods of Data Collection and Analysis

A multimethod approach including two questionnaires, taped interviews, participatory observations, application forms, and journal notes were used to generate both narrative and analytic data. The survey instruments that were used included (1) the Adoption Tour Survey Questionnaire on expectations and experiences of the motherland tour project, which contained fifteen items on a 10-point Likert scale and one narrative open-ended essay on the meaning of the homeland trip and (2) the Self-Identity Acculturation Scale (Koh, 1994) to measure cultural identity on twenty-two items, including historical backgrounds and more recent behaviors related to cultural identity. Additional data collection strategies employed were participatory observation notes, journal notes, and during- and after-tour responses from the participants on videotape. For data analysis, both descriptive statistics and content analysis techniques were used where appropriate. To measure the effects of participating in the homecoming tour project, both an identity scale and a survey questionnaire were administered and a t-test was used to measure statistical significance at a 0.05 level.

FINDINGS AND DISCUSSIONS

This section presents both narrative and statistical data according to the major themes of this study, including

1. the meaning of search for roots;
2. behavioral and affective changes;
3. factors associated with ethnic identity;
4. the healing aspects of the homecoming experience, and
5. the importance of building peer social networks.

The Meaning of Searching for Roots

Several themes emerged from the narratives of the respondents to the question *"What does the homeland trip mean to you personally?"* at the onset of the homeland trip, as shown in Exhibit 18.1. They include (1) an increased knowledge about Korea, Korean culture, and ethnic backgrounds; (2) an elevated sense of connectedness; (3) an increased motivation to search for personal roots. Additional themes that are more salient emerged

EXHIBIT 18.1. Narrative Assessment of Pretrip Expectations

Theme	Narratives	Source (study subject number)
Knowledge	*It means a voyage to learn more about my culture and who I really am.*	S2
	It will be true when we can learn about our country with others in the same situations.	S7
	Experience Korea, its people, and my roots.	S20
	I like to experience the culture and learn more about my background.	S21
	One should see how the country has changed and how it was in the past. Get used to Korea and compare to the US. It means to find what you can about your homeland and remembering it.	S25
	It means a chance to go visit to my homeland, and it's time to know more about Korea.	S27
Personal Roots	*My goal is to try to locate my orphanage and get a feel at the atmosphere there and also to live everyday life of a Korean.*	S15
	This trip is very important to me, chance for me to visit my home and relive. Going back to the roots is always important, very personal. Hopefully it will be fulfilled in some way.	S22
	Being a place where I was born and looking for my bio-family.	S28
Connect-edness	*Rediscover the friends left behind and to find them again.*	S8
	Being able to meet my blood family and orphanage is the highlight of the trip. The whole trip is fantastic, hopefully.	S17

from the posttrip response narratives to the question *"What was the most significant aspect of this homeland trip?"* as presented in Exhibit 18.2. They include (1) ethnic identity; (2) healing effects, and (3) self-growth experience in addition to what they had initially expected from this tour.

Behavioral and Affective Change

In assessing behavioral and affective change, the author's survey questionnaire with fifteen variables was used at the pre- and the post-homeland-tour. The mean and standard deviation of the pretest and posttest in these variables are presented in Table 18.3. The *t*-test shows that there were at least five variables that had statistically significant change as the result of their participation in homeland tour experiences. The knowledge level of native country increased the most significant at $p < .001$ level, followed by sensitivity to culture at $p < .01$ level, degree of self-acceptance, level of comfort in meeting other Korean adoptees, and feeling toward U.S. families each at $p < .05$ level. As noted in the narrative section, these statistical find-

---

EXHIBIT 18.2. Narrative Assessment of Posttrip Experiences

Theme	Narratives	Source
Knowledge	*It really showed me what my history and culture was or is like. It opened my doors for me to study my heritage. The trip helped me come to some important connections about me, my life, and my history. It was a wonderful trip regardless of the minor problems, and it gave me many important decisions that I'll have to make in the future. It was a successful trip, and I would suggest for others to go in the future.*	S2
	It will be true when we can learn about our country with others in the same situations.	S7
	Learned more Korean history and culture that I have been lost.	S27

Personal Roots

Another part of this trip that was very important to me was my visit to the orphanages. After seeing the kids, I knew that I would want to adopt someday and give one of these kids a good life (at least give it my best shot in raising them). The first orphanage could be described as "inadequate." It was dirty, run down, understaffed, and very old. The second orphanage was in much better condition, up-to-date, and seemed to have a good structure/program for the kids. I just thought to myself, I was one of them, and now it's my turn to help them.   S7

My most significant aspect about my homeland trip is the fact that I found out about my past, why I was given up, etc. This was painful for me, but it has also helped me to fill in some empty spaces. I would definitely do this again, it was worthwhile.   S15

The most significant aspect of my home-land trip was just seeing the country and seeing the orphanage. These parts of the trip were important to me personally because it helped me learn more about my cultural backgrounds. Visiting the orphanage made me think about my adoption more.   S17

The most significant aspect of this trip was meeting my blood relatives (family) and my old orphanage. Also discovering my family root was significant. This trip answered 99% of my unknown past. I hope all the adopted people get an opportunity to seek and search their family history. A fantastic trip.   S19

Seeing the orphanage I came from, because it's a part of my life that was unknown and part of my origin. Also just to see Korea is significant because my roots stem from there.   S20

(continued)

(continued)

Theme	Narratives	Source
	The next time I go to visit Korea I would like to visit some orphanages. That would let me understand a little more about what my life was like before I was adopted, because I have no knowledge and would like to gain some.	S21
Ethnic Identity	The most significant aspect of my home-land trip was developing a deeper aware-ness of who I am; I am Korean. All this involved by the fabrication of meeting other Koreans (host family, other Kore-ans I've met each day), Korean culture (history class and sightseeing we did each day). Before I just looked Korean; now, I not only look Korean, I know more about what it is to be Korean. I still have a long way to go but at least my quest has begun.	S7
	I really liked meeting Matt. He is so cool. The trip gave me a better understanding of who I am and where I come from. The trip meant something different for everyone.	S11
Connect-edness	It was great to see my family again and I really enjoyed meeting other adoptees; however, at my age, I would have pre-ferred an individual trip with more free-dom to pursue my own agenda as I will be going back in the next two years.	S1
	The things I enjoyed are meeting host families, the Korean people, going to see my hometown, and all of the Korean peo-ple along, and how helpful they were, I can't explain in words the feelings or emotions I went through finding about my mom and meeting my family. The best are the Korean people, and going home-town, meet people; everyone was willing to help way beyond what is expected of them.	S3

I really liked meeting little Liz. She's just adorable.	S4
The most rewarding experience I had was with my host family. They were so generous and happy people. It made me feel proud to have a connection with them. It also gave me the opportunity to see how Korean family life is and all the cultural similarities and difference. The friendship I made with Hye-Young is one that I hope will continue for a long time.	S10
Visiting my homeland trip means so much to me. Because I was adopted by American family when I was sixteen. I felt more comfortable about Korean and Korean culture. During this trip I went to visit my family at an orphanage. They all welcomed me with big hand.	S14
The other significant aspect was meeting other adopted Koreans. There was that instant connection. We found that we had a lot of feelings about adoption that were the same. It's just good to know you're not alone. This also helps the confusion and feelings about adoption. I feel we all gained friends and a chance to find out about ourselves.	S16
I enjoyed the trip and would come back anyway in a second. It was nice to know there are others with the same back-grounds that you have. I made new friends that will hopefully last a lifetime.	S24
I really enjoyed spending time and getting to know others are in the same situation as me. It was also nice to first visit the country and get to understand the culture and people better.	S21
The most significant aspects of my home-land trip was touring with other adopted Koreans also understand me. Also staying with host families made me see how Koreans really live (their lifestyle). I think	

(continued)

(continued)

Theme	Narratives	Source
	touring with other adopted Koreans are very important because of similar backgrounds. There is an understanding and great bonding with each other.	S28
Self-Growth	*This trip was a time of self-growth for me! I learned much more than just about the surface of Koreans and their society. This is a trip that is very special and hopefully all of the friends. Memories will stay with me forever.*	S9
	Learned more about one's culture for personal growth.	S26
Healing Effects	*The greatest thing about this tour was the opportunity to meet people with very similar backgrounds that were just as extreme and traumatic as your own, but having the underlying understanding*	S5
	that connect us all is a very deep way. Also, the acceptance of not ever leaving my past has helped me deal with a lot of healing in my own life. With this tour, I have felt a deep sense of my Korean culture has been rooted into me that help me to identify myself better as a Korean-American adoptee. I felt the uniqueness in the people give us a sense of having yet our own identity and race. This has been a wonderful experience that I will cherish always.	
	For me, there were two very significant aspects. The first one being the inner healing and personal growth. I feel that I have begun to find part of the missing piece of my life. I understand more of Koran culture and the people. This has helped me understand more of my birth parents and ultimately myself. The more I understand, the more the confusion goes away.	

TABLE 18.3. Pre- and Posttest Behavioral and Affective Changes

Variables[a]	Pretest Mean (SD)	Posttest Mean (SD)	F value
1	3.93 (2.07)	6.78 (1.59)	−8.86[*]
2	7.25 (1.69)	7.65 (1.50)	−0.46
3	5.89 (2.28)	7.00 (1.68)	−2.14[**]
4	4.42 (3.11)	4.64 (3.22)	−0.14
5	5.22 (2.10)	5.78 (3.07)	−1.18
6	6.67 (2.48)	6.00 (2.55)	1.20
7	7.04 (1.93)	7.70 (1.56)	−1.28
8	8.52 (1.44)	9.41 (1.09)	−3.17[***]
9	8.78 (1.25)	9.35 (1.07)	−2.71[**]
10	7.85 (2.15)	8.17 (1.67)	−1.06
11	7.85 (2.14)	8.17 (1.67)	−1.89
12	8.17 (2.17)	8.30 (2.00)	−0.72
13	3.30 (3.55)	4.82 (3.75)	−2.12[**]
14	8.22 (1.65)	8.33 (1.52)	0.34
15	8.08 (1.74)	8.36 (1.84)	−0.23

[a]1: Knowledge level of native country, 2: Attitude toward Korea, 3: Sensitivity to culture, 4: Fantasy or mystique about Korean society, 5: Feelings about biological relatives, 6: Discovery of past, 7: Impressions of Korean society, 8: Degree of self-acceptance, 9: Level of comfort meeting Korean adoptees, 10: Level of self-awareness, 11: Attitude toward Korea's international adoption, 12: Feelings about own adopted situation, 13: Feelings toward U.S. family, 14: Excitement about homeland trip, 15: Recommendations about trip.

[*]$p < .001$
[**] $p < .05$
[***] $p < .01$

ings are complementary to some extent to the significant aspects of the participants' homeland tour experiences. As their knowledge has increased in appreciation of their native country, its culture, and people, this tour also benefited them by connecting them with other Korean adoptees who share similar backgrounds and needs for bonding in pursuit of their roots. It is noteworthy that they became more appreciative of their adopted parents and families despite their searching for their roots through this homeland tour.

Factors Associated with Ethnic Identity

To assess any changes in the ethnic identity of Korean adoptees who participated in this homeland tour, Koh's (1994) Self-Identity Acculturation

Scale (SIA) was used. This scale is a twenty-one-item, multiple-choice questionnaire covering language (four questions), identity (four questions), friendship choice (four questions), behaviors (five questions), generation/geographic history (three questions), and attitudes (one question). This was modified by Koh from the Suinn-Lew Asian-Identity Acculturation Scale (SL-ASIA). The correlation effects between the twenty-one paired items did not yield any statistical significance except food preference at home between male (4.0/.95) and female (3.27/.80) at $p < 039$.

Ten days might have been too short to observe any significant changes on the measurements of this scale. This instrument was found to be not well adapted to the assessment of the changing effects on ethnic identity for Korean adopted youths and young adults. The language skills in speaking ($r = .483, p < .05$) and reading ($r = .473, p < .05$) had positive correlations with the overall variables of Lee's Korean Adoptees' Homeland Tour Questionnaire. As language is an essence of culture and a medium of understanding, it can be conjectured here that knowledge acquisition depends on the level of language competence, which in turn facilitates cognitive change.

The Healing Aspects of Motherland Tour Experience

As noted in the narrative section, it was a profound experience for those who discovered their past with more realistic views of their roots and the socioeconomic circumstances that led to their adoption. When the adoptees visited orphanages and baby homes, they saw these children and babies through empathic eyes as if they themselves were there. It was a touching moment for me to observe some of the adoptees who were sobbing while holding and cuddling these babies. It was a precious healing time for them to reconcile intrapsychically with their own capacity to accept who they were. No words could adequately describe such expressed vulnerability and grief of abandonment. The healing process makes self-integration more complete, as one participant who wrote:

> For me, there were two very significant aspects, the first one being the inner healing and personal growth. I feel that I have begun to find part of the missing piece of my life. I understand more of Korean culture and the people. This has helped me understand more of my birth parents and ultimately myself. The more I understand, the more the confusion goes away.

Other adoptees spoke of the importance of locating themselves in their birth country:

> The most significant aspect of my homeland trip was just seeing the country and seeing the orphanage. These parts of the trip were important to me personally because it helped me learn more about my cultural backgrounds. Visiting the orphanage made me think about my adoption more.

And other participants spoke of the importance of seeing themselves in those biologically related to them:

> The most significant aspect of this trip was meeting my blood relatives (family) and my old orphanage. Also discovering my family root (tree) was significant. This trip answered ninety-nine percent of my unknown past. I hope all the adopted people get an opportunity to seek and search their family history.

Peer Social Network Building

Unlike many adoptees who visited their homeland individually in search for their roots, the benefits of an organized group tour, composed of adoptees who share relatively similar backgrounds and motivation, are noteworthy. Not only do they serve as psychological buffers for each other, but also, more importantly, they built a lasting supportive social network based upon their shared experiences. This is a hallmark of homeland tours for adoptees as many of the participants have remained in contact till today, after eleven years. In the narrative section, many participants stated that meeting other adoptees whose backgrounds were similar made their homeland trip worthwhile. Nationwide networks such as the Korean American Adoptee Adoptive Family Network (KAAN) have been established to promote informational exchange and the rights of Korean adoptees and adoptive families (Winston, 2004).

Expectations and Outcomes

Analysis of the videotape, which captured the daily activities of tour and after-tour group gatherings, clearly revealed the synergy that stems from the need for ethnic identity and connectedness among those who share similar adoption backgrounds in young adults. The videotape was viewed by myself and a Loyola University Chicago social work graduate assistant, and the contents were coded and verified by both to ensure accuracy. In this section, only relevant findings are presented in Table 18.4. While traveling, one of the senior participants took the lead in asking each participant *"Why did you come on this trip and what do you like about it?"*

TABLE 18.4. Reasons for Coming on the Trip and Favorite Experiences of the Trip[a]

Participant	Why did you come on this trip?	What did you like about it?
1	To get in touch with my cultural background	[Response missing]
2	To get information on my birth family	Getting to know other Korean adoptees
3	Want to see Korea	Interested, surprised
4	Learn about culture	Therapeutic
5	To see country and learn	Unsure about looking for parents
6	Going home	Feeling numb and overwhelmed
7	To visit motherland and orphanage	The weather has been hard
8	I forgot Korea, feels nice to be there	Want to come back
9	See my homeland	It's incredible
10	To go back to Korea	Like it and am enjoying myself
11	To discover my heritage	Liked my host family
12	Interested in Korea	It's been a shock, enjoyed the orphanage
13	To see homeland	Pretty cool
14	Find out about culture	The weather has been unreal
15	Wanted to see Korea	Back to motherland, sightseeing and meeting people
16	Wanted to see Korea	Most everything has been good
17	See the people, find out who they are	See the country; the food is excellent
18	See my people; learn about the customs	Meeting people
19	I have been keeping contact with a man who might be my biological dad for a year now, and want to meet him and figure out if he is	Answered a lot of questions I had about myself
20	Decided to come at last minute; no expectations	Have enjoyed everything
21	Wanted to see the land, especially the culture	Meeting other people has been the most fun, both adoptees and locals
22	Wanted to teach children about Korea	Trip a big learning experience
23	See the culture; wanted to visit home town. Wanted to see mom	Best was meeting people, host family. Wanted to see mom. Visited hometown and found her, but she did not come out to meet (only reason given was that she had a hard life). Met aunt and first cousin. Bonding with people a lot of fun

TABLE 18.4 *(continued)*

Participant	Why did you come on this trip?	What did you like about it?
24	Family reunion	Fifteen folks; met relatives–cousin, half-brothers, (three or four half-brothers and one half-sister who was adopted in Switzerland). Bonding with people a lot of fun. Feeling about trip unbelievable. Want to go back and live there for a year or two.
25	Family reunion	Great experience, met brother, sister, mother, niece, and nephew. Way more than expected. Want to go back

[a]These responses were video-recorded on-the-spot while traveling by one of the participating adoptees during the middle and later parts of the homeland tour as a midterm assessment of their experiences in the host country. Three subjects were not available to respond during the taping period.

As noted in Table 18.4, there were several reasons given for participating in this homeland trip. Many of them wanted to visit their motherland to learn more about its people, land, and culture, while others wanted to meet their biological family and relatives with whom they had prior contact or to find out if they could trace their biological roots. For those who did not have any information about their kin, they wanted to go back to the orphanage or to the village in which they grew up. The majority of the participants were satisfied with their experiences, with three participants having met their biological kin for the first time during this trip.

Several salient aspects of their homeland trip experiences can be highlighted in terms of response characteristics. First, an array of emotional responses were shown differently from adoptee to adoptee; from a "feeling of numbness and [being] overwhelmed," to "shock," to "enjoying self," and "enjoying everything," to finding it "therapeutic." Second, it was a bonding experience that made the family reunion between adoptees and their natal families and relatives the most fulfilling part of their trip. Third, through their quest for their ethnic roots, the trip helped many of the adoptees to develop a sense of connectedness with Koreans in and out of their social network, including other adoptees, host families, old friends at the orphanage, village people, and other Koreans they came in contact with. Fourth, the trip helped one participant to clear her self-doubt and gave her a lot of answers.

Fifth, because it was such a fulfilling experience for some, they wanted to come back to explore more. Sixth, others were simply "interested and surprised" or described it as being "incredible," "pretty cool," "unbelievable," or "way beyond expected." Finally, the muggy summer weather was "unbearable," but the food was "great."

CONCLUSION

On the basis of the empirical findings and other supporting data, I conclude the following:

1. The Korean adoptees who participated in this homecoming tour project confirmed the major research assumptions about their search for new meanings in the process of reconstructing their psychosocial world.
2. The needs for finding out *who they are, where they came from,* and *what pushed them for adoption* were real and profound for the adoptees. The quest provided them with a light to the shadowed past of their birth, ethnic roots, biological kin, the natal environments, and the circumstances under which they were adopted.
3. The range of emotional experiences that resulted from exploring the painful realities of their past and the current situations of their native country reflected individual differences, from a feeling of numbness in some to healing among others.
4. Many positive cognitive and behavioral changes, in terms of self-awareness, self-acceptance, and integration of ethnic pride, took place as the result of affirming their own ethnic and self-identity.
5. The participants became more appreciative of their American adoptive families.
6. The gained knowledge and understanding of, and connection to, Korea, its people, culture, history, and geography increased motivations for further explorations as well as for making necessary adjustments to their preconceived notions.
7. The participants highly valued the supportive peer networking among Korean adoptees having similar backgrounds and predicaments.

The following comments came in a letter from one of the Korean adoptees (Elizabeth R., adult adoptee) who participated in the homecoming tour, and depicts many of the salient points highlighted in the preceding list.

The trip to my motherland meant a lot to me, I will never forget this once in a lifetime experience. I learned many new and interesting things about Korea through this trip. Now that I have returned to my motherland and experienced her culture, I feel that I have a better sense of pride in whom I am and where I come from.

I realize that many people had doubts on whether I could handle such a big step in discovering who I am and where I come from; even I had a little hesitation on being able to go back to Korea. Now that I've successfully achieved this step in my self-discovery I am able to say that this time in my life was perfect for a trip like this. Although there were the strong emotions and "culture shock," this trip made me feel so much more comfortable with my heritage. I have never been ashamed of being Korean but up until now, I have never been completely comfortable about being Korean. I don't exactly know how to put my feelings into words. All I can do is give you this very recent example and hope you understand what I am trying to say.

While at work, one of my customers asked me if I was related to a Chinese girl who sang in his church choir. Understand that I have been mistaken for being Chinese since I can remember. And for the first time in my life my reply was "I'm not Chinese, I'm Korean." Saying that made me feel proud to be who I am, a Korean-American. The man replied with the ignorant statement of, "You don't look Korean," and I replied back wisely by saying, "Sorry to disappoint you."

REFERENCES

Cederblad, M. (1982). Utlandska adoptivbarn som kommit till Sverige efter tre års ålder: Anpassningsprocessen under det forste året i familjen [*Foreign adoptees who have come to Sweden after the age of three years: The adaptation process during the first year with the family*]. Stockholm: Statens Namnd for Internatonallea Adotivfrågor (NIA).

Clark, E., & Hainisee, J. (1982). Intellectual and adaptive performance of Asian children in adoptive American settings. *Journal of American Academy in Child and Adolescent Psychiatry, 27*(1), 111-115.

Deacon, S. (1997). Intercountry adoption and the family life cycle. *The American Journal of Family Therapy, 25*(3), 245-260.

DiVirglio, L. (1956). Adjustment of foreign children in their adoptive homes. *Child Welfare, 35,* 15-21.

Feigelman, W., & Silverman, A. (1983). The long-term effects of tranracial adoption. *Social Service Review, 58,* 588-602.

Friedlander, M. L. (January 1999). Ethnic identity development of internationally adopted children and adolescents: Implications for family therapists. *Journal of Marital and Family Therapy, 25*(1), 43-60.

French, G. (1986). Intercountry adoption: Helping a young child deal with loss. *Child Welfare, 65*(3), 272-279.

Hoksbergen, R. A. (1991). Intercountry adoption coming of age in the Netherlands: Basic issues, trends and developments. In H. Altstein & R. J. Simon (Eds.), *International adoption: A multinational perspective.* New York: Praeger.

Hübinette, T. (2003). [Mental health among international adoptees in Sweden], *Psykisk: Hälsa: Suenska föreningen för psykisk hälsovård* no. 1/2003 (vol. 44), pp. 17-30.

IEKAS. (2005, April 8). Korea must stop overseas adoption. *The Information Exchange for Korean American Scholars, 5*(13). Retrieved on April 20, 2005, from http://www.skas.org.

Kim, D. S. (1977). How they fared in American homes: A follow-up study of adopted Korean children. *Children Today, 6*(2), 2-6.

Kim, W. J. (1995). International adoption: A case review of Korean children. *Child Psychiatry and Human Development, 25*(3), 141-154.

Koh, T. (1994). Ethnic identity in first, 1.5, and second generation Korean-Americans: An exploratory study. In H. Kwon (Ed.), *Korean Americans: Conflict and harmony* (pp. 43-53). Chicago: North Park College and Theological Seminary Press.

Liow, S. R. (1994). Transracial adoption: Questions on heritage for parents, children, and counselors. *Counseling Psychology Quarterly, 7*(4), 375-384.

Pacheco, F., & Eme, R. (1993). An outcome study of the reunion between adoptees and biological parents. *Child Welfare, 72*(1), 53-65.

Rathburn, C., McLaughlin, H., Bennet, C., & Garland, J. (1965). Later adjustment of children following radical separation from family and culture. *American Journal of Orthopsychiatry, 35,* 604-609.

Smit, E. (2002). Adopted children: Core issues and unique challenges. *Journal of Child and Adolescent Psychiatric Nursing, 15*(4), 143-150.

Tizard, B. (1991). Intercountry adoption: A review of the evidence. *Journal of Child Psychiatry, 32*(5), 743-756.

Verhulst, F., Althaus, M., & Versluis-Den Bieman, H. (1990). Problem behavior in international adoptees: An epidemiological study. *Journal of American Academy of Child and Adolescent Psychiatry, 29*(1), 94-111.

Wilkinson, H. S. (1995). Psychological process and issues in international adoption. *The American Journal of Family Therapy, 23*(2), 173-163.

Winston, C. (2004). *"Meeting the needs": Korean American adoption community perspective on more effective placement services.* A paper presented at the 4th International Seminar on post-adoption services. Available at http://www.haanet .com/news/holt_korea_presentation.html.

PART VII:
RESOURCES

International adoption has been the focus of numerous scholarly, professional, and popular writings. The body of literature and media is widespread and often unpublished—as in theses and dissertations—and there is no central repository or indexed reference for this growing collection. Therefore, in our final section, we provide a thoughtfully prepared selected bibliography for those readers who desire to pursue further study of Korean or other international adoption. The bibliography includes scholarly works as well as popular literature, films, and resources on the World Wide Web.

Chapter 19

International Korean Adoption: A Selective Bibliography

Janet H. Clarke

While there are research and other cultural productions in many languages on the subject of international Korean adoption, only works written in or translated into English are included here. However, insofar as English language materials are concerned, the attempt has been to be comprehensive. Because research and other discourses on Korean adoption are often grouped with other Asian groups or other international adoptions, this bibliography is divided into two broad categories: *Korean Adoption* and *Asian Adoption*. The entries under *Korean Adoption* are primarily about Korean adoption or include Korean adoption as a significant part of the discussion. The entries under *Asian Adoption* are primarily about one or more Asian adoption groups and/or include them in a discussion of international adoption in broader terms.

Within these broad categories of *Korean Adoption* and *Asian Adoption,* the entries are listed chronologically by decade starting in 1950 to show common themes (e.g., children's physical and psychological adjustments), shifts (e.g., adoptees as research subjects to adoptees as researchers, writers, filmmakers, etc.), and new developments (such as the use of feminist or postcolonial theoretical frameworks to critique Eurocentric modes of discourse) in the history of the literature on international Korean adoption. Each decade is then divided by genre: *Research and Scholarship, Nonfiction, Fiction,* and, where applicable, *Poetry, Films/Videos,* and *Web Sites. Research and Scholarship* includes scholarly writings, research findings, reports, case studies, and other professional literature, such as professional brochures or booklets. *Nonfiction* includes news reports, human-interest

International Korean Adoption
© 2007 by The Haworth Press, Inc. All rights reserved.
doi:10.1300/5734_19

features, autobiography, and biography. *Fiction* is reserved for book-length monographs as well as short stories. Although there is much poetry about the Korean adoption experience, there are few book-length works specifically devoted to this group; thus there is only one English-language volume listed in this category. In keeping with the English-language focus of this bibliography, the selections in *Films/Videos* include works in, or available in, English. Web sites were chosen based on relevance and breadth of information. While there are many excellent local organizations represented on the Web, only those local or regional organizations that provide extensive resources beyond their local community are included. Chat groups, LIST-SERVs, and adoption agencies in general are not included. Similarly, adoption guidebooks and/or handbooks are not included. Finally, juvenile and children's books are omitted in this bibliography.

KOREAN ADOPTION

1950-1959

Research and Scholarship

DiVirglio, L. (1956). Adjustment of foreign children in their adoptive homes. *Child Welfare, 35,* 15-21.
Valk, M. A. (1957). *Korean-American children in American adoptive homes.* New York: Child Welfare League of America.

Nonfiction

Holt, B., & Wisner, D. (1956). *Seed from the East* [s.l.]: Holt International Children's Services.

Films/Videos

Law, G. (Director). (1959). The Conley family. In W. Kayden (Producer), *On the go* (Show no. 18B). CBS Television Network.

1960-1969

Research and Scholarship

Chakerian, C. G. (1962). *First report on Korea* (Rev. ed.). Chicago: [s.n.].
Chakerian, C. G. (1963). *Second report on Korea.* New York: National Council of the Churches of Christ in the United States of America; Church World Service, Immigration Services.

Hurh, W. M. (1969). *Marginal children of war: An exploratory study of American-Korean children.* (Paper presented at the Joint Meeting of Midwest and Ohio Valley Sociological Societies, May 3, 1969). (ERIC Document Reproduction Service No. ED 047 781).

International Social Service. (1960). *Adoption of Oriental children by American White families.* New York: Child Welfare League of America.

Keltie, P. E. (1969). *The adjustment of Korean children adopted by couples in the Chicago area.* Unpublished master's thesis, Jane Addams Graduate School of Social Work, University of Illinois, Chicago.

O'Conner, L., Jr. (1964). *The adjustment of a group of Korean and Korean-American children adopted by couples in the United States.* Unpublished master's thesis, University of Tennessee, Knoxville.

Rathbun, C., McLaughlin, H., Bennet, C., & Garland, J. (1965). Later adjustment of children following radical separation from family and culture. *American Journal of Orthopsychiatry, 35,* 604-609.

Nonfiction

Anthony, J. (1960). *The rascal and the pilgrim: The story of the boy from Korea.* New York: Farrar, Straus, and Cudahy.

1970-1979

Research and Scholarship

Adams, J., & Kim, H. B. (1971). A fresh look at inter-country adoptions. *Children, 18,* 214-221.

Carroll, T. G., & Kim, C. (1975). Intercountry adoption of South Korean orphans: A lawyer's guide. *Journal of Family Law, 14,* 223-254.

Chartrand, W. R. (1978). Applications of selected components of a correspondence theory of cross-cultural adjustment to the adjustment of white families who have adopted older children from Korea (Doctoral dissertation, University of Minnesota, 1978). *Dissertation Abstracts International, 39,* 5749.

Children's Bureau (1975). *Tips on the care and adjustment of Vietnamese and other Asian children in the United States* [Handbook]. Washington, DC: H. Miller.

Guilbault, C., & Guilbault, J. (1972). *A descriptive study of the adjustment of Korean children adopted by families in Minnesota.* Unpublished master's thesis, University of Wisconsin.

Joe, B. (1978). In defense of intercountry adoption. *Social Service Review, 52,* 1-20.

Kim, D. S. (1976). Intercountry adoption: A study of self-concept of adolescent Korean children who were adopted by American families (Doctoral dissertation, University of Chicago, 1976). *Dissertation Abstracts International,* 215.

Kim, D. S. (1977). How they fared in American homes: A follow-up study of adopted Korean children. *Children Today, 6*(2), 2-6.

Kim, D. S. (1978). From women to women with painful love: A study of maternal motivation in intercountry adoption process. In H. H. Sunoo & D. S. Kim (Eds.), *Korean women: In a struggle for humanization.* Memphis, TN: The Association of Korean Christian Scholars in North America, Inc. (AKCS).

Kim, D. S. (1978). Issues in transracial and transcultural adoption. *Social Casework, 59*(8), 477-486.

Kim, H. C. (1974). *Intercountry adoption: American and Danish parents who adopted Korean-born children.* Unpublished master's thesis, Ohio State University, Columbus.

Kim, H. T., & Reid, E. (1975). After a long journey: A study on the process of initial adjustment of the half and full Korean children adopted by American families and the families' experiences with these children during the transitional period. In B. Kramer (Ed.), *The unbroken circle: A collection of writings on interracial and international adoption* (pp. 306-427). Minneapolis, MN: Organization for a United Response.

Kim, S. P., Hong, S., & Kim, B. S. (1979). Adoption of Korean children by New York area couples: A preliminary study. *Child Welfare, 58,* 419-427.

Laning, S. (1978). *The socialization of the adopted Korean child* [Technical Report]. Medford, MA: Tufts University.

Miller, H. (1971). Korea's international children. *Lutheran Social Welfare, 11*(2), 12-23.

Miller, H. (1971). Recent developments in Korean services for children. *Children, 18*(1), 28-30.

Pruzan, V. (1977). Born in a foreign country—adopted in Denmark. *International Child Welfare Review, 36*(2), 41-47.

Silverman, A. R., & Feigelman, W. (1977). Some factors affecting adoption of minority children. *Social Casework, 58,* 554-561.

Simon, R. J. (1974). An assessment of racial awareness, preference, and self-identity among white and adopted non-white children. *Social Problems, 22*(1), 43-57.

Stansbury, G. (1974). *A child of two worlds: The older Korean orphan comes to Utah.* Unpublished master's thesis, University of Utah, Salt Lake.

Westhues, A., & Cohen, J. S. (1977). A comparison of the adjustment of adolescent and young adult inter-country adoptees and their siblings. *International Journal of Behavioral Development, 20,* 47-65.

Winick, M., Meyer, K. K., & Harris, R. C. (1975, December 19). Malnutrition and environmental enrichment by early adoption. *Science, 190,* 1173-1175.

Nonfiction

America is all they know, but they're not quite at home. (1977, March 1). *New York Times,* p. 27.

Brooton, G. (1971, September 26). The multiracial family. *New York Times Magazine,* pp. 78-80.

Dullea, G. (1977, April 4). For Korean lepers' children, it's America the beautiful. *New York Times,* p. 34.

Malcolm, A. (1977, August 10). South Korea seeks to end flow of orphans to families abroad. *New York Times*, p. 2.

Mathews, L. (1977, January 7). Despite popularity, cute Korean babies aren't for export. *Wall Street Journal*, pp. 1, 8.

Films/Videos

McCann, D., Korty, J., & Lockhart, W. (Producers). Korty, J. (Director) (1977). *Who are the DeBolts, and where did they get 19 kids?* Video, 72 min., English.

1980-1989

Research and Scholarship

Ahn, H. N. (1989). *Identity development in Korean adolescent adoptees: Eriksonian ego identity and racial-ethnic identity* [Technical Report]. Berkeley: University of California, School of Social Welfare.

Andreasen, J., Melsen, B., Miletic, T., & Wenzel, A. (1986). Dental and skeletal maturity in adoptive children: Assessments at arrival and after one year in the admitting country. *Annals of Human Biology, 13,* 153-159.

Cederblad, M. (1982). *Children adopted from abroad and coming to Sweden after age three.* Stockholm: The Swedish National Board for Intercountry Adoption.

Chun, B. H. (1989). Adoption and Korea. *Child Welfare, 68,* 255-260.

Clark, E., & Hanisee, J. (1982). Intellectual and adaptive performance of Asian children in adoptive American settings. *Developmental Psychology, 18,* 595-599.

Dole, K., Hostetter, M. K., Iverson, S., & Johnson, D. (1989). Unsuspected infectious diseases and other medical diagnoses in the evaluation of internationally adopted children. *Pediatriya, 83,* 559-563.

Erickson, M. J. (1980). *Racial identity, awareness, and preferences of transracially adopted Koreans and their Caucasian siblings.* Unpublished master's thesis, Moorhead State University, Minnesota.

Feigelman, W., & Silverman, A. R. (1984). The long-term effects of transracial adoption. *Social Service Review, 58*(4), 588-602.

Frydman, M., & Lynn, R. (1989). The intelligence of Korean children adopted in Belgium. *Personality and Individual Differences, 19,* 1323-1325.

Hoksbergen, R. A. C. (1986). *Adoption in worldwide perspective: A review of programs, policies, and legislation in 14 countries.* Berwyn, PA: Swets North America.

Huh, N. S. (1985). Adopted Korean children's adjustment in American families. *Korean Social Welfare, 83,* 82-101.

Kim, S. P. (1980). Behavior symptoms in three transracially adopted Asian children: Diagnosis dilemma. *Child Welfare, 59,* 213-224.

Kim, S. P., & the American Academy of Child Psychiatry (1981). *Special adoptions: An annotated bibliography on transracial, transcultural, and nonconventional adoption and minority children.* Rockville, MD: National Institute of Mental Health.

Kim, W. J., Davenport, C., Joseph, J., Zrull, J., & Woolford, E. (1988). Psychiatric disorder and juvenile-delinquency in adopted children and adolescents. *Journal of the American Academy of Child and Adolescent Psychiatry, 27*(1), 111-115.

Koh, F. (1981). *Oriental children in American homes.* Minneapolis, MN: EastWest Press.

Kreider, S. D., Lange, W. R., & Warnock-Eckhart, E. (1987). Hepatitis B surveillance in Korean adoptees. *Maryland Medical Journal, 36*(2), 163-166.

Kuhl, W. (1985). *When adopted children of foreign origin grow up.* Osnabruck, Germany: Terre des Hommes.

Lange, W. R., & Warnock-Eckhart, E. (1987). Selected infectious disease risks in international adoptees. *The Pediatric Infectious Disease Journal, 6,* 447-450.

Laning, B. K. (1989). Intercountry adoption in the 1980s. *Korean and Korean-American Studies Bulletin, 3*(3), 20-22.

Lydens, L. A. (1988). A longitudinal study of crosscultural adoption: Identity development among Asian adoptees at adolescence and early adulthood (Doctoral dissertation, Northwestern University, 1988). *Dissertation Abstracts International, 49,* 3882.

Riggle, S. A. (1989). *International adoption: Cross-cultural marketing implications: A study of orphanages in Malaysia, Thailand, India, and South Korea.* Unpublished master's thesis, Johns Hopkins University, New York.

Rubin, K. A. (1987). *An investigative study of the adoption of Korean children by Caucasian families in New Mexico.* Unpublished master's thesis, Antioch University.

Ryan, A. S. (1983). Intercountry adoption and policy issues. *Journal of Children in Contemporary Society, 15*(3), 49-60.

Silverman, A. R. (1980). Transracial adoption in the United States: A study of assimilation and adjustment (Doctoral dissertation, University of Wisconsin, Madison, 1980). *Dissertation Abstracts International, 41,* 2311.

Trueman, M. (1985). Malnutrition and environmental enrichment: A statistical reappraisal of the finds of the adoption study of Winick et al. *Early Child Development and Care, 21,* 277-280.

Understanding the adopted E.S.L. student: A guide for teachers. (1984). Baltimore, MD: FACE, Inc.

Wilkinson, H. S. P. (1985). *Birth is more than once: The inner world of adopted Korean children.* Bloomfield Hills, MI: Sunrise Ventures.

Nonfiction

Barker, K. (1988, May 26). "Official language" bills spark debate at GWU: Unity weighed against ethnic identities. *Washington Post,* p. B13.

Chira, S. (1988, April 21). Babies for export: And now the painful questions. *New York Times,* p. A4.

Demak, R. (1989, July 24). An all-star father. *Sports Illustrated,* p. 69.

Dunphy, C. (1986, January 4). How love saved 14 "doomed" kids. *Toronto Star,* p. L1.

Golden, D. (1989, June 11). When adoption doesn't work. *Boston Globe,* p. 16.

Greer, W. R. (1986, June 26). The adoption market: A variety of options. *New York Times,* p. C1.

Growe, S. J. (1986, July 29). Naomi Bronstein: She risks all for needy kids. *Toronto Star,* p. H1.

Haberman, C. (1984, May 4). A papal visit for the lepers of Korea. *New York Times,* p. A9.

Han, H. S., & Spencer, M. E. (1987). *Understanding my child's Korean origins* (Rev. ed.). St. Paul, MN: Children's Home Society of Minnesota.

Henderson, K. (1985, August 8). Couples welcome overseas children. *Christian Science Monitor,* 29.

Klemesrud, J. (1984, November 19). Number of single parent adoptions grows. *New York Times,* p. C13.

Kutner, L. (1989, September 28). Parent & child. *New York Times,* p. C8.

LaRue, W. (1987, November 14). Elbridge's newest Americans: Three Korean-born children find a family's love in a new country. *Post-Standard* (Syracuse, NY), p. A7.

Melvin, T. (1983, June 12). A reunion of Korean, 81, and adoptees. *New York Times,* p. 11.

Rothschild, M. (1988, January). Babies for sale: South Koreans make them, Americans buy them. *The Progressive,* pp. 18-23.

Self-denial is at the root of South Korea's baby export. (1988, May 9). *New York Times,* p. A18.

Skalka, P. (1984, November). What this baby needs is love. *Reader's Digest,* 88-93.

Strick, L. W. (1985, December). A most precious Hanukkah gift. *Good Housekeeping,* pp. 122, 124, 128.

Tabor, M. (1989, November 6). Opting for adoption: Fewer Korean babies available. *Boston Globe,* p. 36.

Telfer, J., & Telfer, J. (1986). *Bridges: A guide for those associated with building a Korean-Australian family through adoption in South Australia.* [Adelaide, South Australia]: Korean Friendship Group Inc.

Vellante, J. (1988, November 24). Couple is bowled over by their adopted twins. *Boston Globe,* p. A4.

Wolter-Carlson, L. (1986, November). I couldn't give up my foster baby. *Redbook,* pp. 82-86.

Woolley, S. (1988, June 20). When it comes to adoption, it's a wide, wide world. *Business Week,* p. 164.

Zullo, A. (1982, March 22). Suzanne Williams: An eager escort for U.S.-bound orphans. *Christian Science Monitor,* 17.

Films/Videos

Junger, K. (Director) (1988). *Birthplace unknown.* 16 mm, 55 min., Dutch with English subtitles.

1990-1999

Research and Scholarship

Altstein, H., & Simon, R. J. (1997). The relevance of race in adoption law and social practice. *Notre Dame Journal of Law, Ethics, & Public Policy, 11,* 171-195.

Ando, M-K. (1994). Between two worlds. *Women Working in Film and Video, 2*(4), 23.

Andresen, I. L. K. (1992). Behavioural and school adjustment of 12-13-year-old internationally adopted children in Norway: A research note. *Journal of Child Psychology and Psychiatry, 33,* 427-439.

Aronson, J. C. (1997). *Not my homeland: A critique of the current culture of Korean international adoption.* Unpublished manuscript, Hampshire College, Amherst, Massachusetts.

Aukes, S. R. (1993). *Clinical implications for working with adopted Korean adolescents.* Unpublished master's thesis, College of St. Catherine and University of St. Thomas, St. Paul, Minnesota.

Benson, P. L., Sharma, A. R., & Roehlkepartain, E. C. (1994). *Growing up adopted: A portrait of adolescents & their families.* Minneapolis, MN: Search Institute.

Bergquist, K. L. (1997). *Identity formation in adult Korean adoptees.* Unpublished master's thesis, Norfolk State University, Virginia.

Bernthal, N. L. G. (1990). Motherhood lost and found: The experience of becoming an adoptive mother to a foreign-born child (Doctoral dissertation, The Union Institute, 1990). *Dissertation Abstracts International, 51,* 3120.

Boer, F., Versluis-den Bieman, H. J. M., & Verhulst, F. C. (1994). International adoption of children with siblings: Behavioral outcomes. *American Journal of Orthopsychiatry, 64,* 252-262.

Brooks, D., & Barth, R. P. (1999). Adult transracial and inracial adoptees: Effects of race, gender, adoptive family structure, and placement history on adjustment outcomes. *American Journal of Orthopsychiatry, 69,* 87-99.

Brooks, L. K. (1990). Temperament in five- and six-year-old Anglo-American, Korean-American, and adopted Korean children (Doctoral dissertation, University of Chicago, 1990). *American Doctoral Dissertations 1989-1990* (p. 498). Ann Arbor, MI: UMI.

Carlson, R. R. (1994). The emerging law of intercountry adoptions: An analysis of the Hague Conference on intercountry adoption. *Tulsa Law Journal, 30,* 243-304.

Cederblad, M., Hook, B., Irhammar, M., & Mercke, A. (1999). Mental health in international adoptees as teenagers and young adults: An epidemiological study. *Journal of Child Psychology and Psychiatry and Allied Disciplines, 40,* 1239-1248.

Cole, J. C. (1992). Perceptions of ethnic identity among Korean-born adoptees and their Caucasian-American parents (Doctoral dissertation, Columbia University, 1992). *Dissertation Abstracts International, 54,* 0317.

Curtis, J., Benuska, M., & Dinnel, D. (1998-1999). Korean Identity Development Society: Profile of Korean culture camp participants. *Korean American Historical Society Occasional Papers, 4,* 63-84.

des Jardins, K. S. (1996). Racial identity development and self concept in adopted Korean women (Doctoral dissertation, Boston University, 1996). *Dissertation Abstracts International, 56,* 5166.

Didier, S. (1998). *"Just a drop in the bucket": An analysis of child rescue efforts on behalf of Korean children, 1951 to 1964.* Unpublished master's thesis, Portland State University, Oregon.

Elsinger, R. J. K. (1997). *The adopted Korean American diaspora: Forces behind identity construction.* Unpublished manuscript, Macalester College, St. Paul, Minnesota.

Fauve-Chamoux, A. (1998). Introduction: Adoption, affiliation, and family recomposition: Inventing family continuity. *The History of the Family, 3,* 385-392.

Gildea, L. A. (1992). The academic achievement of adopted Korean children: Factors of intellect and home educational environment (Doctoral dissertation, Boston University, 1992). *Dissertation Abstracts International, 52,* 6106.

Gonzalez, E. G. (1990). Effects of age at placement and length of placement on foreign and domestic adopted children (Doctoral dissertation, University of Akron, 1990). *Dissertation Abstracts International, 51,* 1013.

Harp, A. (1999). *Korean adoptees communicating identities and negotiating the hyphens between selves and others.* Unpublished master's thesis, San Diego State University, California.

Herrmann, K. J., Jr., & Kasper, B. (1992). International adoption: The exploitation of women and children. *Affilia, 7*(1), 45-58.

House International Affairs Committee. (1999, October 20). *Hague Convention Policy Joint Council on International Children's Services.* (Testimony of S. A. Freivalds).

Huh, N. S. (1993). Services for out-of-wedlock children in Korea. *Early Child Development and Care, 85,* 35-46.

Huh, N. S. (1997). Korean children's ethnic identity formation and understanding of adoption (Doctoral dissertation, SUNY-Albany, 1997). *Dissertation Abstracts International, 58,* 0586.

Humphrey, M., & Humphrey, H. (Eds.) (1993). *Intercountry adoption: Practical experiences.* London: Routledge.

Johnson, W. J., & Kim-Johnson, M. (1998-1999). Sometimes love isn't enough: The voices of some adult Korean adoptees in Minnesota. *Korean American Historical Society Occasional Papers, 4,* 99-109.

Juffer, F., Hoksbergen, R. A. C., Riksen-Walraven, J. M., & Kohnstamm, G. A. (1997). Early intervention in adoptive families: Supporting maternal sensitive responsiveness, infant-mother attachment, and infant competence. *Journal of Child Psychology & Psychiatry & Allied Disciplines, 38,* 1039-1050.

Juffer, F., & Rosenboom, L. G. (1997). Infant-mother attachment of internationally adopted children in the Netherlands. *International Journal of Behavioral Development, 20*(1), 93-107.

Kane, S. (1993). The movement of children for international adoption: An epidemiologic perspective. *Social Science Journal, 30*(4), 323-339.

Kang, H. Y. (1998). Re-membering home. In E. Kim & C. Choi (Eds.), *Dangerous women: Gender and Korean nationalism* (pp. 249-290). New York: Routledge.

Kidd, S. M. (1993). *A comparison of the self-concepts of Korean children adopted by Caucasian parents and Caucasian children adopted by Caucasian parents.* Unpublished master's thesis, University of Alaska, Fairbanks.

Kim, W. J. (1995). International adoption: A case review of Korean children. *Child Psychiatry and Human Development, 25*(3), 141-154.

Kim, W. J., Shin, Y., & Carey, M. P. (1999). Comparison of Korean-American adoptees and biological children of their adoptive parents: A pilot study. *Child Psychiatry & Human Development, 29*(3), 221-228.

Koh, F. M. (1993). *Adopted from Asia: How it feels to grow up in America.* Minneapolis, MN: EastWest Press.

Kwak, T. H., & Lee, S. H. (Eds.) (1991). *The Korean-American community: Present and future.* Masan, Korea: Kyungnam University Press.

Lytle, K. J. (1993). *Outreach and families who have adopted Korean children.* Unpublished master's thesis, College of St. Catherine and University of St. Thomas, St. Paul, Minnesota.

Mancini, K. S. (1995). *A study of Korean-born adoptees: Identity, self-esteem, and relationship with adoptive parents.* Unpublished master's thesis, University of California, Los Angeles.

Meier, D. I. (1998). Loss and reclaimed lives: Cultural identity and place in Korean American intercountry adoptees (Doctoral dissertation, University of Minnesota, 1998). *Dissertation Abstracts International, 59,* 0580.

Meier, D. I. (1999). Cultural identity and place in adult Korean-American intercountry adoptees. *Adoption Quarterly, 3*(1), 15-48.

Mullen, M. (1995). Identity development of Korean adoptees. In W. L. Ng., S. Chin, J. S. Moy, & G. Y. Okihiro (Eds.), *ReViewing Asian America: Locating diversity* (pp. 61-74). Pullman: Washington State University Press.

Nagy, J. E. (1995). Deborah Johnson Flournoy on identity and self-esteem for Korean American adoptees: A workshop report. *Korean and Korean-American Studies Bulletin, 6*(2-3), 54-55.

Park, P. (1999, Autumn). Deconstructing race: Intercountry adoptees and the discourse of authenticity. *Transcultured Magazine, 2*(1), 10-11.

Park, S. H. (1994). Forced child migration: Korea-born intercountry adoptees in the United States (Doctoral dissertation, University of Hawaii, 1994). *Dissertation Abstracts International, 55,* 1654.

Penner, E. E. (1996). *Comparative analysis of international child adoption practices and policies in Korea and China.* Unpublished master's thesis, McGill University, Montreal, Quebec, Canada.

Peterson, M. (1996). *Korean adoption and inheritance: Case studies in the creation of a classic Confucian society.* Ithaca, NY: Cornell University East Asia Program.

Politte, J. L. (1993). Self esteem among Korean adopted preadolescents (Doctoral dissertation, Walden University, 1993). *Dissertation Abstracts International, 55,* 3644.

Politte, J. L. (1994). A study of adopted Korean children and their self-esteem. *FACE Facts, 17*(4), 24-26.

Ramos, J. D. (1990). Counseling internationally adopted children. *Elementary School Guidance & Counseling, 25*(2), 147-152.

Reader, K. A. G. (1996). Adjustment characteristics and ego formation of transracial Korean adoptees: A phenomenological study (Doctoral dissertation, Union Institute, Cincinnati, Ohio, 1996). *Dissertation Abstracts International, 57,* 2181.

Rorbech, M. (1990). *Denmark— my country: The conditions of 18-25 year old foreign born adoptees in Denmark* (Booklet No. 39). Copenhagen: The Danish National Institute of Social Research.

Sarri, R. C., Baik, Y., & Bombyk, M. (1998). Goal displacement and dependency in South Korean-United States intercountry adoption. *Children and Youth Services Review, 20*(1/2), 87-114.

Silverman, A. R. (1993). Outcomes of transracial adoption. *The Future of Children, 3*(1), 104-118.

Simon, R. J. (1994). Transracial adoption: The American experience. In I. Gaber & J. Aldridge (Eds.), *In the best interests of the child: Culture, identity, and transracial adoption* (pp. 136-150). London: Free Association Books.

Simon, R. J., & Altstein, H. (1992). *Adoption, race, and identity: From infancy through adolescence.* New York: Praeger.

Sjogren, J. S. (1996). A ghost in my own country. *Adoption & Fostering, 20*(2), 32-35.

Sjogren, J. S. (1997). Dream's end. *Adoption & Fostering, 21*(2), 16-18.

Stock, K. K. H. (1999). Rise of a fourth culture: Korean adoptees. *Transcultured, 1*(4), 11.

Stolley, K. S. (1993). Statistics on adoption in the United States. *The Future of Children, 3*(1), 26-42.

Tizard, B. (1991). Intercountry adoption: A review of the evidence. *Child Psychology and Psychiatry, 32*(5), 743-756.

Triseliotis, J. (1993). Intercountry adoption: In whose best interest? In M. Humphrey & H. Humphrey (Eds.), *Intercountry adoption: Practical experiences* (pp. 119-137). London: Routledge.

van den Oord, E. J. C. G., Boomsma, D. I., & Verhulst, F. C. (1994). A study of problem behaviors in 10- to 15-year-old biologically related and unrelated international adoptees. *Behavior Genetics, 24*(3), 193-205.

Verhulst, F. C., Althaus, M., & Versluis-den Bieman, H. J. M. (1990). Problem behavior in international adoptees: I. An epidemiological study. *Journal of the American Academy of Child and Adolescent Psychiatry, 29*(1), 94-103.

Verhulst, F. C., Althaus, M., & Versluis-den Bieman, H. J. M. (1990). Problem behavior in international adoptees: II. Age at placement. *Journal of the American Academy of Child and Adolescent Psychiatry, 29*(1), 104-111.

Verhulst, F. C., Althaus, M., & Verslius-den Bieman, H. (1992). Damaging back-grounds: Later adjustment of international adoptees. *Journal of the American Academy of Child and Adolescent Psychiatry, 31,* 518-524.

Verhulst, F. C., & Versluis-den Bieman, H. J. (1995). Developmental course of problem behaviors in adolescent adoptees. *Journal of the American Academy of Child and Adolescent Psychiatry, 34,* 151-159.

Westhues, A. (1998). Ethnic and racial identity of internationally adopted adoles-cents and young adults: Some issues in relation to children's rights. *Adoption Quarterly, 1*(4), 33-55.

Westhues, A., & Cohen, J. S. (1998). The adjustment of intercountry adoptees in Canada. *Children and Youth Services Review, 20*(1-2), 115-134.

Wickes, K. L. (1993). Transracial adoption: Cultural identity and self-concept of Korean adoptees (Doctoral dissertation, Ball State University, 1993). *Dissertation Abstracts International, 54,* 4374.

Wickes, K. L., & Slate, J. R. (1997). Transracial adoption of Koreans: A preliminary study of adjustment. *International Journal for the Advancement of Counselling, 19*(2), 187-195.

Winn, B. J. (1994). *Korean adult adoptees: Adlerian personality characteristics.* Unpublished master's thesis, University of Arizona, Phoenix.

Yoon, D. P. (1997). Psychological adjustment of Korean-born adolescents adopted by American families (Doctoral dissertation, University of Illinois, Champaign-Urbana, 1997). *Dissertation Abstracts International, 58,* 2396.

Nonfiction

About the Association of Korean Adoptees. (1998, May 31). *Korea Times,* p. 24.

Adopted Koreans honor G.I.'s at Washington War Memorial. (1999, September 13). *New York Times,* p. A13.

Adoptions rise as hardships in Korea persist. (1999, May 4). *Desert News* (Salt Lake City, Utah), p. A4.

Ando, M. (1995). Living in half tones. In S. Wadia-Ells (Ed.), *The adoption reader: Birth mothers, adoptive mother's and adopted daughters* (pp. 179-189). Seattle, WA: Seal Press.

Anthony, T. (1994, September 28). Bucks case highlights foreign adoption prob-lems: Cultural demands vary from country to country. *Legal Intelligencer,* p. 3.

Baker, M. (1997, November 17). South Korea struggles to free itself from adoption stigma. *Christian Science Monitor, 89*(246), 6.

Beason, T. (1997, July 11). Adoptees realize they are not alone—Bothell Camp brings together children whose home once was Korea. *Seattle Times,* p. B1.

Bishoff, T., & Rankin, J. (Eds.) (1997). *Seeds from a silent tree: An anthology.* Glen-dale, CA: Pandal Press.

Bishop, J. (1996). Adopted. In E. H. Kim & E. Yu (Eds.), *East to America: Korean American life stories* (pp. 306-313). New York: New Press.

Braum, M. (1995, December 31). Korean adoptee travels thousands of miles to re-unite with biological family. *Asian Pages (St. Paul),* p. 12.

Bruining, M. O. (1995). A few thoughts from a Korean, adopted, lesbian, writer/ poet, and social worker. *Journal of Gay & Lesbian Social Services, 3*(2), 61-66.

Capell, J. (1997, April 29). Best interests of the child. *Korea Times,* p. 23.

Chappell, C. L. H. J. (1996, December 29). International adoption: Korean-American adoptees organize for support. *The Star Tribune (Minneapolis),* p. 7E.

Chappell, C. L. H. J. (1996, December 29). International adoption: Now I'm found. *The Star Tribune (Minneapolis),* p. 1E.

Clement, T. P. (1998). *The unforgotten war: Dust of the streets.* Bloomfield, IN: Truepeny Publishing Company.

Copeland, L. (1999, September 11). From fire to melting pot: 400 born in Korea, raised in America meet to tell their stories. *Washington Post,* p. C01.

Cox, S. S-K. (1999). *Voices from another place: A collection of works from a generation born in Korea and adopted to other countries.* St. Paul, MN: Yeong & Yeong.

Dirks, C. (1999, July 16). Korean adoptees return to homeland. *London Free Press,* p. A3.

Dole, C. H. (1998-1999). International and private adoption: One family's story. *Korean American Historical Society Occasional Papers, 4,* 89-97.

Dorow, S. (1999). *I wish for you a beautiful life: Letters from the Korean birthmothers of Ae Ran Won to their children.* St. Paul, MN: Yeong & Yeong.

Doten, P. (1991, April 4). Adopting from abroad: Clinics help anxious parents cope with a difficult but rewarding process. *Boston Globe,* p. 65.

Eisenberg, B. (1990, February 28). Road to foreign adoptions gets rockier. *Christian Science Monitor,* p. 13.

Elliott, L. (1994, December). 1,000 men and a baby. *Reader's Digest,* 49-54.

Elson, S., & Yoon, C. S. (1999, September 27). Livin' in two cultures. *The Asian Reporter* (Portland), p. 1.

Enrico, D. (1995, September). How I learned I wasn't Caucasian. *Glamour, 93,* 106.

Enrico, D. (1999, September 8). Connecting with our Korean heritage. *USA Today,* p. D1.

Fayerman, P. (1994, February 10). Third World adoptees face prejudice, study says: Taunting could be reduced through help from schools, report claims. *Vancouver Sun,* p. B7.

Fields-Meyer, T. (1996, March 4). For a native son. *People Weekly,* 52-54.

Foo, S. S. (1990, February 1). Adoptees adept at adapting group supports moms, children in their growth. *Post-Standard* (Syracuse, NY), p. 7.

Gertjegerdes, C. (1998, December 15). Korea invites worldwide orphans. *Columbus Times,* p. A1.

Gorman, P. (1999). The Korean adoption experience: A look into our future? In A. Klatzkin (Ed.), *A passage to the heart: Writings from families with children from China* (pp. 271-274). St. Paul, MN: Yeong & Yeong.

Ha, T. (1998, August 31). Resources available for Korean adoptees and their families. *Asian Pages* (St. Paul), p. 7.

Holder, L. (1998-1999). Raising young Americans in Korean skin. *Korean American Historical Society Occasional Papers, 4,* 85-88.

Hong, S. (1998, August 31). Sung-duk Bauman meets birth mother on last day of home visit. *Korea Times,* p. 17.

Hong, S. (1999, January 17). Subsidy for families adopting disabled orphans to double. *Korea Times.* Retrieved April 17, 2005, from http://times.hankooki.com/.

Hong, T. (1997, June/July). Beyond biology. *A. Magazine,* 34-41.

Houtz, J. (1992, February 13). Tot's death dividing adoption community. *The Seattle Times,* p. G1.

Jackson, C. (1992, June 28). Abandoned girl graduates at top of class. *Post-Standard* (Syracuse, NY), p. A1.

Jones, F. (1992, August 22). Adoptee's self-discovery: A long and winding road. Nancy (Mi Ryung) MacDonald puts a face to her homeland, Korea. *Toronto Star,* p. K2.

Kahn, J. P. (1992, August 27). Mama Mia: The Allen scandal threatens the role Farrow holds most dear: Motherhood. *The Boston Globe,* p. 81.

Kichen, I. (1995, June 12). Long journey, happy ending: Adopting a foreign child. *Business Week,* 102-103.

Ko, N. (1994, June 25). Interracial adoptions increase. *Northwest Asian Weekly,* p. 9.

Koenig, K. (1995, August 25). Asia's precious export: Americans looking to adopt healthy babies are flocking to China and Korea. *AsianWeek (San Francisco),* p. 10.

Koenig, K. (1998, December 18). Ritual brings families together, say parents of adopted children. *Jewish Bulletin,* p. 6.

Korean adoptee finds his family: Now he chooses to live with them for nine months. (1996, August 31). *Asian Pages (St. Paul),* p. 5.

Lee, M. G. (1994). Made in Korea: Korean adoptees go home. *Colors, 3*(1), 44-47.

Lewin, T. (1990, February 12). South Korea slows export of babies for adoption. *New York Times,* p. B10.

Lewin, T. (1994, June 23). Adopted youths are normal in self-esteem. *New York Times,* p. A14.

Life isn't dull in family with 21 children. (1990, April 3). *Toronto Star,* p. B4.

Lipsher, S. (1999, June 27). Staying in touch with a far-off heritage: Adoptees learn Korean culture at annual camp. *Denver Post,* p. F4.

Lipton, M. A. (1997, December 8). Baby on board. *People Weekly,* pp. 137-138.

Livingston, C. (1995, June 8). Students learn of classmates' Korean culture: An Auburn mother takes time to share a lesson in cultural differences. *Post-Standard* (Syracuse, NY), p. B1.

MacDonald, M. (1995, October 18). Korean American identity: Why should adoption make a difference? *Korea Times,* p. 5.

Malone, H. (1999, December 2). Adoption subsidies assist families. *Boston Globe,* p. B4.

Marks, J. (1993, May 23). How we adopted me. *New York Times Magazine,* pp. 32-34.

Marks, J. (1993, August). An adopted child's journey. *Parents,* pp. 36, 38-39.

Mathee, I. (1998, January 1). Group could help Asian adoptees adapt: Tackling identity issues a priority. *Seattle Post-Intelligencer,* p. E1.

McCallum, J. (1993, April 26). Family matters. *Sports Illustrated,* 32-36.

McGowan, S., & Gilman, L. (1996, July). It took two moms to save one son. *McCall's*, pp. 50-55.

Meltz, B. F. (1995, February 2). The transracial adoption: Child caring. *Boston Globe*, p. A1.

Miller, J., & Gatehouse, J. (1997, October 12). Rainbow families: Canadians are adopting more babies from other countries than from Canada. *The Gazette (Montreal, Quebec)*, p. D3.

Mom, dad thankful for help in adoption. (1994, November 30). *Vancouver Sun*, p. B12.

Nieves, E. (1992, August 15). With adoption, a future; with effort, a past; New Jersey camp brings history and pride to Korean-born children. *New York Times*, p. I25.

Nishioka, J. (1998, December 2). An adopted way of life. *Asian Week (San Francisco)*, p. 11.

Oleck, J. (1999, June 14). Wanted for adoptions: Worldwide standards. *Business Week*, p. 71.

Omori, C. (1999, June 2). Asian adult adoptees struggle with dual identities. *International Examiner* (Seattle), p. 9.

Parton, N. (1994, May 7). Mother's Day better by the dozen for Cloverdale family. *Vancouver Sun*, p. A4.

Pash, B. (1998, March 6). They too are chosen: How international adoption is changing the Jewish community. *Baltimore Jewish Times*, p. 70.

Pertman, A. (1999, September 12). Korean adoptees gather to share history: Meeting blends celebration, research. *Boston Globe*, p. A14.

Rankin, J. (1999, February 28). My first hanbok. *Korea Times*, p. 16.

Register, C. (1991). *Are those kids yours? American families with children adopted from other countries.* New York: Free Press.

Reitman, V. (1999, March 6). S. Korea tries to take care of its own with domestic adoptions. *Los Angeles Times*, p. 2.

Richard, R. (1991, January 31). A happy, hopeful return: Norwell student waits for a marrow donor. *Boston Globe*, p. 17.

Ritts, L. (1999, June 2). Asian babies, American parents: Rejection, reconciliation, and unconditional love. *International Examiner* (Seattle), p. 8.

Robertson, L. (1997, January 14). Reflections: Watering cultural roots. *Asian Pages* (St. Paul), p. 4.

Rovner, S. (1992, February 4). Adopting from abroad: Parents may face perplexing health problems when they bring home children from other countries. *The Washington Post*, p. Z12.

Sharp, D. (1992, December 31). Korean adoption: An adoptee speaks openly about her experiences. *Asian Pages* (St. Paul), p. 4.

Song, Y. I., & Moon, A. (1998). *Korean American women: From tradition to modern feminism.* Westport, CT: Praeger.

Stage, J. (1993, August 10). An adoptive family network. *Post-Standard* (Syracuse, NY), p. C1.

Summer camp with a twist. (1999). *American Teacher, 83*(5), p. 9.

Swardson, A. (1995, June). A father's trial. *Good Housekeeping,* pp. 102-105, 155-156.

Tevlin, J. (1992, December). Was I ever a baby? *McCall's,* pp. 81-82, 84, 88-89, 91-93.

Theater Mu to present mask dance (1995, December 15). *Asian Pages* (St. Paul), p. 6.

Trost, A. (1996, January 14). Tonya Sookhee Bishoff: Korean adoptee shares experiences. *Asian Pages* (St. Paul), p. 11.

Trost, A. (1997, April 14). Korean adoptee speaks out against international adoption. *Asian Pages* (St. Paul), p. 8.

Trost, A. (1998, April 14). Korean adoptees share experiences through documentary. *Asian Pages* (St. Paul), p. 9.

Tyre, P. (1999, March 1). We gave him up to save his life. *New York,* pp. 30-35, 121.

Vickery, M. (1996, August 31). Elementary teachers visit Korean institute. *Asian Pages* (St. Paul), p. 8.

White, L. S. (1995). *Chesi's story: One boy's long journey from war to peace.* Tallahassee, FL: Father & Son Pub.

Winston, C. (1995). Bridging ethnic communities from here to there. Part II: Making the connection. *Roots and Wings, 7*(1), 14-18.

Wood, E. (1998, October 2). More foreign adoptees return to homelands to adopt children. *Houston Chronicle,* p. 7.

Wood, E. (1998, November 20). Bringing kids' culture home: Adoptive families work to teach children. *Austin American-Statesman* (Texas), p. F5.

Yanigisawa, A. (1999, January 1). Home for Christmas . . . 67 children! American couple adopt to give Asian kids a home. *Northwest Asian Weekly,* p. 1.

Yoon, S. (1997, October 28). Korean-American adoptees visit their homeland with much emotion, interest. *Korea Times,* p. 23.

Fiction

Baker, L. (1997). *The flamingo rising.* New York: Knopf.

Hom, S. G. (1999). Double lifeline. In S. Ito & T. Cervin (Eds.), *A ghost at heart's edge: Stories and poems of adoption* (pp. 248-257). Berkeley, CA: North Atlantic Books.

Lee, M. G. (1993). *If it hadn't been for Yoon Jun.* Boston: Houghton Mifflin.

Lee, M. G. (1999). Summer of my Korean soldier. In S. Ito & T. Cervin (Eds.), *A ghost at heart's edge: Stories and poems of adoption* (pp. 204-211). Berkeley, CA: North Atlantic Books.

Pak, T. (1999). *Cry Korea cry.* New York: The Woodhouse.

Films/Videos

Adolfson, N. (Producer & Director) (1998). *Passing through: A personal diary documentary.* NAATA. Video. 27 min., English.

Ahn, M. K. (Producer & Director) (1994). *Living in half tones.* Video, 9 min., English.

Ahn, M-K. (Director) (1996). *Undertow.* 16 mm, 18 min., English.

Arndt, J. C. Y. H. (Director) (1998). *Crossing chasms: A documentary.* Video. 58 min., English.

Borshay Liem, D. (Producer & Director) (2000). *First person plural.* [Video]. United States: Deann Borshay Liem & NAATA. Video, 56 min., English and Korean with English subtitles.

Cherbak, C. A., & Stein, H. (Producers). Stein, H. (Director) (1991). *American eyes.* Video, 30 min., English.

Holt International Children's Services. (Producer) (1992-1993). *One boy and one girl at a time: Korean legacy.* Video, English.

Hunter, S. (Producer & Director) (1996). *Born journey.* Video, 30 min., English.

Kim, U. (Producer). Tolle, T. (Director & Producer) (1998). *Searching for go-hyang.* Video and 16 mm, 31 min., English and Korean with English subtitles.

Koh, J. (Producer & Director) (1999). *True.* 16 mm, 90 min., English.

Lee, C. (Director) (1999). *Love.* Video, 100 min., English.

Lemoine, M. (Director) (1996). *45% Korean.* Video, 15 min., French and Korean with English subtitles.

Roe, S. Y. (Co-Producer & Director) (1994). *Basilio's family.* Video, 53 min., English.

Schulte, T. (Producer), & Park, Y. J. (Director) (1991). *The long journey home: The story of Katie and her new American family.* Video, 22 min., English.

Spaulding for Children (Producer) (1994). *Asian/Asian American culture: A perspective from history and child welfare.* Video, 60 min., English.

Taub, L., & Chase, D. (Producers). Cole, M. (Director). (1999). *Narrow escape.* Video, 92 min., English.

Theiler, K. S. (Producer & Director) (1994). *Great girl.* 16 mm, 14 min., English.

Tomes, K. S. (Director) (1997). *Looking for Wendy.* Video and 16 mm, 18 min., English.

2000–

Research and Scholarship

Armstrong, S., & Slaytor, P. (2001). *The colour of difference: Journeys in trans-racial adoption.* Annandale, New South Wales, [Australia]: Federation Press.

Australian Institute of Health and Welfare (AIHW) (2004). *Adoptions Australia 2003-04* (AIHW cat. No. CSW 23). Canberra: AIHW.

Bergquist, K. J. S. (2000). Racial identity, ethnic identity, and acculturation in Korean adoptees (Doctoral dissertation, College of William and Mary, 2000). *Dissertation Abstracts International, 61,* 3769.

Bergquist, K. J. S. (2003). Exploring the impact of birth country travel on Korean adoptees. *Journal of Family Social Work, 7*(4), 45-61.

Bergquist, K. J. S. (2004). Expanding the definition of Asian diasporic studies: The immigrant experiences of Korean adoptees. *Journal of Immigrant and Refugee Services, 1*(3/4), 21-39.

Bergquist, K. J. S., Campbell, M. E., & Unrau, Y. A. (2003). Caucasian parents and Korean adoptees: A survey of parents' perceptions. *Adoption Quarterly, 6*(4), 41-58.

Breyer, J. (2004). *Korean adoptees: Colonial legacies, transformative possibilities.* Unpublished master's thesis, University of California, Los Angeles.

Choy, C. C., & Choy, G. P. (2003). Transformative terrains: Korean adoptees and the social constructions of an American childhood. In C. F. Levander & C. J. Singley (Eds.), *The American child: A cultural studies reader* (pp. 262-279). New Brunswick, NJ: Rutgers University Press.

Dalen, M. (2001). School performances among internationally adopted children in Norway. *Adoption Quarterly, 5*(2), 39-57.

Eng, D. L. (2003). Transnational adoption and queer diasporas. *Social Text, 21*(3), 1-37.

Fahnbulleh, J. A. (2002). *Transcultural adoptions and the formation of cultural identity.* Unpublished master's thesis, California State University, Long Beach.

Freundlich, M. (2000). *Adoption and ethics: Vol. 1. The role of race, culture, and national origin in adoption.* Washington, DC: Child Welfare League of America, Inc: The Evan B. Donaldson Adoption Institute.

Freundlich, M. (2001). *Access to information and search and reunion in Korean American adoptions: A discussion paper.* El Dorado Hills, CA: Korean American Adoptee Adoptive Family Network. Retrieved April 9, 2005, from the Korean American Adoptee Adoptive Family Network at http://www.kaanet.com/Whitepaper.pdf.

Freundlich, M., & Lieberthal, J. K. (2000). *The gathering of the first generation of adult Korean adoptees: Adoptees' perceptions of international adoption* (Technical Report). New York: The Evan B. Donaldson Adoption Institute.

Friedlander, M. L., Larney, L. C., Skau, M., Hotaling, M., Cutting, M. L., & Schwam, M. (2000). Bicultural identification: Experiences of internationally adopted children and their parents. *Journal of Counseling Psychology, 47,* 187-198.

Fujimoto, E. (2001). Korean adoptees growing up in the United States: Negotiating racial and ethnic identities in White America (Doctoral dissertation, Arizona State University, 2001). *Dissertation Abstracts International, 62,* 389.

Gilmer, J. (2001). *Korean adoptees: Parental involvement and the experience of ethnicity.* Unpublished master's thesis, San Francisco State University.

Groza, V., & Ryan, S. D. (2002). Pre-adoption stress and its association with child behavior in domestic special needs and international adoptions. *Psychoneuroendrocrinology, 27*(1-2), 181-197.

Hers, K. (2001, Summer). Overseas adopted Koreans, where do we belong? Criticism of the standards of selecting artists in Korea. *Korea Fulbright Review,* 26-27.

Hjern, A., Lindblad, F., & Vinnerljung, B. (2002, August 10). Suicide, psychiatric illness, and social maladjustment in intercountry adoptees in Sweden: A cohort study. *Lancet, 360,* 443-448.

Hoksbergen, R., & van Dijkum, C. (2001). Trauma experienced by children adopted from abroad. *Adoption & Fostering, 25*(2), 18-25.

Horan, A. K. Y. (2002). *Guests or family? Korean adoptees at the door of Asian American studies.* Unpublished master's thesis, Ohio State University, Columbus.

Howell, S. (2003). Kinning: The creation of life trajectories in transnational adoptive families. *Journal of the Royal Anthropological Institute, 9*(3), 465-484.

Hübinette, T. (2004). Adopted Koreans and the development of identity in the "third space." *Adoption & Fostering, 28*(1), 16-24.

Huh, N. S., & Reid, W. J. (2000). Intercountry, transracial adoption and ethnic identity: A Korean example. *International Social Work, 43,* 75-87.

Hurdis, R. (2002). Heartbroken: Women of color feminism and the third wave. In D. Hernandez & B. Rehman (Eds.), *Colonize this! Young women of color on today's feminism* (pp. 279-292). New York: Seal Press.

International adoption medical specialists rank leading nations on health of adopted children [Special issue]. (2002). *Adoption/Medical News, 8*(1-2), 1-11.

Johansson-Kark, M., Rasmussen, F., & Hjern, A. (2002). Overweight among international adoptees in Sweden: A population-based study. *Acta Paediatrica, 91*(7), 827-832.

Kim, E. (2000). Korean adoptee auto-ethnography: Refashioning self, family, and finding community. *Visual Anthropology Review, 16*(1), 43-70.

Kim, E. (2003). Wedding citizenship and culture: Korean adoptees and the global family of Korea [Special issue]. *Social Text, 21*(1), 57-81.

Kim, E. (2004). Gathering "roots" and making history in the Korean adoptee community. In M. Checker & M. Fishman (Eds.), *Local actions: Cultural activism, power, and public life in America* (pp. 208-230). New York: Columbia University Press.

Kim, S. (2003). *Narratives of individual cultural and racial identity experiences of Korean adoptees in the United States.* Unpublished master's thesis, University of Oregon, Eugene.

Kim, W. S. (2002, August 10). Benefits and risks of intercountry adoption. *Lancet, 360*(9331), 423-424.

Lee, D. C. (2000). Ethnic perspective-taking ability and ethnic attitudes in development of Korean-born adoptee youth (Doctoral dissertation, University of Wisconsin, Madison, 2000). *Dissertation Abstracts International, 61,* 6737.

Lee, J. (2004). Asian America is in the heartland: Performing Korean adoptee experience. In E. Ty & D. C. Goellnicht (Eds.), *Asian North American identities: Beyond the hyphen* (pp. 102-116). Bloomington, Indianapolis: Indiana University Press.

Lee, R. M. (2003). The transracial adoption paradox: History, research, and counseling implications of cultural socialization. *Counseling Psychologist, 31*(6), 709-742.

Lieberman, K. (2001). The process of racial and ethnic identity development and search for self in adult Korean transracial adoptees (Doctoral dissertation, Massachusetts School of Professional Psychology, 2001). *Dissertation Abstracts International, 62,* 2066.

Lindblad, F., Hjern, A., & Vinnerljung, B. (2003). Intercountry adopted children as young adults: A Swedish cohort study. *American Journal of Orthopsychiatry, 73*(2), 190-202.

Locke, K. S. (2003). *The role of cultural identity for transracially adopted Korean adults.* Unpublished master's thesis, College of St. Catherine and University of St. Thomas, St. Paul, Minnesota.

Lovelock, K. (2000). Intercountry adoption as a migratory practice: A comparative analysis of intercountry adoption and immigration policy and practice in the United States, Canada and New Zealand in the post WW II period. *International Migration Review, 34,* 907-949.

Mack, K. (2002, November/December). International adoption medicine. *Children's Voice,* 28-29.

Megyeri, K. A. (2002). The Minnesota international adoption project [Special issue]. *Adoption/Medical News, 8*(4), 1-4.

Mumma, D. (2001). *Chakbyolin sa wa annyonghasipnigga (good-by and hello): A travelogue of two cultures and one family.* Unpublished master's thesis, Hamline University, St. Paul, Minnesota.

Nielson, E. K. (2002). *Fostering a child's cultural identity: A study of Korean heritage camp participants* (University scholar project). Brigham Young University, Provo, Utah.

Pallier, C., Dahaene, S., Poline, J. B., LeBihan, D., Argenti, A. M., & Dupoux, E., & Mehler, J. (2003). Brain imaging of language plasticity in adopted adults: Can a second language replace the first? *Cerebral Cortex, 13*(2), 155-161.

Sacerdote, B. (2004). *What happens when we randomly assign children to families?* Cambridge, MA: National Bureau of Economic Research.

Selman, P. (2000). The demographic history of intercountry adoption. In P. Selman (Ed.), *Intercountry adoption: Developments, trends and perspectives* (pp. 15-39). London: British Agencies for Adoption and Fostering.

Selman, P. (2002). Intercountry adoption in the new millennium: The "Quiet Migration" revisited. *Population Research and Policy Review, 21,* 205-225.

Shiu, A. (2001). Flexible production: International adoption, race, Whiteness. *Jouvert: A Journal of Postcolonial Studies, 6*(1-2). Retrieved April 17, 2005, from http://social.class.ncsu.edu/jouvert/v6i1-2/shiu.htm.

Spencer, M. E. (2001, June). Successful Korean adoptions: The Spencer study. Part 1: Introducing the study [Special issue]. *Adoption/Medical News, 7,* 6.

Spencer, M. E. (2001, July-August). Successful Korean adoptions: The Spencer study. Part 2: Data about adult adopted persons [Special issue]. *Adoption/Medical News, 7,* 7-8.

Spencer, M. E. (2001, September-October). Successful Korean adoptions: The Spencer study. Part 3: Responses of parents of young adults adopted from Korea [Special issue]. *Adoption/Medical News, 7,* 9.

Spencer, M. E. (2001, November-December). Successful Korean adoptions: The Spencer study. Part 4: Family issues related to Korean adoptions [Special issue]. *Adoption/Medical News, 7,* 10.

Stams, G. J. M., Juffer, F., Rispens, J., & Hoksbergen, R. A. C. (2000). The development and adjustment of 7-year-old children adopted in infancy. *Journal of Child Psychology & Psychiatry & Allied Disciplines, 41,* 1025-1037.

Stams, G. J. M., Juffer, F., & van Ijzendoorn, M. H. (2002). Maternal sensitivity, infant attachment, and temperament in early childhood predict adjustment in middle childhood: The case of adopted children and their biologically unrelated parents. *Developmental Psychology, 38*(5), 806-821.

Stewart, Y. K. (2002). *Ethnic identity formation among female Korean intercountry adoptees living with Caucasian-American parents.* Unpublished master's thesis, Arizona State University, Phoenix.

Thorud, J. (2000). *My second status: An autobiography.* Unpublished manuscript, Coe College, Cedar Rapids, Iowa.

Traver, E. K. (2000). Dethroning invisibility: Talk stories of adult Korean adoptees (Doctoral dissertation, University of Denver, 2000). *Dissertation Abstracts International, 61,* 3774.

Varnis, S. L. (2002). Regulating the global adoption of children. *Society, 38*(2), 39-47. Retrieved April 9, 2005, from MasterFILE Select.

Ventureyra, V. A. G., & Pallier, C. (2004). In search of the lost language: The case of the adopted Koreans in France. In M. Schmid, et al. (Eds.), *First language attrition: Interdisciplinary perspectives on methodological issues* (pp. 207-221). Amsterdam, Philadelphia: John Benjamins.

Ventureyra, V. A. G., Pallier, C., & Yoo, H. Y. (2004). The loss of first language phonetic perception in adopted Koreans. *Journal of Neurolinguistics, 17*(1), 79-91.

Verhulst, F. C. (2000). The development of internationally adopted children. In P. Selman (Ed.), *Intercountry adoption: Developments, trends and perspectives* (pp. 126-142). London: British Agencies for Adoption and Fostering.

Williams, C. M. (2001). *The impending revolution: The prospect for openness in Korean-American adoptions.* Unpublished manuscript, Massachusetts Institute of Technology, Cambridge.

Yngvesson, B. (2000). Un nino de cualquier color: Race and nation in inter-country adoption. In J. Jenson & B. Santos (Eds.), *Globalizing institutions: Case studies in regulation and innovation* (pp. 169-204). Burlington, VT: Aldershot.

Yngvesson, B., & Mahoney, M. A. (2000). "As one should ought, and wants to be": Belonging and authenticity in identity narratives. *Theory, Culture and Society, 17*(6), 77-110.

Yoon, D. P. (2001). Causal modeling predicting psychological adjustment of Korean-born adolescent adoptees. *Journal of Human Behavior in the Social Environment, 3*(3-4), 65-82.

Yoon, D. (2004). Intercountry adoption: The importance of ethnic socialization and subjective well-being for Korean-born adopted children. *Journal of Ethnic & Cultural Diversity in Social Work, 13*(2), 71-89.

Nonfiction

A beautiful Wedding. (2004, October 13). *The Korea Herald.* Retrieved April 9, 2005, from Lexis-Nexis Academic Universe.

Adoptee makes helping other adoptees his life-long goal. (2004, January 17). *Korea Times.* Retrieved April 9, 2005, from Lexis-Nexis Academic Universe.

Adoptees bear their hearts through "Letter never sent." (2005, February 16). *Korea Times*. Retrieved April 9, 2005, from Lexis-Nexis Academic Universe.

Adoption Day to be established. (2005, March 23). *Korea Times*. Retrieved April 9, 2005, from Lexis-Nexis Academic Universe.

Adoptions on the rise. (2003, June). *Swedish Press* (Vancouver), 74(6), p. 13.

Allen, K. M. (2003, March 28). Mixed-race conference: No more assumptions. *Northwest Asian Weekly* (Seattle), 22 (12), p. 11.

Allen, O. (2002, January 16-February 5). A dream fulfilled: State Senator Paull Shin delivers speech at Martin Luther King, Jr. celebration. *International Examiner* (Seattle), 29(2), p. 5.

Anoka sheriff's candidate has ties to Korean-American community. (2002, September 14). *Asian Pages* (St. Paul), 13(1), p. 2.

Beason, T. (2003, April 12). Face still familiar to foster mom an Idaho teen in search of his roots finally meets the woman who cared for him as a child in South Korea. *The Seattle Times,* p. B1.

Branswell, B. (2003, February 15). The challenge of adoption: Parents who bring babies to Quebec from overseas are ready for the rewards but are often ill-equipped to deal with the inevitable hardships. *The Gazette* (Montreal), p. E1.

Branswell, B. (2005, February 25). The lucky ones: A lack of services and support is a problem for many parents who adopt children from other countries—but then there is the joy the kids bring. *The Gazette* (Montreal), p. A10.

Breslin, B. (2004, June 3). Cypress resident explores Korean roots; Adoptee returns to birth country, helping others during her trip. *The Houston Chronicle,* p. 1.

Brett, J. (2003, October 6). Southerner finds her Asian roots; Student trip to Korea lets adopted teen meet birth mother. *The Atlanta Journal-Constitution,* p. 1B.

Briggs-Harty, L. (2002, May 23). Adoptive parents take travel barriers in stride; people who seek children accept lines, scans; some countries loosen red tape. *St. Louis Post-Dispatch,* p. 1.

Broadwater, C. (2004, December 25). From Korea, with love. Family adopts 4 Korean kids since so many needed help. *Charleston Gazette* (West Virginia), p. 1A.

Bronston, B. (2003, November 27). Family ties; Some 20 years ago, two children—first a boy and later a girl—came from Korea into the lives and hearts of a New Orleans couple. On this day devoted to counting blessings, their story of becoming a family is well worth telling. *Times-Picayune* (New Orleans), p. 1. Retrieved April 9, 2005, from Lexis-Nexis Academic Universe.

Chipping a niche for himself. (2002, February 10). *The Boston Globe,* p. 1.

Choe, C. (2001, April 30). Pearl Buck's contribution to Korea. *Korea Times,* p. 15.

Chow, M. (2002, November 20). Over 100 APAs elected to office in last week's election. *AsianWeek* (San Francisco), 24(13), p. 8.

Chow, M. (2004, May 20-26). Laughing out loud; "AsianWeek" brings humor to APA Heritage Month. *AsianWeek* (San Francisco), 25(28), p. 17.

Colon, V. (2004, December 27). Adopted daughter learns heritage: Clovis couple wanted their child to know of her Korean culture. *Fresno Bee,* p. B1.

Conaboy, C. (2005, February 16). Adoptee finds birth family, answers. *The Concord Monitor* (Bow, NH). Retrieved April 9, 2005, from Lexis-Nexis Academic Universe.

Couvillion, E. (2003, November 30). A promise fulfilled: Catholic community services office helps Walker family adopt infant from South Korea. *Sunday Advocate* (Baton Rouge). Retrieved April 9, 2005, from Lexis-Nexis Academic Universe.

Creager, E. (2005, April 4). Tours forge links for adopted kids and their American families. *Detroit Free Press*. Retrieved April 9, 2005, from Lexis-Nexis Academic Universe.

Creamer, A. (2003, January 24). For many American families, worries about Korea hit home. *Sacramento Bee,* p. E1.

Crien, E. (2004, October 14-20). Nearly half of foreign-born adoptees are Asian. *AsianWeek* (San Francisco), *25*(59), p. 8.

Eaton, J. (2001, January 30). Group puts Korean culture in spotlight. *Asian Reporter* (Portland), 11(5), p. 9.

Eaton, J. (2001, April 24). Growing up Asian in a Caucasian world: Ah-gah Project benefits adoptive services. *The Asian Reporter* (Portland), p. 1.

Faciane, V. (2003, May 8). Adopted children make each day special; Catholic Charities assists local parents. *Times-Picayune* (New Orleans), p. 1.

Fanning, K. (2004, November/December). One life, two countries. *Scholastic Choices, 2*(3), 6-9.

Frank, J. (2003, November 14). API concerns addressed at community summit. *Asian Pages* (St. Paul), 14(5), p. 5.

Gay Swedes free to adopt, but foreign agencies balk. (2004, January 30). *Agence France Presse*. Retrieved April 9, 2005, from Lexis-Nexis Academic Universe.

Ginsburg, J. (2003, January 23). Conversions emerging as major issue facing adoptive Jewish parents. *Jewish News* (Whippany, NJ), 57(4), p. 12.

Ginsburg, J. (2004, February 29). For those who "don't look Jewish," the search for acceptance is no joke. *Jewish News* (Whippany, NJ), 58(5), p. 17.

Goetze, J. (2001, February 15). Forging Korean connections. *The Oregonian*, p. 1.

Government to review quota system on foreign adoption. (2000, April 30). *Korea Times,* p. 12.

Graves, H. (2001, April 29). Adoptees from Korea reach across the years and miles siblings via adoption, pair take separate paths to find birth families. *The Boston Globe*, p. 11.

Han, H. S., & Ruth, K. (2004). *Many lives intertwined: A memoir.* St. Paul, MN: Yeong & Yeong.

Har, J. (2001, February 15). International adoption changes family's culture, race; UO sociologists examine the ethnic identities of people who don't look like all their relatives. *The Oregonian,* p. A1.

Holt, M. (2001, July 31). Thoughts of the times: My trip to Diamond Mountain. *Korea Times* (Los Angeles), p. 14.

Hong, T. (2002, September 25). Picturing the worlds of Chris Soentpiet. *AsianWeek* (San Francisco), p. 19.

Hübinette, T. (2005, March 1). Overseas adoption. *The Korea Herald.* Retrieved April 9, 2005, from Lexis-Nexis Academic Universe.

Hwang, S. (2001, September 14). Paull Shin links his motherland, fatherland. *Northwest Asian Weekly* (Seattle), 20(37), p. 8.

Jin, H. (2004, April 19). More Koreans adopt children openly at home; A larger number of parents do not hide adoptions despite lingering prejudice. *The Korea Herald.* Retrieved April 9, 2005, from Lexis-Nexis Academic Universe.   .

Johnson, O. (2002, August 6). Author shares story of adoption and search for roots. *The Asian Reporter* (Portland), p. 13.

Jones, R. (2002, July 15). Homeland on the range; heritage camps immerse foreign-born kids in native cultures. *Rocky Mountain News* (Denver), p. 3D.

Joshi, M. (2002, January 25). INS offers citizenship to 27 adopted children. *India Abroad* (New York), *32*(17), p. 12.

Khang, H. (2004, September 13). Sweet intent, bitter legacy. *South China Morning Post,* p. 20.

Kim, D. H. (2001). *Who will answer?* Eugene, OR: Holt International Children's Services.

Kim, E. (2000). *Ten thousand sorrows: The extraordinary journey of a Korean War orphan.* New York: Doubleday.

Kim, K. (2004, January 12). Overseas Korean artists are O.K.A.Y. *The Korea Herald.* Retrieved April 9, 2005, from Lexis-Nexis Academic Universe.

King, C. (2004, October 12). Korean American community celebrates ChuSok. *Asian Reporter* (Portland), *14*(42), p. 12.

Kinney, R. J. (2004). Seoul searching. In A. Han & J. Hsu (Eds.), *Asian American X: An intersection of 21st century Asian American voices* (pp. 52-57). Ann Arbor: University of Michigan Press.

Koenig, M. A. (2000). *Sacred connections: Stories of adoption.* Philadelphia: Running Press.

Korea ranks first in U.S. adoptee list. (2004, September 25). *Korea Times.* Retrieved April 9, 2005, from Lexis-Nexis Academic Universe.

Korean Institute of Minnesota to celebrate 26th anniversary (2001, June 14). *Asian Pages* (St. Paul), 11(18), p. 15.

Lakeville athlete heads for World Cup tournament in Korea (2002, June 14). *Asian Pages* (St. Paul), 12(19), p. 10.

Larsen, P. (2003, November 2). All in the family. *Sarasota Herald-Tribune,* p. 45.

Lee, C. (2001, September 30). Adoptees visit in search of heritage, identity. *Korea Times,* p. 16.

Lee, J. (2004, August 7). When blood is thicker than a border; Adoptees revisit Korea in hopes of finding roots, re-establishing family ties. *The Korea Herald.* Retrieved April 9, 2005, from Lexis-Nexis Academic Universe.

Lee, M. (2001, March 14). A day in the working life: Joe Symeonides, high school English teacher. *Asian Pages* (St. Paul), 11(13), p. 11.

Lee, M. (2001, July 31). A day in the working life: Suzanne Burrows, a Taiko drummer. *Asian Pages* (St. Paul), 11(22), p. 11.

Lee, W. (2003, December 24). Discovering their roots through dancing. *The Korea Herald.* Retrieved April 9, 2005, from Lexis-Nexis Academic Universe.

Lieser, E. (2001, October 3). Adoption: And the long road ahead. *AsianWeek* (San Francisco), p. 17.

Louie, R. (2005, January 6). A place to call home: A generation of adopted women has paved the way for the next. *Daily News* (New York), p. 48.

Macdonald, E. (2004, November 26). Overseas adoptions reach a 10-year high. *Canberra Times* (Australia), p. 1.

Marshal recalls growing up at Boys Town. (2000, November 21). *Columbus Times,* p. 6.

McKenzie, A. (2004, July 10). A long road to home. *Courier Mail* (Queensland, Australia), p. L6.

McTee, S. (2003). *Song from Seoul: A daughter's journey, a mother's story.* Salt Lake City, UT: SMC Ventures.

Meier, P. (2002, May 24). All grown up, with places to go; A Lakeville teen who came from Korea as an infant is going back to coach soccer, to lecture and to see the World Cup. *Star Tribune* (Minneapolis), p. 1B.

Mentor plan for adoptees. (2003, July 28). *Sunday Mail* (South Australia), p. 25.

Miller, J. (2001, May 31). God had a plan for me: Adam King. *Korea Times* (Los Angeles), 10(5), p. 16.

Min, S. J. (2003, August 13). Home away from Seoul: An examination of Korean adoption. *AsianWeek* (San Francisco), 24(50), p. 16.

Miner, L. (2004, September 28). "Welcome to your motherland:" Adoptee Kim Kereluik gave her Korean heritage little thought while growing up in the suburbs. Then, she traveled back to the country of her birth. *Chicago Daily Herald,* p. 1. Retrieved April 9, 2005, from Lexis-Nexis Academic Universe.

Mistretta, E. (2003, November 23). Lifelink to celebrate adoption program with gala. *Chicago Daily Herald,* p 1. Retrieved April 9, 2005, from Lexis-Nexis Academic Universe.

Moline, A. (2002, October 31). Opening gates of emotion. *International Examiner* (Seattle), p. 25

Namm, L. (2001, April 6). Phoenix adoption group holds first meeting. *Jewish News of Greater Phoenix, 53*(27), p. 4.

Namm, L. (2003, October 24). Kreplach and wontons: Asian-American Havurah helps blend two cultures, traditions. *Jewish News of Greater Phoenix, 56*(5), p. 18.

National Adoption Information Clearinghouse. (2000). *Korean adoption resources.* Washington, DC: National Adoption Information Clearinghouse.

Nishiwaki, C. (2004, July 10-16). July 4 award honors Sen. Paull Shin: Once a "street urchin," now an elected official. *Northwest Asian Weekly* (Seattle), *23*(28), p. 4.

Noerper, M. (2004). A little too Asian and not enough white. In A. Han & J. Hsu (Eds.), *Asian American X: An intersection of 21st century Asian American voices* (pp. 92-99). Ann Arbor: University of Michigan Press.

Noone, L. (2003). *Global mom: Notes from a pioneer adoptive family.* Baltimore, MD: Gateway Press.

O'Neal, J. (2004, December 16-22). White parents struggle to adjust with transracial adoptions. *New York Amsterdam News, 95*(51), p. 4.

Paull Shin receives Spirit of Liberty Award. (July 6, 2004). *Asian Reporter* (Portland), *14*(28), p. 1.

Peifer, C. (2003, August 18). Their mission was to adopt Korean orphans: Holts were moved to act, changing a nation in the process. *The Seattle Post-Intelligencer,* p. A8.

Peifer, C. (2003, August 18). Twin adoptees search for their Korean roots. *The Seattle Post-Intelligencer,* p. A1.

Peifer, C. (2003, August 19). Joyful surprise on the phone, A. *The Seattle Post-Intelligencer,* p. A1.

Protyniak, N. (2002, February 5). Fall in call to adopt. *Herald Sun* (Melbourne, Australia), p. 15.

Pyle, E. (2002, March 17). "A Credit to God": Plain City-area couple see adoption as life calling. *Columbus Dispatch* (Ohio). Retrieved April 9, 2005, from Lexis-Nexis Academic Universe.

Ramirez, M. (2005, February 1). Adoptees and identity: Answering "who am I?" can be a long, complicated journey. *Seattle Times.* Retrieved April 9, 2005, from Lexis-Nexis Academic Universe.

Rawstone, T. (2001, January 20). Thousands of babies up for sale on the Net. *The Daily Telegraph* (Sydney, Australia), p. 6.

Register, C. (2005). *Beyond good intentions: A mother reflects on raising internationally adopted children.* St. Paul, MN: Yeong & Yeong.

Reilly, R. (2000, August 28). Seoul searching. *Time, 156,* 42.

Rivera, E. (2003, July 27). After adoptions, Korean children celebrate kinships: Conference in N. Va unites families with dual cultures. *The Washington Post,* p. C3.

Robinson, K. (2002). *A single square picture: A Korean adoptee's search for her roots.* New York: Penguin Group.

Roman, K. (2001, September 13). Adopted baby stranded in B.C. *The Ottawa Citizen.* Retrieved April 9, 2005, from Lexis-Nexis Academic Universe.

Root, C. (2004, May 31). Korean adoptee experience in Minnesota. *International Examiner* (Seattle), *15,* p. 5.

Saltzman, J. (2002, June 2). Adopting a new culture, families are digging deep into the roots of their children. *The Boston Globe,* p. 1.

Schindler, J. (2005, March 24). Born in Korea, teen helps other adoptees: She wins award for revitalizing KARE. *Times-Picayune* (New Orleans). Retrieved April 9, 2005, from Lexis-Nexis Academic Universe.

Seo, H. (2001, June 8). Adoptive parents strive to change adoption culture. *The Korea Herald.* Retrieved June 8, 2001, from http://www.koreaherald.com.

Soh, J. (2001, September 30). After 26 years, Korean adoptee reunited with biological mother. *Korea Times,* p. 17.

Soong, A. (2001, July 19). New Orleans couples adopt Korean babies. *Times-Picayune* (New Orleans), p. 9. Retrieved April 9, 2005, from Lexis-Nexis Academic Universe.

Steuber, C. (2004). Creating myself. In A. Han & J. Hsu (Eds.), *Asian American X: An intersection of 21st century Asian American voices* (pp. 118-121). Ann Arbor: University of Michigan Press.

The Power of Asian American women. (2001, May 11). *Northwest Asian Weekly* (Seattle), *20*(19), p. 4.

The world is changing. (2004, September 7). *The Oregonian*, p. C01.

Town, J. (2001, July 14). Melding community and academics: The Twin Cities' Asian American community offers insight and inspiration. *Asian Pages* (St. Paul), 11(21), p. 12.

Transracial adoption should be a last resort. (2003, August 27). *The Oregonian*, p. E1.

Trenka, J. J. (2003). *The language of blood: A memoir.* St. Paul, MN: Borealis Books.

Trost, A. (2002, September 14). Author Helie Lee inspires with honesty, confidence, and happiness. *Asian Pages* (St. Paul), 13(1), p. 10.

Tsui, C. (2005, January 23). Cross-cultural Seoul searching to find a place to call home. *South China Morning Post*, p. 6.

van Praag, J. (2005, January 19-February 1). Museum delves into Asian adoptee experience in new exhibit. *International Examiner* (Seattle), *32*(2), p. 10.

Vance, J. J. (2003). *Twins found in a box: Adapting to adoption.* Bloomington, IN: 1st Books.

Vaughn, C. (2002, May 9). Homeland tour helps family discover daughter's heritage. *The Houston Chronicle*, p. 1.

Vu, C. (2001, May 30). Painting a rainbow: *Colors NW* tells stories of all people of color. *Northwest Asian Weekly* (Seattle), *20*(13), p. 1.

Wallgren, C. (2002, February 10). Chipping a niche for himself. *The Boston Globe*, p. 1.

Warren, B. (2001, May 21). Mothers journey to Korea. *St. Louis Post-Dispatch*, p. 1.

Wilkinson, H. S. P., & Fox, N. (Eds.) (2002). *After the morning calm: Reflections of Korean adoptees.* Bloomfield Hills, MI: Sunrise Ventures.

Winfrey, Y. (2000, April 21). Actress Amy Kim Waschke takes center stage. *Northwest Asian Weekly* (Seattle), p. 3.

Wolf, M. (2001, January 22). GW student rediscovers her culture. *Rocky Mountain News* (Denver), p. 5D.

Woosley, L. (2004, October 26). Korean film crew captures Dillon adoptees' stories. *Tulsa World* (Oklahoma), p. D6.

Yu, J. (2001, April 30). The other 100,000 Korean Americans. *Korea Times*, p. 22.

Zamichow, N. (2004, November 28). Searching for missing pieces of a painful past; A millionaire's son was adopted in the U.S., unknown to his mother. He wants answers. *Los Angeles Times*, p. A1.

Fiction

Lee, M. M. (2005). *Somebody's daughter.* Boston: Beacon Press.

Lee, V. (2001). *Princess June: A novel.* Santa Barbara, CA: Fithian Press.

Scott, J. C. (2002). *The lucky gourd shop.* Denver, CO: MacMurray & Beck.

Shiomi, R. A. (2001). Mask dance. In R. Srikanth & E. Y. Iwanaga (Eds.), *Bold words: A century of Asian American writing* (pp. 351-386). New Brunswick, NJ: Rutgers University Press.

Tyler, A. (2006). *Digging to America: A novel.* New York: Alfred A. Knopf.

Poetry

Kwang, C. L. B. (2002). *Copia.* Portland, OR: Pinball Pub.

Films/Videos

Blum, A. (Director) (2002). *Perspectives on adoption: International adoptees tell their stories.* Video, 38 min., English.

Douglas-Henry, J., & Thorburn, C. (Producers). Cummins, J. (Director) (2003, January 26). *From Korea with love.* Sydney [New South Wales, Australia]: SBS. Video, 52 min., English.

Hallmark Hall of Fame Productions (Producer). Coolidge, M. (Director) (2001). *The flamingo rising.* Video, 90 min., English.

Lee, H. (Producer & Director) (2000). *Subrosa.* Video, 22 min., English and Korean with English subtitles.

Seo, D. (Director) (2003). *Made in Korea.* Video, 52 min., English.

Web Sites

Adopted Korean Connection, http://www.akconnection.com/. Support network for Korean adoptees with educational, cultural, and social focus; based in Minnesota.

Adoptee Solidarity Korea, http://adopteesolidarity.org. Activist group dedicated to ending intercountry adoption of Koreans.

Adopterade Koreaners Forening (Sweden), http://www.akf.nu. Swedish association of Korean adoptees.

Arierang, http://www.arierang.nl/. Dutch Association for Korean adoptees.

Dongari, http://www.dongari.ch/index.html. Association for Korean adoptees in Switzerland.

Forum for Koreansk Adopterte, http://www.fkanorway.org/. Resource and networking organization for Korean adoptees in Norway.

Global Overseas Adoptees Link, http://www.goal.or.kr/. Organization assisting adoptees returning to Korea.

International Korean Adoptee Associations, http://ikaa.org. An umbrella organization connecting independent Korean adoptee networks in Europe, United States, and Korea.

International Korean Adoptee Services, http://www.inkas.or.kr/. Cultural and educational site for adopted Koreans, based in Korea.

Korean@doptees Worldwide (K@W), http://www.koreanadoptees.net. International organization for Korean adoptees resources.

Korean American Adoptee Adoptive Family Network, http://www.kaanet.com/. Education, resource, and networking organization, annual conference information.

Korean Focus, http://www.koreanfocus.org/. Cultural resources for Korean adoptive families and Korean Americans based in northern Virginia.

Korean Identity Development Society (KIDS), http://www.koreanidentity.org. Support network and resource for Korean heritage.

Korean Klubben, http://koreaklubben.org/. Association of Korean adoptees in Denmark.

Korean Quarterly Online, http://www.koreanquarterly.org/. Award-winning journal by adopted Koreans, Korean Americans, and adoptive parents.

Mission to Promote Adoption in Korea (MPAK), http://www.mpak.com/Home English.htm. Christian organization that seeks to promote adoption of Korean orphans by Koreans in Korea.

Overseas Adopted Koreans, http://oaks.korean.net. A program sponsored by the Overseas Koreans Foundation [http://www.okf.or.kr] whose goal is to connect all overseas Koreans.

Racines Coreennes, http://www.racinescoreennes.org/. French association of Korean adoptees.

U.S. State Department's Office of Overseas Citizens Services for International Adoption from Korea, http://travel.state.gov/family/adoption/country/country_410.html. U.S. government site with current laws and guidelines for Korean adoption.

ASIAN ADOPTION—GENERAL

1950-1959

Research and Scholarship

Kirk, H. D. (1953). Community sentiments in relation to child adoption (Doctoral dissertation, Cornell University, 1953). *Dissertation Abstracts International, 247.*

1960-1969

Research and Scholarship

Baham, R. V. (1963). *Adjustment of foreign-born Oriental children adopted by Caucasian families.* Unpublished master's thesis, University of Southern California, Los Angeles.

Bowman, L. R., Gjenvick, B. A., Harvey, E. T. M. (1961). *Children of tragedy.* New York: Church World Service National Council of the Churches of Christ in the U.S.A.

Chakerian, C. G. (1966). *Children of hope.* Chicago: Department of Church and Community McCormick Theological Seminary.

Chakerian, C. G. (1968). *From rescue to child welfare.* Chicago: Department of Church and Community McCormick Theological Seminary.

Fricke, H. (1965). Interracial adoption: The little revolution. *Social Work, 10,* 92-97.

Rathbun, C., & Kolodny, R. (1967). A groupwork approach in cross-cultural adoptions. *Children, 14*(3), 117-121.

Rosenberg, A. H. (1968). *The adoption of Oriental children by Caucasian-American parents.* Unpublished master's thesis, University of Wisconsin.

Young, M. J. (1963). Inter-racial adoption: An exploratory study of non-Oriental parents who adopted Oriental children. Unpublished master's thesis, Bryn Mawr College, Pennsylvania.

Nonfiction

Trumbull, R. (1967, April 30). Amerasians. *New York Times Magazine,* pp. 112-114.

Fiction

Gallant, M. (1968). April fish. In M. Gallant, *The collected stories of Mavis Gallant* (pp. 306-309). New York: Random House.

1970-1979

Research and Scholarship

Hoopes, J. L., Sherman, E. A., Lawder, E. A., Andrews, R. G., & Lower, K. D. (1970). *A follow-up study of adoptions (Vol. II): Post-placement functioning of adopted children.* New York: Child Welfare League of America, Inc.

Jacka, A. A. (1973). *Adoption in brief: Research and other literature in the United States, Canada and Great Britain, 1966-72: An annotated bibliography.* Windsor, England: National Foundation for Educational Research.

Jones, C.E., & Else, J. F. (1979). Racial and cultural issues in adoption. *Child Welfare, 58,* 373-382.

Kim, T., & Reid, E. (1970). *After a long journey.* Unpublished master's thesis, School of Social Work, University of Minnesota, Minneapolis.

Ladner, J. A. (1977). *Mixed families: Adopting across racial boundaries.* New York: Anchor Press.

Simon, R. J., & Altstein, H. (1977). *Transracial adoption.* New York: Wiley.

Smith, J. M. (1970). Planning for homeless children: A study of Chinese girls adopted in American families (Doctoral dissertation, Harvard University, 1970). *Dissertation Abstracts International,* 115.

Nonfiction

Judge upholds adoptions that he had ruled illegal (1977, July 26). *New York Times,* p. 16.

Lifton, B. J. (1976, May 1). Orphans in limbo. *Saturday Review,* pp. 20-22.

Thailand cracks down on adoptive baby trade (1977, May 2). *New York Times,* p. 38.

The Vietnam babylift. (1976). *Commonweal, 53*(20), 617-621.

Torment over the Viet non-orphans (1976, May 9). *New York Times Magazine,* pp. 14-15, 76-78, 83, 86-87.

U.S. Department of Health, Education, and Welfare (1979). *Intercountry adoption guidelines.* Washington, DC: Government Printing Office.

U.S. Department of Health, Education, and Welfare (1979). *National directory of intercountry adoption service resources.* Washington, DC: Government Printing Office.

1980-1989

Research and Scholarship

Anagnost, A. (1988). Family violence and magical violence: The woman as victim in China's one-child birth policy. *Women and Language, 9*(2), 16-22.

Baker, R. (1984). Parentless refugee children: The question of adoption. In P. Bean (Ed.), *Adoption: Essays in social policy, law, and sociology* (pp. 254-272). London: Tavistock Publications.

Balanon, L. G. (1989). Foreign adoption in the Philippines. *Child Welfare, 68,* 245-254.

Baldwin, M. L. (1984). *An exploration of the needs and concerns of Caucasian families who have adopted Asian children: A workshop model.* Unpublished master's thesis, San Francisco Theological Seminary.

Dalen, M., & Saetersdal, B. (1987). Transracial adoption in Norway. *Adoption & Fostering, 11,* 41-46.

Feigelman, W., & Silverman, A. R. (1983). *Chosen children. New patterns of adoptive relationships.* New York: Praeger.

Fletchman-Smith, B. (1984, Spring). Effects of race on adoption and fostering. *International Journal of Social Psychiatry, 30,* 121-128.

Friede, A., Harris, J. R., & Kobayashi, J. M. (1988). Transmission of hepatitis B virus from adopted Asian children to their American families. *American Journal of Public Health, 78,* 26-29.

Gill, O., & Jackson, B. (1983). *Adoption and race: Black, Asian and mixed race children in white families.* New York: St. Martin's Press.

Jenista, J. A., & Chapman, D. (1987). Medical problems of foreign-born adopted children. *American Journal of Diseases of Children, 141*(3), 293-302.

National Committee for Adoption (1989). *1989 Adoption factbook: United States data, issues, regulations, and resources.* Washington, DC: National Committee for Adoption.

Ngabonziza, D. (1988). Intercountry adoption: In whose best interests? *Adoption & Fostering, 12,* 35-40.

Rue, M., & Rue, L. (1984). Reflections on bicultural adoption. In P. Bean (Ed.), *Adoption: Essays in social policy, law, and sociology* (pp. 243-253). London: Tavistock Publications.

Silverman, A. R. (1980). Transracial adoption in the United States: A study of assimilation and adjustment. (Doctoral dissertation, University of Wisconsin, Madison, 1980). *Dissertation Abstracts International, 41,* 2311.

Simon, R., & Altstein, H. (1981). *Transracial adoption: A follow-up.* Lexington, MA: Lexington Books.

Simon, R., & Altstein, H. (1987). *Transracial adoptees and their families: A study of identity and commitment.* New York: Praeger.

Small, J. W. (1984, Spring). The crisis in adoption. *International Journal of Social Psychiatry, 30,* 129-142.

Smith-Garcia, T., & Brown, J. S. (1989). The health of children adopted from India. *Journal of Community Health, 14,* 227-241.

Weil, R. H. (1984). International adoption: The quiet migration. *International Migration Review, 18,* 276-293.

Nonfiction

Sandness, G. L. (1978). *Brimming over.* Minneapolis, MN: Mini-World Publications.

Sheehy, G. (1986). *Spirit of survival.* New York: Morrow.

Teltsch, K. (1982, October 1). Many agencies joined in retrieving Vietnam children. *New York Times,* p. A6.

Fiction

Dixon, S. (1983). Not Charles. In S. Dixon, *Movies: Seventeen stories* (pp. 47-57). San Francisco: North Point Press.

Shi, T. (1985). One winter's evening (A. Bailey, Trans.). In M. S. Duke, (Ed.), *Contemporary Chinese literature: An anthology of post-Mao fiction and poetry* (pp. 129-133). Armonk, NY: M. E. Sharpe.

Stokkelien, V. (1984). A Vietnamese doll. In K. Hanson (Ed.), *An everyday story: Norwegian women's fiction* (pp. 187-191). Seattle: Seal Press.

1990-1999

Research and Scholarship

Altstein, H., Coster, M., First-Hartling, L., Ford, C., Glascoe, B., Hairston, S., Kasoff, J., & Grier, A. W. (1994). Clinical observations of adult intercountry adoptees and their adoptive parents. *Child Welfare, 73,* 261-269.

Altstein, H., & Simon, R. J. (Eds.) (1991). *Intercountry adoption: A multinational perspective.* New York: Praeger.

Bagley, C. (1992). The psychology of adoption: Case studies of national and international adoptions. *Bulletin of Hong Kong Psychological Society, 28/29,* 95-115.

Bagley, C. (1993). Chinese adoptees in Britain: A twenty-year follow-up of adjustment social identity. *International Social Work, 36,* 143-157.

Bagley, C., Young, L., & Scully, A. (1993). *International and transracial adoptions: A mental health perspective.* Brookfield, VT: Ashgate Publishing Co.

Balanay, C. A. (1996). *Cultural issues related to Caucasian families who have adopted Asian children.* Unpublished master's thesis, California State University, Long Beach.

Banks, R. R. (1998). The color of desire: Fulfilling adoptive parents' racial preferences through discriminatory state action. *Yale Law Journal, 107*(4), 875-964.

Baran, A., & Lifton, B. J. (1995). Adoption. In W. T. Reich (Ed.), *Encyclopedia of bioethics* (Rev. ed.) (pp. 71-75). New York: Simon & Schuster Macmillan.

Barret, S. E., & Aubin, C. M. (1990). Feminist considerations of intercountry adoption. *Women and Therapy, 10*(1-2), 127-138.

Bartholet, E. (1993). *Family bonds: Adoption and the politics of parenting.* Boston: Houghton Mifflin.

Bartholet. E. (1993). International adoption: Current status and future prospects. *The Future of Children, 3*(1), 89-103.

Benson, P., Sharma, A., & Rohelkepartain, E. (1994). *Growing up adopted: A portrait of adolescents and their families.* Minneapolis, MN: Search Institute.

Berg-Kelly, K., & Eriksson, J. (1997). Adaptation of adopted foreign children at mid-adolescence as indicated by aspects of health and risk taking—a population study. *European Child & Adolescent Psychiatry, 6*(4), 199-206.

Brenner, E. M. (1993). Identity formation in the transracially-adopted adolescent (Doctoral dissertation, California School of Professional Psychology, Berkeley/Alameda, 1993). *Dissertation Abstracts International, 54,* 3871.

Cecere, L. A. (1998). *The children can't wait: China's emerging model for intercountry adoption.* Cambridge, MA: China Seas.

Cermak, S., & Groza, V. (1998). Sensory processing problems in post-institutionalized children: Implications for social work. *Child & Adolescent Social Work Journal, 15*(1), 5-37.

Collmeyer, P. M. (1995). From "Operation Brown Baby" to "Opportunity": The placement of children of color at the Boys and Girls Aid Society of Oregon. *Child Welfare, 74,* 242-263.

Deacon, S. A. (1997). Intercountry adoption and the family life cycle. *American Journal of Family Therapy, 25,* 245-260.

English, B. A., et al. (1990). *Intercountry adoption: An annotated bibliography and review of the international literature.* Kensington, New South Wales: School of Librarianship, University of New South Wales.

Fieweger, M. E. (1991). Stolen children and international adoptions. *Child Welfare, 70,* 285-291.

Friedlander, M. L. (1999). Ethnic identity development of internationally adopted children and adolescents: Implications for family therapists. *Journal of Marital and Family Therapy, 25*(1), 43-60.

Gusukuma, I. V. (1997). Intercountry adoption: The experiences and adjustments of families adopting children from Latin America, China, and the United States (Doctoral dissertation, University of Texas, Austin, 1997). *Dissertation Abstracts International, 58,* 2850.

Hayes, P. (1993). Transracial adoption: Politics and ideology. *Child Welfare, 72,* 301-310.

Hibbs, E. D. (Ed.) (1991). *Adoption: International perspectives.* Madison, CT: International Universities Press.

Hostetter, M. K., Iverson, S., Thomas, W., McKenzie, D., Dole, K., & Johnson, D. E. (1991). Medical evaluation of internationally adopted children. *New England Journal of Medicine, 325,* 479-485.

Human Rights Watch/Asia. (1996). Death by default: A policy of fatal neglect in China's state orphanages. New York: Human Rights Watch.

Johansson, S., & Nygren, O. (1991). The missing girls of China: A new demographic account. *Population and Development Review, 17,* 35-51.

Johnson, K. (1993). Chinese orphanages: Saving China's abandoned girls. *Australian Journal of Chinese Affairs, 30,* 61-87.

Johnson, K. (1996). The politics of the revival of infant abandonment in China, with special reference to Hunan. *Population and Development Review, 22,* 77-98.

Johnson, K. A., Huang, B., & Wang, L. (1998). Infant abandonment and adoption in China. *Population and Development Review, 24,* 469-510.

Kallgren, C. A., & Caudill, P. J. (1993). Current transracial adoption practices: Racial dissonance or racial awareness? *Psychological Reports, 72,* 551-558.

Ketchin, M. J. (1999). *The psychosocial implications of international adoption: A theoretical study of adopted Chinese females: A project based upon an independent investigation.* Unpublished master's thesis, Smith College School for Social Work, Northampton, MA.

Kim, S. J. (1999). *Adult transracial adoptees and their ethnic identity.* Unpublished master's thesis, California State University, Long Beach.

Kistler, M. F. (1995). *The transcultural adoption experience.* Unpublished master's thesis, California State University, Long Beach.

Kwok, K. D. (1999). *American couples who adopt Chinese children: Perceptions about cultural issues.* Unpublished master's thesis, California State University, Long Beach.

Ladner, J. A., & Gourdine, R. (1995). Transracial adoptions. In C. Willie, P. Ricker, B. Kramer, & B. Brown (Eds.), *Mental health, racism, and sexism* (pp. 171-197). Pittsburgh, PA: University of Pittsburgh Press.

Lanz, M., Iafrate, R., & Rosnati, R. (1999). Parent-child communication and adolescent self-esteem in separated, intercountry adoptive and intact non-adoptive families. *Journal of Adolescence, 22*(6), 785-794.

Lifton, B. J. (1994). *Journey of the adopted self: A quest for wholeness.* New York: Basic Books.

Maclear, K. (1995). Drawing dividing lines: An analysis of discursive representations of Amerasian "occupation babies." *Resources for Feminist Research, 23*(4), 20-34.

McRoy, R. G. (1991). Significance of ethnic and racial identity in intercountry adoption within the United States. *Adoption & Fostering, 15*(4), 53-61.

O'Brian, C. (1994). Transracial adoption in Hong Kong. *Child Welfare, 73,* 319-330.

Riley, N. E. (1997). American adoptions of Chinese girls: The socio-political matrices of individual decisions. *Women's Studies International Forum, 20*(1), 87-102.

Rorbech, M. (1991). The conditions of 18- to 25-year-old foreign-born adoptees in Denmark. In H. Altstein & R. Simon (Eds.), *Intercountry adoption: A multinational perspective.* New York: Praeger.

Silverman, A. R., & Feigelman, W. (1990). Adjustment in interracial adoptees: An overview. In D. M. Brodzinsky & M. D. Shechter (Eds.), *The psychology of adoption* (pp. 187-200). New York: Oxford University Press.

Simon, R., Altstein, H., & Melli, M. (1994). *The case for transracial adoption.* Washington, DC: The American University Press.

Smith, D. G. (1994). *Transracial and transcultural adoption.* Rockville, MD: National Adoption Information Clearinghouse.

Social, Health, and Family Affairs Committee, Council of Europe. (1999, December 2). *International adoption: Respecting children's rights.* Retrieved April 17, 2005, from http://assembly.coe.int/Documents/WorkingDocs/doc99/EDOC8592.htm.

Telfer, J. (1999). Relationships with no body? "Adoption" photographs, intuition and emotion. *Social Analysis, 43*(3), 144-158.

Tessler, R. C., Gamache, G., & Liu, L. (1999). *West meets East: Americans adopt Chinese children.* Westport, CT: Bergin & Garvey.

Thurston, A. F. (1996, April). In a Chinese orphanage. *Atlantic Monthly,* 28-41.

Trolley, B. C. (1995). Grief issues and positive aspects associated with international adoption. *Omega: The Journal of Death and Dying, 30,* 257-268.

Trolley, B. C., Wallin, J., & Hansen, J. (1995). International adoption: Issues of acknowledgement of adoption and birth culture. *Child & Adolescent Social Work Journal, 12,* 465-479.

van Gulden, H., & Bartels-Rabb, L. M. (1995). *Real parents, real children.* New York: Crossroad.

van Leeuwen, M. (1999). The politics of adoptions across borders: Whose interests are served? (A look at the emerging market of infants from China.) *Pacific Rim Law and Policy Journal, 8*(1), 189-218.

Versluis-den Bieman, H. J., & Verhulst F. C. (1995). Self-reported and parent reported problems in adolescent international adoptees. *Journal of Child Psychology and Psychiatry, 36,* 1411-1428.

Vonk, M. E., Simms, P. J., & Nackerud, L. (1999). Political and personal aspects of intercountry adoption of Chinese children in the United States. *Families in Society: The Journal of Contemporary Human Services, 80,* 496-505.

Wilkinson, H. S. (1995). Psycholegal process and issues in international adoption. *American Journal of Family Therapy, 23,* 173-183.

Nonfiction

Daniels, L. (1999, August 8). Adoptees from China spark quest for culture: A growing number of Oregon parents join forces to give their Asian American children a proud sense of their heritage. *The Sunday Oregonian,* p. E1.

Davie, S. M. (1995). An adoptee's journal. In S. Wadia-Ells (Ed.), *The adoption reader: Birth mothers, adoptive mothers and adopted daughters* (pp. 237-250). Seattle, WA: Seal Press.

Dutt, E. (1999, June 11). Keeping children connected to the heritage of their birth. *India Abroad,* p. 22.

Give me your squalling masses: Coming to America 1. (1996, February 3). *The Economist,* p. 22.

Janowitz, T. (1998). Bringing home baby. In J. Bialosky & H. Schulman (Eds.), *Wanting a child* (pp. 92-100). New York: Farrar, Straus and Giroux.

Jones, B. (1998). Heedless love. In J. Bialosky & H. Schulman (Eds.), *Wanting a child* (pp. 9-14). New York: Farrar, Straus and Giroux.

Klatzkin, A. (1999). *A passage to the heart: Writings from families with children from China.* St. Paul, MN: Yeong & Yeong.

Levin, J. (1998). Scarlett O'Hara at the moonlit pagoda. In J. Bialosky & H. Schulman (Eds.), *Wanting a child* (pp. 158-170). New York: Farrar, Straus and Giroux.

Lewin, T. (1998, October 27). New families redraw racial boundaries. *New York Times,* pp. A1, A18.

Li, N. (1992, June 29). Foreign adoption of Chinese children legalized. *Beijing Review,* 23-25.

Liedtke, J. A., & Brasseur, L. E. (1997). *New American families: Chinese daughters and their single mothers: Adoption stories about hope and love from Our Chinese Daughters Foundation.* Bloomington, IL: Our Chinese Daughters Foundation.

Serrill, M. S. (1991, October 21). Going abroad to find a baby. *Time,* 86-88.

Stroshane, S. W. (1999). Unborn song. In S. Ito & T. Cervin (Eds.), *A ghost at heart's edge: Stories and poems of adoption* (pp. 232-234). Berkeley, CA: North Atlantic Books.

Szabo, J. (1997, September 30). Keeping their culture: Chinese adoptees find friends in new group. *Anchorage Daily News,* p. 2D.

Tawa, R. (1999, December 17). For Asian kids, a healthy new self-image: Line of products from Asia for Kids helps children to value their own cultural identities. *Vancouver Sun,* p. E7.

Transnational adoption (1998, September 28). *Beijing Review,* p. 22.

Wadia-Ells, S. (1995). The Anil journals. In S. Wadia-Ells (Ed.), *The adoption reader: Birth mothers, adoptive mothers and adopted daughters* (pp. 114-122). Seattle, WA: Seal Press.

Wait, L. (1995). Expectations . . . and realities. In S. Wadia-Ells (Ed.), *The adoption reader: Birth mothers, adoptive mothers and adopted daughters* (pp. 150-158). Seattle, WA: Seal Press.

Wheeler, E. (1998, October 8). Adoption brings bundle of joy to family. *Ventura County Star (California),* p. B4.

Wheeler, K., & Werner, D. (1999). *Adopting in China: A practical guide, an emotional journey.* Chula Vista, CA: Tracks Pub.

White, N. J. (1995, December 3). Single woman a winner in adoption minefield. *Toronto Star,* p. E1.

WuDunn, S. (1991, February 26). China's castaway babies: Cruel practice lives on. *New York Times,* p. A4.

Fiction

Hicks, B. J. (1998). *China doll.* Sisters, OR: Palisades.

Films/Videos

Blewett, K., & Woods, B. (Producers & Directors) (1996). *Return to the dying rooms.* Video, 50 min., English.

Brown, N. (Director) (1997). *Letter to Maya.* Video, 22 min., English.

Davidson, C., & Rogosin, D. (Producers). Davidson, C. (Director) (1993). *East wind, west wind.* Video, 95 min., English.

Evans, J., Merwin, C., O'Halloran, B., & Phelps-Owens, L. (Producers). Merwin, C. (Director) (1998). *Good fortune.* Video, 60 min., English

Farnsworth, E. (Producer). Farnsworth, E., & Knoop, J. (Directors) (1990). *Thanh's war.* Video, 58 min., English.

FCC-New England, (Producer). Chase, J., Fry, S., Guastella, R., & Klatzkin, A. (Directors) (1999). *Please don't forget me.* Video, 20 min., English.

Lo, C. M. (Producer & Director) (1999). *Catfish in black bean sauce.* Video, 119 min., English.

Rosenberg, R., Shields, B., & Christiansen, B. (Producers). Korty, J. (Director) (1995). *Redwood curtain.* Video, 105 min., English.

Taylor, H. (Director) (1995). *A mother's journey.* Video, 57 min., English and Chinese with English subtitles.

2000–

Research and Scholarship

Adamec, C., & Pierce, W. L. (Eds.) (2000). *The encyclopedia of adoption* (2nd ed.). New York: Facts on File.

Adams, G., Tessler, R., & Gamache, G. (2005). The development of ethnic identity among Chinese adoptees: Paradoxical effects of school diversity. *Adoption Quarterly, 8*(3), 25-46.

Anagnost, A. (2000). Scenes of misrecognition: Maternal citizenship in the age of transnational adoption. *Positions: East Asia Cultures Critique, 8*(2), 389-421.

Bergquist, K. J. S. (2004). International Asian adoption: In the best interest of the child? *Texas Wesleyan Law Review, 10*(2), 343-350.

Bimmel, N., Juffer, F., van IJzendoorn, M. H., & Bakermans-Kranenburg, M. J. (2003). Problem behavior of internationally adopted adolescents: A review and meta-analysis. *Harvard Review of Psychiatry, 11*(2), 64-77.

Briggs, L. (2003). Mother, child, race, nation: The visual iconography of rescue and the politics of transnational and transracial adoption. *Gender & History, 15*(2), 179-200.

Bryant, M. R. (2001). *Decision making and the adoption process for American families of Chinese children: An application of rational choice theory.* Unpublished master's thesis, Virginia Polytechnic Institute and State University, Blacksburg.

Carstens, C., & Julia, M. (2000). Ethnoracial awareness in intercountry adoption: U.S. experiences. *International Social Work, 43,* 61-73.

Cartwright, L. (2003). Photographs of "waiting children": The transnational adoption market [Special issue]. *Social Text, 21*(1), 83-109.

Congressional-Executive Commission on China. China's children: Adoption, orphanages, and children with disabilities: Roundtable before the Congressional-Executive Commission on China, 107th Cong., 2nd Session (2003, October 21).

Coutin, S. B., Maurer, B., & Yngvesson, B. (2002). In the mirror: The legitimation work of globalization. *Law & Social Inquiry, 27*(4), 801-843.

Dorow, S. K. (2000). Narratives of race and culture in transnational adoption. In P. Kivisto & G. Rundblad (Eds.), *Multiculturalism in the United States: Current issues, contemporary voices* (pp. 135-148). Thousand Oaks, CA: Pine Forge Press.

Dorow, S. K. (2002). "China 'R' Us"?: Care, consumption, and transnationally adopted children. In D. T. Cook, (Ed.), *Symbolic childhood* (pp. 149-168). New York: Peter Lang.

Dorow, S. K. (2002). Spirited crossings: The political and cultural economy of transnational adoption (Doctoral dissertation, University of Minnesota, 2002). *Dissertation Abstracts International, 63,* 3740.

Dorow, S. K. (2006). *Transnational adoption: A cultural economy of race, gender, and kinship.* New York: NYU Press.

Feigelman, W. (2000). Adjustments of transracially and inracially adopted young adults. *Child & Adolescent Social Work Journal, 17*(3), 165-183.

Feng, W. (2005). Can China afford to continue its one-child policy? *AsiaPacific Issues, 77,* 1-12. Retrieved April 21, 2005, from http://www.eastwestcenter.org/stored/pdfs/api077.pdf.

Fong, R., & Wang, A. (2001). Adoptive parents and identity development for Chinese children. *Journal of Human Behavior in the Social Environment, 3*(3-4), 19-33.

Friedlander, M. L., Larney, L. C., & Skau, M. (2000). Bicultural identification: Experiences of internationally adopted children and their parents. *Journal of Counseling Psychology, 47*(2),187-198.

Garbus, C. (2000). *The impact of racism on the adjustment of adult intercountry adoptees: A project based upon an independent investigation.* Unpublished master's thesis, Smith College, Northampton, Massachusetts.

Goodman, J. F., & Kim, S. S. (2000). "Outcomes" of adoptions of children from India: A subjective versus normative view of "success." *Adoption Quarterly, 4*(2), 3-27.

Hayes, P. (2000). Deterrents to intercountry adoption in Britain. *Family Relations, 49*(4), 465-471.

Hjern, A. (2004). Illicit drug abuse in second-generation immigrants: A register study in a national cohort of Swedish residents. *Scandinavian Journal of Public Health, 32*(1), 40-46.

Hjern, A., & Allebeck, P. (2004). Alcohol-related disorders in first- and second-generation immigrants. *Addiction, 99*(2), 229-236.

Hjern, A., Vinnerljung, B., & Lindblad, F. (2004). Avoidable mortality among child welfare recipients and intercountry adoptees: A national cohort study. *Journal of Epidemiology and Community Health, 58*(5), 412-417.

Hoksbergen, R., & van Dijkum, C. (2001). Trauma experienced by children adopted from abroad. *Adoption & Fostering, 25*(2), 18-25.

Hollinger, J. H. (2004). Intercountry adoption: Forecasts and forebodings. *Adoption Quarterly, 8*(1), 41-60.

Holt International Children's Services. (2000). International adoption statistics: Significant source countries of immigrant orphans 1985-1996. Retrieved September 11, 2004, from http://www.holtintl.org/insstats.html.

Howell, S. (2003). Kinning: The creation of life trajectories in transnational adoptive families. *Journal of the Royal Anthropological Institute, 9*(3), 465-484.

Johnson, K. (2002). Politics of international and domestic adoption in China. *Law & Society Review, 36*(2), 379-396.

Johnson, K. (2004). *Wanting a daughter, needing a son: Abandonment, adoption, and orphanage care in China.* St. Paul, MN: Yeong & Yeong.

Klein, C. (2000). Family ties and political obligation: The discourse of adoption and the Cold War commitment to Asia. In C. G. Appy (Ed.), *Cold War constructions: The political culture of United States imperialism, 1945-1966* (pp. 35-66, 285-289). Amherst: University of Massachusetts Press.

Luo, N., & Bergquist, K. J. S. (2004). Born in China: Birth country perspectives on international adoption. *Adoption Quarterly, 8*(1), 21-39.

Manning, L. D. (2002). Communicative construction of collective family identity in families with children from China (Doctoral dissertation, University of Denver, 2002). *Dissertation Abstracts International, 63,* 1187.

Mannis, V. S. (2000). The adopting single mother: Four portraits of American women adopting from China. *Adoption Quarterly, 4*(2), 29-55.

Martinez, D. (2001). Body rocking as an indicator of disordered attachment in internationally adopted children (Doctoral dissertation, University of Hartford, 2001). *Dissertation Abstracts International, 62,* 2067.

Masson, J. (2001). Intercountry adoption: A global problem or a global solution? *Journal of International Affairs, 55*(1), 141-166.

McIntyre, S. R. (2001). Portraits of culturally competent adoptive parenting: A phenomenological study of white adoptive parents of intercountry transracial young adults (Doctoral dissertation, Gonzaga University, 2001). *Dissertation Abstracts International, 62,* 3936.

Miles, C. G. (2000). Bonding across difference. In S. Akhtar & S. Kramer (Eds.), *Thicker than blood: Bonds of fantasy and reality in adoption* (pp. 19-59). Northvale, NJ: Jason Aronson.

Moosnick, N. R. (2000). Challenged mothers: Women who adopt transracially and/or transnationally (Doctoral dissertation, University of Kentucky, 2000). *Dissertation Abstracts International, 61,* 2933.

Nelson, R. (2000). The developmental status and expressive behavior of ex-institutionalized female Chinese infants: The early months (Doctoral dissertation, DePaul University, 2000). *Dissertation Abstracts International, 61,* 4419.

O'Donovan, K. (2002). "Real" mothers for abandoned children. *Law & Society Review, 36*(2), 347-378.

Ortiz, A. T., & Briggs, L. (2003). The culture of poverty, crack babies, and welfare cheats: The making of the "healthy white baby crisis." *Social Text, 21*(3), 39-57.

Ouellette, F., & Belleau, H. (2001). Family and social integration of children adopted internationally: A review of the literature. Montreal: INRS-Universite du Quebec.

Reed, K. (2000). Separation-individuation theory and interracial adoption. In S. Akhtar & S. Kramer (Eds.), *Thicker than blood: Bonds of fantasy and reality in adoption* (pp. 61-89). Northvale, NJ: Jason Aronson.

Roby, J. L. (2005). Openness in international adoptions: A study of U.S. parents who adopted children from the Marshall Islands. *Adoption Quarterly, 8*(3), 47-71.

Rojewski, J. W., & Rojewski, J. L. (2001). *Intercountry adoption from China: Examining cultural heritage and other postadoption issues.* Westport, CT: Bergin & Garvey.

Scroggs, P. H., & Heitfield, H. (2001). International adopters and their children: Birth culture ties. *Gender Issues, 19*(4), 3-30.

Selinkse, J., Naughton, D., & Flanagan, K. (2001). Ensuring the best interest of the child in intercountry adoption practice: Case studies from the United Kingdom and the United States. *Child Welfare, 80,* 656-667.

Simon, R., & Altstein, H. (2000). *Adoption across borders: Serving the children in transracial and intercountry adoptions.* Lanham, MD: Rowman and Littlefield.

Solchany, J. E. (2000). The nature of mothers' developing relationships with their internationally adopted Chinese daughters (Doctoral dissertation, University of Washington, 2000). *Dissertation Abstracts International, 61,* 2994.

Stiles, C. F., Dhamaraksa, D., & Rosa, R. (2001). Families for children: International strategies to build in-country capacity in the Philippines, Thailand, Romania, and India. *Child Welfare, 80,* 645-655.

Tan, T. X. (2004). Child adjustment of single-parent adoption from China: A comparative study. *Adoption Quarterly, 8*(1), 1-20.

Tan, T. X., & Nakkula, M. J. (2004). White parents' attitudes towards their adopted Chinese daughters' ethnic identity. *Adoption Quarterly, 7*(4), 57-76.

Telfer, J. (2003). The imagined child: Ambiguity and agency in Australian intercountry adoption. *Australian Journal of Anthropology, 14*(1), 72-79.

Trenka, J. J., Oparah, J. C., & Shin, S. Y. (2006). *Outsiders within: Writing on transracial adoption.* Cambridge, MA: South End Press.

Tu, W. (2001). Cultural identity in Chinese-born children adopted by White American parents: Chinese inside their hearts (Doctoral dissertation, Indiana University, 2001). *Dissertation Abstracts International, 62,* 2679.

United States Congress House (2000). Intercountry Adoption Act of 2000. 107th Cong. H.R. 2909.

Volkman, T. A. (2003). Embodying Chinese culture: Transnational adoption in North America [Special issue]. *Social Text, 21*(1), 29-55.

Volkman, T. A. (2005). *Cultures of transnational adoption.* Durham, NC: Duke University Press.

Vonk, M. E. (2001). Cultural competence for transracial adoptive parents. *Social Work, 46*(3), 246-255.

Vonk, M. E., & Angaran, R. (2001). A pilot study of training adoptive parents for cultural competence. *Adoption Quarterly, 4*(4), 5-18.

Vonk, M. E., & Angaran, R. (2003). Training for transracial adoptive parents by public and private adoption agencies. *Adoption Quarterly, 6*(3), 53-62.

Yngvesson, B. (2002). Placing the "gift child" in transnational adoption. *Law & Society Review, 36*(2), 227-256.

Yu, Y. (2000). Intercountry adoption: Attitudes, needs, and beliefs of American parents who have adopted Chinese children (Doctoral dissertation, Florida State University, 2000). *Dissertation Abstracts International, 61,* 4568.

Nonfiction

Bhatt, S. (2003, October 3). Born Indian, reborn American. *India Abroad (New York Edition), 34*(1), p. M2.

Champnella, C. (2003). *The waiting child: How the faith and love of one orphan saved the life of another.* New York: St. Martin's Press.

Cunningham, L. S. (2005). Two daughters, two destinies. In P. Kruger & J. Smolowe (Eds.), *A love like no other: Stories from adoptive parents* (pp. 44-55). New York: Riverhead Books.

Frank, C. (2005). She is among us. In P. Kruger & J. Smolowe (Eds.), *A love like no other: Stories from adoptive parents* (pp. 11-21). New York: Riverhead Books.

Gubernick, L., & Shen, L. (2000, September 14). Hancock ad raises alarm in adoption community. *Wall Street Journal,* p. B1.

Higginson, J., & Kearly, P. (2003). *Unlocking the past.* Flat Rock, MI: A.N.Y.O. Pub. Co.

Hood, D. (2005). The orphan myth. In P. Kruger & J. Smolowe (Eds.), *A love like no other: Stories from adoptive parents* (pp. 226-238). New York: Riverhead Books.

Jake Asenjo is a lucky 3-year-old boy. (2003, October 9). *Filipino Reporter (New York), 31*(42) p. 1.

Keefer, B., & Schooler, J. E. (2000). *Telling the truth to your adopted or foster child: Making sense of the past.* Westport, CT: Bergin & Garvey.

Levin, J. (2005). Special needs. In P. Kruger & J. Smolowe (Eds.), *A love like no other: Stories from adoptive parents* (pp. 239-254). New York: Riverhead Books.

Prager, E. (2001). *Wuhu diary: On taking my adopted daughter back to her hometown in China.* New York: Random House.

Prager, E. (2005). Across two cultures. In P. Kruger & J. Smolowe (Eds.), *A love like no other: Stories from adoptive parents* (pp. 217-225). New York: Riverhead Books.

Smolowe, J. (2005). Color her Becky: Grappling with race. In P. Kruger & J. Smolowe (Eds.), *A love like no other: Stories from adoptive parents* (pp. 93-104). New York: Riverhead Books.

Treen, J. (2005). Reluctant no more (not that I ever was). In P. Kruger & J. Smolowe (Eds.), *A love like no other: Stories from adoptive parents* (pp. 195-205). New York: Riverhead Books.

Tully, M. (2000, Sept. 23). Senate ratifies international adoption pact. *CQ Weekly,* p. 2228.

White, M. (2001, August 3). Sugar and spice: They are Indian, American, adopted, blended. *India Abroad,* p. M14.

Woodard, S. L. (2002). *Daughter from afar: A family's international adoption story.* San Jose, CA: iUniverse.

Zhao, Y. (2002, April 9). Living in two worlds, old and new: Foreign-born adoptees explore their cultural roots. *New York Times,* pp. B1, B2.

Fiction

Ball, D. W. (2002). *China run: A novel.* New York: Simon & Schuster.

Phan, A. (2004). *We should never meet.* New York: St. Martin's Press.

Russell, B. N. (2004). *Offspring of a deathless soul: A timeless journey to spiritual triumph.* McLean, VA: Big Mind Publishing, Inc.

Films/Videos

Burnette, M., & Bronstein, S. (Producers). Bronstein, S. (Director) (2004). *China's lost girls.* DVD, 43 min., English.

Cecere, L. (Director). (2000). *Saving girls' lives: International adoptions from China* (Lou Douglas lecture, Kansas State University.) Video, 74 min., English.

Chang, C. (Producer & Director) (2003). *Love without boundaries.* Video, 60 min., English.

Chang, C. (Producer & Director) (2003). *My unforgotten daughter.* Video, 48 min., English.

Cheung, L. (Director) (2003, June 17). Baby for sale: Child trafficking growing in Asia; drainage design in public housing flats. In *Inside story.* Asian Television Ltd.

Dolgin, G. (Producer & Director). Franco, V. (Director) (2002). *Daughter from Danang.* DVD, 83 min., English.

Gardner, J. (Producer). (2003, April 26). *Experiences of Operation Babylift adoptees.* Washington, DC: National Cable Satellite Corp; West Lafayette, IN: C-SPAN Archives.

Inkster, D. (Director) (2003). *The art of autobiography.* Video, 47 min., English.

Kuipers, R. (Producer). Bancroft, L. (Director) (2001). *Missing Vietnam.* Video, 104 min., English.

Mason, D. (Producer & Director) (2003). *Three Khmer flowers.* DVD, 60 min., English.

Oskam, J. (Producer & Director) (2003, December 14). *International adoption: Changing culture one child at a time.* Lubbock, TX: KTXT-TV.

Tam, S. (Producer). Lee, K. (Director) (2001). *Made in China: The story of adopted Chinese children in Canada.* Video, 48 min., English.

Thai, P. Q., & Gardner, J. (Producers). Gardner, J. (Director) (2001). *Precious cargo.* Video, 56 min., English.

Wise, N., & Lin, D. (Directors) (2003). *Chinese daughters.* Video, 27 min.

Web Sites

Adopted Vietnamese International, http://www.adoptedvietnamese.org. International network of Vietnamese adoptees based in Australia.

Adoptie Driehoek Onderzoeks Centrum (ADOC), http://www.adoptionresearch.nl. Adoption research center at Leiden University, the Netherlands.

Also-Known-As, Inc., http://www.alsoknownas.org/. National organization for inter-country adoption community.

Amerasian Foundation, http://www.amerasianfoundation.org/. Maintains a search registry for children of wars in Asia.

Asian Adult Adoptees of Washington, http://www.aaawashington.org/. Networking and educational resource for Asian/Pacific adoptees in Washington state.

Child Welfare Information Gateway, http://childwelfare.gov. Governmental clearinghouse for statistics, research, and birth family search information.

Families with Children from China, http://fwcc.org/. National organization with links to regional FCC organizations.

In Third Space, http://www.inthirdspace.net/. E-magazine by and for transnational adoptees.

Kinsearch Registry, http://www.kinsearchregistry.org. Search registry using participants' DNA profiles.

SOS Children's Villages-USA, http://www.sos-usa.org/. SOS villages provide alternative permanent care for abandoned and abused children, emphasizing sibling cohesion, stability, and community, with villages around the world.

Vietnamese Adoptee Network, http://www.van-online.org. National networking organization for Vietnamese adoptees.

War and Children Identity Project, http://www.warandchildren.org/index.html. Norwegian service for children fathered by foreign or enemy soldiers, with registration system and scholarly reports.

Conclusion

M. Elizabeth Vonk
Kathleen Ja Sook Bergquist

The works contained in this collection are representative of the breadth
and depth of scholarly interest in the adoption of Korean-born children into
the homes of Western, primarily white families over the past fifty years.
While the collection is of interest purely for its historical and anthropological
value, the work of the authors contained here may be of greater value for its
implications for current and future international adoptees and their families.

International adoption has continued to increase in numbers over the
fifty years since adoption from Korea began. In 2002, more than 20,000
children were adopted by families in the United States from sending countries in Asia, Eastern Europe, and South America (http://travel.state.gov/
orphan_numbers.html). This represents a 310 percent increase from the
number of international adoptions just a decade earlier in 1992. The authors
of this collection provide information, gleaned from a half-century of Korean adoption, which is significant to the well-being of all international
adoptees. Adult international adoptees, families formed through international adoption, professionals who work in the area of adoption, policymakers, and researchers may all find thought-provoking and relevant
information here.

International adoptees may find both solace and provocation in the essays that reflect on loss and identity struggles related to Korean adoption
(Chapters 7, 8, 9, and 10). Through the variety of ways in which the authors
describe Korean adoptees' journeys toward an integrated sense of self, the
journey itself is perhaps normalized. Seen clearly through these authors'
works, international adoptees may be willing to see and accept in themselves a longing for birth mothers and a true sense of belonging, a deep-
rooted protest against the racism inherent in Western culture and the stigma
associated with circumstances of birth, and reconciliation with a unique
identity that is some part Korean and another part Western. The "voice" of

International Korean Adoption
© 2007 by The Haworth Press, Inc. All rights reserved.
doi:10.1300/5734_20

adult international adoptees is a crucial source of information and it needs to be heard.

Implications for parents are also apparent in the chapters. First, the need is evident to help children find a bridge over which they may experience socialization within their birth cultures. Huh shows a connection between cultural socialization activities and Korean adoptees' ability to integrate Korean and American aspects of identity. In addition, the importance of helping children learn to cope with racism and discrimination is underscored by Feigelman's findings that adoptees do indeed experience discrimination and discomfort with their appearance. Both Gray and Juffer et al. show that adoptees' issues related to race and culture are evident in Australia and the Netherlands in addition to the United States. While these and other chapters make it clear that parents have responsibilities to help their internationally adopted children with issues related to racial identity and ethnic socialization, Vonk et al. show that parents of children adopted from Korea and China are still struggling with the value and execution of these responsibilities. These findings are compelling and point to the need for parents to push themselves to meet their children's needs.

Adoption professionals also may find implications in these chapters. Again, while evidence such as Yoon's mounts in support of the salience of race and culture in international adoption, Shiao and Tuan demonstrate that the issue of race has been severely minimized in international adoption practice. Brian reiterates this view and shows how international adoption facilitators have participated in minimization of racial identity concerns. Adoption professionals' responsibility to evaluate readiness of and prepare prospective parents for the unique responsibilities of international adoptive parenting is clear. In addition, professionals need to be prepared to provide adequate support for families and adoptees for whom challenges related to ethnic identity may arise developmentally. Both Bergquist and Lee provide promising examples of adoption practice with adoptees.

The chapters address policy at several levels. First, D. S. Kim provides a context for the advent of the practice of international placement of children from Korea. As in many sending countries, the practice might be seen as a response to internal social problems that ultimately adversely affected the welfare of children. Choy expands the view by examining the beginnings of adoption from Korea in the United States. Bai, B. J. Lee, and Hübinette provide insights into the current practice of international adoption in Korea. The power dynamics both within and between the two countries are striking, leading the reader to question whether it is possible to separate the personal from the political when examining international adoption. At a minimum, the authors underscore the necessity of development and enforcement of policies that will ensure ethical practice with all members of the adoption triad. In addition, these authors ask policymakers to examine whether the practice of international adoption is a help or a hindrance to the welfare of children in the sending countries.

Finally, these chapters point to the need for further research. In practice, more information is needed concerning the ways in which parents may be able to help their children develop positive ethnic identity. Are there specific attitudes or skills of parents that are related to positive outcomes for children who were adopted internationally? Are there parents who are not suited for international adoptive parenting, and if so, is there a good method for evaluation of suitability? Are there practices that promote healthy international adoptive families and positive racial identity in adoptees? For policymaking, more information is needed regarding the effect of international adoption on the welfare of children in the sending countries. Does international adoption discourage in-country problem solving for social issues affecting children? What positive and negative effects have Western adoption agencies had on the child welfare systems of sending countries?

In sum, the chapters collected here provide an invaluable look into the fifty-year-old practice of adopting children from Korea. By no means providing a complete picture, this book nonetheless is a window into the historical, sociopolitical, anthropological, and psychological world of international adoption. Our hope is that this collection will inspire thought and future research that will help improve the well-being of the many thousands of transplanted children who have joined families far from their places of birth.

Index

Page numbers followed by the letter "f" indicate figures; those followed by the letter "t" indicate tables.

"Abandoned Child" song, 228, 230
Abandoned children
    literature, 305
    as motivation for international
        adoption, 9-10
    number of adoptions, 197-198, 199t
"Abandoned Children" song, 229
Aborigines, white dominance of, 245
Abortion
    decline of availability of babies, 26
    legalization, 10
    Roe v. Wade court case, 10
ABS (Affect Balance Scale), 285
Abuse of children, 36, 194-195
Adjustment after adoption, 14-15
Adopted from Asia, 299t, 300, 302
Adopter-centered marketing model, 62
Adoption, defined, 189
Adoption Act, 237
Adoption agency
    closed adoptions, 211. *See also*
        Closed adoption
    Internet information, 65
    open adoption. *See* Open adoption
    private vs. public sector adoptions, 66
Adoption History Project, 32-33
Adoption Law, 214-215
Adoption Tour Survey Questionnaire,
    324
Adoptive Families, 6, 7
Adoptive Families of America (AFA),
    6, 19
Adoptive Parental Support of Adoptee's
    Ethnic Socialization
    (APSAES), 284
AFA (Adoptive Families of America),
    6, 19

Affect Balance Scale (ABS), 285
African-American adoptions
    difficulty of placement, 11
    dysfunctionality by characteristics,
        52t, 53
    follow-up studies, 47
    by white families, 16, 157-159
Afro-Caribbean experience, 244
Age and adjustment problems, 57
Ages for ethnic identity development
    four to six years, 85-86
    nine to eleven years, 88-90
    seven to eight years, 86-88
    twelve to fourteen years, 90-92
Alger, Horatio, 146
Allen, Horace N., 173
Allison, 299
Alone album, 229
Althaus, M., 317
Altstein, H., 47
Altstein, J., 74
American dream, 146-147
American Dream, 226
American-Indians, 16, 26
American-Korean Foundation, 36
Anagnost, A., 142, 143
Analysis of variance (ANOVA) test, 51
Andre, Ty, 247
ANOVA (analysis of variance) text, 51
Appadurai, A., 230
Appearance discomfort, 54-55, 55t
APSAES (Adoptive Parental Support
    of Adoptee's Ethnic
    Socialization), 284
Arierang. See Susanne Brink's Arirang
Asian-American experience, 160-161
Assimilation, segmented, 162

International Korean Adoption
© 2007 by The Haworth Press, Inc. All rights reserved.
doi:10.1300/5734_21

Attachment security studies, 268-269, 273

Australian adoptions
  Aborigines, white dominance of, 245
  Adoption Act, 237
  adoption legislation, 251
  background, 237-238
  Commonwealth Government under the Immigration Act, 237
  construction of "difference," 249-250
  cultural identity issues, 243-245
  culture camps, 252-253
  culture issues, 238-239, 243-245
  data analysis, 241
  data collection, 240-241
  differences in adoptee experiences, 245-246
  government support, lack of, 238
  Guardianship of Children Act, 237
  Korean-Australian identities, 250-254
  multiculturalism, 249-250, 259
  open adoption, 251
  participants, 240-241
  racism issues, 238-239, 241-243, 254-257
  reasons for few placements, 238
  research discussion and conclusions, 257-259
  research methodology, 239-240
  research results, 246-249
  sociopolitical context, 241-243
  Vietnamese adoptions, 239, 242-243. *See also* Vietnamese adoptions
  white policy, 245, 247, 249-250

Baden, A., 80-81
Bagley, C., 281, 282
Bai, Tai Soon, 187, 191-192, 207, 386
Bal, M., 147
Barth, R. P., 48
BDI (Beck's Depression Inventory), 285
Be Strong concert, 228
Beckett, Jeremy, 243
Beck's Depression Inventory (BDI), 285
Behavior problem studies, 270-271, 273-274, 317
Behavioral and affective change after Motherland Tour, 326, 331, 331t

Benson, P., 82
Bergquist, Kathleen Ja Sook, 100, 109-110, 277, 295, 385, 386
Berlin Report, 226-227, 228, 230
Bernal, M., 87
Berry, M., 203
Best interests of the family, 191
Between Love, 223
Bibliography
  Asian adoption
    1950-1959, 369
    1960-1969, 369-370
    1970-1979, 370-371
    1980-1989, 371-372
    1990-1999, 373-376
    2000-, 377-384
    fiction, 370, 372, 377, 382
    films/videos, 377, 382-383
    nonfiction, 370, 371, 372, 376-377, 381-382
    research and scholarship, 369-376, 377-381
    Web sites, 383-384
  background information, 341-342
  Korean adoption
    1950-1959, 342
    1960-1969, 342-343
    1970-1979, 343-345
    1980-1989, 345-347
    1990-1999, 348-357
    2000-, 357-369
    fiction, 356, 367-368
    films/videos, 342, 345, 347, 356-357, 368
    nonfiction, 342-347, 352-356, 361-367
    poetry, 368
    research and scholarship, 342-346, 348-352, 357-361
    Web sites, 368-369
Bibliotherapy
  for Asian-American adoptees, 308-311, 309t
  authenticity criteria, 307, 310
  criteria for using, 307, 309t
  realities of adoption, 305
  use of literature, 296-298
Biethnic identity, 93
Biological kin, search for, 320

Biracial children
    adoption. *See* Transracial child
        placement
    international adoption of, 10
    ostracizing of, 7-9
    preference by race and gender, 137
    preference patterns, 137
    as supply of adoptable children, 26
    U.S. soldiers as fathers, 136-137
Birmingham school, 222
Birth certificates, 142. *See also* Records
Birth control and increased adoption
    field, 10, 26
Birth country perspectives, 187
    on domestic adoption. *See* Domestic
        adoption
    popular culture. *See* Popular culture
    recent trends. *See* Trends in child
        welfare and adoption in Korea
Birth mothers
    adoption impact, 113, 131-134
    affect economy, 142-145
    categories of women, 139
    circumstances of relinquishment,
        131. *See also* Reasons for
        child relinquishment
    engaged in sex industry, 139-140
    as factory workers, 140, 176
    first stage: Cold War, 136-137
    gift rhetoric, 145-147
    illegitimate motherhood, 176-178
    industrialization and factory
        workers, 140, 176
    intercountry adoption and Korea,
        135-139
    memory activation of, 147-149
    narratives, 148
    second stage: economic
        development, 137-138
    social reality, 134
    teenage girls, 140
    third stage: globalization, 138-139
    trauma of, 134-135
    as unwed mothers. *See* Unwed mothers
    young factory workers, 140
Birth records
    birth certificates, 142
    destroyed in war, 257-258
    family registry, 210-211

Black children, adoption of. *See*
    African-American adoptions
Blainey, Geoffrey, 243
Blood-relatedness
    Confucianism, 191-192, 200
    importance of, 200, 211-212
Boat people, 243
Books. *See* Literature
Brennan, G., 238
Brian, Kristi, 43, 61, 386
Brink, Susanne. *See Susanne Brink's*
    Arirang
Brooks, D., 48
Bruining, Mi Ok Song, 180
Buck, Pearl S., 27, 28
Buddhism, 4

Campbell, M. E., 100, 109-110
Camps. *See* Culture camps
Capitalism, neoliberal, 122
Care of children in the system, 216t
Carp, E. Wayne, 25-26
Caruth, Cathy, 134
Case examples. meaning of
    homecoming, 318-320
Caucasian, defined, 76
CBCL (Child Behavior Check List),
    270-271
Chamberlin, Lucile, 36
Chan, Sucheng, 172-173
Chastity, 176
Chavira, V., 281, 282
Cheng, A. A., 147
Child Behavior Check List (CBCL),
    270-271
Child Placement Service, 28, 136
Child Welfare Law, 194, 215, 217
Child Welfare League of America,
    11-12
Childhood studies
    attachment security, 268-269, 273
    behavior problems, 270-271,
        273-274, 317
    child and family characteristics,
        266-267, 272-274
    child temperament, 267
    cognitive development, 271-272,
        273, 274

Childhood studies *(continued)*
competence, 267-268
discrimination, 272
early childhood
attachment security, 268-269, 273
child and family characteristics,
266-267
child temperament, 267
competence, 267-268
literature, 296
maternal instructive behavior,
269-270, 273
maternal sensitive
responsiveness, 269, 273
IQ development, 271-272, 273, 274
latency and industry stage, 296, 301
literature, 296
maternal instructive behavior,
269-270, 273
maternal sensitive responsiveness,
269, 273
middle childhood
behavior problems, 270-271,
273-274, 317
cognitive development, 271-272,
273, 274
discrimination, 272
IQ development, 271-272
peer group popularity, 271, 274
social development, 271, 274
peer group popularity, 271, 274
social development, 271, 274
Children on the Brink 2004, 12
Children's Christian Fund, 29
China
Kids Like Me in China, 299t, 300,
302, 304, 306
Korean War involvement, 5
roots tours, 124
Ching, S., 297
Choi, Chungmoo, 135
Choice makes commitment, 74
Ch'ôl-su, Pak, 226, 227
Choy, Catherine Ceniza, 1, 25, 386
Christ Is the Answer Foundation, 38
Christianity
Christ Is the Answer Foundation, 38
Everett Swanson Evangelistic
Association, 39

Christianity *(continued)*
humanitarian reasons for adoption,
307
in Korean history, 172-176
Korean War and, 172-176
prerequisite for adoption, 33
proselytizing ban, 173
Chun, Byong, 175, 176
Citizenship
cultural, 118
honorary, 125-127
naturalization, 179-180
wedding culture and, 124-127
Clarke, J. Calvitt, 29-30
Clarke, Janet H., 341
Clon hip-hop band, 228, 230
Closed adoption
child's name in family registry,
210-211
impact on adoptees, 203
importance of blood-relatedness,
211-212
likelihood of secrecy, 210-211
prevalence in international
adoptions, 142
problems of, 213
secrecy as negative influence,
209-210
Cognitive development studies,
271-272, 273, 274
Cold War, 135, 136-137, 174
Cole, J., 81, 86
Collective self-esteem, 284-285,
289-291
Collective Self-Esteem Scale (CSE),
285
Color-blind approach to cultural
differences, 81, 110
*The Colour of Difference; Journeys in
Transracial Adoption,* 240,
250
Comforters, 10
Commonalities, 119-120
Commonwealth Government under the
Immigration Act, 237
Competence studies of children,
267-268
Concerned United Birthparents (CUB),
142

Confucianism
    adoption beliefs, 176-177
    blood-relatedness, 191-192, 200
    family values, 191
    gender hierarchies, 68
    prevalence of, 4
    saving face, 195
    virtue and chastity beliefs, 176
Consensual Qualitative Research
    (CQR), 102
Continuity needs of children, 214-215,
    216t
Contraception and increased adoption
    field, 10, 26
Coopersmith, S., 281
Corbin, J., 241
Costs, application and processing fees,
    67
Cota, K., 87
Counseling for emotional problems, 50
Court case, Roe v. Wade, 10
Cox, D. R., 242
Cox, Susan Soon-Keum, 119-120, 127
CQR (Consensual Qualitative
    Research), 102
Cratty, Lark, 180
Cross, W. E., 89, 93
Crothers, Samuel, 296
CSE (Collective Self-Esteem Scale),
    285
CUB (Concerned Untied Birthparents),
    142
Culturalist essentialism, 63, 71
Culture
    adjustment after adoption, 14-15
    adoptee culture dimension, 81
    Australian issues, 238-239
    background, 4
    complexity of issues, 103t, 105-106
    Cultural Awareness Training
        Program for Overseas Adopted
        Koreans, 116, 117-118
    cultural citizenship, 118
    cultural genocide, 157
    cultural sensitivity, 72-73
    culturalist essentialism, 63, 71
    Cultural-Racial Identity Model,
        80-81
    culture camps. *See* Culture camps

Culture *(continued)*
    ethnic identity. *See* Ethnic identity
    hiding of culture, 61
    integrating Korean heritage, 90-92
    multicultural planning, 296
    multiculturalism. *See*
        Multiculturalism
    one shared culture, 244
    parental cultural competence. *See*
        Parents, study of cultural
        competence
    parental culture dimension, 81
    perception problems, 63-64
    popular. *See* Popular culture
    problem-oriented view, 74-76
    in the United States, 63
    wedding citizenship and, 124-127
Culture camps
    in Australia, 252-253
    for ethnic identity development,
        84-85, 86, 87
    Saet Byol Korean Adoptive
        Families, 240
Cumulative intercountry adoptions,
    155, 156f

D'Angelo, A., 298
Darwinian racial theories, 242
Daughters of the ghost, 178-184
de Hartog, Jan, 264
De Kinderen, 264
Demilitarized Zone (DMZ), 125
Desirability of Asian adoptees, 157
Development of ethnic identity
    ages four to six years, 85-86
    ages nine to eleven years, 88-90
    ages seven to eight years, 86-88
    ages twelve to fourteen years, 90-92
    impact of adoption, 80-83
    interaction and, 164-166
    Korean adoptees in America study,
        164-168
di Leonardo, Michaela, 63
Diaspora, 120
Dietrich, D., 297
Discourse on adopted Koreans,
    229-231
Discrimination studies, 272

Disidentification, 127-128
Displaced Persons Act, 6
Divorce rates, 190
Dixey, B., 298
DMZ (Demilitarized Zone), 125
Domain 1 of cultural competence
        study, 103-105, 103t, 109-110
Domain 2 of cultural competence
        study, 103t, 105-106, 109-110
Domain 3 of cultural competence
        study, 103t, 106-108, 110
Domain 4 of cultural competence
        study, 103t, 108, 110
Domestic adoption, 216-217
    adoptee's need for roots, 213
    blood lineage, 211-212
    children's need for continuity,
        214-215, 216t
    of handicapped children, 16, 210, 211t
    need for continuity, 209-210
    overseas and domestic adoptions,
        18-19, 18t
    positive impact of overseas
        adoption, 207-208
    self-help group for parents, 213-214
    statistics, 208t
    trends, 204
Dorow, S., 146
DTQ (Dutch Temperament
        Questionnaire), 267
Dutch Temperament Questionnaire
        (DTQ), 267
Dysfunctionality by characteristics,
        50-53, 52t

Economics
    affect economy and birth mothers,
        142-145
    of caring for homeless children, 15-16
    International Monetary Fund, 18
    Korean economic development plan,
        137-138
    neoliberal capitalism, 122
    poor country to rich country
        adoption trends, 17
    recession of 1997, 18
    stage of intercountry adoption,
        137-138

Education
    creative programming, 111
    Cultural Awareness Training
        Program for Overseas Adopted
        Koreans, 116, 117-118
    ethnic identity issues, 94-95
    postadoptive, 103t, 108
    preadoptive, 103t, 108
    pregnant girls, 140
    schools. *See* Schools
    sex education, 141
    for transracial adoptive parents,
        103t, 108
Emotional adjustment after adoption,
        14-15
Employment of overseas adoptees,
        316-317
Eng, David, 134
Erikson's theory of psychosocial
        development, 209
"Eternity" song, 228, 230
Ethnic identity. *See also* Racism;
        Transracial child placement
    adoptee culture dimension, 81
    adoption impact, 83
    assessment after Motherland Tour,
        331-332
    Australian issues, 238-239, 243-245
    biethnic identity, 93
    color-blind approach, 81, 110
    concerns of, 79-80
    Cultural Awareness Training Program
        for Overseas Adopted Koreans,
        116, 117-118
    Cultural-Racial Identity Model,
        80-81
    daughters of the ghost, 178-184
    defined, 80, 281
    development of
        ages four to six years, 85-86
        ages nine to eleven years, 88-90
        ages seven to eight years, 86-88
        ages twelve to fourteen years,
            90-92
    impact of adoption, 80-83
    interaction and, 164-166
    Korean adoptees in America
        study, 164-168
    development theory, 280-282

Ethnic identity *(continued)*
  differences in adoptee experiences,
    245-246
  discussion of study, 92-94
  disidentification, 127-128
  educational assistance, 94-95
  extent of identity, 84-85
  group identity, 89, 317
  importance of, 47
  Korean-Australian identities,
    250-254
  literature, 301-304
  loss of, 46
  new ethnicity research, 161-162
  open adoption and, 203
  parental culture dimension, 81
  parental influence, 93, 386
  personal identity, 89
  practice implications, 94-95
  pride of, 121
  psychosocial issues. *See*
    Psychosocial reconstruction
  reasons for issues, 243-245
  self-designations, 85
  self-identity. *See* Self-identity
  study method, 83-84
  study results, 84-92
Everett Swanson Evangelistic
    Association, 39
Extraordinary Law, 8
Extraordinary Law of Adoption for the
    Orphan Child, 6

Facilitators of adoptions
  consumer needs of the target
    market, 65-67
  cultural aspects, 67-69
  race consciousness assumptions,
    70-74
Factory workers as birth mothers, 140,
    176
Family
  blood-relatedness. *See* Blood-
    relatedness
  Confucianism family values, 191
  development of ethnic identity, 282,
    290

Family *(continued)*
  early childhood studies, 266-267,
    272-274
  *Family Matters: Secrecy and
    Disclosure in the History of
    Adoption,* 25-26
  Family Planning Program, 137
  family registry, 67, 76, 210-211
  foster care, 199-200, 214, 216t
  global family of Korea, 119-124
  homecoming experiences, 320. *See
    also* Homecoming
  impact of conflict, 4-5
  modern trends, 190
  separation impact, 230-231
Fanon, Frantz, 244
Feigelman, W., 43, 45, 81, 282, 316,
    317, 386
Feldman, S. S., 281
Fiction resources
  Asian adoption, 370, 372, 377, 382
  Korean adoption, 356, 367-368
Films/videos
  American Dream, 226
  Asian adoption, 377, 382-383
  Berlin Report, 226-227, 228, 230
  Between Love, 223
  discourse on adopted Koreans,
    229-231
  A Guilty Woman, 223
  importance of, 223
  Korean adoption, 342, 345, 347,
    356-357, 368
  Korean Film Database, 223
  Love, 228, 230
  Oseam Hermitage, 226, 227
  The People in White, 227
  Push! Push!, 227
  Susanne Brink's Arirang, 224-226,
    228, 230, 264
  Too Tired to Die, 227
  When April Goes By, 223
  Wild Animals, 227, 230
Final Fantasy, 228
Finalization of adoption, 75
First World privileges, 177-178
Fiske, John, 229
Fitness of families for adoption, 34-35

Follow-up of transracially adopted children
  age and adjustment problems, 57
  appearance discomfort, 54-55, 55t
  counseling for emotional problems, 50
  cultural identity issues, 46
  discussion of results, 56-58
  dysfunctionality by characteristics, 50-53, 52t
  gender and adjustment, 52t, 53
  methods of study, 48-50, 51t
  National Longitudinal Survey of Youth, 48
  overview, 45-48
  racial antagonism, 53-54, 54t
  racism issues, 54-55
  results of study, 50-56, 51t, 52t, 54t, 55t
  school expulsion, 50
  youth difficulties, 50, 51t
Foreign adoption, defined, 131
Foster care, 199-200, 214, 216t
Fry, Ying Ying, 306
Funky Together, 228

GAIPS (Global Adoption Information & Post Service), 19
Garza, C., 87
GAS (Global Assessment Scale), 49
Gathering conferences
  first Gathering, 117
  International Gathering of Korean Adoptees, 119-124
  purpose of, 116
GDP (Gross Domestic Product) of Koreans, 15-16
Gender
  adjustment and, 52t, 53
  Korean traditions, 68
  preference patterns, 137
Genocide, cultural, 157
Geography of Korea, 3
Ghostly Matters, 171-172
Ghosts, 171-172, 178-184
Gift rhetoric, 145-147
Gill, O., 282
Glaser, B., 241

Global Adoption Information & Post Service (GAIPS), 19
Global Assessment Scale (GAS), 49
Global ethnoscape, 230
Global family of Korea, 119-124
Global Overseas Adoptees' Link (GOA'L), 117, 125
Globalization
  global ethnoscape, 230
  of Korean internation adoption, 11-14
  marketing, 66
  perspectives on adoption, 235
  private vs. public sector adoptions, 66
  stage of intercountry adoption, 138-139
GOA'L (Global Overseas Adoptees' Link), 117, 125
Goode, J., 63, 71
Gordon, Avery, 134, 171-172
Government support
  Child Welfare Law, 215
  for illegitimate children, 177
  Korea's Adoption Law, 214-215
  principle of welfare policy, 189
  state public welfare, 32-33
  Whitlam Federal Labor Government, 242
Gray, Kim, 235, 237, 386
Green Meadows Orphanage, 39
Gross Domestic Product (GDP) of Koreans, 15-16
Grotevant, H., 101, 110
Group identity, 89, 317
Groups 1-4 studies, 164-167
Guardianship of Children Act, 237
A Guilty Woman, 223
Gumbel, Bryant, 68

Haerangsa, 228
Hague Convention on International Adoption, 14, 264
Hall, S., 222, 244-245, 246, 259
Handicapped children
  adoption subsidy, 201
  disability status of adoptees, 197, 198t

Handicapped children *(continued)*
domestic and overseas adoption, 210, 211t
number of adoptions, 197, 198t
as social problem, 16
special needs, defined, 200-201
trends for adoption, 199-200
Hardt, Michael, 142
Harvey, I. J., 242
Haunting, 171-172
Health problems on arrival to adoptive family, 273
Hee-ho, Lee, 117, 120-121, 122-123
Hermit Kingdom, 3
Herrmann, Kenneth J., 177-178
Hill, C. E., 102
Hirsch, M., 133, 148-149
Historical background
Adoption History Project, 32-33
adoption in Korea, 191-195
biracial children, 7-9
Christianity and the Korean War, 172-176
conflicts and family impact, 4-5
generally, 1, 3-4, 385-387
geography, 3
institutional adoption, 25-28
motivation for international adoption, 9-11
origin of adoptions, 5-7
sociohistorical background, 1, 385-387
trends in child welfare and adoption in Korea, 191-195
Ho, Robert, 243
Hojuje (family registry), 67, 76, 210-211
Hoksbergen, 17
Holland, W., 245
Hollingsworth, L. D., 17
Holt, Harry and Bertha
abuse of children by adoptive parents, 37
adoption of eight children, 30-31, 207
Asian adoption phenomenon, 155-156
first adoptions, 6
history of adoptions, 27, 28

Holt, Harry and Bertha *(continued)*
Holt Adoption Program, Inc., 136-137
Holt International Children's Services, 175-176
Holt Korea, 319
humanitarian reasons for adoption, 307
proxy adoptions, 33-36
tours to birth country, 19
Holy King Orphanage, 39
Homecoming
adoptee's need for roots, 213
adoption impact, 208
birth mothers and children uniting, 143-145
case examples, 318-320
International Gathering of Korean Adoptees, 119-124
research project. *See* Psychosocial reconstruction
search for biological kin, 320
during Seoul Olympic Games, 116-118
trip services, 320
Homosexuals prohibited from adoption, 67
Hong, Oak Soon, 38
H.O.T. group, 229
Howard, John, 243
Hübinette, Tobias, 187, 221, 316-317, 386
Huh, N. S., 43, 79, 100, 110
Humanitarianism of international adoptions, 11
Hurdis, Rebecca, 113, 171
Hurh, W., 137

I Wish for You a Beautiful Life, 10
ICASN (Inter-Country Adoptee Support Network), 240
Identity
ethnic. *See* Ethnic identity
family questions and, 75
group, 89, 317
personal, 89
If It Hadn't Been for Yoon Jun, 299t, 300, 302-303, 307

Illegitimate children
government support, lack of, 177
mixed race, 7. *See also* Biracial
children
out-of-wedlock births, 67, 68
Illegitimate motherhood, 176-178
Immigration
of children, 28-29
Immigration and Nationality Act, 6,
32
Immigration Restriction Act of
1901, 241-242
laws, 28-29
Independent adoption schemes, 27,
38-40
Indian Child Welfare Act of 1978, 158
Indians, 16, 26
Industrialization
birth mothers and, 140, 176
modern trends, 190
Infertility
importance of blood-relatedness,
211-212
prejudice, 212
as reason for adoption, 10, 11, 264
Institutional discourse
consumer needs of the target
market, 65-67
ethics questions, 68-69
family registry, 67
gender issues, 68
illegitimate children, 67, 68
race consciousness assumptions,
69-74
research, 64-65
Institutionalizing international adoption
historical origins, 25-28
independent adoption schemes, 27,
38-40
rescue to rivalry, 31-37
world vision, 28-31
Instructive behavior studies, 269-270,
273
Intelligence development studies,
271-272, 273, 274
Interaction and development of racial
identity, 164-166
Inter-Country Adoptee Support
Network (ICASN), 240

Intercountry adoption, defined, 131
International adoption trends, 202-203
International Gathering of Korean
Adoptees, 119-124
International Migration Services, 26
International Monetary Fund, 18
International Social Service (ISS),
26-27, 38-39
Internet
for adoption agency information, 65
Gathering conference connections,
117
Investigation of Asian adoption, 159
IQ development studies, 271-272, 273,
274
ISS (International Social Service),
26-27, 38-39
ISS-USA (ISS-United States of America
Branch), 27-28, 31-36

Jackson. B., 282
Japan
Christian resistance to imperialism,
173
domination of Korea, 4
Korean liberation, 174
JCICS (Joint Council on International
Children's Services), 15
Johnson, P., 47, 89
Joint Council on International Children's
Services (JCICS), 15
Juffer, Femmie, 235, 263, 386
Jun, Moon Hee, 229
Jung, Kim Dae, 117, 120, 139, 224, 230

KAAN (Korean American Adoptee
Adoptive Family Network),
19, 333
Kangdong-gu honorary citizenship,
125-127
Kasper, Barbara, 177-178
Katz, P. A., 82
Kelley, V. A., 38
Kennedy, Lucile, 34-35
Kids Like Me in China, 299t, 300, 302,
304, 306

Kil-su, Chang, 224
Kim, C. H., 191
Kim, D., 1, 3, 93, 282, 386
Kim, Eleana, 113, 115
Kim, Hosu, 113, 131
Kim, So-yong, 226
Kim, W. J., 316
Kirk, H. D., 281, 289
Kivisto, P., 243
Klein, C., 29, 137
Klineberg, O., 86
Knight, G., 87
Koh, T., 331-332
Korea Motherland Tours, 19
Korean Adoptees' Homeland Tour
    Questionnaire, 332
Korean American Adoptee Adoptive
    Family Network (KAAN), 19,
    333
Korean Coalition for Peace Movement,
    321
Korean Family Law, 192-193
Korean Film Database, 223
Korean Focus, 19
Korean War
    casualty statistics, 5
    Christianity and, 172-176
    history of Korea, 135
    impact on families, 4-5
Koreanness of adopted Koreans, 119-124
Kramer, Betty, 6
Kraus, Joanna Halpert, 303, 304, 308
Kwang-su, Park, 226
Kwon, J. H., 193-194
Kwon, Madame, 121
Kyung, Min, 251-252

Lambert, W. E., 86
Language, 316
Larsen, Alice, 302
Latency and industry development
    stage, 296, 301
Latino adoptees
    counseling for emotional problems,
        50
    dysfunctionality by characteristics,
        52t, 53
    school expulsion, 50

Lee, Bong Joo, 187, 189, 386
Lee, Daniel B., 277, 315
Lee, Marie, 300
Lee, R. M., 80, 83, 101, 110
Lee's Korean Adoptee's Homeland
    Tour Questionnaire, 332
Legal perspective of adoption, 189,
    192-195
Legislation
    Adoption Act, 237
    Adoption Law, 214-215
    Australian Adoption Act, 237
    Australian policies, 251
    Child Welfare Law, 194, 215, 217
    Commonwealth Government under
        the Immigration Act, 237
    Displaced Persons Act, 6
    Extraordinary Law, 8
    Extraordinary Law of Adoption for
        the Orphan Child, 6
    Guardianship of Children Act, 237
    Hague Convention, 14, 264
    Immigration and Nationality Act, 6,
        32
    immigration laws, 28-29
    Immigration Restriction Act of
        1901, 241-242
    Indian Child Welfare Act of 1978,
        158
    Korean Family Law, 192-193
    legal perspective of adoption, 189,
        192-195
    Minnesota Act of 1917, 203
    Race Discrimination Act of 1975,
        242
    recognition of adoptees, 120
    Refugee Relief Act of 1953. *See*
        Refugee Relief Act of 1953
    Roe v. Wade court case, 10
    Security Council Resolution 83, 4-5
    Special Act Relating to the
        Promotion and Procedure of
        Adoption, 116
    Special Adoption Assistance Act,
        192-193
Lemoine, Mihee-Nathalie, 117
Levine, Bettijane, 25
Liow, S. R., 317
LISTSERV, 250

Literature
  authenticity, 297-298
  bibliography. *See* Bibliography
  bibliotherapy. *See* Bibliotherapy
  children's adoption literature,
      295-296
  equitable representation, 297-298
  identity themes, 301-304
  for preadolescent Asian adoptees,
      298-300, 299t
  relationships to adoptive and birth
      families, 305-306
  resources. *See* Bibliography
  SEM reviews, 280-282
  sociopolitical context, 306-307
  survey for Asian literature, 298-300,
      299t
  themes of books, 301-307
      identity, 301-304
      relationships to adoptive and
          birth families, 305-306
      sociopolitical context, 306-307
Location, cultural importance of,
      103-104, 103t
Longitudinal adoption study, 265-266
Loss. *See* Remembering loss
Louie, Andrea, 124
Love, 228, 230
Lowe, Lisa, 122-123, 127-128
Lu, M. Y., 297
Luke, A., 251
Luke, C., 251

Magazines. *See* Media
Mail-Order Kid, 299t, 300, 303
Mallick, M., 281
Mapo Orphanage, 39
Marketing
  adopter-centered model, 62
  consumer needs of the target
      market, 65-67
  globalization, 66
  marketing meetings, 65
Marriage requirement for adoption, 67
Massatti, Richard R., 43, 99
Maternal instructive behavior studies,
      269-270, 273

Maternal sensitive responsiveness
      studies, 269, 273
McDonald, Joyce, 303
McGoldrick, M., 281
Media. *See also* Bibliography;
      Literature
  development of adoption issue,
      223-224
  films. *See* Films/videos
  popular culture. *See* Popular culture
  reporting of abuse and neglect, 194
  research source of information, 240
  search for birth parents, 208
  sympathy for orphans, 174-175
  television. *See* Television
Melli, M. S., 47
Melosh, Barbara, 25-26
Melting pot, 63
Melucci, A., 244
Memory activation of birth mothers,
      147-149
Messiah complex, 35
Military prostitutes, 10, 136, 139-140
Minnesota Act of 1917, 203
Miracle of the Han, 140
Mission to Promote Adoption in Korea
      (MPAK), 19, 69, 213-214
Mixed race children. *See* Biracial
      children
Model minority myth, 147, 182
Moo-hyun, Roh, 121
Moon, K., 135
Moon, Seungsook, 68
Moral perspective of adoption, 190
Morrison, 61, 70
Motherland and Family Tours, 19
"Motherland" song, 228, 230
Motherland Tour, 113, 124
Mothers. *See* Birth mothers; Unwed
      mothers
Motivation for adoptions. *See* Reasons
      for child relinquishment
MPAK (Mission to Promote Adoption
      in Korea), 19, 69, 213-214
Multiculturalism
  adopter-centered model, 62
  in Australia, 249-250, 259
  consumer needs of the target
      market, 65-67

Multiculturalism *(continued)*
   cultural sensitivity, 72-73
   dominant institutional discourse,
       64-74
   ethics questions, 68-69
   family registry, 67
   gender issues, 68
   illegitimate children, 67, 68
   impact on Korean adoptees, 64
   marketing models, 61-62
   perception problems, 63-64
   planning, 296
   problem-oriented view, 74-76
   race consciousness assumptions,
       69-74
   research, 64-65
Multilateral international adoptions,
   11-12, 12f

NABSW (National Association of Black
       Social Workers), 142, 157-158
Nagel, J., 162
Names of adopted Koreans, 122
Nation of immigrants, 63
National Association of Black Social
       Workers (NABSW), 142,
       157-158
National Longitudinal Survey of
       Youth, 48
National security concerns, 136
Naturalization, 179-180
Neglect of children, 194-195
Neoliberal capitalism, 122
Netherlands adoptions
   background, 263-264
   early childhood studies, 266-270,
       272-274
   Hague Convention on International
       Adoption, 14, 264
   middle childhood studies, 270-274
   research discussion and conclusions,
       272-274
   research methodology, 263, 265-266
Networks, 19, 240, 333
Neuberger, Richard, 30-31
Newspapers. *See* Media
Niles, Su, 181, 183

Nonfiction resources
   Asian adoption, 370, 371, 372,
       376-377, 381-382
   Korean adoption, 342-347, 352-356,
       361-367
Non-Invited Guests, 231
North Korea
   adoption policies, 16
   formation of republic, 174

Ocampo, K., 87
OECD (Organisation for Economic
       Co-operation and
       Development), 15, 208
OKF. *See* Overseas Koreans
       Foundation (OKF)
Older child placement, 199-201
Olympics. *See* Seoul Olympic Games
One shared culture, 244
Open adoption
   in Australia, 251
   defined, 203, 205
   self-identity and, 210
   trends, 203-204
Operation Babylift, 246-247
Organisation for Economic Co-operation
       and Development (OECD), 15,
       208
Organization for a United Response
       (OURS), 6
Origin of international adoption, 5-7
Orphanages
   Green Meadows Orphanage, 39
   Holy King Orphanage, 39
   Mapo Orphanage, 39
Orphans
   daughters of the ghost, 178-184
   defined, 29
   from Korean War, 5
   media sympathy for, 174-175
   Special Adoption Assistance Act,
       192-193
Oseam Hermitage, 226, 227
Ott, Edith, 37
Ott, Wendy Kay, 37
OURS (Organization for a United
       Response), 6

Overseas adoption
  of handicapped children, 210, 211t
  by year, 7-8, 8t, 208t
Overseas Koreans Foundation (OKF)
  Cultural Awareness Training
    Program for Overseas
    Adopted Koreans, 116,
    117-118
  Gathering conferences, 116, 117
  Motherland Tour, 113, 124

PACS (Parent-Adolescent
    Communication Scale), 283-284
Pardeck, J. T., 298, 308, 310
Parents
  APSAES, 284
  cultural competence, 99-101
  development of ethnic identity, 282,
    386
  ethnic identity influence, 93, 386
  measuring parent-child
    relationships, 283-284
  Parent-Adolescent Communication
    Scale, 283-284
  Parental Acceptance-Rejection
    Questionnaire, 283
  parental culture dimension, 81
  Parents for Overseas Adoption, 36
  Parents of Korean and Korean-
    American Children, 6
  same ethnicity as child, 103t, 105
  self-help group for parents, 213-214
  single parents, 26
  study of cultural competence
    discussion of results, 108-110
    domain 1, 103-105, 103t, 109-110
    domain 2, 103t, 105-106, 109-110
    domain 3, 103t, 106-108, 110
    domain 4, 103t, 108, 110
    implications, 110-111
    method of study, 101-102
    overview, 99-101
    results of study, 102-108
  training and education, 103t, 108
Park, Pauline, 64
Park, Wansoo, 43, 99
PARQ (Parental Acceptance-Rejection
    Questionnaire), 283

Pataray-Ching, J., 297
Peer group
  networks, 19, 240, 333
  popularity studies, 271, 274
The People in White, 227
Peoples' Republic of China. *See* China
Personal identity, 89
Pettiss, Susan, 32, 33, 35-36, 39
Phinney, J. S., 80, 281, 282
Pierce, Bob, 29, 32
Poetry resources, 368
Politics
  political emancipation, 122-123
  political embarrassment of child
    exports, 16, 116
  recognition of adoptees, 120
  sociopolitical context, 241-243,
    306-307
  sociopolitical context of adoption
    literature, 306-307
  sociopolitical context of Australian
    adoptions, 241-243
  welfare of children, 386-387
Poor country to rich country adoption
    trends, 17
Popular culture
  adoption issue in, 221-222
  discourse on adopted Koreans,
    229-231
  films, 223, 226-228
  importance of, 222-223
  songs about adoption, 223, 228-229
  Susanne Brink's Arirang, 224-226,
    228, 230, 264
Postadoptive support, 103t, 108
Poverty as cause for child
    relinquishment, 141
Practice implications, 277
Preadoptive training and education,
    103t, 108
Pride of ethnicity, 121, 285
Problem-oriented view of adoption
    culture, 74-76
Proselytizing ban, 173
Prostitution, 10, 136, 139-140
Proxy adoptions, 32-36
Proxy for race, 71
Psychological adjustment after
    adoption, 14-15

Psychological well-being, 285. *See also*
    Structural Equation Modeling
    (SEM)
Psychosocial development theory, 209
Psychosocial reconstruction
    employment issues, 316-317
    language issues, 316
    meaning of homecoming, 318-320
    racial characteristics, 315-316
    research project
        behavioral and affective change,
            326, 331, 331t
        conclusion, 336-337
        data collection and analysis, 324
        ethnic identity factors, 331-332
        expectations and outcomes, 333,
            334t-335t, 335-336
        findings and discussions, 324-336
        healing aspects of tour, 332-333
        meaning of searching for roots,
            324-330
        participant profile, 322-324,
            322t, 323t
        peer social network, 333
        posttrip experiences, 326-330
        pretrip expectations, 325
        purpose of, 321-322
        tour participants, 320-321
    search for biological kin, 320
    search for cultural roots, 320
Push! Push!, 227

Quiet migration of international
    adoptees, 155

Race
    Australian issues, 238-239
    Race Discrimination Act of 1975, 242
    racial awareness, 296
    racial identity development, 164-168
    racial isolation, 241
    as social construction, 162-163
Racism
    antagonism and dysfunctionality,
        53-54, 54t
    appearance discomfort, 55-56, 55t
    Australian issues, 238-239, 241-243,
        254-257

Racism *(continued)*
    Australian white policy, 245, 247,
        249-250
    biracial children. *See* Biracial
        children
    black and Indian children, 16
    complexity of issues, 103t, 105-106
    Cultural-Racial Identity Model,
        80-81
    ethnic identity. *See* Ethnic identity
    inferior races, 241-242
    race consciousness assumptions,
        69-74
    Race Discrimination Act of 1975,
        242
    racial matching, 238
    religion and, 103t, 107
    Social Darwinian theories, 242
    studies of young adults, 54-55
RACIT (Revised Amsterdam Child
    Intelligence Test), 272
Raetz, Erwin, 30, 31-32
Ralph, K. S., 297
Rankin, Jo, 181-182
Reasons for child relinquishment
    adoptions as closed transactions,
        142
    domestic care system, 216t
    engaged in sex industry, 139-140
    industrialization and factory
        workers, 140, 176
    motivation for international
        adoption, 9-11
    number of adoptions, 197-198, 199t
    poverty, 141
    social constraints, 131
    unwed mothers, 131-132, 140,
        198-199. *See also* Unwed
        mothers
    voluntary relinquishment, 10
Recent developments, 17-20, 18t
Recession of 1997, 18
Reconnection to Korea, 19
Records
    of adoptions, 26-27
    birth certificates, 142
    birth records, 210-211, 257-258
    birth records destroyed by war, 257
    family registry, 67, 76, 210-211

Red Cross, 231
Redefining adoption, 190-191
Refugee Relief Act of 1953
    expiration of, 31
    provisions for adoptions, 6, 33
    quotas for adoptions, 175
    visas, 29, 30
Register, Cheri, 176
Reid, W., 43, 100, 110
Religion
    Buddhism, 4
    Christianity. *See* Christianity
    Confucianism. *See* Confucianism
    as prerequisite for adoption, 33
    racism issues, 103t, 107
    Shamanism, 4
Relinquishment of children, 10. *See
    also* Reasons for child
    relinquishment
Remembering loss
    citizenship and culture wedded,
        124-127
    conclusion, 127-129
    global family of Korea, 119-124
    overview, 115-116
Republic of Korea National Red Cross,
    231
Rescue to rivalry
Research
    Asian adoption resources, 369-376,
        377-381
    Asian-American experience, 160-161
    attachment security studies,
        268-269, 273
    Australian adoptions. *See* Australian
        adoptions
    behavior problems, 270-271,
        273-274, 317
    childhood. *See* Childhood studies
    cognitive development, 271-272,
        273, 274
    competence studies, 267-268
    discrimination, 272
    discussion of results, 56-58
    ethnic identity. *See* Ethnic identity
    follow-up of adoptees. *See* Follow-
        up of transracially adopted
        children
    future of, 387

Research *(continued)*
    Groups 1-4 studies, 164-167
    homecoming experiences. *See*
        Psychosocial reconstruction
    information on adoption, 204
    IQ development, 271-272, 273, 274
    Korean adoptees in America study,
        163-167
    Korean adoption resources,
        342-346, 348-352, 357-361
    longitudinal adoption study,
        265-266
    maternal instructive behavior
        studies, 269-270, 273
    maternal sensitive responsiveness
        studies, 269, 273
    methods of study, 48-50, 51t
    middle childhood studies, 270-272
    multiculturalism, 64-65
    National Longitudinal Survey of
        Youth, 48
    Netherlands adoptions. *See*
        Netherlands adoptions
    new ethnicity research, 161-162
    parental cultural competence
        discussion of results, 108-110
        domain 1, 103-105, 103t, 109-110
        domain 2, 103t, 105-106, 109-110
        domain 3, 103t, 106-108, 110
        domain 4, 103t, 108, 110
        implications, 110-111
        method of study, 101-102
        overview, 99-101
        results of study, 102-108
    peer group popularity, 271, 274
    race as social construction, 162-163
    results of study, 50-56, 51t, 52t, 54t,
        55t
    SEM. *See* Structural Equation
        Modeling (SEM)
    sensitive responsiveness studies,
        269, 273
    social development, 271, 274
    temperament studies, 267
Resources. *See* Bibliography
Returning to Korea. *See* Homecoming
Revised Amsterdam Child Intelligence
    Test (RACIT), 272
Rivalry among organizations, 31-37

Rizza, M., 298
Robertson, Heber, 35
Roe v. Wade court case, 10
Rohelkepartain, E., 82
Roots
    differences in adoptee experiences,
        245-246
    homecoming search for, 320
    importance of finding, 212, 213
    meaning of homecoming, 318-320
    meaning of searching for roots,
        324-330
    resolution of ethnic identity, 317
    roots tours to China, 124
    search for. *See* Tours to birth
        country
    seeking in Korea. *See* Homecoming
Rosenthal, D. A., 281
Russell Sage Foundation, 163
Russian influence in North Korea, 174
Ruth, Kari, 180

Saet Byol Korean Adoptive Families,
    240
Saigon, fall of, 242
Sam, Kim Young, 120
Satisfaction with Life Scale (SWLS),
    285
Saving face, 195
Schemes for adoption, 27, 38-40
Schools
    acceptance challenges, 161
    cultural importance of, 103t, 104
    expulsions, 50
    teacher sensitivity to adoptee need,
        94-95
Sealed adoptions. *See* Closed adoption
Search for birth families, 116-118
Search for truth, legitimacy, and justice
    Christianity and the Korean War,
        172-176
    daughters of the ghost, 178-184
    ghosts, 171-172
    illegitimate motherhood, 176-178
Second World exploitation, 177-178
Secretive adoption. *See* Closed
    adoption
Security Council Resolution 83, 4-5

The Seeds from the East, 6
Segmented assimilation, 162
Self-concept theory, 280-282
Self-designations, ethnic, 85
Self-esteem of adoptees
    collective self-esteem, 284-285,
        289-291
    family influence, 281
Self-help group for parents, 213-214
Self-identity
    defined, 209
    in domestic adoptions, 212
    need for continuity, 209-210
    resolution of ethnic identity, 317
    secrecy in adoption and, 212
    Self-Identity Acculturation Scale
        (SIA), 324, 331-332
SEM. *See* Structural Equation
    Modeling (SEM)
Sensitive responsiveness studies, 269,
    273
Seoul Olympic Games
    homecoming of adoptees, 116-118
    Korean ethics questions, 68-69
    recognition as exporter of children,
        18, 116, 138, 224
    recognition as industrial nation, 116
Sex education for unwed mothers, 141
Shamanism, 4
Shame of ethnicity, 285
Sharkey, P. M. B., 298
Sharma, A., 82
Shiao, Jiannbin L., 113, 155, 386
Shireman, J., 47, 89
SIA (Self-Identity Acculturation
    Scale), 324, 331-332
Silverman, A., 81, 159, 282, 316, 317
Simon, R., 47, 74
Sinawe, 228, 230
Single parenthood and decline of
    availability of babies, 26
Siu, Lok, 118
Sky pop group, 228, 230
SL-ASIA (Suinn-Lew Asian-Identity
    Acculturation Scale), 332
Smith, E. J., 281, 282, 289
Smith, Lillie Reed, 38
Smith, Rebecca, 180, 182
Smith, V., 133, 148-149

Social adjustment after adoption, 14-15
Social construction of race, 162-163
Social Darwinian racial theories, 242
Social development studies, 271, 274
Social reality of birth mothers, 134
Social workers, learning from SEM study, 291
Socialization
APSAES, 284
parental support for, 290, 386
psychosocial development theory, 209
Sociohistorical background, 1, 385-387
Sociological approach
Asian adoption phenomenon, 155-157
Asian-American research, 160-161
black-white placements, 157-159
cumulative intercountry adoptions, 155, 156f
desirability of Asian adoptees, 157
Groups 1-4 studies, 164-167
investigation of Asian adoption, 159
Korean adoptees in America study, 163-167
new ethnicity research, 161-162
race as social construction, 162-163
racial identity development, 164-168
segmented assimilation, 162
Sociopolitical context
of adoption literature, 306-307
of Australian adoptions, 241-243
Sokoloff, B. Z., 192
Songs about adoption
discourse on adopted Koreans, 229-231
importance of, 223
popular songs, 228-229
Susanne Brink's Arirang, 224-226, 228, 230, 264
Source countries for international adoptions, 12-13, 13t
South Korea
adoption policies, 16
formation of republic, 174
Special Act Relating to the Promotion and Procedure of Adoption, 116
Special Adoption Assistance Act, 192-193

Special needs children, 200-201. *See also* Handicapped children
Sponsorship programs
birth country visits, 253
Everett Swanson Evangelistic Association, 39
Homecoming Tour, 320-321
World Vision, 29-32
Stages of intercountry adoption and Korea
first stage: Cold War, 136-137
second stage: economic development, 137-138
third stage: globalization, 138-139
STAI (State-Trait Anxiety Inventory), 285
Stalin, 174
Standards for adoptions, 32-33
State public welfare, 32-33
State-Trait Anxiety Inventory (STAI), 285
Statistics
children needing protection, 195, 196t
cumulative intercountry adoptions, 155, 156f
current countries of origin, 156
disability status, 197, 198t
domestic and overseas adoption, 208t
domestic and overseas adoption of handicapped children, 210, 211t
foreign-born adopted children, 46
Korean GDP, 15-16
Korean War casualties, 5
multilateral international adoptions, 11-12, 12f
number of adoptions, 196, 197t
overseas adoption by year, 7-8, 8t
reasons for entry into substitute care, 197-198, 199t
source countries for adoptions, 12-13, 13t
total Korean overseas adoptions, 316
Stereotypes, model minority myth, 147, 182
Steward, R., 80-81

*Story of Adoption: Why Do I Look
    Different?,* 300
Strange Situation Procedure, 268
*Strangers and Kin: The American Way
    of Adoption,* 25-26
Strauss, A., 241
Structural Equation Modeling (SEM)
    APSAES, 284
    collective self-esteem, 284-285,
        289-291
    data analysis, 285-286
    data collection, 283
    descriptive analyses, 286, 287t
    development of, 282
    ethnic identity development theory,
        280-282
    limitations of study, 291
    literature review, 280-282
    measurement evaluation, 287-288,
        288f
    parent-child relationship, 283-284
    psychological well-being, 285
    purpose of, 279-280
    research discussion, 289-291
    research methodology, 283-285
    research results, 286-289, 287t,
        288f, 289t
    sampling, 283
    self-concept theory, 280-282
    structural evaluation, 288-289, 289t
    testing the model, 287
    theoretical backgrounds, 280-282
    variables and instruments, 283-285
    well-being, 285
Studies. *See* Research
Subsidy for special needs children, 201
Suicide rates of adoptees, 317
Suinn-Lew Asian-Identity Acculturation
    Scale (SL-ASIA), 332
Sun, Kwon Young, 223
Supply of adoptable children in the
    U.S., 11
Surveys. *See* Research
Survival skills, 296
Susanne Brink's Arirang, 224-226,
    228, 230, 264
Swanson, Everett, 38, 39
SWLS (Satisfaction with Life Scale),
    285

Tae, Kim Geun, 119
Tall Boy's Journey, 299t, 300, 304,
    305, 308
TAPS (Transracial Adoption Parenting
    Scale), 101-102
Teacher's Report Form (TRF), 270-271
Television
    cultural work, 144-145
    narratives of birth mothers, 148
    research source of information, 240
    search for birth parents, 208
    showing reunions of birth mothers
        and children, 144
Temperament studies of children, 267
Theory
    ethnic identity development, 280-282
    psychosocial development, 209
    self-concept, 280-282
    Social Darwinism, 242
Therapy. *See* Bibliotherapy
They Are Nothing Different with Us
    album, 229
Third World exploitation, 177-178
Thompson, B. J., 102
Thompson, Sibyl, 34
Tizard, B., 316, 317
Too Tired to Die, 227
Tours to birth country
    Adoption Tour Survey
        Questionnaire, 324
    China root tours, 124
    Holt's tours to birth country, 19
    homecoming research tour. *See*
        Psychosocial reconstruction
    Korea Motherland Tours, 19
    Lee's Korean Adoptee's Homeland
        Tour Questionnaire, 332
    Motherland and Family Tours, 19
    Motherland Tour, 113, 124
Training. *See also* Education
    creative programming, 111
    Cultural Awareness Training
        Program for Overseas Adopted
        Koreans, 116, 117-118
    for transracial adoptive parents,
        103t, 108
Transcultural child placement, 17
Transracial Adoption Parenting Scale
    (TAPS), 101-102

Transracial child placement
    age and adjustment problems, 57
    appearance discomfort, 54-55, 55t
    black-white placements. *See*
        African-American adoptions
    counseling for emotional problems,
        50
    discussion of results, 56-58
    doubts about, 17
    dysfunctionality by characteristics,
        50-53, 52t
    follow-up. *See* Follow-up of
        transracially adopted children
    gender and adjustment, 52t, 53
    methods of study, 48-50, 51t
    racial antagonism, 53-54, 54t
    racism issues, 54-55
    results of study, 50-56, 51t, 52t, 54t,
        55t
    school expulsion, 50
    Vietnam. *See* Vietnamese adoptions
    youth difficulties, 50, 51t. *See also*
        Follow-up of transracially
        adopted children
Trauma of birth mothers, 134-135
Trends in child welfare and adoption in
        Korea
    best interests of the family, 191
    children needing protection, 195,
        196t
    disability status, 197, 198t
    family foster care, 199-200, 214,
        216t
    family norms, 190
    history of, 191-195
    international adoption, 202-203
    legal perspective, 189, 192-195
    moral perspective, 190
    number of adoptions, 196, 197t
    open adoption, 203-204
    policy reform, 204-205
    principle of welfare policy, 189
    reasons for entry into substitute
        care, 197-198, 199t
    redefining adoption, 190-191
    research and data-gathering, 204
    saving face, 195
    special needs children, 199-201
TRF (Teacher's Report Form), 270-271

Triangulation, 239
Truman, Harry, 174
Tuan, Mia H., 113, 155, 386

U.N. madams, 10
United States
    adoption Web sites, 385
    aid to Korea, 135
    American dream, 146-147
    Asian-American experience, 160-161
    culture, 63
    history of adoptions, 192
Unity through diversity, 63
Unofficial ambassadors, 139-140
Unrau, Y. A., 100, 109-110
Unwed mothers
    as birth mothers. *See* Birth mothers
    reasons for child relinquishment,
        131-132, 140, 198-199
    sex education, 141
    single parents, 26
    as social problem, 138
    social stigma, 140-141
    source of children for foreign
        adoption, 138-139

van IJzendoorn, Marinus H., 263
Vasta, E., 249
Verhulst, F., 317
Verma, L., 281
Versluis-Den Bieman, H., 317
Videos. *See* Films/videos
Vietnamese adoptions
    to Australia, 239, 242-243
    birth records destroyed in war, 257
    boat people, 243
    differences in adoptee experiences,
        246-248
    racial isolation, 241
    transracial adoptions, 45-46
    Vietnam airlift of 1975, 237
Visas, 29, 30, 117-118
Visiting Korea by adoptees. *See*
        Homecoming
Viviani, N., 242

*Voices from Another Place: A
    Collection of Works from A
    Generation Born in Korea
    and Adopted to Other
    Countries,* 240
Voluntary relinquishing of children, 10
Vonk, M. Elizabeth, 43, 99, 296,
    301-302, 385, 386
Vroegh, K., 47

Watson, K., 89
*We Don't Look Like Our Mom and
    Dad,* 299t, 300, 302
Web sites
    adoptee/adoptive family, 19
    AFA, 19
    Asian adoption resources, 383-384
    dilemmas of adoption, 77
    Korean adoption resources, 368-369
    Korean Film Database, 223
    SOS Villages, 76
    Susanne Brink's Arirang, 264
    United States adoptions, 385
Wedding citizenship and culture,
    124-127
Weil, R. H., 155
Welfare. *See* Government support
Well-being, 285. *See also* Structural
    Equation Modeling (SEM)
Western queens, 10
When April Goes By, 223
When You Were Born series, 299t,
    300-302, 306, 308

Whitlam Federal Labor Government,
    242
Wild Animals, 227, 230
Wilkinson, H., 82, 320
Wilkinson, S. H. P., 281
Williams, E. N., 102
Williams, I. A., 246-248
Williams, Raymond, 63
Winters, John, 39
Won-Seok, Jin, 227
Woo, Cheong Jin, 223
World vision, 28-31
World Vision, 29-32
Wu, Frank, 63

Yang, Hyunah, 176
Yang-suk, Kwon, 121
Yangyenohwe, 175
Yong, Lee Du, 223
Yong-gyun, Pae, 227
"Yông-mi Robinson" song, 228
Yoon, D. P., 277, 279, 280, 282,
    284-285, 289
Youn Hee and Me, 299t, 300, 302, 303,
    304
Young, Chung Won, 228
Young, L., 281, 282
YoungHee, 180-181
Youth difficulties study. *See* Follow-up
    of transracially adopted
    children
Yuh, J., 146
Yun, Sung Hyun, 43, 99